Advocacy

Advocacy

Championing Ideas
& Influencing Others

JOHN A. DALY

Yale

UNIVERSITY

PRESS

New Haven and London

Yale University Press books may be purchased in quantity for
educational, business, or promotional use. For information, please
e-mail sales.press@yale.edu (U.S. office) or sales@yaleup.co.uk
(U.K. office).

Designed by Nancy Ovedovitz and set in Janson and Gotham types by
Keystone Typesetting, Inc. Printed in the United States of America.

Library of Congress Cataloging-in-Publication Data
Daly, John A. (John Augustine), 1952–
Advocacy : championing ideas and influencing others / John A. Daly.
p. cm.
Includes bibliographical references and index.
ISBN 978-0-300-16775-7 (alk. paper)
1. Branding (Marketing). 2. Social interaction.
3. Communication in marketing. I. Title.
HM1166.D35 2011
302.2 — dc22
2011008294

A catalogue record for this book is available from the British Library.

This paper meets the requirements of ANSI/NISO Z39.48-1992
(Permanence of Paper).

10 9 8 7 6 5 4 3 2 1

Contents

Advocacy

1

The Politics of Ideas

It is harder to get a good idea accepted
than to get a good idea.
STEPHEN FRIEDMAN

If we had an Innovators' Hall of Fame, it would include Tim Berners-Lee; William Campbell, Mohammed Aziz, and Roy Vagelos; Patsy Mink and Edith Green; David Warren; Clair Patterson; Joan Ganz Cooney; and Jim Delligatti. Their names may be unknown to you, but each is responsible for at least one extraordinary innovation that affects us every day. They have something else in common, too. Each faced strong resistance from others — bosses, colleagues, and other decision makers — who often blithely dismissed their brainstorm, publicly challenged its value, or, in some cases, tried to sabotage it. Each of these intrepid innovators came to learn what so many other creative researchers, scientists, engineers, and business leaders recognize: It is not enough to come up with a brilliant idea. You also need to galvanize support through effective advocacy.

Not only did Tim Berners-Lee come up with what we know today as the World Wide Web, but he also had to convince his employer, the European Organization for Nuclear Research (CERN), to support his work on the Web. After pushing indefatigably for his notion, he finally won management's support. But then he faced a second advocacy challenge: to persuade CERN to make his brainchild freely available to the public. "It took

1

18 months . . . to persuade CERN directors not to charge royalties for use of the Web," Berners-Lee says. "Had we failed, the Web would not be here today."[1]

William Campbell was a drug researcher who discovered a cure for river fever, a malady that every year blinded millions of people living in the tropics. Campbell, along with his colleague Mohammed Aziz, persuaded Roy Vagelos, then head of research and development at Merck, to develop the drug, now called Mectizan. Then Campbell, Aziz, and Vagelos faced a daunting advocacy challenge: convincing Merck executives to spend enormous amounts on a pill that wouldn't make the company a penny, because the people who needed the drug were some of the poorest in the world. They succeeded, and Merck has since donated more than 2.5 billion tablets (worth close to $4 billion). Today more than 25 million people receive the drug annually — and have their sight — because of Campbell, Aziz, and Vagelos's advocacy. In fact, the World Health Organization recently announced that river blindness may soon be eliminated in Africa.

If you have a daughter who plays soccer or volleyball today, you should thank Patsy Mink and Edith Green. In the late 1960s, Mink and Green were two of the few female members of the U.S. Congress. Struck by the absurd limits placed on women's involvement in college activities, they shepherded through Congress, despite blatant sexist opposition, an innovative piece of legislation called Title IX, which today guarantees girls and women opportunities in education and athletics. In 1972, when the law was passed, girls accounted for only 7 percent of all athletes in high school; by 2008 they accounted for almost half.[2]

Every time you board an airplane, you might think kindly of David Warren. Working at the Aeronautical Research Laboratory in Melbourne in the 1950s, he dreamed up what we now know as the cockpit voice recorder. Putting recorders on planes would seem to be an obvious step for an industry that celebrates safety. But when Warren pitched his notion, he was turned down flat. The Royal Australian Air Force claimed that his device would "yield more expletives than explanations." The Federation of Australian Air Pilots declared that "no plane would take off in Australia with Big Brother listening." He finally persuaded British aeronautics experts to test his idea. Today, every commercial airplane contains a recorder in a "black box," and we are all safer because of Warren's advocacy.[3]

Do you use unleaded gasoline? If so, Clair Patterson deserves your thanks. He pioneered the idea of eliminating harmful lead from fuel. Another obvious innovation, right? Yet it took more than ten years for him to get his idea adopted, so great was the political opposition. Energy companies tried to stop his research funding; powerful industry opponents asked his university, the California Institute of Technology (Caltech), to fire him. But because of his tenacious advocacy, all of us breathe cleaner air today.

When the Carnegie Foundation raised the idea of funding an educational television show for children, Joan Ganz Cooney's boss at New York City's Channel 13, Lewis Freedman, said he didn't think she would be interested in the project. She interrupted to say that she most definitely would be. As discussion of the project proceeded, Freedman kept turning her down because he wanted her to continue to work on public affairs documentary projects (she had won an Emmy on one). She thought getting involved in the education show for children was hopeless until her husband had lunch (on an unrelated matter) with Lloyd Morrisett, head of the Carnegie Foundation. Ganz Cooney's husband told Morrisett of his wife's interest in doing the research. That prompted Morrisett to call Ganz Cooney's boss and tell him she was the person he wanted to lead the effort. As Ganz Cooney will admit, it was "a little bit tricky" going around her boss.[4] In fact, she said later, the job would not have been hers if she hadn't done so.[5] Her involvement didn't grow any easier. When she finally completed the project and presented it to top executives, one of those attending the meeting asked, "Who are you? . . . Why would anyone be interested in your opinion? . . . I just think it's crazy."[6] Luckily, Ganz Cooney turned out to be a relentless advocate. Today, thanks to her, we all enjoy Big Bird, Elmo, and the rest of the gang on *Sesame Street*.

Ever had a Big Mac? You can cheer Jim Delligatti, who owned some McDonald's franchises in the Pittsburgh area in 1967. Disturbed that profits were not increasing, he borrowed an idea from the Big Boy restaurant chain and created the double burger on a bun. Did McDonald's executives like his idea? Not at first. Fred Turner, the company's president, didn't want to expand the menu. But Delligatti persevered. His regional manager bought the idea and made the case to senior executives. McDonald's leadership finally told Delligatti that he could test his fancy new sandwich — but only at one of his restaurants, and he had to use McDonald's products. The latter restriction sentenced his idea to failure, because the traditional hamburger bun was too small for two all-beef patties, special sauce, lettuce, cheese, pickles, and onion. So Delligatti ignored instructions and ordered large sesame rolls to create the Big Mac. After sales at his Uniontown restaurant shot up, he piloted the idea at other stores in the Pittsburgh area. Soon other McDonald's stores started selling his sandwich.[7] Thanks to Delligatti's advocacy, burger lovers throughout the world can sink their teeth into Big Macs.

Each of these innovators, and many others introduced in the pages ahead, came to recognize that creative genius is seldom sufficient to make great ideas viable. Persistent, well-considered advocacy is just as important. And advocacy is what this book is about.

The products you find on store shelves, the processes that make organizations safer, more efficient, and profitable, the innovations that let you live longer and better — all originally sprang from somebody's mind. But these innovative products and processes didn't magically appear the moment they were imagined. Instead, the idea for each one needed to be sold inside some organization before it became a reality.

Victor Hugo was wrong when he wrote that an idea whose time has come cannot be stopped. Ideas can be stopped. Too often, brilliant ideas flounder because of the inability or unwillingness of their creators to sell them to others. Indeed, how many great ideas for lifesaving drugs, world-changing technologies, and innovative business processes have fallen by the wayside simply because their proponents were unable to successfully advocate for their adoption? As the writer David Bornstein said: "An idea is like a play. It needs a good producer and a good promoter even if it's a masterpiece. Otherwise the play may never open; or it may open but, for lack of an audience, close after a week."[8] Organizations are crowded and noisy marketplaces of ideas. Every one of them has more needs than resources. The notions that get adopted win out not only because of their objective value but also because of their proponents' skill at selling them.

Skill at pitching ideas is well worth acquiring. People who can sell ideas are generally more successful and happier than those who have never developed that skill. Not being able to market their ideas, not reaping the rewards of being creative, can make people feel impotent and ultimately cynical. Consider a few cases. In a California technology firm, a talented engineer is disgruntled because another engineer keeps getting funded and he doesn't, even though he has many more patents. A mid-level executive in a British financial firm recognizes a fellow walking past as a former employee and now his boss. A dedicated scientist in India complains that a colleague gets credit for an idea that was hers long before he talked it up and persuaded the company decision makers of its merits.

These individuals are all bright and energetic. They didn't begin their careers as whiners or cynics. In their own minds, they have done everything right — they have worked diligently, demonstrated creativity, and exhibited loyalty and dependability — yet others in their organizations have more money, status, and influence. They make the mistake, however, of assuming that having good ideas is enough. This point is crucial. What they fail to grasp is how vital advocacy is to success. Chuck Fox, appointed in 2009 to manage the environmental quality of the world's largest estuary, the Chesapeake Bay, addresses this point. When advocating, he says, "you need to have the science completely on your side. You need to have a policy well thought out. But if you don't have the politics on your side, you lose."[9]

The Idea-Advocacy Matrix

How do you get politics on your side when you have an idea to pitch? That is what this book is about. Figure 1 lays out the two key dimensions that we will be discussing. One dimension relates to the *quality of an idea*. Some notions are really dumb; others are brilliant. (Most ideas, of course, fall somewhere in the middle of the quality dimension.) In a perfect world, good ideas win out over bad ones. If someone proposes a brilliant notion, it is adopted (and its inventor is rewarded handsomely). And if someone

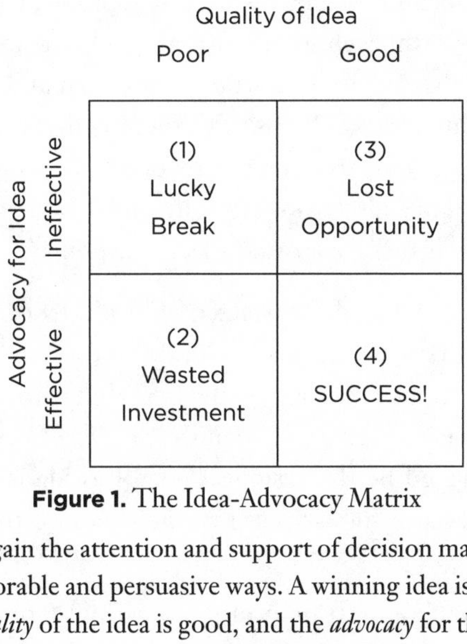

	Quality of Idea	
	Poor	Good
Ineffective	(1) Lucky Break	(3) Lost Opportunity
Effective	(2) Wasted Investment	(4) SUCCESS!

(Advocacy for Idea)

Figure 1. The Idea-Advocacy Matrix

If new ideas are to gain the attention and support of decision makers, they must be touted in memorable and persuasive ways. A winning idea is strong in two dimensions: the *quality* of the idea is good, and the *advocacy* for the idea is effective.

pitches a stupid idea, it is dismissed out of hand. In the real world, good ideas frequently falter, alas, and bad ideas too often receive accolades. Vital to getting an innovation adopted is a second dimension — advocacy. If new ideas are to win the attention and support of decision makers, they must be touted in memorable and persuasive ways. Combining the dimensions of quality and advocacy yields four quadrants.

Quadrants 1 and 2: Poor Ideas

The first two quadrants relate to poor ideas that are advocated with varying degrees of skill.

Quadrant 1: Lucky Break. People sometimes have really bad ideas, and we are all relieved when they can't find buyers. Poor ideas that can't be sold fall into quadrant 1. It is a *lucky break* for all when someone can't sell a bad idea.

Quadrant 2: Wasted Investment. When someone succeeds in selling a bad idea, money, time, and energy are expended on what is a *wasted investment.* We have all seen it happen. Someone with great advocacy skills convinces decision makers to adopt an idea that won't sell, will be too costly, will create unnecessary work, or will cause harm. Think of the successful advocacy for the massive use of DDT in agriculture, which led to deaths of some animal species and increases in certain sorts of cancer, the introduction of nonnative species like kudzu or the Asian carp that wipe out native plants or animal populations, the recommendation in Europe that pregnant women combat morning sickness with Thalidomide, which resulted in the birth of many deformed children, the hype about not vaccinating children against fatal diseases such as whooping cough and measles, which has brought fatalities in its wake, British Petroleum's decision to use apparently cheap methods when constructing a deep ocean oil rig in the Gulf of Mexico, which resulted in a disastrous oil spill. The list is endless.

Some flawed ideas revolve around specific products.

In 1972, experts persuaded the state of Florida to dump a million used tires into the waters off the coast. Goodyear even distributed pamphlets that said, "Worn out tires may be the best things that have happened to fishing since Izaak Walton." The author of *The Compleat Angler* would have been horrified by the results. Today Florida is engaged in a massive cleanup because the tires are ruining natural reefs and destroying fish life.[10]

Remember "New Coke"? If its promoters within Coca-Cola hadn't been successful in pitching the idea inside the company, it never would have hit the shelves — and sat there unbought. Its failure is a legendary instance of a wasted investment.

Consultants and employees alike sold United Airlines on an automatic baggage-handling system at the Denver International Airport. After spending over a quarter of a billion dollars on the system, United decided, in 2005, that going automatic was a lousy idea and switched back to a traditional system.

In October 2007 the drug giant Pfizer took Exubera, an inhaled diabetes medication, off the market, taking an almost $3 billion loss. Why? Not because it didn't work and not because it was unsafe. Inhaling a medication simply didn't appeal to customers. People inside Pfizer had successfully advocated for an idea that turned out to be a flop.

Environmentalists in the Netherlands cheered when they discovered that a palm oil from Southeast Asia might replace petroleum as a biofuel. They successfully advocated for government subsidies for companies that produced generators to burn palm oil. But they soon discovered that their idea to help stop global warming and save the environment was counterproductive. Meeting the demand for palm oil had horrifying environmental consequences in Southeast Asia: millions of acres of rain forest were devastated, rich soil was destroyed through the overuse of chemical fertilizers, and huge amounts of carbon emissions were released from draining and then burning peatlands.[11]

Other flawed ideas concern less tangible items. In one company, a seasoned advocate sold the idea of moving customer support offshore. As it turned out, customers wanted support personnel with an intuitive understanding of their individual issues. They mutinied against the company and migrated to competitors. In another firm, corporate communication managers touted moving their company's internal newsmagazine to the Web. The rationale was simple: it would save lots of money. Six months later, after an expensive switchover, company executives were stunned to discover that no one was reading the Web-based materials. Vital information was not reaching employees. So the company had to go back to the old print format, which people could take home, to lunch, to the restroom.

Most advocates don't know their ideas will backfire. Their notions seem great at first. Wilhelm Normann created what we now know as trans fats (bad for your body); Thomas Midgely invented and campaigned for Freon (bad for the atmosphere) as well as leaded gasoline (bad for the body).

And even failed ideas can teach valuable lessons. Some argue that Coke gained a huge marketing advantage from the failure of New Coke (in selling "Classic Coke").[12] But such lessons are often quite costly, and many of the people involved in a botched project wish the failed idea had never seen the light of day.

Quadrants 3 and 4: Good Ideas

Let's look at the other two quadrants of figure 1, which show what happens with good ideas.

Quadrant 3: Lost Opportunity. If you have a genuinely great idea but can't get decision makers to adopt it, your idea becomes a *lost opportunity*. It is the ideas in this quadrant that led to the writing of this book. When good ideas languish, companies lose the prospect of making money, and creative employees leave or become cynical.

Business history is dotted with stories of opportunities lost because people within companies were unsuccessful in pitching their ideas. And those neglected opportunities were consequential. Competitors seized market share that could have been kept and increased if the good idea had been adopted. Take the minivan. Who came up with that idea — Chrysler? No. Ford engineers came up with that idea — they called it the van-wagon — but they couldn't convince management that customers would buy it. In fact, one executive who endorsed it, Hal Sperlich, was fired and went on to lead the effort at Chrysler, which then dominated the minivan world for many years.[13] Ford lost out.

In 1998, Andrew Burrell and his colleagues at a computer firm called DEC created a tiny music player called the Personal Juke Box. DEC was being sold to Compaq at the time, and Burrell tried to sell his idea to executives at Compaq. But as one researcher reports, "When Compaq bought DEC, they basically got the whole research thing completely by accident. Once they found out it was there, a number of VPs started putting plans in place to kill it. We tried pretty hard to interest product groups, but they didn't have the vision that this thing [the digital music player] could have a very wide audience."[14] The executives at Apple were more receptive to the idea of a tiny music player and made history — and pots of money — with the iPod. Nokia engineers had the idea of a large touch screen for phones long before Apple introduced the iPhone, but management rejected the notion. Opportunities lost!

Failure to advocate a good idea effectively may mean that competitors gain an edge. But it may also mean that the development of a great idea is delayed. Many years ago, Sony engineer Ken Kutaragi was convinced that his company should be in the video-game business. So he proposed that Sony create what we now know as the PlayStation. Sony executives dismissed his idea and moved Kutaragi to a small office outside Tokyo where he nonetheless continued his campaign. He finally succeeded, but only after selling computer chips that handled sound to Nintendo (if competitors are interested in sound technology, we should be, too) and convincing the head of Sony Music that a PlayStation with a compact disc could be a good platform for people wanting to play Sony Music CDs. He told *Fast Company* that his "success had come despite the system, not because of it."[15]

Companies unreceptive to advocacy efforts often discover that their brightest "idea people" leave in search of more hospitable homes elsewhere. Some of today's most successful companies were created by individuals who were unable to convince movers and shakers within their former organizations of the merits of their ideas.

Sam Walton, the founder of Walmart, started his career as a franchisee in the Ben Franklin chain of stores. Walton tried to convince the Ben Franklin executives that his model of buying directly from manufacturers and offering deep discounts would lead to incredible opportunities. They didn't listen, Walton implemented the idea himself, and Walmart became an international phenomenon.

Ron Hamilton came up with the idea of making disposable contact lenses while working at CooperVision. After discovering a way to cheaply mass-produce lenses that could be changed monthly, Hamilton pitched his idea to management. He was turned down flat. Why? His idea threatened the part of the company's business that included cleaning fluids: with disposable lenses, people could toss away their lenses instead of cleaning them. So Hamilton left CooperVision and started a company that two years later was purchased for close to $40 million. Today almost everyone who wears contacts uses disposable ones.[16]

Eugene Kleiner and many other early innovators left William Shockley's Semiconductor Laboratory in the late 1950s when they failed to convince him of the merits of silicon. Joining a small company named Fairchild, these rebels soon dominated the semiconductor industry. Later Gordon Moore and other creative thinkers at Fairchild left to create Intel for a similar reason. Moore recalls that he was frustrated at Fairchild because "it was increasingly difficult to get our new ideas into the company's products. As the company grew, it became more and more difficult to transfer the ideas and the new technology."[17]

Steve Wozniak, a cofounder of Apple Computers, was working at Hewlett-Packard when he and Steve Jobs designed their first personal computer. Wozniak had signed a document at HP saying that whatever he designed as an employee belonged to HP. He said, "I loved [HP]. That was my company for life. So I approached HP. . . . Boy, did I make a pitch. I wanted them to do it. I had the Apple I, and I had a description of what the Apple II could do. I spoke of color. I described an $800 machine that ran BASIC (an early computer language), came out of the box fully built and talked to your home TV. And Hewlett-Packard found some reasons it couldn't be a Hewlett-Packard product."

Later, when HP began work on a computer, Wozniak approached the project managers and asked to work on it. "I really wanted to work on computers. And they turned me down for the job. To this day I don't know why. I said, 'I don't have to run anything,' even though I'd done all these things and they knew it. I said, 'I'll do a printer interface. I'll do the lowliest engineering job there is.' I wanted to work on a computer at my company and they turned me down."[18] Think how different the computer industry would be if Wozniak had successfully pitched his ideas to HP.

John Warnock and Chuck Geschke, the founders of Adobe, the second-biggest company in the world making software for personal computers, were working at Xerox when they came up with their idea of computer-based publishing, known as Postscript. As Warnock told a San Jose newspaper, "We started [Adobe] out of frustration with the employer that we had because we were building great stuff and there was no way that this stuff was ever going to get into the hands of the people who could use it."[19] The inventors spent two years trying to sell the idea within Xerox before they left to create their own company.

Craig Venter left the National Institutes of Health when his proposal to use "whole-genome shotgun sequencing" was rejected. He went on to create his own company, where the first decoding of a whole bacterial genome was completed. That discovery was heralded by Nobel laureate James Watson as a "great moment in science."[20]

At first reading, you might think that the real issue in these cases is not advocacy but rather the unwillingness of companies to listen to gifted employees. You would be right. These organizations weren't attentive enough, and brilliant individuals jumped ship in search of more receptive audiences. It is essential that executives create cultures in which good ideas are recognized and supported. Leaders too often have no idea of who is doing the most innovative work. Koichi Tanaka, for instance, shared the Nobel Prize in Chemistry in 2003 for his work on protein-molecule analysis. The company he worked for, Shimadzu, a Japanese precision-engineering firm, saw little value in commercializing his invention until after researchers in other nations had done so and had given Tanaka recognition for the work. In fact, until he won the Nobel Prize, he was a low-level "salary man." Afterward, the president of Shimadzu told reporters that although he had met Tanaka a few years earlier, he "could not have imagined" that he would ever be a Nobel laureate.[21] Only after receiving the Nobel Prize was Tanaka promoted to a senior position.

The inability of leadership to recognize and commercialize great ideas is only part of what happens when ideas fall into Quadrant 3. Responsibility also lies with the people who came up with the ideas in the first place. In many cases, innovative people are not effective salespeople. They either don't know how to promote their ideas or don't want to. Either way, their ideas falter. Promising ideas must be merchandised.

The paradigmatic case of a lost opportunity must be Xerox. In the early 1970s, the company assembled some of the world's brightest computer scientists at its Palo Alto Research Center (PARC) in California. Their task was wide open: push forward with vital, interesting projects. Out of this lab came extraordinary innovations. One was the first PC to include graphical user interface (the Xerox Alto). Another was Ethernet. But Xerox, at the corporate level, did amazingly little to capitalize on these inventions. Beyond the reputational loss, how much money did Xerox lose by not exploiting the scientists' work? Billions. According to Steve Jobs, if Xerox had harvested all of the PARC inventions, today it would be richer than IBM, Microsoft, and Xerox combined.[22]

Why did Xerox miss its opportunity? Perhaps because PARC researchers didn't understand that they not only had to invent things but also had to sell their inventions. Douglas Smith and Robert Alexander, in their classic study of the Xerox debacle, argue that much of the problem at Xerox was a culture clash between young scientists and corporate executives. Most of the researchers had just finished school. Pony-tailed mavericks, they had little respect for people in suits. As one scientist recalls, "When we felt sometimes that someone was not worth talking to, we sometimes told them that."[23] These inventors burned rather than built bridges. Even the more mature leaders of PARC sometimes didn't grasp the value of pitching ideas as commercial opportunities. For example, when George Pake, a scientific leader at PARC, presented one of the center's ideas to executives at Xerox, he emphasized the technological challenges that still needed to be overcome, not the idea's business potential.[24] And Robert Taylor, one of the founders of PARC, famously said, "I was hired to produce the best technology I could. If the product group [at Xerox] was not able to take advantage of our technology a lot of people are culpable, not me."[25]

Quadrant 4: Success. Quadrant 4 is the home of good ideas that have been promoted effectively. Great ideas that have been successfully sold within organizations fall in this box.

Construction: In 1941, the many thousands of people working in Washington, DC, for the United States Army were spread across more than seventeen buildings. General Brehon Somervell, an accomplished administrator, imagined a single mammoth building to house them all. Because of his successful advocacy, the government constructed the largest building in the world. First labeled "Somervell's Folly," it is now considered a national landmark: the Pentagon.

Automobile Industry: J. Mays and Freeman Thomas worked at Volkswagen's California Design Center. It took them three years to convince the leadership of VW to resurrect the famous Beetle. "The design only took three days," says Mays. "Selling the project took three years."[26]

Agriculture: G. C. "Jack" Hanna, a professor of vegetable crops at the University of California, Davis, teamed with an engineering faculty member, Coby Lorenzen, to create a mechanical tomato harvester. Hanna's colleagues thought the idea ridiculous, but six years later, Hanna's equipment was harvesting virtually 100 percent of California's tomato crop.[27]

Computer Technology: Bernie Meyerson, an IBM researcher, contended that far greater processing speeds could be achieved if germanium were added to computer chips. For years, nobody at IBM accepted his notion. He kept campaigning and convinced his skeptics. IBM made billions as a result.

Consumer Products: Art Fry of 3M created the Post-it Note. His managers saw little value in a small sticky piece of paper. So, without anyone's permission, he created prototypes and even built a machine to make them. He distributed prototypes to secretaries of 3M executives. Days later, the secretaries asked Fry for more. Fry told them he didn't have any more. They ought to persuade their bosses to support his idea. And now we have Post-it Notes.[28]

Lighting: Japanese engineer Shuji Nakamura spent ten years creating blue LEDs at Nichia, a tiny chemical company on Shikoku island. Managers continually urged him to work on other projects, and his coworkers harassed him, telling him that he should quit, that he was wasting company money, but he kept insisting that he was close to an important discovery. He finally created an effective blue LED, and Nichia has reaped millions from his innovation.[29]

Technology: Tetsuya Mizoguchi, an engineer at Toshiba, argued with company executives about the importance of devising a portable computer. They dismissed the idea: it would never amount to much. Mizoguchi kept making his case, and the leadership finally saw the light. Today millions of people own a laptop.[30]

Photoduplication: Xerox entered the laser-printer market mostly because of a strong selling job by the head of the company's printing division, Jack Lewis. Lewis pushed for the printer despite direct orders from senior leaders to kill the project that eventually led to the printer.[31] If Lewis had stopped pushing, the company would have lost a hugely lucrative opportunity.

Pharmaceuticals: Richard Miller, a researcher in 3M's pharmaceutical unit, developed a new sort of immune-response modifier to treat genital and perianal warts. His bosses were so skeptical of his work that they told him to move on to another project. Miller persisted anyway. Today his product, marketed under the name Aldara, yields millions in annual sales.

Financial Services: In 1997, David Pottruck, a senior executive at the Charles Schwab brokerage firm, persuaded his firm's leadership to make a very risky move: to create a full-service Internet brokerage business and charge a commission of only $29.95 for up to 1,000 shares. Pottruck knew the move would initially reduce earnings commissions the company received for trading equities. In fact, since the company's leaders' compensation was tied to earnings, his idea would probably take money out of executives' pockets. Making the move was a huge gamble. But Pottruck succeeded in his advocacy, and Schwab took a leadership role in Internet-based trading. Over the next three years, trading volume skyrocketed 183 percent, and profits doubled.[32]

Medicine: Two Australian physicians, Barry Marshall and Robin Warren, spent almost twenty years trying to convince peers that bacteria cause peptic ulcers. Prestigious doctors ignored and ridiculed the notion, and medical journals were reluctant to publish their research. Before their advocacy was successful, peptic ulcers were often linked to stress and were treated by surgery. Today, patients swallow a pill, and their ulcers disappear, while Marshall and Warren enjoy a Nobel Prize in Medicine in recognition of their work.

Mail Delivery: Joe Perrone worked at FedEx in New York City. He often saw harried customers rushing right past a FedEx truck on their way to a FedEx drop box. "Hey," Perrone wondered, "why not cut a slot in each FedEx truck? That way customers, when spying a truck, could drop their packages into the slot." Customers would save time, and pickups might be faster, too. Perrone had to get a stamp of approval from seven different company units, which he procured by asking people in each unit how he could make it work for them. As he told the *Washington Post*, "Since I was the one willing to [do] all the legwork, they said, 'If you want to knock yourself out, go right ahead.' "[33] Today, thousands of FedEx trucks have little slots on their side panels thanks to Perrone's successful advocacy.[34]

What do all of these idea champions, some famous and others less so, have in common? They understood that for their ideas to be realized, they had to become advocates. Advocacy is an exhausting but necessary skill. Thomas Edison, a model of advocacy, was brilliant at generating publicity for his ideas and obtaining funding for them. Robert Fulton didn't invent the steam engine, but he successfully advocated using a steam engine to power boats; even before he tested his version of a steam engine, he had to sell his idea to wealthy investors. When the creator of Ethernet, Robert Metcalfe, took aspiring entrepreneurs for tours around his Boston Back Bay mansion, he reminded them that he didn't acquire the mansion because he invented the Ethernet. He acquired it after spending a decade promoting the idea.[35]

Don't misunderstand. Although many of the ideas described above are world-shaking, most ideas advocated in organizations every day are mundane. They involve reorganization, or product modification, or a different approach to an issue, or an improvement in a process. They are about using a different vendor, promoting an employee, or convincing management to change work hours. They are still important. Most of the things that today make organizations successful and jobs pleasant were small ideas that employees successfully sold within their firms.

Advocacy is not limited to convincing skeptical leaders to try out something new; colleagues need convincing, too. Bringing ideas to market nowadays almost always requires team efforts. Advocates also often need to sell ideas to subordinates — which means that top executives need to be brilliant advocates. The chief executive officer who turned J. C. Penney around, Allen Questrom, told the *Wall Street Journal* that one of the biggest challenges in leading a large organization through change was selling the strategy to employees.[36] Perhaps Boeing's CEO, James McNerney, said it best when describing his board of directors: "I'm just one of eleven with a point of view. I have to depend upon my power to persuade."[37]

What Is Advocacy?

Advocacy means persuading people who matter to care about your issue. It is about getting listened to, being at the table when decisions are made, being heard by people who make decisions. It is about facing and overcoming resistance. It is about speaking and writing in compelling ways that make decision makers want to adopt your ideas.

Sometimes advocates champion brand-new ideas, and sometimes they suggest modifications to existing processes, products, and problems. Henry Ford didn't invent the car, but he created a new process to make it; Michael Dell didn't invent the computer, but he came up with an innovative process to sell it; Amazon didn't invent books, but it devised a new way to distribute them, as did Netflix for films. Advocates might propose decreasing or increasing the investment their firm makes in an initiative; they might request changes to budgets, promote the reorganization of work processes, sell a training initiative, accelerate development cycles, argue that a project needs to be kept alive, or suggest candidates for important positions.

Advocacy means overcoming obstacles. Unsophisticated advocates think they have been successful when decision makers give them a first nod; wise advocates know they must keep selling long after an idea is launched.

Studies of product development find that administrative activities account for 90 percent of the time it takes to get products to market.[38] So successful advocates often must persuade slow organizational bureaucrats to speed up processes.

Advocacy is also involved in attempts to stop or delay bad ideas. Indeed, when people pitch ideas that fall in Quadrant 2 (Wasted Investment), the arguments that others make to oppose those ideas are prime examples of advocacy. While working as a scientist at the Food and Drug Administration, Frances Kelsey was an extraordinary advocate against the introduction of thalidomide into the United States. The drug, created in the 1950s in Europe to reduce morning sickness among pregnant women, often resulted in serious birth defects. She persuaded the FDA's leadership that further testing was necessary before the drug could be approved. And she relentlessly challenged the drug's manufacturer for data that they tried to hide. For her work she received the President's Award for Distinguished Federal Civilian Service — the highest honorary award the federal government grants career civilian employees. More important, children in the United States never suffered the horrendous problems that came from thalidomide.

Advocacy is as important in nonprofit settings as in for-profit settings. Fund-raisers must coax people to donate money, time, and ideas. In government, the ability to sell agendas and propose alternatives to agenda items requires incredible advocacy skills. Robert Rubin, former secretary of the treasury and former head of Goldman Sachs, summarized the role of advocacy in government this way: "Having a significant influence ordinarily requires not only an important piece of work but also a shrewd sense of how to get attention in the media, Congress, and elsewhere in official Washington."[39]

Finally, advocacy is about empowerment — about giving smart and dedicated people the opportunity to have an impact, to make sure their hard work is recognized, appreciated, and used. People want to make their ideas happen, partly for the psychic rewards — being listened to and making a contribution — and partly for material rewards, since successful advocates of transformational ideas can reap huge commercial payoffs. Of course, many advocates never get credit for their work. Even through Charles Momsen invented and campaigned for a diving bell to rescue sailors stuck in submarines, the United States Navy opted to name the bell the McCann Rescue Chamber. Certain Naval leaders felt that Momsen had embarrassed them with his insistent advocacy, so they gave the laurel instead to one of Momsen's colleagues who had contributed to the project.[40] General William "Billy" Mitchell fared even worse than Momsen. Mitchell's strong advocacy for air power in the military in the early twentieth century ultimately proved successful, but it also led to his court-martial.

Advocacy isn't only about getting personal credit for an innovation, gratifying though that can be. Organizations profit, too. The future of any firm depends on the ability of its talented people to passionately and successfully promote innovative ideas. Successful advocates are catalysts for change. Organizations prosper because innovations are directly associated with revenue growth, market share, market value, and even the survival of the firm. Societies, too, advance through innovations. Economists estimate that half of the economic growth in the world over the past fifty years can be attributed to technological innovations.[41] Every one of those innovations had to be advocated within some organization before it appeared in the marketplace.

Advocacy Skills for Everyone

Business scholars Gina O'Connor and Mark Rice studied the development of many significant innovations in large companies such as IBM, DuPont, and General Motors. They found that low- and mid-level researchers were often the first to recognize new opportunities. However, recognition is only the first step. Advocacy must follow. Influential managers who understood both the markets and the new ideas were crucial for pushing innovations.[42] Successful CEOs certainly champion innovations. Legendary business leaders like Darwin Smith (Kimberly-Clark), James Burke (Johnson & Johnson), and William Allen (Boeing) each faced huge challenges in convincing employees, board members, and customers that major changes were needed: Kimberly-Clark needed to sell everything that had made the company great for almost a century, Johnson & Johnson needed to handle a massive product-tampering problem, and Boeing needed to move from being solely a defense contractor to creating planes that virtually every major commercial airline in the world could — and does — use. Each of these executives had splendid advocacy skills. But people at the lowest levels of a firm can find themselves advocating for ideas. A janitor may have a great notion for rearranging the sequence in which equipment is maintained. An experienced administrative assistant may discover a useful technique for dealing with a difficult client. A security guard may pitch an idea for enhancing the safety of a facility.

Someone doesn't have to have an original idea to be an advocate. Advocates can play the vital role of selling other people's ideas to decision makers. A major responsibility of managers is to sell the ideas of their subordinates to high-level decision makers. Indeed, employees are far more satisfied with their supervisors when they perceive that their supervisors can influence those higher up.[43]

Regardless of how crucial advocacy is, most people know surprisingly little about how to pitch ideas successfully. In one study, conducted by Swiss researchers, 98 percent of executives from throughout the world who were surveyed reported that they had experienced difficulty selling an idea within their organization.[44] While many executives and business pundits praise the value of innovation, few highlight the importance of selling innovations. Instead, we read commentaries like one found in the *Economist Technology Quarterly*: "Above all, companies need to separate their perception of the value of an idea from the way it is presented, or the track record of the person proposing it."[45] Value, presentation, and individual can't really be separated. A valuable idea that is not sold within a firm is not going to see the light of day, no matter what its merits.

Most books and articles about product development ignore the marketing of innovations *within* organizations. The texts make product development sound impeccably logical, even sterile. They describe what make some products more successful in the marketplace, the stages of new product development (e.g., strategy development, idea generation, product screening, business analysis, product development, test marketing, commercialization), formal decision-making criteria (go/no-go tollgates; sensitivity analysis; risk analysis), the availability of new technologies, and so on.

What you don't read about in those books are the emotions, misunderstandings, rivalries, bureaucratic hurdles, politics, and other interpersonal dynamics that experienced product developers know they have to deal with to get an idea adopted. Anyone who has worked in an organization knows that politics can matter as much as business issues when decisions are made.[46] Everyone in an organization is vying for money, people, space, and other resources. As Bill Drayton, the founder of the social entrepreneurship organization Ashoka, says, "I don't believe that *conceiving* an idea and *marketing* an idea are different."[47] "Politics is as important as the policy," says former treasury secretary Robert Rubin, "because if the politics doesn't work, the policy—no matter whether the decisions are sensible or not—won't be implemented."[48] Moving from idea to implementation is as much a social and political process as it is a rational one—and maybe even more so.

Some people believe the ability to advocate is something you either have or don't have. As an engineer at a large oil-services firm said, "I'm just not good at that sort of stuff," referring to his inability to champion ideas. At first glance, he may be right. Academic studies show that people who successfully champion ideas in organizations are innovative risk-takers who have a strong need to achieve.[49] They are adaptive and believe they have a great deal of control over their lives.[50] As leaders, they are self-confident, inspirational, and charismatic, as well as intellectually stimulating.[51] They probably have a great deal of "emotional intelligence."

Yet personality doesn't account for everything. In any organization you hear stories about people who successfully pitched ideas but who had none of the advocacy characteristics identified in personality studies.

Anyone, at any age, can learn to effectively pitch ideas. With time, experience, and the skills discussed here, people of all types and backgrounds can become successful advocates. Even experienced advocates must hone their skills when their jobs change. George Marshall, in reflecting on his first years of being chief of staff of the U.S. military during the Second World War, said: "It became clear to me at the age of 58 I would have to learn new tricks that were not taught in the military manuals or on the battlefield. In this position [chief of staff] I am a political soldier and will have to put my training in rapping-out orders and making snap decisions on the back burner, and have to learn the arts of persuasion and guile. I must become an expert in a whole new set of skills."[52]

The Downside to Advocacy

Let's acknowledge that advocacy has its negative aspects. First, advocacy skills can be used to resist good ideas. If an idea is a bad one, successful advocacy lets people effectively oppose it. Yet, in the political give-and-take of an organization, advocates can also use the skills described in this book to crush valuable ideas for their own advantage: An executive argues to maintain a unit that obviously needs to be shut down just because he wants more "head count"; a manager persuades her boss not to adopt another person's brilliant idea because it might make her look bad; a scientist squashes an innovative grant proposal because it threatens to make some of his research irrelevant.

Second, advocacy can be used to champion bad ideas (think back to quadrant 2 in figure 1). Since the quality of an idea can matter less than the politics surrounding it, crafty advocates can cajole people into supporting ideas that fail miserably. Eve successfully persuaded Adam to eat that apple: good-bye, Eden. At NASA, some engineers and scientists urged the launch of *Challenger* in the cold January weather (the space shuttle was torn apart) and convinced their colleagues to ignore the tiles that fell off during the launch of *Columbia* (it broke up). Similarly, certain managers at Toyota downplayed the problems the company was facing in 2009 with the accelerator pedal that stuck in open position.

In fact, a major reason why products fail in the marketplace is the over-enthusiasm of managers during the development process.[53] Highly involved champions often wear blinders when it comes to their ideas. Indeed, they are especially overconfident with pioneering ideas.[54] They ignore market evidence that fails to support their ideas.[55] While enthusiasm, focus, and confidence are definitely plusses in promoting good ideas, these factors are equally compelling when promoting bad ideas. Sophisticated advocates can argue for bad ideas as well as good ones, and once ideas take hold in an organization, they are often hard to root out.[56] Even if advocates cannot successfully turn an idea into a reality, they can prolong decision making, costing organizations enormous amounts of money. The later the decisions are made to kill a project, the more expensive it is to kill it. "Fail early, fail cheap" is a wise maxim. Good advocacy can sometimes lead a company to persist with a bad plan or product for too long.

Third, advocacy is associated with political risks. An advocate's credibility may well be shattered if she bungles an attempt to advocate. An advocate's reputation can be threatened if he touts a lemon. If the idea is rebuffed by management, ends up costing far more than it's worth, or is rejected in the marketplace, the advocate is the one held responsible.

A Framework for Advocacy

More than twenty-five years ago, Gifford Pinchot wrote a book celebrating "intrapreneuring." Its thesis was that successful companies let their employees' great ideas blossom. Pinchot's book was quite popular for a time, but attention to the topic faded, perhaps because the specific ways in which people successfully sell ideas were never spelled out. The current book fills that void by describing what successful advocates do when pitching ideas. The chapters that follow illuminate the major skills required for successful advocacy.

Effective advocates communicate clearly and memorably. Chapter 2 focuses on what it takes to ensure that people understand and remember the ideas being advocated. Chapter 3 shows how advocates frame their ideas so they have impact.

Effective advocates build credibility and generate affinity. People won't willingly buy ideas from people they don't like or trust. An advocate's reputation is crucial to inspiring confidence in his or her ideas. Chapter 4 offers a catalog of ways that advocates use to build and maintain their reputation.

Effective advocates build relationships that let ideas prosper. It is almost impossible to successfully push big or even small ideas all by yourself. The processes are too complicated; the issues are too complex. Sophisticated advocates are often in the role of coordinator—marshaling relationships to ensure that ideas are heard and adopted. Shrewd advocates rally support through alliances (chapter 5) and networking (chapter 8).

Effective advocates presell their ideas. One thing that is crystal clear about advocacy is that important decisions are often made long before formal meetings happen. Superb idea champions know how to presell their ideas. They build the groundwork before springing their ideas on decision makers. Preselling successfully requires the advocate to understand who makes decisions (chapter 7), time pitches perfectly (chapter 9), and offer vivid messages (chapter 12).

Effective advocates influence others. At its core, advocacy is about persuasion. Good advocates grasp the value of narrative (chapter 6), understand techniques of persuasion (chapters 10 and 11), sound confident (chapter 13), and know how to manage meetings to gain the attention they think their ideas deserve (chapter 14).

A hoary maxim says, "If you build a better mousetrap, people will beat a path to your door." That maxim is wrong. People won't beat a path unless they know you have a mousetrap, like and respect you, and are persuaded that your mousetrap is indeed better. When you finish reading this book, you will have the tools to successfully sell your mousetrap.

2

Communicate Your Idea with Impact

Self-expression must pass into
communication for its fulfillment.

PEARL BUCK

Imagine that tomorrow morning you meet with your organization's senior executives to pitch an idea you have been working on for the past six months. Your twenty-minute session is part of what your company calls its annual project reviews, when top decision makers hear from employees about their projects and budget needs for the coming year. A week from now, the executives will hold a private session to discuss all the projects, and you know that only a few will be vividly remembered, and even fewer will receive generous support. Most projects will have been all but forgotten by the time the executive session is held. What can you do to make sure decision makers remember your proposal amid the clutter of the many ideas that were raised in the review sessions?

Part of the answer to this question lies in how clearly you communicate your idea. As the man who brought us the Post-it Note, 3M's Art Fry, says, "It's one thing to have an idea but if you can't communicate it to others . . . you're dead in the water."[1] Too often, people don't communicate their ideas clearly enough. And even when the ideas are perfectly clear, decision makers frequently forget most of what they have heard. In fact, people recall less than 15 percent of what they have heard in recent conversations—and about one-fourth of what they do recall is inaccurate.[2] In this chapter, we will discover what successful advocates do to clearly communicate their ideas in memorable ways.

Know What You Want People to Know

One of the biggest mistakes that unsophisticated advocates make is pitching their ideas before knowing exactly what they want decision makers to remember. They have a sense that something in the organization or one of its products or processes needs to change, but before taking the time to think through their ideas completely, they start to talk. Wise proponents, on the other hand, decide what they want to communicate before they start talking. They have a laserlike focus on the essential points that decision makers need to understand. These savvy proponents accept that not everything about their ideas is equally important. Some information is helpful but not essential; and some information, though interesting, is superfluous. Remember, the Declaration of Independence has fewer than 1,500 words; the Gettysburg Address, only 272 words. John Kennedy's famous inaugural address lasted less than fifteen minutes. The average television sound bite for a presidential candidate in the 2004 election was less than eight seconds long![3]

Try this exercise. Think of what you are proposing. Can you encapsulate the idea in fewer than 100 words? 50 words? 10 words? Look at a billboard on the street. With just a picture and a few words, you get the message. So what is your billboard? Young financial analysts at Fidelity Investments quickly learned when pitching ideas to Peter Lynch, the company's legendary stock picker, that "he really wanted to hear the story in a simplified way. What's the main factor that's driving this company? What's going to make people want this stock?"[4] Similarly, A. G. Lafley, the successful former CEO of Procter & Gamble, when presented with overly complex pitches, used to say, "Give me the *Sesame Street* version."[5]

Stay on Message with Repetition and Redundancy

Early in election campaigns, successful politicians, who are professional advocates by definition, identify themes that they want reporters and voters to pay attention to. Then they religiously stay "on message" in their speeches and ads. James Carville, the successful manager of Bill Clinton's first presidential campaign, constantly reminded staffers during the campaign that the key message was "It's the economy, stupid."

One way of staying on message is repetition. Years ago psychologists discovered the "mere exposure effect": the more often people see an object, the more positive they feel about it.[6] There is a wonderful story of a man who was so in love with a woman who lived far from him that every day, for 500 days, he mailed a love letter to her. On the 500th day, she married the postman. Exposure works. Up to a point, it can enhance decision makers' feelings toward an idea.[7]

When Intuit's Dan Robinson wanted to convince colleagues that the company should develop software to help people manage medical expenses, he started off every conversation with "Health care is a $1.3 trillion business, and we [Intuit] don't have a piece of it. Health care is messed up. There ought to be lots of ways to make it easier, and people will pay for that help." Repetition worked. Intuit finally adopted his idea.[8]

John Loose, former CEO of Corning, told of a similar approach. "We believe in the Rule of Six. When there is a message . . . you have to say it six times. You can't have a meeting one day and check it off. You have to keep going back."[9]

But repetition isn't always helpful. It doesn't work, for instance, when people don't understand what is being said. In an intriguing series of studies, communication researchers had someone pretend to be lost. The "lost" person approached people in Davis, California, requesting directions to a well-known location. After getting directions, the lost individual acted confused and said he didn't understand. At this point, what did many direction givers do? They gave the same directions in louder voices.[10] How helpful was that? If someone doesn't understand what you are saying the first time, how will repeating it help? Once something has been said a few times in the same way to the same people, that's enough. People get annoyed with needless repetition.

Successful advocates do more than repeat their ideas. They also restate key aspects of their ideas in alternative ways. Let's call this being redundant.[11] As I use the terms here, *repetition* is saying the same thing again in the same way; *redundancy* is saying the same thing in different ways. Do you remember being confused by something a teacher explained in class? You might have approached her after class and asked her to explain the concept to you again. Too often, poor teachers repeated what they had said earlier. What you needed was for the teacher to be redundant — to explain the concept in different ways by offering fresh examples or helpful meta-phors. Effective advocates, like good teachers, are redundant when explain-ing their ideas.

What are the ground rules for being usefully redundant?

- Offer multiple examples.
- Use different modalities.
- Value visual media.
- Move beyond slides and paper.

Offer Multiple Examples

When rescuers search for someone lost on a mountain, they often use signals from that person's mobile phone through a technique called tri-angulation. They take one reading, move some distance and take a second reading, and then move in a different direction and take a third. They lo-cate the person where those readings intersect. The same principle works when pitching ideas. Explaining ideas in multiple ways helps decision makers home in on what's being proposed. So smart advocates normally employ at least two examples when introducing a concept. They know that if they offer only one, decision makers might confuse the concept with the example.

Suppose you are explaining to a child how a lever and a fulcrum work. You show the child a picture of a farmer lifting a rock using them.

"Ah," the youngster says, "levers and fulcrums are farming equipment."

"No," you reply, "not exactly." Then you offer a second picture, this time of a seesaw at a playground. Now the child grasps the concept. This is why teachers, when assigning word problems in high-school math, never assign just one problem. Were students to do just a single item, they might confuse the specific problem with the underlying mathematical concept. Complet-ing several problems helps them grasp the basic principle that the word problems were designed to teach.

Redundancy of this sort works in organizations, too. Six Sigma is a col-lection of techniques used in companies to reduce unwanted variation, improve quality, and better manage processes. But Six Sigma advocates, to their chagrin, often find that decision makers fail to understand how helpful the techniques can be outside of manufacturing and logistics. In fact, the methods employed in Six Sigma can be used to enhance almost any orga-nizational function (e.g., sales, financial management). Decision makers think of Six Sigma so narrowly because proponents traditionally offer man-ufacturing or logistics examples. If they want people to see the generality of the approach, they could offer both a manufacturing example and an exam-ple drawn from, say, sales or human resources.

Use Different Modalities

People's primary sensory preferences are visual, auditory, and kinesthetic (tactile). Visually oriented people need to *see* the information; those who process information primarily in auditory ways prefer *hearing* it; and kines-thetic listeners like to *touch* things. Wise proponents use the preferred style of their listeners when pitching ideas. A prototype of a cell phone or an energy-efficient washing machine has more impact with kinesthetically and visually oriented people than it does with those who prefer auditory infor-mation.[12] People who have a strong need to touch things feel far more confident in judging products they can touch, while people with less need to touch are comfortable making similar judgments without handling prod-ucts.[13] Visually oriented decision makers have stronger positive reactions to aesthetically pleasing versions of products than do those who are less fo-cused on their visual aspects.[14]

While each of us may have a preferred modality, smart advocates use multiple modalities — auditory, visual, and kinesthetic — when communi-cating their ideas. There are three good reasons for doing so. First, advo-cates often address a diverse group of decision makers — some are visually oriented, others more auditory or tactile — so using all three modalities raises the chance that the proponents will connect to every one in the audience. Second, it is difficult to identify even an individual's media prefer-ence. Third, even if people's preferences are obvious, there is still value in using different modalities.

People process visual and auditory information in different parts of their brain. When proponents both talk about their ideas and provide working models of what they are proposing, their message ignites two parts of the brain. Abraham Lincoln's law partner, William Herndon, said that Lincoln often sprawled out on a sofa and read aloud. Asked why he wouldn't read quietly, Lincoln replied, "I catch the idea by two senses . . . when I read aloud I hear what I read and I see it, and hence two senses get it and I remember it better."[15] Academic research supports Lincoln's belief: words accompanied by pictures are more persuasive than words alone.[16]

Value Visual Media: Seeing Is Believing

Hospitals are unsafe places. One major reason that patients get sick (or sicker) is because hospital staff don't wash their hands frequently enough. Just talking about the importance of washing hands and placing antibiotic soap in convenient locations doesn't seem to work. Doctors and nurses still examine patient after patient without washing their hands in between. Rekha Murthy, an epidemiologist at the Cedars-Sinai hospital in Los Angeles, was stymied: How could she foster hand washing? Then she came up with a powerful persuasive technique. At a meeting of the hospital's top twenty physicians she asked each to press a palm into an agar plate, saying she "would love to culture your hand." After the cultures developed, she photographed the bacteria that were present. The pictures were "disgusting and striking, with gobs of colonies of bacteria." One vivid photograph was made into a screen saver and placed on every computer in the hospital. Soon there was almost 100 percent compliance with the hospital's hand-washing regimen.[17] People understood the message when they heard it, but they really understood it when they saw the picture.

The maxim "A picture is worth a thousand words" is true. Visuals garner attention and humans have well-honed visual skills. We have used pictures for communication much longer than we have used words. Visuals are also efficient for communicating many kinds of information. Wouldn't you rather show someone a map than give directions in mere words? Wouldn't you rather display an organizational chart than describe the same complex organizational structure verbally? Wouldn't you rather demonstrate an Apple iPad than explain its capabilities with words alone?

Visuals make advocates more persuasive.[18] Graphic pictures on cigarette packages are more effective at communicating the risks of smoking than text warnings are.[19] For years, Montgomery Ward produced an annual children's Christmas story to promote the store's brand name. In 1939, Robert Mays, a copywriter employed by Montgomery Ward, created one of the most memorable holiday stories we have: "Rudolph the Red-Nosed Reindeer." When he first pitched his story, his boss balked at the idea of a red-nosed deer. In those days, red noses implied drunkenness. Mays asked a colleague and illustrator, Denver Gillen, to go to Lincoln Zoo in Chicago and sketch what a red-nosed deer might look like in a children's tale. Mays brought Gillen's drawing back to his boss, and the picture convinced him that they could charm children with a deer with a large red nose — as indeed they have, for decades.

While studying eBay auctions of nineteenth-century coins, two research-ers, Charles Wood and Robert Kaufman, found that when pictures ac-companied information about a coin's age and condition, sellers received 12 percent more money than when they provided text-only offerings of the same coins. In addition, buyers gave sellers a higher "reputation score" when pictures were included in their auctions.[20]

Throughout history, scientists, too, have used visuals as a crucial way of persuading doubters.[21] Geophysicist Clair Patterson, the scientist who made the case to stop using toxic leaded gasoline, persuaded many people of his argument by showing them three cartoon drawings, the famous "mea-sles" cartoons (fig. 2). The first fellow had one dot on his chest, which represented the natural level of lead in a human body. The second man had 500 dots, representing the typical level of lead in an American in 1980. The third had 2,000 dots, representing the amount at which symptoms of lead poisoning are obvious. What was the point? People were slowly being poisoned to death by lead.[22]

Politicians, those masters of advocacy, understand the value of the visual. As Charlene Barshefsky, President Clinton's trade representative, said, "All the statistics in the world about export-related jobs don't offset one picture of a closed factory whose loss is blamed on foreign competition."[23]

David Stockman was head of the U.S. Office of Management and Budget (OMB) during the early part of Ronald Reagan's administration. Charged with balancing the budget, he sought to control military spending. Secre-tary of Defense Caspar Weinberger adamantly opposed Stockman's pro-posals to cut the military budget. In meeting with Reagan to make the military's case, Weinberger displayed a cartoon showing three soldiers. As Stockman tells it, "One was a pygmy who carried no rifle. He represented the Carter budget. The second was a four-eyed wimp who looked like Woody Allen, carrying a tiny rifle. That was . . . me? . . . the OMB's [proposed] defense budget. Finally, there was G.I. Joe himself, 190 pounds of fighting man, all decked out in helmet and flak jacket and pointing an M-60 machine gun menacingly. . . . This imposing warrior represented, yes, the Department of Defense budget plan."[24] Weinberger won the day.

One reason why visuals are often more effective than words is because people remember visual information better than verbal information. Data presented in graphical form (e.g., a simple bar graph) have more impact

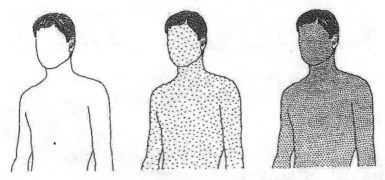

Figure 2. Lead in the Human Environment

Clair Patterson's cartoon depicts the amount of lead found in early humans, the average amount in Americans in 1980, and the amount symptomatic of lead poisoning. (Reprinted with permission from *Lead in the Human Environment* [1980], by the National Academy of Sciences. Courtesy of the National Academies Press, Washington, DC.)

than the same data presented as simple numbers.[25] During Reagan's presidential reelection campaign, CBS aired a story showing him cutting a ribbon at a new nursing home and distributing medals to handicapped children who completed a race. As the video played on the home television screen, CBS correspondent Lesley Stahl told viewers how Reagan had tried to cut funding for both nursing homes and the handicapped. Later that evening, one of Reagan's aides phoned Stahl thanking her for the broadcast. She was surprised because she'd been pointing out hypocrisy in Reagan's administration. But Reagan's staff member knew that no one really listened to what she said; they looked at the pictures and gained an impression of Reagan's kindness and generosity.[26]

To be effective, visuals should match how decision makers think. For example, since people believe that upward slopes represent increasing rates, any graph showing growth should show upwardness. Visuals should be uncluttered, including only information directly relevant to the point being made. Bad PowerPoint presentations are filled with clutter—words come from every direction, sound effects evoke a bad karate movie, colors change randomly, distracting images fill the background. The audience can become more intrigued by the seductive details of the slides than by what the speaker is saying. Finally, visuals should be simple. The simpler the visual, the easier it is for others to understand it and the more persuasive it is.

The British Conservative Party, in its successful 1979 election campaign,

Figure 3. "Labour Isn't Working"

Visuals are compelling. This striking poster was used by Margaret Thatcher's Conservative Party in the 1979 election campaign in Great Britain. The Labour Party lost. (Everett Collection, New York.)

used a striking visual: a picture of a long line of people waiting outside an unemployment office. Printed across the picture was the phrase "Labour isn't working" (fig. 3).[27] The Labour Party was the party of the incumbent prime minister, whom Margaret Thatcher hoped to replace. Since she was campaigning in a year when there was massive unemployment in Britain, that simple billboard communicated brilliantly her entire plan to fix the economy by replacing the current government.

At the end of the U.S. invasion of Iraq, the U.S. military identified top Iraqi leaders whom it wanted to arrest. Rather than just listing names on a sheet of paper, the military created fifty-five playing cards, each containing the name, title, and photograph of one of the "most wanted." Simple but powerful.

Move Beyond Slides and Paper

In the early twentieth century, U.S. military leaders were adamantly opposed to creating a powerful air force. They preferred giant battleships for waging war at sea. But General Billy Mitchell, a decorated First World War aviator, disagreed and, in the early 1920s, convinced military leaders to let him test his notion of using airplanes in sea battles. Several old battleships were taken to sea, and Mitchell's planes flew over them, dropping bombs. Every ship was sunk. That demonstration was a big reason why U.S. airpower developed within the military. Mitchell understood that when decision makers *see* something, they have a hard time disbelieving it. Mitchell didn't use slides or handouts. His visual was more striking—a demonstration of what he was proposing. Like Mitchell, many successful proponents go beyond slides and paper and persuade decision makers through working models and prototypes, real-life examples, personal experience, or visual props.

One way of using visuals is to present a *working model* of the idea. The U.S. Patent Office, from its beginnings in 1790 until 1880, required inventors to submit actual working models for inventions that they were seeking to patent. The reasoning was that an actual replica of the invention would prove its viability. If people could see it, they would believe it. Many innovations have been promoted by offering decision makers working models. Consider a few.

Lew Urry devised the small alkaline battery in 1955 to replace the traditional carbon zinc battery. Management at his company, Eveready, wasn't convinced that Urry's proposed technology was a winner until he brought the company's vice president of technology, R. L. Glover, into the company's cafeteria, where Urry had two model cars waiting. One car used a traditional battery; the other used his new alkaline battery. The first car barely moved; the second car went several lengths of the room — so far, in fact, that people in the cafeteria grew tired watching and went back to work. Next, Urry arranged to have the research director put two glowing flashlights in his desk drawer, one powered by the carbon zinc battery, the other by an alkaline one. Opening the drawer hours later the director found the alkaline-powered flashlight still shining brightly. The flashlight using the carbon zinc battery was dead. As Urry said, "When you come up with an idea, you have to sell it to your bosses." He sold his idea by demonstration.[28]

David Warren's attempts to promote his idea of a black box for airplanes were stymied until 1958, when the secretary of the Air Registration Board of the United Kingdom happened upon his demonstration unit while visiting the organization where Warren worked. The secretary asked Warren to demonstrate the cockpit voice recorder in the United Kingdom, and the response was phenomenal.[29] Had Warren not built his demonstration unit, his idea would have languished and died.

Thomas Edison faced an uphill battle convincing the public to switch from gas lighting to electric lighting. So he demonstrated his electric lights in offices that were easily seen by people working in the financial district of New York and in the offices of major New York newspapers.[30] Edison knew that the financial industry and the news business had to buy his idea if it was to succeed, and the best way to persuade them was to let them *see* his invention in action. It worked. Here's what the *New York Times* said the day after Edison's lights went on. "It was not till about 7 o'clock, when it began to grow dark, that the electric light really made itself known and showed how bright and steady it is. . . . It was a light that a man could sit down under and write for hours without the consciousness of having any artificial light about him. . . . The light was soft, mellow, and grateful to the eye, and it seemed almost like writing by daylight to have a light without a particle of flicker and with scarcely any heat to make the head ache."[31] Mission accomplished!

Some working models are *prototypes* — physical representations of what advocates have in mind. Prototypes often serve as proofs of concepts. If you make it — a model of a product or a working piece of software — you have proven that it can be put into use. Prototypes can convince decision makers that an idea is worth exploring. At the MIT Media Lab, a center for technology innovation, the motto was "Demo or die." Without a demonstration, visitors wouldn't understand the concepts that the scientists came up with. Prototypes work in every arena of innovation.

Some prototypes are spare; they look like a completed product but are empty inside. The originator of the Palm PDA used a simple wooden block to communicate his idea of the size of the object he had in mind. The block fit neatly into the breast pocket of his shirt. Spare prototypes are preferred when building a complete model is too expensive or when advocates want initial reactions to their notion. Sometimes, too, a spare prototype is designed to answer some basic questions, like size or shape. An architect's model of a building is a spare prototype. There is nothing inside, but both the architect and the client can grasp what the finished building will look like.

When you pitch an idea to experts, prototypes don't have to be perfect; but for a naive or inexperienced audience, prototypes should look good and work perfectly. If you create a prototype of a piece of equipment with two panels out of alignment, some executives who are inexperienced in the product design process may reject the entire idea; experienced engineers would know that the misalignment was a minor problem that could easily be fixed later. Similarly, many consumers determine the quality of a new computer program by how it looks on the screen, not by its functionality. You don't want to give decision makers any reason to dismiss your idea.

In addition to working models, proponents sometimes use *real-life examples* of their ideas to convince decision makers.

Whenever Jan Eliasson, president of the General Assembly of the United Nations in 2005, wanted to make the case about the need for unpolluted water in poor countries, he held up a full glass of water. He would say: "This glass of fresh, clean water is a common sight to us. But to two billion people in the world, it's a luxury. I have seen a mother receiving a bottle [of water] while she has a child on her arm and witnessed that smile that says she knows that the only alternative is to walk for two or three miles, and then only to get polluted water." He contrasts this sort of visual image with statistics: "You can break down figures that show that 300 million people south of the Sahara don't have clean water. But working with images may be more important. If we can see relief in these concrete terms and remember this glass of water, then maybe we can be more action-oriented."[32]

He might have learned this technique from James Grant, who served as the director of UNESCO for many years. Grant was convinced that the severe diarrhea that killed millions of children each year could be eliminated for a paltry sum if governments would hand out kits containing oral rehydration salts. So every time he met with a nation's leader, he would pull a packet of these salts from his pocket. Holding the packet in his hand, he would ask the leader, "Do you know that this costs less than a cup of tea and it can save hundreds of thousands of children's lives in your country?"[33] The impact of Grant's message was amplified by the presence of the packet.

Physicist Richard Feynman explained why the O-rings had failed, causing the space shuttle *Challenger* to be torn apart, by using a visual prop during a congressional hearing. Feynman dropped an O-ring into a glass of ice water, pulled it out, and then showed the committee how brittle the ring had become. The weather on the day of the explosion had been unusually cold, which led to failure of the O-ring, which led in turn to the shuttle falling apart. The demonstration made his point persuasively.

Cemex executive Luis Farias convinced his company's leadership to use petroleum coke, a residual material derived from processing petroleum, as an energy-efficient fuel source for making cement. He was successful in his argument only after he took executives to a cement plant in Spain that already used the technology. Seeing the technology sold the idea.[34]

When President Ronald Reagan wanted to celebrate American heroism, he began a trend in State of the Union speeches that continues to this day. While addressing Congress, Reagan pointed to a man sitting in the gallery, Lenny Skutnik, who had heroically rescued a woman from the freezing Potomac River after an airplane crash. Reagan could have simply said that Americans are brave, but the presence of Skutnik made it palpable. In 2009, when another president stood at the podium, US Airways pilot Chesley "Sully" Sullenberger, who had safely landed an A320 on the Hudson River, sat in the same seat, personifying American heroism.

Advocates sometimes find that the most successful "visual" involves participation by the decision makers themselves, who personally *experience* what is being proposed. Car salespeople let you drive the model you are considering; perfume store clerks provide testers at their counters. If you drive that car, you are more likely to buy it. If you wear that scent, you are more likely to choose it the next time you purchase perfume. Examples abound.

Galileo Galilei, the great scientist and inventor, had an advocacy problem with his first telescope. No one believed that it worked. How could anyone see something far away with pieces of glass? Galileo overcame people's doubts by having them peer through his telescope and read the writing on far-off buildings.

When Sony introduced its now-famous Walkman, the company needed to convince journalists that the product was marketable. Remember, the Walkman was a radical idea—a tape recorder that couldn't record. So Sony took journalists to Yoyogi Park in Tokyo, where each received headphones and a Walkman, and invited them to listen to a description of the product as they strolled through the park. This immediate experience helped journalists understand the idea of the Walkman.

Motorola spent an enormous amount of money on a gamble: They created the first cell phone before the Federal Communications Commission (FCC) had released frequencies for such a phone. But when the commission met to assign frequencies, it immediately awarded sole rights to the crucial high-frequency spectrum to AT&T, at that time the dominant telecommunication company in the United States. Stunned, Motorola asked for, and got, a second hearing. At that hearing, John Mitchell, the Motorola executive responsible for its cell-phone program, handed a Motorola cell phone (called the DynaTac) to one of the commissioners and let him make a call. Amazed, commission members reversed their prior decision and allowed competition for high-frequency bands.[35] As one of the phone's creators, Marty Cooper, says, "The phone was pivotal. The FCC would never have made those moves without those demonstrations." AT&T was stunned. "Motorola was politically much cleverer than we were. We were technical geniuses, but we didn't know anything about lobbying and political stuff," said Joel Engel, who led AT&T's efforts.[36]

Edwin Land, the inventor of polarized lenses, needed to convince the American Optical Company to buy his idea, so he invited company executives to a Boston hotel suite. Land placed a bowl filled with goldfish near the sunny window. Land apologized for the glare and said he was sorry the executives couldn't see the fish. "What fish?" the executives wondered. But when Land handed each of them a polarized lens (which eliminated the glare), the fish came into view. That demonstration persuaded them to make his product. Voilà, sunglasses.[37]

In poor countries, inexpensive yet effective stoves are vital not only for cooking but for health. Wood-burning stoves that leak gases and smoke poison millions of people each year. In Oregon, near the Willamette River, the Aprovecho Research Center is where aficionados of stoves create cheaper, safer, more durable stoves. A few decades ago, the dominant model stove was a clay one named the Lorena stove. It was easy to build and could be used even in the poorest parts of the world. Larry Winiarski, a local inventor, believed an alternative, something called a rocket stove, was much more effective. But people working at Aprovecho loved the old clay stove and ignored Winiarski's initiatives. They "knew" the Lorena was best. So Winiarski designed an experiment. Next to the clay oven he built a rocket stove. He lit both stoves. The rocket stove, fueled with just a few twigs, got hot in less than a quarter hour. The traditional Lorena stove, filled with wood, wasn't hot enough to cook bread after an hour. That demonstration won people over. Today the rocket stove is considered one of the best models for cooking in the world.[38] The proof of Winiarski's claim lay in the demonstration.

Organize a Memorable Presentation

Savvy advocates know that artful organization of persuasive messages is crucial to their effectiveness. The keys to good organization are:

- chunking information
- structuring the presentation
- using signposts

Chunk Your Information

When you have lots of information to convey, organize it into "chunks" to make it easier to remember. Try saying your telephone number aloud. If you live in the United States, you will probably pause slightly at the dashes. Each dash creates a chunk of numbers. In Mexico City, you don't find dashes, but there are spaces between groups of numbers. Seeing numbers in chunks makes it easier for us to remember them. In school, you learned the value of completing an outline before writing an essay. The outline forced you to chunk your ideas into meaningful units. Creating PowerPoint slides often serves the same function by forcing users to chunk ideas into bullet points.

When information is chunked, three is the usual number of items. People in many cultures think in threes. According to southern German folk wisdom, all good things come in three. Ancient Greeks thought three was the perfect number. The Bible tells us about three wise men. More to the point here, a good presentation has an introduction, a body, and a conclusion. Great speakers know the further value of threes. At Gettysburg, Lincoln reminded us that ours is a government "of the people, by the people, for the people." In World War II, Churchill told his compatriots, "Never was so much owed by so many to so few." In an interesting series of studies, linguists found that people assume three points when listening to speeches.[39] Make two points and applause seldom erupts; make four points and applause begins as you start your fourth point. So, if you want people to remember what you are proposing try chunking the points you want to make into three major ones.

Structure Your Presentation

In an experiment done years ago, psychologists told subjects to listen to a list of thirty words. Later, these people were asked to recall the words. Interestingly, they remembered far more words from the beginning and the end of the list than from the middle. Psychologists dubbed this finding the *primacy-recency effect*. For advocates, the primacy-recency effect means putting your key points at the beginning and the end of your presentation: start with the big news and finish with a bang. The authors of the 1994 Republican Contract with America strategically placed the two most important items — a balanced budget and term limits — first and last, since they understood that most Americans would read only the beginning and the end of the document.[40] Unsophisticated advocates typically chatter pointlessly at the start of their pitch, put the critical material in the middle, and blather again at the end. No wonder people leave their presentations uncertain of their crucial ideas and not able to remember them.

To take advantage of the primacy-recency effect, you must do more than just put your best arguments first and last. You would be unwise, for example, to lead off with a highly controversial argument. Instead, begin with a strong point that is both important to your audience and apt to have their support. Now that your audience is disposed to listen and respond positively, you can transition to issues that are more controversial. Many successful advocates begin their pitches with statements of principles — things everyone can agree upon and, even more important, things they care about.

What if you don't have enough time to make an argument at both the beginning and the end of your pitch? Should you put your best issue first or last? The answer is that if you plan to present only your own side of the issue, put your strongest argument first, especially if decision makers are highly involved in the issue. But when presenting both sides of the argument, state your own position last.[41] If your audience is highly involved in what you are pitching, you should put your best argument first because highly involved people listen carefully at the start, and once they have reached a decision, they are unlikely to change their mind. But if the decision makers have little interest in what you are pitching, or little familiarity with it, you should put your strongest argument last, since they are more likely to remember the last thing you say.[42]

What if a decision will be made as soon as you finish talking? Then it is wise to place the most important thing last (recency). If, by contrast, there will be a delay after you have pitched your idea — a lunch break or another meeting — put your key thought near the beginning.

Advocates must also consider the attention span of decision makers. If their attention is likely to fade quickly, you might put your strongest arguments first. What you say at the beginning may affect the decision makers' moods. George W. Bush's acceptance speech at the 2004 Republican national convention was structured strategically. The first half was easygoing, indeed gentle. The second half was much stronger and tougher. Why? Bush's advisors felt that a harsh start might scare swing voters. And they might change channels soon after the speech began. At the same time, hardcore Bush supporters would be glued to their televisions for the entire speech and would appreciate Bush's strong close.

Use Signposts

Organized messages are better remembered than disorganized ones, and people who present well-organized messages are more positively regarded than those whose messages are chaotic.[43] One way of sounding organized is through "signposting." In textbooks all sorts of signposts tell readers where they are and what to focus on: there are headings and subheadings; there are introductory paragraphs informing readers of what's coming next; there are summary paragraphs reminding readers of what they just read. Signposts like these help people comprehend and remember. Signposts also help when making presentations at meetings. Smart advocates offer signposts by using their voice to highlight critical information; by offering people overviews before going into the body of their pitch; by providing succinct, compelling, clear summaries of what they say; and by often enumerating their points (e.g., *"First*, we will talk about the problem we discovered; *second*, we will look at various possible solutions; and *third*, we will make a recommendation").

Advocate Face-to-Face

In 1939, New York City financier Alexander Sachs had a vital meeting scheduled with his good friend President Franklin Roosevelt. Sachs carried a letter from Albert Einstein warning Roosevelt that German scientists were developing an atomic bomb. Knowing that if he just mailed the report, it would get buried in a pile of memos on the president's desk, Sachs instead stood in front of his desk and read a summary of Einstein's letter aloud. That got Roosevelt's attention, and he quickly initiated a project to both stop what the Nazis were doing and create an atomic bomb for the United States.[44] Like Sachs, good proponents know the wisdom of face-to-face communication. They meet with people rather than send e-mails and letters.[45] As Robert Zoellick, head of the World Bank, says, "I like to see people face-to-face even if it means traveling halfway around the world. You can read, you can study, but to see people and circumstances, it's a motivator."[46] Ideas can get lost in mounds of papers and flurries of e-mails, but people are more cooperative and far more likely to commit to working together on issues when they meet in a group.[47] People trust you more when they converse with you in person. You can't shake a hand over the phone; you can't see nods of agreement and looks of confusion using e-mail.

One important reason for preferring face-to-face exchanges for advocacy is that it is much harder for decision makers to reject people and their ideas when meeting them in the flesh. This is why experienced salespeople willingly travel thousands of miles for brief meetings with potential clients. Customers can ignore e-mails, and they can put off decisions over the phone, but saying no to someone sitting in front of you is harder to do. Jack Welch, former CEO of General Electric, after reading a proposal for a large investment in Thailand, turned to his wife and said: "Look at this deal here. This guy, this nut, wants us to invest $1 billion in autos. I'm going to blow him out of the water tomorrow. I mean, this guy's got no chance." The next day, the man with the proposal, Mark Norbom, head of GE Capital's office in Thailand, walked into the board meeting and in forty-five minutes turned both Welch and the board into supporters. "So we bet on it," says Welch. "What it was is this guy flying over from Bangkok, and he was in there, and he was making the case. . . . We were convinced. If you asked me five minutes before the meeting, I'd say 'Get out of here. What are you, nuts?' And yet he made a great case, and you love him for doing it."[48] Norbom understood how important face-to-face communication was when selling ideas. Distance does *not* make the heart grow fonder.

So what do you do if you can't meet face-to-face? First, use all of the techniques discussed in this book when composing memos and e-mails and when preparing for teleconferences. Second, use the richest media you can. New video-conferencing systems like HALO mimic face-to-face interactions far better than a phone call or e-mail because feedback is immediate. Third, know the communication culture of the organization's decision makers and use their preferred media. Some companies still rely on face-to-face meetings for important decisions, others use text messages intensively, and others prefer written documents. Don't pitch your idea by e-mail if the firm has a phone culture — it won't get the attention it deserves.

Watch the Jargon

Advocates understand that using appropriate language legitimizes their efforts to champion ideas. If you use words that signal to decision makers that you are deeply conversant with the issue you are pitching and with the way decision makers think, you enhance your credibility. Words show people whether or not you belong to the club. A person championing a technology solution before a highly technical audience should use appropriate technical terminology. Talking to a group of lawyers may require different language choices about the same solution. Staffers in the federal government may pitch an idea by saying, "OMB wants us to coordinate this proposal with both DOJ and DOD. The project will be led by a couple of SESs" (translation: The Office of Management and Budget [at the White House] wants us to coordinate this proposal with the Justice Department and the Defense Department. The project will be led by some senior government executives [Senior Executive Service personnel]). In the military, an officer may say, "We are going to staff the proposed project with a couple of O-6s brought in from CENTCOM" (translation: The staff will be a couple of colonels from Central Command).

Although using these sorts of acronyms might enhance a proponent's credibility when speaking with government employees or army officers, they would backfire with an audience with no government or military experience. And using acronyms incorrectly would hurt the advocate's credibility. If you tell people in Washington that HHS will be taking care of border security, for example, some strange looks would be aimed your way. HHS is the Department of Health and Human Services. What you probably meant was DHS — the Department of Homeland Security.

Assessing your audience and choosing appropriate jargon is important. But seasoned champions are careful about all the words they select, not just the jargon. How many times have you heard people complain, "I told them that! Why can't they listen?" or "It's right there in writing. Can't they read?" Statements like these reflect a faulty assumption that everyone shares the same meanings for words. Not true. What does the word "turkey" mean? In the United States it can mean a bird, a country, three strikes in bowling, or a jerk you would not invite to go bowling. How about the phrase "a lot of money"? A price of $50,000 might seem expensive to one person and a bargain to another.

People in different cultures may also interpret the same word differently. When Nancy McKinstry became CEO of Wolters Kluwer, a major Dutch publisher, she found herself pitching her plans as "aggressive," using a term she had successfully used in the United States. But the word, she quickly learned, turned off Europeans. So she switched to "decisive," which helped her get what she needed.[49] Similarly, William Amelio, former CEO of the Chinese computer manufacturer Lenovo, tells about a time when design teams from the West and East suddenly stopped working well together. Why? After reflection, they discovered that the thwarted teamwork was due to a misunderstanding tied to words. Someone on the Western team had said that the two teams should have a "common design element" — appropriate jargon for computer designers wanting to share, except that in Mandarin "common" means uninteresting and boring.[50]

People in what may seem to be the same culture can even misinterpret numbers, with massive consequences. As NASA's Mars Climate Orbiter approached Mars in the late 1990s, its software miscalculated distances, leading it to be inserted into orbit 170 kilometers lower than planned. As a result, the orbiter was destroyed in the atmosphere of Mars. Why did this happen? It turned out that the team managing the probe, based in the United States, calculated distances in imperial units (feet and miles), while the European team, which had programmed the software, used metrical units. As NASA reported, "The 'root cause' of the loss of the spacecraft was the failed translation of English units into metric units in a segment of ground-based, navigation-related mission software."[51]

Even the colors that advocates use in their pitches can have different meanings in different cultures. Craig Smith, a reporter for the *New York Times*, relates the story of an agriculture official from the state of Washington who went to China to hawk his state's products. After handing out bright green caps to all, he failed to notice that none of the men put them on, and many of the women nervously laughed. Why? In China, a green hat is the symbol of someone who has been cuckolded. Similarly, one company in China took the white ribbons off the boxes that held gifts and replaced them with red ribbons. Why? White in China implies death, while red stands for luck.[52]

Seek Questions

An important, and often overlooked, technique for ensuring that your advocacy message is clearly understood involves generating discussion among decision makers. Rather than monopolizing meetings with long-winded presentations, canny proponents induce people to ask questions and talk about their ideas. There are good reasons to invite questions.

First, questions help advocates assess whether their messages have been accurately understood. When someone raises a question that hints at a possible misunderstanding, smart advocates clarify. Should you tell audience members to hold their questions until the end of presentation? In most cases, the answer is no. Your goal is to make sure people understand what you are talking about. If someone misses a point, you want to clear up their misunderstanding right away. There are exceptions to welcoming questions as you go along — for instance, for a formal speech in front of a large group of people. But most effective proponents don't make presentations so much as they have conversations with decision makers who ask lots of questions — and are encouraged to do so.

Second, questions help advocates grasp what the decision makers think is important. Next time you attend a meeting, listen carefully to the questions that people ask. You will often learn more about the people asking the questions than you learn from the answers to the questions. The questions that people ask hint at what matters to them, what they need, what they are worried about. Even supportive questions can aid advocacy efforts. They can encourage proponents to think more deeply about their ideas and prompt them to generate related ideas. Edwin Land was asked by his young daughter why she couldn't see her photographs as soon as she took them. Land took her question seriously and created Polaroid.

Third, good questions about a new idea encourage people in meetings to spend more time discussing the idea. Those discussions lead individuals to engage in what psychologists call elaboration. When people elaborate on a new idea, they clarify, in their minds, what is being proposed. They connect the new idea to familiar notions and consequently begin to feel some psychological ownership of the new proposal.

Fourth, questions present wonderful opportunities for advocates to prove their competency. As we will discuss in a later chapter, a good measure of your perceived competency lies in how you respond to questions and objections. If you answer tough questions well, decision makers will gain confidence in backing you and your proposal.

How do you encourage people to raise questions? The obvious way is to ask for questions. But remember to formulate an open-ended invitation. Wise advocates never end presentations with "Any questions?" The appropriate answer would be a simple yes or no. Instead, they might say, "What are your questions?" or "Who has the first question?" You should also reward questions.

A final piece of advice is to avoid getting defensive or responding angrily in ways that might humiliate those who ask questions. Alan Greenspan, former head of the U.S. Federal Reserve, was brilliant at responding to questions from members of Congress. His principle is worth bearing in mind: Make "every member of Congress look like a genius for asking a particular question, even when the question is truly idiotic."[53]

3

Frame Your Message

It isn't that they cannot see the solution,
it is that they cannot see the problem.

G. K. CHESTERTON

Winnie-the-Pooh visits Rabbit's hole and gleefully feasts on his friend's honey. Much plumper for the culinary experience, Pooh attempts to squeeze out of the hole. Half in and half out, Pooh is trapped.

"The fact is," says Rabbit, "you're stuck."

"It all comes," replies Pooh crossly, "of not having front doors big enough."

"It all comes," responds Rabbit sternly, "of eating too much."[1]

Each frames Pooh's predicament differently. People, too, like Pooh and Rabbit, frame ideas in terms of how they understand those ideas. And how advocates frame issues affects how persuasive they are.

Humans are a categorizing species. We mentally sort events, objects, and ideas into categories, or schemas. Schemas are the cognitive file cabinets we use to organize information. Pooh's schema for his problem was different from Rabbit's. And how each defined the problem — the schema — shaped how each imagined resolving it.

Schemas Shape Understanding

Scientific advances often occur when a classificatory schema emerges to organize existing knowledge — when drawers and files are created in our mental file cabinets about some phenomenon. In the eighteenth century, for example, Carolus Linnaeus created our naming and organizing system for classifying organisms. Using concepts like genus, species, and phylum, familiar to all of us still today, he organized the study of plants into a science. Linnaeus was only one such categorizer. Glance at a sky dotted with clouds, and what do you see? Maybe some cirrus clouds? Maybe a puffy cumulus cloud? These familiar categories for clouds didn't exist until 1802, when Luke Howard, an English amateur scientist, devised them. Before Howard, there were just clouds; now we can name distinctive types of clouds, each with its own character and significance. In 1869, purportedly while sleeping, Russian chemist Dmitri Mendeleev dreamed up the periodic table of elements. Mendeleev's table included the sixty-three elements known at that time. But it had gaps where there ought to be elements. Mendeleev's table, or schema, anticipated elements like gallium, scandium, and germanium, which indeed were later discovered.

Classificatory schemas are everywhere. Try this exercise. Ask software engineers the first computer language they learned. If they say BASIC, FORTRAN, or COBOL, you can bet they went to school sometime before the mid-1980s. If they say Pascal, they went to school in the 1980s or early 1990s. If they say C++ or Java, they began in the 1990s or later. Today they learn HTML. Each generation did not simply learn a different software language, however; they learned an alternative schema that shapes, even today, how they conceive of code. FORTRAN is linear (remember the GO TO loops?). Pascal is a structured language. C++ is more object-oriented. HTML is for Web pages.

Languages represent category schemas. For instance, in some languages, there are two categories of second-person pronouns: a familiar one for addressing close friends and relatives (e.g., in French, *tu*; in German, *du*; in Bengali, *tumi*) and a more formal one for addressing superiors and people with whom we are not well acquainted (in French, *vous*; in German, *Sie;* in Bengali, *apni*). English has only one such pronoun (we long ago abandoned "thee" and "thou").[2] No wonder native speakers of English are often viewed as less formal than others. If you grow up using a language in which you have to assess, and implicitly announce, your relationship with another person every time you speak, you see the world differently than if your first language, like English, blurs such distinctions.

The same is true when languages use gendered nouns. The gender of a noun shapes how people see what that noun represents. In German, the word for "bridge" is feminine. In Spanish, it is masculine. Not surprisingly, when shown a bridge, German speakers suggest adjectives such as "beautiful," "fragile," and "pretty," while Spanish speakers, shown the same bridge, offer terms like "big," "strong," and "sturdy."[3]

Schemas for ideas can vary in many ways. Like Pooh and Rabbit, two people might frame the same issue differently. That explains many misunderstandings. Or two people's schemas for an idea could vary in complexity. One person's schema for an issue could be well developed; another's, meager. People with well-developed schemas about an issue have an easier time grasping and remembering new material about ideas related to that issue. People with rudimentary schemas about that issue find it harder to understand and recall the same material.

Imagine two people, Gerri and Sandra. Gerri follows sports religiously — baseball, soccer, football, hockey, cricket, basketball, rugby, and even NASCAR. And she's a fan of every level of play — high school, college, and professional. She knows sports history. Gerri has a well-developed schema for all this arcana; she has many categories for mentally storing information about sports. Sandra, on the other hand, has few categories when it comes to sports. In fact, the only thing she knows for sure is that her favorite television shows are sometimes canceled because of late-running sports events.

Suppose Gerri and Sandra are both told that the first World Series in baseball occurred in 1903 with Boston beating Pittsburgh. Who is more likely to remember this detail? Gerri, of course. She will recall it because she has a file drawer to store it in — a category that might be labeled "baseball/professional/1900s." With Sandra, though, the new information goes in one ear and right out the other since she has no distinctive place to store it. We have all had Sandra's experience. We will finish reading a magazine article and suddenly realize we have no idea of what we just read. But that seldom happens when we are experts about a topic. Then, when we read something about that topic, we can readily recall it later.

Advocates must consider how well developed decision makers' categories are before presenting them with a proposal. Why? If advocates incorrectly assume that decision makers have well-organized, highly detailed schemas on the subject of the pitch, they may quickly lose decision makers' attention if the decision makers' schemas are simple. Alternatively, decision makers may feel talked down to, even insulted, when advocates assume incorrectly that they have modest schemas about the subject of the pitch.

People with well-developed schemas for an issue typically respond more extremely to proposals about that issue than do people with simpler schemas. For example, people who are highly involved in politics tend to have more entrenched reactions to arguments about political issues than do apolitical people.[4] Brilliant scientists will react more strongly to ideas related to their areas of expertise than to ideas that fall far from what they know. When pitching a technical idea to engineers steeped in the topic, you can bet they will be more critical of it than nonengineers would be.

When the decision maker's schema for an idea matches the advocate's schema, the decision maker will easily comprehend what is being proposed. Two civil engineers can chat comfortably with one another about an engineering project. Two physicians with the same specialty find conversations about a patient's malady straightforward. No wonder work teams composed of members with similar mental models tend to be efficient.[5] In some successful new product development teams, people from every major relevant discipline are placed on the teams and attend meetings at which decision makers, with different backgrounds and expertise, evaluate the ideas. That way, if the chief financial officer asks a complex question, the team member with a finance background can respond. If the general counsel raises an issue, the individual with legal experience can answer.

But more often than not, advocates face the challenge of talking with people who don't share their schemas. What often results? Misunderstandings and confusion. Marketing people can experience difficulty talking to engineers about advertising initiatives; engineers' eyes glaze over when accounting teams start discussing new project controls. In medicine, physicians' schemas shape how they evaluate medical difficulties. If we go to a neurologist because of back pain, she would probably treat us differently than a rheumatologist would. And a rheumatologist might, in turn, treat us in ways a surgeon would never consider. Each medical specialty sees the same concern differently because each begins with an alternate frame of reference.

Successful advocates communicate their ideas in ways that fit decision

makers' schemas. They use the skills described in the chapter on communicating ideas (chapter 2) and are especially clear about the frame of
reference — the schema — within which they want decision makers to view
their ideas. They do this because they want to ensure that decision makers
understand and remember what they are saying and because they know that
how decision makers categorize ideas shapes how they will respond to those
ideas. If a notion is located in a "risky" category, for instance, decision
makers are less likely to adopt it than if it fits in a more comfortable, "safe"
category. Suppose an advocate proposes to reorganize her unit. Is she addressing a human resources (HR) issue or a budget concern? Since people
generally believe that HR issues are more political than finance issues,
which are seen as more rational, framing the reorganization as an HR move
may make listeners wonder about political machinations instead of the
bottom line. Framing the reorganization as a financial move would make
them more likely to view it as logical.[6]

How do advocates discover decision makers' schemas for ideas? This isn't
much of a challenge when advocates are familiar with decision makers and
their organizations. But if advocates are new to the firm or are unfamiliar
with the decision makers (e.g., a new executive brought in from outside the
company), they must assess how the decision makers think, how they organize their worlds. Smart advocates may scrutinize decision makers' backgrounds (e.g., previous places of work, favorite hobbies and sports, majors
in college, accomplishments) to grasp their schemas. If a decision maker
worked for many years in a firm that described project management with
rah-rah sports metaphors, a savvy advocate might use sports metaphors
when pitching her notion. Decision makers from a military background
may categorize people's roles differently than decision makers who spent
years in a university do. In meetings, advocates listen carefully to what
decision makers say. What units, for example, do they think are substantively different (e.g., Do they consider sales and marketing one unit, or do
they see clear distinctions? Do they think of R&D as a single activity, or do
they regard research as separate from development?).

Definitions Shape Problems

Read the case in box 1.[7] Then select one of the six problem statements
listed there and imagine solutions.

BOX 1. WHAT IS THE PROBLEM?

The manager of a large office building has been receiving a growing number of complaints about its elevator service, particularly during rush hours. Several long-term tenants have threatened to move out unless service improves. In response, the manager researched the possibility of adding one or two elevators. He learned that the idea was feasible, but the only elevator company in the area has a six-month backlog of orders. The manager then turned to you, his assistant, and asked you to devise a plan to get two new elevators installed within three months. You must present the plan at the next staff meeting.

Problem Statements

1. To get two elevators within three months.
2. To improve elevator service in the building.
3. To get more people out of the building faster.
4. To keep the tenants happy.
5. To keep upset tenants from moving.
6. To keep the building fully leased.

Now let's consider solutions to each problem statement.

1. *To get two elevators within three months:*
   Find a contractor outside the local area.
   Pay a premium to get a local contractor to move you up the list.
   Buy the contractor's company.
2. *To improve elevator service in the building:*
   Speed up the elevators.
   Sequence the elevators so they stop only at certain floors.
   Limit the availability of elevators at lower floors.
3. *To get more people out of the building faster:*
   Create a health program encouraging people to use the stairs.
   Build escalators.
   Connect the upper floors of the building to the building next door.
4. *To keep the tenants happy:*
   Explain to them the situation and the timeline for getting elevators.

Distract them during their waits by providing reading materials.

Invite them to generate ideas.

5. *To keep upset tenants from moving:*

   Offer rent rebates.

   Offer them special amenities.

   Offer them extra entitlements.

6. *To keep the building fully leased:*

   Reduce rents.

   Start an advertising campaign to attract new tenants who care more about exercise than elevators.

   Change the function of the building (e.g., make it a storage facility).

Notice how each problem statement yields some solutions and not others. If the problem is about providing new elevators (statement 1), the solutions emphasize acquiring elevators. The second and third problem statements yield solutions focused on moving people. The last three problem statements generate tenant-focused notions. How a problem is stated shapes the solutions that people propose.

What are doctors paid for? Diagnosis. For most maladies, once a diagnosis is made, there are accepted treatment guidelines. Misguided doctors treat people before they have a good understanding of what ails them. What causes crime — poverty, opportunity, education, or greed? If we think it is caused by poverty, we find ways of reducing the number of poor people. If we believe the problem is opportunity, we start installing cameras and fences everywhere. If we think it is education, we fund more schools.

The direction that new projects take in organizations is often a function of the problem statement that decision makers select. In project management, is the issue staying on schedule or managing costs? Strategically, is the company focused on market share or margins? If market share, discounting might be appropriate; margins imply less discounting. Why do technology companies tussle so much to set standards? Because whichever standard is adopted shapes who wins in the marketplace.[8]

In 2005 the pharmaceutical giant Merck created a vaccine for some forms of cervical cancer, a cancer often caused by sexual activity. For its proponents, the problem was obvious: many thousands of lives were endangered by cervical cancer, and a vaccine could save some people from death. But some conservative politicians in the United States saw a different problem. Believing in chastity before marriage and sexual monogamy after marriage, they feared that a new vaccine would encourage promiscuity, so they campaigned against funding the medicine.[9] Here, alternative problem statements led to completely different responses to the release of the vaccine.

Whoever Defines the Problem Wins

When pitching proposals, wise proponents seek agreement on the problem before discussing possible solutions. Doing this saves time *and* makes the proponents more influential. Consider the typical meeting. Almost as soon as the session starts, people begin to discuss solutions. "We should do this," insists one person. "No, we should try this instead," says another. At some point, somebody sees the futility of the discussion and says, "Wait a moment, why are we here in the first place?" This question prompts a discussion about possible problems, followed, in the end, by agreement on what the problem is and a much quicker dialogue about a limited pool of solutions that match the chosen problem statement. Here is a suggestion: in future meetings, begin by defining a problem and agreeing on a problem statement. Meetings will go faster.

Indeed, if you want to go right to crucial issues in meetings, create decision-focused agendas instead of topical agendas. Most agendas are topical: "We'll be talking about A, B, and C." Topical agenda items often lack focus, so participants can't adequately prepare for discussions. Imagine that you receive a topical agenda listing "Human Resource Issues" or "Budget." What might those topics mean? How would you prepare to discuss those issues? Instead, suppose you receive a decision agenda with items like these: "We need to transfer two people to Akron. Who goes?" or "We need to cut the budget by 3 percent. What should be axed?" Decision-agenda items focus attention on specific decisions to be made at the meeting. Now you can arrive at the meeting with names of candidates for possible transfer or budget items that could be trimmed.

Getting buy-in to a problem statement right at the beginning does more than make meetings more efficient. It also gives advocates influence, since problem statements create boundaries for what can and cannot be proposed.[10] One problem statement yields solutions that another problem statement about the same issue might not. So wise advocates lobby for their problem definition. They know that if they have specified a problem well enough, solutions emerging from discussions about that problem will be reasonably close to the solution they had in mind in the first place.

Think back to the elevator problem. An advocate who wants tenant-focused solutions like meetings and incentives might pitch a problem statement about how to keep tenants happy. His problem statement would probably lead participants to generate solutions similar to those he had in mind. Had he, on the other hand, suggested solutions at the start of the session — "Let's meet with tenants" or "Let's lower the rent" — other participants might have seen him as pushy. And they might have come up with very different solutions to the elevator problem, unrelated to the tenants.

The next time you want to pitch a proposal, start with a discussion of what exactly the problem is. Encourage people to buy into the problem the way you want it defined. Then write the problem statement in big, bold letters on a whiteboard or flip chart. If someone raises an idea that is not relevant to the problem statement, you may be able to postpone discussion of that idea until later since it doesn't address the stated problem.

New Schemas Can Create Solutions

When pitching ideas, proponents have a choice between referencing existing categories ("It's like X," "It fits with our current product mix," "It's an extension of Y") or suggesting that their proposals represent entirely new categories. Clearly, most advocates in most situations pitch ideas using established categories. Take a beginning marketing course and you'll be told, "Think like your customer!" Take a beginning speech class and you'll hear, "Adapt to your audience!" This advice is excellent: ideas that make good sense to decision makers (they fit their schema) are often easy to sell. Wise advocates often talk about their notions using terminology the decision makers are familiar with. Advocates latch onto metaphors used regularly within the firm and tie their ideas to past ideas (e.g., "This is just like what we did in Europe a few years ago").

It is especially wise to link proposals to familiar categories when addressing cautious decision makers. Many conservative decision makers — who are comfortable with what they already know — are uneasy with anything too unorthodox. They won't embrace unfamiliar and unpredictable notions. For example, Lord Kelvin, brilliant as he was (think the Kelvin scale), could never escape from his need for a mechanical model to understand James Maxwell's electromagnetic theory of light. Nor could Tycho Brahe, the eminent Danish astronomer, accept the Copernican notion of a nonstationary earth.[11] Both of these scientists knew what they knew, and dismissed ideas that were too foreign to them. With cautious decision makers, successful advocates introduce ideas as though they fit established categories or frameworks.

Sometimes it is wiser, however, to create new schemas. Rather than adapting to how decision makers think, savvy advocates may offer decision makers a new way of thinking by creating an entire new framework for understanding an issue. Novel categories intrigue people, ignite entirely new product lines, and can open doors to radical ideas that decision makers would otherwise never consider.

In business, great success often comes to people who create new categories. Chrysler created a new category with the minivan; *Time* magazine's 2010 Person of the Year, Mark Zuckerberg, created Facebook, a new type of social media; Victor Gruen created the indoor shopping mall surrounded by huge parking lots; Trammell Crow introduced buildings that housed fancy office suites and warehouses in the same structure; Capital One came up with a new credit business when it let people transfer their credit-card balances to new cards with lower interest rates; Ted Turner created the all-news network; Sony provided all-music listening with the Walkman (Sony's Akio Morita used to say that business success is satisfying appetites people don't know they have). Business history is filled with such cases.

In 1988, Kraft Foods created an entire new market with the introduction of Lunchables — a new category of prepackaged meals that children could take to school for lunch. To this day, Kraft has more than half the market for prepackaged foods.[12]

When the retail chain called The Container Store was established, potential investors had difficulty understanding the store's concept. Why would anyone want to open stores containing nothing but empty boxes? Stores had always offered a few storage containers, but until the founders, Kip Tindell and Garrett Boone, came up with the category, no one had imagined entire stores filled with empty containers.[13]

Dietrich Mateschitz, today one of the richest men in Europe, created a new beverage category — energy drinks — when he started marketing Red Bull. Now grocery stores and fast-food refrigerator units are filled with energy drinks of every flavor and degree of punch.

FedEx created a new category when it built an airline that delivered packages rather than people. Today FedEx is worth more than most of the major passenger airlines.

Harry Markowitz created a concept, popularized by John Bogle, called the index fund. Stock index funds are one of the largest investment categories today. Even before index funds, three smart financiers developed and marketed, in 1924, the Massachusetts Investors Trust: the first mutual fund. No such category existed before, and today most investors opt for mutual funds to fill out their portfolios.

In each of these examples, proponents created a new category of business as a way of pushing their ideas. Without doubt, the creativity of great leaders often lies in the generation of new categories.

Redefining Problems Can Create Solutions

It is clear by now that the solutions that people generate to problems are shaped by how those problems are defined. But what if you have a clear problem statement and no viable solution? Redefine the problem. New solutions often emerge when old problems are reframed.

Let's consider a variant on the elevator problem in box 1. This case, which comes from a perhaps apocryphal story told in the hospitality industry, is about a high-rise hotel built with insufficient elevators. Guests were constantly complaining about interminable waits. Installing new elevators in an existing high-rise structure is extraordinarily difficult. What to do? The hotel company hired consultants to craft new solutions. Most were unable to generate any real innovation. One consultant, however, asked management what the "real" problem was.

Management replied that guests were waiting too long for elevators to arrive.

The consultant asked, "Are the guests waiting too long, or do they *think* they are waiting too long?"

"What's the difference?" management responded.

"A big one," the consultant said.

Once everyone agreed that, at least to some degree, the wait was a perceptual problem, the consultant pitched a nifty solution, which you will find in many hotels: hang a mirror on the wall by the waiting area on each floor. Mirrors, it turns out, reduce people's sense of time passing by distracting them. People look at their reflected images, adjust loose hair, check their clothes, and give themselves private greetings. What the consultant did was redefine the problem. As long as management defined the problem as not having enough elevators, they were stuck. A different statement of the problem — altering people's sense of wait time — led to a new solution.

Redefining a problem can profoundly affect how companies conduct business. For many years, the dominant model of business was to fill the "bucket" with as many customers as possible. In the mid-1980s, this model changed. Some very smart people observed that filling the bucket was useless if there was a gaping hole in its side. The goal of business, these critics said, was to plug that hole. Rather than only seeking new customers, business should focus on keeping the ones they already have.

Consider how this redefinition affected travel. Suppose you are a very frequent flier on a particular airline — an Executive Platinum flyer, for instance, on American Airlines. The airline now gives you a special reservation phone number that is promptly and politely answered by a real, live person. Miraculous! Then the airline may upgrade you to first class and let you board first. Because you fly frequently on that airline, you are treated royally. Compare that to the treatment accorded to someone who seldom uses an airline. When calling for a reservation, she endures a long list of options, then a long hold exacerbated by bad music. Once at the airline gate she isn't allowed to board until almost everyone else has boarded. Worse still, she is stuffed into a middle seat in the back of the plane, next to the engines and by the bathroom. Celebrate the loyal customer and punish the occasional one: it is an interesting model of business. Thirty years ago, airlines did the opposite — gave new customers the red-carpet treatment and ignored established customers. Changing the problem statement from wooing new customers to keeping current customers affected everything the airlines did for customers.

Enterprising businesses often generate new problem statements that create opportunities for innovation. Consider these examples.

The Wright brothers' major advance was to redefine the problem of flight. Whereas previous inventors focused on power, the Wrights saw the problem as one of control. Creating an engine was easy; the real challenge was to make the airplane stable.

Eli Whitney, inventor of the cotton gin, came up with a problem statement that led to his brilliant solution. Rather than focusing on how to pull cotton seeds from the cotton, Whitney asked how to pull the cotton away from the seeds.

Henry Ford reframed automobile manufacturing. Traditionally, workers moved from one assembly point to another. The old problem was, How do we get workers to the car? Ford reframed the issue: How do we get the vehicle to workers? He decided to keep the workers in one place and have the cars move past them on an assembly line, a procedure that proved far more efficient.

Intel's basic problem statement for many years was, How do you make a faster chip? Later, new problem statements emerged: How do you make chips that use less battery power? How do you make smaller chips that are more suitable for laptops? Suddenly the emphasis on speed faded in favor of designing technologies that addressed new problems.

Asustek, a Taiwanese computer manufacturer, introduced small, inexpensive "netbooks" in 2007. The company reframed the concept of the laptop. While companies like Dell and HP focused on making laptops better and faster, Asustek focused on affordability and portability.[14]

Kraft Foods reframed its cheese business. Kraft's new idea was that food should be entertaining. Now Kraft markets cheese sticks and other cheese products that are fun to eat.

Nokia became the dominant cell-phone company in the world at the start of the twenty-first century in part by reframing its business problem. Instead of selling cell phones as well-engineered devices, Nokia decided to sell them as status and fashion symbols. It created sexy phones in striking colors, even introducing them on the fashion runways of Milan and Paris. Later, Nokia lost market share when Apple and Google again reframed the cell phone as a "smart-phone."

In every one of these examples, once a problem was redefined, alternative solutions almost magically emerged.

Scientists have long understood the value of redefining problems. Copernicus's move to a heliocentric theory and Gregor Mendel's theory of genetic inheritance are cases of reframing problems. With diseases, for instance — before Ignaz Semmelweis, Louis Pasteur, Robert Koch, and Joseph Lister made their discoveries about germs and antiseptics — one predominant model of illness was based on the assumption that decaying matter and "bad air" caused sickness. So the preferred preventive for many diseases was fresh-smelling air, sometimes provided by bouquets of flowers. When the French attempted to build the Panama Canal, malaria struck down many workers. The solution was to scent hospitals with flowers in jars of water. Once germs were seen as culprits (a new problem statement), scientists began searching for nasty microbes that caused diseases; and once the bad-air theory of disease was replaced with a germ theory of disease, it was possible to make the connection between mosquitoes and malaria — and to diagnose the standing water in flower jugs as a breeding ground for malaria-bearing mosquitos.[15]

Framing and reframing issues is basic to all kinds of policy debates. Daniel Moynihan, a senator from New York in the 1980s, changed the debate on gun control by arguing that guns don't kill, bullets do. With that reframing, he successfully advocated for legislation that banned what he called "cop-killer bullets." We touched on the crime problem before. What causes it? How do we reduce crime? For decades, law enforcement's aim was to get criminals off the street. After years of effort and expenditures of enormous sums of money, crime only worsened. New solutions emerged when two sociologists, James Wilson and George Kelling, redefined the crime problem. Metaphorically, they suggested that if a warehouse window is shattered and isn't fixed, other windows soon get broken. Alternatively, if the broken window is promptly fixed, others windows stay unbroken. What's the message? If we properly enforce laws against such minor crimes as panhandling and vandalism, worse crimes may fade. Why? First, because quality-of-life enforcement makes communities places where law-abiding citizens want to live. Second, because enforcing quality-of-life crimes lets police officers frisk people for illegal weapons and fingerprint them to check for outstanding warrants, thus reducing the potential for future criminal behavior.[16] Crime in cities like New York decreased substantially after the broken-window theory was introduced.

The U.S. Army in Iraq used the broken-window approach creatively. It found that when Baghdad neighborhoods were made more livable — clean parks, running water, regular electricity — attacks by insurgents decreased.[17] Later, the army's proponent of the broken-window model in Iraq, General Peter Chiarelli, pitched another problem statement for combating insurgency. Noting that so many young men were unemployed, he suggested that violence might decrease if they had jobs. An exhausted twenty-year-old with money in his pocket is not likely to be a terrorist.

In another policy area, environmental protection, the typical approach to controlling pollution was once to enforce a myriad of often complicated and sometimes contradictory regulations — there was one standard for smoke, another for paint, another for degreasing, and so on. Bill Drayton, who served as the assistant administrator of the Environmental Protection Agency (EPA) in the 1970s, redefined the problem of enforcing environmental rules. Rather than focusing on individual pollutants in a manufacturing or chemical plant, he proposed that the EPA set a total emission number for that plant. The plant's managers could then make choices about what to control. Managing pollution was reframed. Rather than having businesses fighting the EPA, why not get them to fight pollution?[18] The plan even created a marketplace model for pollution where companies could trade units tied to a certain level of pollution.

In the political arena, journalists play a major role in framing how people see candidates. Kathleen Hall Jamieson and Paul Waldman have pointed out that in the U.S. presidential election in 2000, journalists framed Albert Gore as deceptive and his competitor George Bush as inexperienced.[19] What that meant was that anything Gore said or did was vetted first in terms of its accuracy. If he made any misstatement, no matter how trivial, he was seen as dishonest. If Bush made a misstatement, it was attributed to his political inexperience. In the end, inexperience was forgiven, especially in combination with Texas folksiness; dishonesty was not. Facts are interpreted differently depending on the frame that people put around the information.

Framing is basic to the internal politics of companies, not just national politics. For example, Phil Purcell was essentially forced out of the CEO position at Morgan Stanley by its board of directors in 2005. At the start of that year, the board had been 100 percent behind Purcell. But as the year progressed, valued employees started leaving, a legal decision cost Morgan Stanley money and reputation, and a group of former managers wrote public letters decrying Purcell's leadership. Board members started quizzing senior employees on the matter. In one of those conversations, a board member asked an employee for a compelling reason to remove Purcell. The employee responded with a question of his own: What was the compelling reason for Purcell to be CEO?[20] That question painfully reframed the debate.

Persuasion is often a function of how an issue is framed. Consider a story of two heavy smokers in a monastery. The two monks fretted about whether it was appropriate to smoke while praying. Seeking direction, the first monk, a less-than-sophisticated persuader, asked his abbot, "Father Abbot, is it permissible for me to smoke while I pray?" "Absolutely not!" responded the abbot. "When you pray, you should only be praying!" The second smoker, a far savvier persuader, approached the abbot. "Father Abbot, I smoke in moments of great weakness. Would it be acceptable at those times of great weakness to pray to the Lord?" "Of course!" said the abbot.

Ever notice that when you buy a new cell phone you almost always find your old charger doesn't work with the new one? The solution is simple: a universal plug for cell phones. What problem statement would convince companies to all agree to a common plug? One problem statement might revolve around the hassles and expenses that consumers face when every phone seems to require a different charger. Perhaps a different problem statement would get more traction. How about the environmental costs of all those discarded chargers piling up in dumps? This problem statement worked in environmentally sensitive Europe. Starting in 2011, the European Union requires every cell phone to use an identical charger.

So how do successful advocates proceed with framing problems? First, they lobby to get their definition of a problem adopted by decision makers. If their definition is adopted, they let decision makers nominate solutions. Doing this lets decision makers feel a sense of ownership for the ideas they come up with. Second, if advocates aren't able to get their problem statements adopted, they subtly shift discussions away from other problem statements to ones that more closely resemble theirs.

Organizations have better and worse ways of defining and redefining issues at different times. When championing ideas in times of chaos and confusion, advocates are wise to frame ideas as proposals that will place their organizations on more stable paths. Alternatively, when business is more stable and predictable, advocates can usefully frame their proposals as opportunities to revitalize.[21] In tough economic times, it is best to frame ideas as ways to save money; in flush times, the same notions can be proposed as ways to make money. They may be the same ideas, but they are framed differently.

Any new proposal can be framed as an opportunity either to gain something or to avoid a threat.[22] So which approach — opportunity or threat — should advocates use? Proposals cast as *opportunities* are seen as positive (e.g., doing this will probably increase our market share) and are perceived as resolvable, controllable, and appropriate for employee involvement.[23] Proposals pitched in terms of *threats* can win support, too: if we don't make changes, we lose something we value (e.g., we'll continue to bleed cash). People are generally more motivated by the fear of losing things than by the possibility of gaining things. We overemphasize negative information when forming our attitudes.[24] We are more sensitive to losses than to gains; the pleasure of winning is less than the pain of losing.[25]

It follows that opportunity-framed proposals are especially attractive when they aren't too radical. If a proposal is perceived as risky, even if there are potential opportunities, people will probably resist it. Why risk losing a sure thing — the status quo? On the other hand, when proposals are framed as ways to avoid bad things (threats), decision makers are more open to taking risks. Why not risk a change if the alternative is worse? The political consultant Dick Morris was one of Bill Clinton's political advisors during his White House years. At one point Morris pitched an idea to Clinton by saying, "I can't guarantee that you win if you follow my advice, but I can guarantee that you lose if you don't."[26] Not surprisingly, politicians are often more successful campaigning using fear-based issues than hope-based issues.

Physicians, too, are often more persuasive with patients when they highlight the negative consequences of not doing something (e.g., "Not having this test lessens our chances of finding your disease in the early, more treatable stage") than when they frame their recommendations in terms of positive consequences (e.g., "Having this test gives us a better chance of finding your disease in the early, more treatable stage").[27]

To sum: When pitching ideas involving some risk, as most proposals do, advocates should emphasize how their ideas could prevent bad things from happening ("If we don't do X, we will get indicted and go to prison") rather than how their ideas could promote positive outcomes ("If we do X, we will stay out of jail"). Combining the two approaches can be best.

Generating Demand Can Create Solutions

Many of our most beloved products were created before we needed them. None of us felt an urgent need for Post-it Notes before we started using them; few of us ever had a hankering for a Walkman, mobile phone, Blackberry, iPad, or even Scotchgard before each was invented. In crafting new schemas, successful advocates are often creating demand for their ideas by creating problems.

Think about it this way. The goal of every great marketer is to make salespeople irrelevant. If a company has great marketing, salespeople become order takers. And what is great marketing but the creation of problems that people never knew they had? The economist Joseph Schumpeter famously said in 1939, "It was not enough to produce satisfactory soap, it was also necessary to induce people to wash." Canny marketers generate demand by creating problems — often problems that consumers never know they have until marketers tell them. Here are some cases in point.

Arm & Hammer baking soda has created novel problems for consumers many times. Historically, baking soda was used in baking. Then it became something people put in refrigerators to eliminate "refrigerator smells" — a problem they had never labeled as such until Arm & Hammer created it. Later yet, people discovered that they needed baking soda to ensure that their garbage disposal didn't smell. What a great business concept: get consumers to spend their hard-earned money on a box of baking soda only to toss its contents down the drain!

The invention of the grocery cart by Oklahoma City grocer Sylvan Goldman spurred sales of groceries in the late 1930s. Before the cart's invention, people hand-carried items to the counter. That worked fine for most people. The introduction of the grocery cart created a problem that consumers never knew they had had before — an empty cart. Today major retailers like Sam's Club, Costco, and Carrefour have rows of super-sized carts that almost scream, "Load up!"

In 1919 the Plumbing-Heating-Cooling Information Bureau, part of the National Association of Master Plumbers, started a major "Bath a Day" campaign. The goal was to convince Americans that it was unhygienic not to take a daily bath (most people in those days didn't bathe every day, nor was that considered a problem). Major soap manufacturers soon joined the campaign. The problem: not bathing enough. The solution: a bathtub (which plumbers need to install) and soap (which soap makers need to sell).

In the 1920s, American booksellers convinced homebuilders that a high-status home had built-in bookcases. The problem for consumers: an empty bookcase. The solution: fill it with books![28]

When the pharmaceutical giant Roche discovered that one of its antidepressant potions relaxed people who suffered from shyness, it started a campaign telling people that shyness was a medical problem, a "social anxiety disorder." In Australia, Roche's crack public relations firm told people that more than a million Australians had an underdiagnosed "soul-destroying" psychiatric disorder called "social phobia," which Roche's drug might resolve.[29]

Baldness became a disease (technically, male-pattern baldness syndrome) when Merck found that one of its drugs encouraged hair growth.

What all of these cases have in common is the decision by marketers to craft new problems. No one knew that baldness was a medical problem until Rogaine hit the market. Shrewd advocates make the same move — they sell problems to decision makers, not solutions. They understand that once decision makers are convinced that they face new problems, they will want solutions. And the ideas that advocates want to sell are the solutions. If you have ever had a great boss, you have seen this move in action. The boss describes a tough problem she is facing. Then she asks, "What do you think we should do?" You respond with an idea, and her eyes light up. "That's a great idea," she says. "Why don't you do just that?" You have been empowered. She has adopted your solution. Of course, she defined the problem well enough that virtually any solution you suggested would be palatable to her.

How do advocates go about creating demand beyond simply describing difficult problems that their ideas will solve? There are an infinite number of ways. Consider some.

Highlight the pain of novelty. Decision makers are generally more comfortable with familiar ideas than with novel ones. That's why computer companies offer college students enormous discounts on both hardware and software. The firms hope that when students eventually find jobs, they will insist on using the same tools they used in school. If, say, an advocate wants the European branch of a company to adopt a process already used in the United States, she might argue that many employees know how to use the process. "It's worked well already, so why not just use it everywhere? Plus, who knows what might happen if the organization adopts an unfamiliar process?" It is easier to adopt what is familiar.

Make it a habit. In April 1926, a novel entitled *Lolly Willowes* arrived in the homes of 4,750 people. It was the first book offered by the Book of the Month Club. Founded by Harry Scherman, the club created a demand for books. Within eight months, more than 46,000 homes were members. Each month, subscribers received notice of a new book that a panel of distinguished literary experts had selected as "must" reading (note the importance of a credible source), and unless members rejected the recommended volume, it would appear in the mail in a few weeks.[30] Membership created automatic demand. Advocates use this technique when they tell decision makers things like "We've done it this way for years."

Highlight customer needs. Charles Foster didn't invent the wooden toothpicks, but he came up with ways to mass-manufacture them. The trouble was that few stores or restaurants stocked them. No one saw much need for them. So Foster hired good-looking young men to stroll into shops and ask clerks if they carried wooden toothpicks. Storekeepers mostly said no. Later the same day, Foster walked into the same shops and pitched his product. Not surprisingly, many of the retailers began stocking Foster's wooden toothpicks. But he didn't stop there. He employed other young fellows to walk in a few days later and buy a box from each retailer. Now the storekeeper was convinced — not only were people requesting the product but they were buying it. Foster did the same thing at fancy restaurants. He hired Harvard students in Boston to throw loud fits when they discovered that no toothpicks were available after meals. Then, a few days later, Foster pitched his product to the restaurant manager. The manager, recalling the unhappy customers, bought some and made them available. Foster knew the value of creating a need to promote his idea.[31]

Generate a crisis. Crises often create demand. Kraft Foods produces 40 percent of the cheese that Americans eat each year. In recent years, one of Kraft's promotional strategies has been to highlight a "calcium crisis." By eating cheese we were building stronger bones. Kraft advertisements told us that "two out of three kids don't get the recommended amount of calcium," and in Asia and Australia, Kraft sold its cheese as "the body-builder for kids."

Emphasize interdependencies. Since many children's toys need batteries, wise retailers place batteries right by the counter. If you buy the toy, you purchase batteries as well. They place razors next to razorblades, printers next to ink cartridges. Walmart discovered that bandage sales increased if it placed bandages next to fishhooks, which can nick fingers.

Create a score-keeping system. A management maxim is that what gets measured, gets done. That rule is useful when advocating ideas. Smart advocates create new problems by generating new metrics. Once they have publicized the metrics, their ideas, which help people achieve those metrics, are "must" notions. Pfizer created demand for its cholesterol drug Lipitor by mass-marketing the notion that you should "know your number" — the level of cholesterol in your body. The best-seller list for books probably accounts for more book sales than any other innovation in publishing.

Link the idea to a problem, even indirectly. In 2005, DuPont successfully lobbied Congress to set deadlines for the National Highway Safety Administration to improve the safety of cars. The congressional legislation included mandates to ensure that people wouldn't be thrown out of a vehicle in an automobile accident. Why was DuPont interested? Perhaps partly because it manufactures laminated glass, which, if used for side and back windows, could significantly reduce the number of crash victims who might be ejected from the car. The deadlines passed by Congress started the process of rule making that ultimately increased demand for DuPont's life-saving product. DuPont wasn't directly pushing its glass. Rather, it was lobbying for a deadline that would, in turn, yield glass sales.

Introduce new criteria for decision makers. An advocate might suggest in a meeting that "when making a decision about A, we should consider V, W, X, Y, and Z." After establishing these criteria in decision makers' minds — after, in effect, creating a schema — the advocate guides decision makers through various possible alternatives in terms of the criteria. Not surprisingly, his idea is the only one that optimally meets the criteria ("Option 1 is good with V, W, and Z; option 2 helps when it comes to V and Z; but only this [my] idea meets all five criteria that we've agreed are important").[32]

Let's look at this last method more closely. Companies often have established criteria for investing in new products. Shrewd advocates know those formal criteria and make sure their ideas pass muster. But they also stealthily encourage decision makers to contemplate additional criteria. Suppose you are pitching a new product idea. You are satisfied that it meets company criteria: It has profit potential and meets customer requirements. It doesn't challenge the current offerings of your company, and it can easily be made with existing resources. But many competing new ideas meet those criteria. So, before the formal decision meeting, while you are chatting with decision makers, you prompt them to think about additional criteria for any new product idea — say, for example, how innovative it is and how it could be packaged more simply than other products are. Right there, you are creating a new problem (a new schema) because you know that your idea meets the new criteria far better than the competing ideas do.

4

Build Your Reputation, Create a Brand

Young man, make your name worth something. . . .
If you can sell a hat for one dollar, you can sell it for
two dollars if you stamp it with your name and make
the public feel that your name stands for something.

Think of some famous brands: Coca-Cola, Nike, McDonald's, Apple. Why do the companies spend so much effort building and protecting their brand names? Because instantly recognized brand names give them enormous advantages in the marketplace.

Recognition. Imagine walking into a store and scanning the shelves. What's in the orange box of detergent over there? Tide. The red can of soda? Coca-Cola. Which shoe has the swoosh sign? Nike. In a crowded marketplace, customers can easily find well-known brands.

Preference. Brands create loyalty. When people don't know what to choose, they pick familiar brand names. Give children carrots in a bag with a Mc-Donald's label on it, and they'll eat more than if they encounter the vegetable in a plain white wrapper.[1] Why? The brand. If you are traveling abroad and can't read the language, at the grocery store you will probably select items with familiar labels. Once people come to like a brand, they choose it every time. Brands become a habit. They make purchasing simpler.

Quality. Brands often bring with them a presumption of quality. In truth, the quality is perceived, not actual. Years ago, in the Pepsi Challenge, a contest started in Dallas by a Pepsi bottler, consumers sipped from two unlabeled cups of cola — one Coca-Cola, the other Pepsi — and were asked which cola they preferred. The winner? Pepsi. Yet most people consider Coca-Cola the preferred brand. Try to remember a time when a waiter asked, "Is Coke okay?" But all of us have been asked, "Is Pepsi okay?" Pepsi may win on taste, but Coke still wins the branding war.

Trust. For most of human history, most people lived in small clusters. They knew who to turn to for food or clothes and who offered high-quality products. When people migrated to cities, it became difficult to know who had good, safe products. Brands emerged as residents sought assurance about what they bought. Good brands offered implicit guarantees. Buy shoes from Nike and they won't fall apart. Buy a cheeseburger from Mc-Donald's, and it will taste the same as any other McDonald's cheeseburger. And if something goes wrong, we believe (perhaps naively) that the company with the brand name will resolve the problem. Indeed, the more important our purchase, the more likely we are to choose a branded product. When buying a $29 phone, we don't fret much about the brand. When purchasing a $5,000 entertainment unit, we probably opt for established brands like Sony and Bose.

Value. When my children were young and the family went shopping, my role was often to sit in the car with a dozing baby (basic parenting principle: never wake a sleeping child) while my wife shopped. Once, with nothing better to do, I watched people approach soft-drink machines in front of the grocery store. One machine dispensed Coke; the other, a private label brand. The Cokes cost $1.00; the private label, exactly half that. Every person but one purchased Cokes, willingly paying double what they had to. Why? Because the Coke brand name had won their trust and loyalty. Their choices were a stunning demonstration of the financial value of a good brand name. People pay for brand names. They will pay extra for Bayer Aspirin even though aspirin has been off patent for years. They will pay extra for clothing and coffee with recognized brand names.

Extensibility. Think of Coca-Cola. What other products could Coca-Cola produce and successfully market under that brand name? Could it sell candy? Probably. How about clothing? Not business suits, but maybe T-shirts with "Coca-Cola" scrawled on them. How about athletic shoes — "Squish" rather than "Swoosh"? Probably not. Or take Nike. Could Nike sell a cola beverage? Nope. But Nike could certainly market an energy drink. A brand allows companies to expand in some directions and stops them from going in others. Dr. Scholl's is an established brand name when it comes to eliminating odors in shoes, but would you buy Dr. Scholl's breath mints? If a company introduces a product that doesn't match its brand name, it will have a difficult time selling the product.

You Are a Brand — and Your Brand Name Counts

Why this discussion of brand names? Because advocates have brand names, just the way products do. An advocate may be known as an innovator, a creative type, a manager, a diligent worker, a joke teller. Advocates' personal brands are the sum of the images that people have of them.

Advocates' brand names are crucial to their success in pitching proposals. If decision makers *recognize* an advocate's name and that name appears on a report, decision makers pick up the report and look at it. Just as Coca-Cola is many people's preferred soda brand, proponents with a great brand name are also *preferred*. They have top-shelf visibility. In companies, the same employees seem to get chosen over and over again when companies choose people to work on important issues — not because these people are necessarily any better than anyone else but because their names come immediately to mind. Decision makers *trust* them to do a good job. Their name on a report makes people think they are getting a *high-quality* product. Indeed, people forgive the blunders and celebrate the successes of people with good reputations. It is the opposite for those with poor brand names: their mistakes are remembered, and their successes are commonly attributed to other factors. And just as Coca-Colas in the machines outside the grocery commanded higher prices than the generic colas, people with trusted brand names often are more *valued* in their organization. The firm will fight to keep them from leaving.

People's brand names shape how others interpret what they say. The same statement extolling rebellion is interpreted quite differently when the purported author is Iraqi dictator Saddam Hussein than when it is attributed to Thomas Jefferson. Same message, different author. In short, you can't separate a persuasive message from the advocate who utters it.

It is important for advocates to remember that it is difficult to pitch proposals that don't match their brand names. This is the notion of brand *extensions*. If you are branded as an HR person, people will listen when you propose ideas for training and recruiting. But if you talk about innovative tax strategies, you probably won't get much traction. Regardless of how good your idea is, if it doesn't fit your brand name, people aren't likely to buy it.[2]

What Is Your Brand Name?

What this means is that advocates must understand how others see them. How do you figure out your brand name? Here are some ways.

Ask trusted colleagues how they view you. What are your perceived strengths and weaknesses? Some organizations use 360-degree feedback — an appraisal method that gives a person opinions from a wide variety of bosses, colleagues, clients, and subordinates. That kind of feedback is invaluable in assessing your brand. What do people think you are great at? What do they see as your weaknesses?

Consider what opportunities you are offered at work. If you know your organization well, you know the high-value areas — the units and jobs that count. If you are never placed in one of those areas, that is a message about your brand.

Volunteer for an assignment that you believe fits your brand and see how people react. If they are keen on having you join, you have probably gauged accurately how you are viewed in the organization. If you get the cold shoulder, maybe people don't see you undertaking that assignment: your brand and what they need in that role don't match.

Sophisticated advocates seldom propose ideas that don't fit their brand names. They sense, given their brand, that they are unlikely to get decision makers' attention. Dan Robinson worked at Intuit (the company that makes Quicken). Because of his personal experience in juggling numerous medical bills, he thought Intuit ought to create software to help people manage their medical expenses. When he first pitched his idea people ignored him. Why? "I was an engineering manager, not a marketer," Robinson says."[3] Marketing people were the ones who generated new markets for software, not engineers.

What happens when people like Robinson have brilliant notions that don't fit their brand name? Sometimes they persuade others in their organization with more appropriate brands to sell their ideas. Hyman Rickover, father of the nuclear-powered navy, understood his brand name in the navy was as an engineer. He had never seen combat. So when he pitched nuclear-powered ships, he made sure his team included naval officers with heroic wartime records. This gave his team a strong brand name among battle-hardened decision makers.[4]

Reinventing Your Brand Name

Advocates without credibility in an area may reinvent how they are perceived. Admittedly, creating a new brand name is difficult. As Prince Sadruddin Aga Khan, who served as the UN's High Commissioner for Refugees, said, "Myths and labels become attached to people, giving them a reputation that does not always correspond to reality."[5] Nonetheless, there are at least five ways to change your personal brand name.

Leave the organization. We have all heard of someone who quit a firm and became incredibly successful elsewhere. People at the former firm ask, "I wonder why we didn't see his talents here." Perhaps the person's brand name — how others viewed him — kept him from accomplishing what he might have. Ed Rasala was a brilliant engineer at minicomputer maker Data General. He had moved to Data General from Raytheon to change his brand name. At Raytheon, he worked on unimportant tasks. His reputation as an average engineer meant that he wasn't handed interesting, high-profile assignments. So he moved to Data General to reinvent his reputation.[6] There he succeeded and found himself included in the development of major new products.

Move within your organization. Sometimes internal transfers let people establish new brand names. They take assignments in other units or locations — places where they don't have an established brand name.

Hang out with different people. You are known by the company you keep. If people always spot you with marketing folks, they will begin to associate you with marketing. If you want to propose a marketing idea, that is the group to be seen with. By the same token, if you spend your time with malcontents, people will assume that you, too, are unhappy. Alternatively, if you are always around creative, energetic, hardworking people, others will assume that you have those qualities. Smart people choose to bask in the reflected glory of successful people.[7] Velcro yourself to stars in your organization — people who have extraordinary reputations as money-earning business people, creative inventors, efficient managers. If someone is deeply respected by executives, there is obviously great value in making sure that person thinks and speaks well of you — and certifies you in the eyes of those leaders.

Hope for a new boss who doesn't know you. You often hear complaints when companies hire leaders from outside the firm. "Why don't loyal employees rise to the top?" That is a valid complaint when you as an employee have the reputation you want. However, if you are seeking to rebrand yourself, an outsider may be your best chance to rework your brand while staying

put. When somebody who already knows everyone in the work pool becomes the new boss, people's brand names — how they are perceived by the
leadership — seldom change. A new outside boss offers everyone fresh opportunities to demonstrate their value.

Develop valuable and scarce resources. Even in the same organization and
under the same boss, people can transform their brand names. They do this
by developing vital and scarce resources.

Transforming Your Brand Name

Try this exercise: Write down five resources you offer to your organization. They might include your knowledge, your ability to work with people,
a language you speak, your skill at a particular task. Now circle the resources that your organization values. The circled items are the beginning
of a transformation effort. The only resources that matter for advocates are
those that the organization values. If you wrote down "strategic vision" and
you work in plant engineering, you have little scope for extending your
work into that area. If you jotted down creativity and you are in accounting,
you might be going to jail.

The resources that count in firms may not be obvious. Lots of little
things matter a great deal in organizations, and people who figure these out
often find niches that afford them substantial power. For example, in October 1940, Lyndon Johnson was a junior member of Congress. Letters that
he wrote to top congressional leaders were seldom answered. One month
later, everything changed. Now senior congressional leaders were writing
to him and addressing him as a good friend. What happened? Johnson
discovered a valuable resource — money. He was single-handedly able to tap
into huge political donations from Texas oilmen. As he liberally dispersed
that money to a number of members of Congress he quickly gained power.
Later, Johnson became assistant minority leader in the U.S. Senate — a
largely ceremonial position. But Johnson, who deeply understood power,
found opportunities in the position that no one had ever considered. One of
his responsibilities was to schedule bills for discussion on the Senate floor.
That information was valuable: he could tell colleagues when they needed
to be on the Senate floor, which gave him influence as the go-to person.[8]

Offering *valued* resources is only the first step toward transforming your
brand name. You must also identify which of those resources are *scarce*
within your organization. In 1990, the Ty Company was a small firm headquartered near Chicago. It manufactured products in Asia and sold them in

hotel and airport stores in the United States. In 1993 the company started selling $5.95 stuffed animals. By 1999, Ty Warner, the owner, was one of the richest individuals in the toy industry and one of the 400 wealthiest people in America. He was so rich that he bought the Four Seasons Hotel in New York City, one of the most expensive hotel properties in the world. What does the Ty Company sell? Little stuffed animals called Beanie Babies.

Why were Beanie Babies so successful? Largely because Warner brilliantly ignored many basic rules of marketing. He spent little on advertising. Instead of letting shops order specific stuffed animals, he sent them whatever *he* wanted. More incredibly still, he constantly took best-selling animals off the market — he "retired" them, in the language of Beanie Baby collectors. What Warner did was create a sense of scarcity. When people found that some of their favorite characters had been retired, they promptly purchased newly introduced Beanie Babies, anticipating that they, too, would disappear from the market — and sooner, rather than later! By randomly allocating the stuffed animals to different outlets, he forced addicted customers to hunt for the little creatures, not knowing which stores might have them. As Warner said, "As long as kids keep fighting over the products and retailers are angry at us because they cannot get enough, I think those are good signs."[9] Consider this: With most children's toys, customers cut off the tags that come with them. But with Beanie Babies, purchasers not only kept the tags on; they actually bought tag protectors! Parents took the toys and put them in plastic bags to make sure their children never touched them. Beanie Babies became successful precisely because of their perceived scarcity.

Warner was certainly not the first to understand the role of scarcity. It wasn't until Catherine the Great fenced in her potato fields and warned peasants not to steal them that potatoes became a popular and valued food in Russia.[10] Fine art, jewelry, old stamps, and ancient coins are all sought after not simply because they are charming but because limited numbers are available. Scarcity implies exclusivity. Not everyone can own Picassos or halfpenny green stamps.

Years ago, the University of Virginia had some old dorms with tiny rooms and no bathrooms. Students avoided them. So the university selected the campus's outstanding seniors and offered them a chance to live in what it declared was the most prestigious place on campus — those dorms. Soon the rooms on the "Lawn" became prized. Not everyone could live there, so having a room there was a mark of status.[11]

Braun, the German company, can also attest to the value of scarcity. When it opted to get out of the stereo business, its warehouses were still filled with valuable inventory, expensive machines that were, however, no longer on the cutting edge of technology and that were being discontinued. Braun's marketing team decided to call these machines Braun's Last Edition. They turned excess inventory into collector items.[12]

The next time you go shopping, you might notice an empty shelf with the words "sold out" on it. Why the sign? It creates a sense of scarcity that encourages consumers to buy similar, even more expensive products.[13]

All of these examples revolve around things. There are many other forms of scarcity — knowledge, networks, languages, even influence, to name a few.

Now examine the list of resources you wrote down. Of those you circled as valued, place a check mark next to those that are also scarce in the firm. Here is where you start transforming your reputation. Develop scarce and valued resources and redefine your brand name.

The Continuum of Brands

Responses to brands fall along a continuum ranging from rejection to insistence. If I bring up someone's name and everyone says "No way!" that person has a *rejection* brand name. Some people have *no* brand name. They are ghosts. They walk through offices every day, and no one knows who they are (think Milton, the stapler guy from the film *Office Space*). Some people have *associative* brand names. You see them and you know them by where they work or what they do. She is an accountant, a lawyer, a salesperson. People may also have *preferred* brand names: "I really want him as part of my team." Finally, some people have *insistence* brand names: "I can't do this without her!"

Where do you want to be on this continuum? Most people initially say "insistence." But wait, think about that. Insistence can trap you. Being pigeonholed could stop you from advancing or even from proposing ideas. If you are the only person who knows how to code in an old computer language like FORTRAN, you will have job security as long as your company uses FORTRAN. But because no one else can code in FORTRAN, the company would be crazy to place you in any other job. You are stuck because of your insistence brand name.

Responsibilities in organizations fall into two major categories: task-focused and people-focused. Task-focused responsibilities might be technical in nature — programming in Java, handling a piece of equipment, being the world's expert on this or that. Task-focused activities can also be established relationships — a client swears by you, saying you are the only person she wants to work with. People-focused tasks are different. They are about leadership, people skills, even advocacy skills. When others describe you as trustworthy, as business savvy, as a brilliant leader, they are thinking about people-focused tasks. For task-focused responsibilities, you do not want insistence brand names. Instead, you want to be preferred. You want people to think you are good at task-focused activities but not essential. But for people-focused tasks you do want insistence. You want to be known as a great person to work with and a wonderfully persuasive spokesperson.

What follows is a description of how you can acquire or maintain an insistence brand name as an advocate.

What Makes a Reputation?

More than 2,300 years ago, Aristotle said that people's ethos — their character, their credibility, their principles and morality — was critical to their success as persuaders. People's ethos in the workplace — that is, their brand names — is a function of whether others perceive them as competent, trustworthy, and passionate and tenacious about their ideas.

It is important to remember that competency, trust, and passion depend upon *perceptions*. It doesn't matter whether proponents themselves think they are smart or trustworthy; what matters is that others see them as smart and trustworthy. Consider the case of former U.S. Senator Rick Santorum, who accepted a donation from a private weather-forecasting company days before introducing legislation limiting what the U.S. Weather Service could provide to the public. In essence, his proposal would have forced citizens to use the company from which he had just received a donation. Santorum's claim that the timing was incidental may have been completely honest, but to the public, his move didn't pass the "I smell a rat" test.[14]

Seasoned advocates know they must continually shape others' perceptions of themselves. Try this exercise. Before you next pitch a proposal, write down the names of the decision makers. Next to each name, rate yourself, on a scale of 0 to 100, in terms of how that person probably regards you with respect to your competency, trustworthiness, and tenacity. If you can confidently say that each decision maker would give you a score of 100 on all three, skip the rest of this chapter.

Successful Advocates Exude Competency

People tend to be willing to support ideas, especially risky ones, proposed by smart, competent proponents with distinguished records of important accomplishments. Typically, decision makers, when listening to pitches, are counterarguing. Someone proposes a notion, and listeners are calculating negatives: "What could go wrong?" "How much is this going to cost?" "How is this better than those other proposals?" Overcoming these sorts of mental arguments is one of the biggest challenges that proponents face. In 2009 brain scientists examined what happened neurologically as people made financial decisions. In some cases, people made financial decisions after hearing an expert make a recommendation. In other cases, they made similar decisions without hearing an expert recommendation. What the researchers found was striking: when people heard an expert recommend a financial move, normal brain activity associated with deep thinking and counterarguing disappeared.[15]

To establish your competency, the guiding principle is to consistently deliver more than others expect. In maneuvering to get proposals adopted, wise advocates work early on to understand decision makers' expectations. They may spend time talking one-on-one with each decision maker to fine-tune their proposals in accordance with what these individuals expect. If one decision maker expects data-driven recommendations, an advocate litters her pitch with numbers. If another decision maker likes brief reports, an advocate prunes the report down to essentials. In addition to adapting to decision makers' expectations, however, perceptive advocates create new expectations. People didn't know that they needed bottled water, cameras on cell phones, or iPads until those innovations were introduced. But it is just as important, maybe even more important, for advocates to pitch only promises that they can keep.

Experienced advocates can actually be handicapped by their very success. If they have distinguished records of accomplishments, people hearing them pitch a new idea may expect more than they used to. Take Ludwig Erhard, who became Germany's minister of economics in 1949. The economy was shattered; Germans were starving. Then the economy started to blossom. Rightly or wrongly, Erhard was branded as responsible for the magnificent economic recovery, which came to be known as the *Wirtschafts-wunder*. In 1963, Erhard replaced Konrad Adenauer as federal chancellor. Given his previous success, Germans figured that Erhard would produce similar miracles in other areas, such as the international arena and the workplace; but Erhard could not possibly live up to their expectations, and many viewed his term as chancellor as disappointing. Had he not been such a capable (and lucky) economics minister, he might have been better regarded as chancellor.

Even when people have previously exceeded decision makers' expectations on one dimension of competence, they can still enhance their brand names by exceeding expectations on other dimensions. What follows are ten ways in which advocates can exceed decision makers' perceptions of their competency and burnish or achieve an insistence brand name.

1. *Prepare, prepare, prepare.* Successful proponents are like former British prime minister Margaret Thatcher. She was a "demon for information, for research, for numbers. She devoured them, she remembered them. . . . No one could out-study or out-prepare her."[16] In debates she overcame objections by knowing more than anyone else. Credible advocates are better prepared than anyone else in meetings. They understand everything about their proposals — not only the technical aspects but also everything else that might be relevant to decision makers.

Bella Moskowitz, a powerful advocate in early-twentieth-century New York, did her homework thoroughly before pitching ideas. In her day, many young women worked in New York City's garment district. Nearby were "dancing academies" offering liquor, bedrooms, and other enticements that could challenge a woman's virtue. When activists complained about these academies, police investigations followed, and the operations disappeared, but only for a while. Moskowitz, seeing how the operations kept reappearing, spent long hours at the city hall identifying who owned the buildings that housed the academies. She discovered, in fact, that prominent city leaders owned many of them. Rather than creating another "investigation," she told these well-known citizens that if they didn't ensure that laws were passed to regulate the academies, their names would be publicized. In short order, laws were passed that significantly improved the "moral surroundings of young girls."[17] Moskowitz did her homework, and that made all the difference.

Proponents have great difficulty promoting ideas if people don't perceive them as technically competent. In meetings, adroit advocates may toss out tidbits of related information simply to show their depth of knowledge. Years ago, Charlotte Beers, then a senior advertising executive, was pitching a proposal to Sears, which sells Craftsman power tools. Most people didn't associate power tools with women in those days. So, as Beers presented her proposal to Sears executives, she picked up a power drill and casually disassembled it. Then, just as casually, she put it back together again. Never once did she say anything about the drill, but her little demonstration communicated her competency about the hardware business.[18]

John Boyd, an advocate within the U.S. Air Force who changed the way the United States fought air wars, once advised a protégé about advocating: "You can never be wrong. You have to do your homework. If you make a technical statement, you better be right. If you are not, they (the opposition) will hose you. And if they hose you, you've had it. Because once you lose your credibility . . . no one will pay attention to you. They won't respect you."[19]

2. Develop a record of accomplishment. Credible proponents have proven that they can accomplish important things. They have track records related to what they are pitching. Joan Ganz Cooney was not a producer of children's television shows when she helped create *Sesame Street*. However, she had won an Emmy for producing public documentaries. That recognition gave her credibility when she began her pitch for better children's television.[20]

Wise advocates never sound egotistical about accomplishments, however meritorious they are. Instead of boasting, they may ask others to describe their deeds — perhaps in an introduction to a report — or they may include brief bios in their written materials. If an advocate is leading a project team, she might introduce each member by describing his or her competencies and allude to her own experience in passing ("When we began this task, I felt lucky. What we were working on fits right in with what I spent three years studying as a postdoc.").

3. See the big picture. Steve Enright held annual meetings for his team during his time as a senior HR executive at Union Pacific. At each meeting a visitor from the financial world (e.g., an analyst from Morgan Stanley) explained to Enright's people how Wall Street viewed Union Pacific. Enright's goal was twofold. First, he wanted his team to grasp what business issues faced Union Pacific and why its stock price was what it was. Second, he hoped that understanding how Wall Street viewed the company would let his team make better pitches to senior executives. Enright understood that senior-level decision makers often complain that employees are too narrowly focused on immediate needs as they do their jobs. Wise proponents enhance their perceived competency by learning about the worlds in which their organizations live. They can contextualize their proposals as part of their firms' competitive strategy and incorporate their ideas within larger business issues.

4. *Be politically savvy.* Successful advocates understand the political environment of their firms. They know how to make the system work for them when pitching their ideas.

Congresswoman Edith Green (along with Congresswoman Patsy Mink) was responsible for the passage of Title IX, the portion of the Education Act of 1972 requiring schools to give women equal opportunities in education. Green also sponsored an earlier act, the Equal Pay Act. During her final term in Congress she gave up a senior position on the Education and Labor Committee of the House of Representatives to join the much more powerful Appropriations Committee. Why? Because Appropriations is where the crucial decisions about money are made — and money drives political issues. She turned down the chance to run for the U.S. Senate (she'd probably have won) because she understood that in the seniority system, her eighteen years in the House of Representatives gave her far more power than she would have had as a junior senator. She used her role as chair of the House's Special Subcommittee on Education to hold seven days of hearings to pave the way for what later became Title IX. Those hearings brought to the fore the massive gender inequities in postsecondary education. At those hearings, she almost never brought up sports. She knew that discussions of equity in sports would create major tiffs. Instead, the panel addressed jobs and educational opportunities.[21] It took her two years to persuade people in Congress to even discuss Title IX. Knowing that people find it hard to say no face-to-face, she finally went door to door on Capitol Hill, chatting up each member of her committee, to get the votes. Only when she had sufficient support did she offer Title IX as an amendment to the Education Act.[22] Green understood the political rules of her organization — what people could do, what was rewarded, and what was ignored or rejected.

5. *Just get it done.* Credible proponents complete projects promptly and well. This means they often end up seeking out "good enough" rather than "best" solutions. William James once said, "The art of being wise is the art of knowing what to overlook." In today's world, James's notion is conceptualized as the distinction between optimizing and satisficing. *Optimizing* means finding the best solution possible. *Satisficing* means discovering one that's good enough. As Voltaire once put it, "The perfect is the enemy of the good." If a grizzly bear is chasing you and a friend, you don't have to be an Olympic runner. You only need to be faster than your buddy. Bill Gates has

proven you can get rich by satisficing — Microsoft would never launch a product if the company waited until a perfect code was created. The Flip video camera isn't fancy. It has very few of the frills that more expensive cameras have. But it works just fine for everyday video recording, and it is cheap. No proposal is perfect. So at some point advocates just go ahead and pitch a good idea, not a great one, but one that will suffice — at least for now.

Bert Keely did much of the foundational work on what we know today as the Tablet PC. He understood the necessary business approach to product development. "Creativity is highly regarded for a short time, but the primary thing is to ship a product. It involves taking this passion of yours and running it through a humiliating, exhausting process. You can't believe how many ego-deflating compromises people have to make to get it out."[23] Engineers working on the Prius hybrid car at Toyota wanted to postpone releasing the vehicle until some technical issues were resolved. But Toyota decided to debut the Prius despite the flaws because none were dangerous. "If this had been left to the R&D guys," said Toyota's CEO, Fujio Cho, "we'd probably still be tinkering with it."[24] Advocates can happily settle for good enough.

6. *Align with the right people.* We already saw that you can change your brand by hanging out with different people. Smart proponents also bolster their brand name by associating with people who are respected for their knowledge and wisdom. They build teams composed of people with enviable reputations. They use evidence from unimpeachable sources.

Aligning with competent people is especially important when touting ideas that don't clearly fall within an advocate's realm of perceived expertise. When public figures, like U.S. presidents, address charged political issues, they physically surround themselves with people who exude competency about those topics. When discussing law enforcement, presidents stand with rows of uniformed police officers. If the issue is health related, physicians in white coats line up behind them. Being surrounded by these presumably competent people bolsters the president's perceived competency.

Equally important, advocates avoid being associated with people who might hurt their chances of selling ideas. Congresswoman Edith Green resisted being viewed as part of a "woman's caucus" in the U.S. House of Representatives in the 1960s. Why? She felt that in the sexist environment of the time, being pigeonholed as a feminist might undercut her effectiveness in getting what amounted to a feminist agenda passed.[25]

7. *Show up when it matters; seek out crises.* Crises are opportunities for proponents to enhance their perceived credibility. Many successful leaders

have made their reputation on the basis of how they handled crises. Take Rudy Giuliani. He emerged as a hero after the September 11 terror attack on the World Trade Center. And how about "Sully" Sullenberger, the US Airways pilot who safely landed his plane on the Hudson River? Because he was so credible, airline pilots' unions in November of 2010 used him as a spokesperson to successfully convince the Transportation Security Administration not to require uniformed pilots to go through the intense scrutiny everyone else must experience at airports prior to boarding planes. Crises need not be cataclysmic to bolster a proponent's reputation, however. Just being part of important events and decisions counts. For many years, John Breaux, the senior senator from Louisiana, was perceived as one of the most influential people in the Senate. Political observers often wryly observed that he was always in the action. "He's the Forrest Gump of Washington," said one person. "He's always there when something important is going down."[26]

8. *Develop multiple competencies.* People with sterling brand names earn tributes to their multiple areas of expertise: "She's a great marketer who began her career as an engineer," or "He's amazing — good at numbers and also wonderful with people," or "She started in product design, but the company put her in charge of Korea, and she turned the business there around." If you are a gifted engineer, work on your selling skills. If you are a talented salesperson, learn to manage balance sheets. Not only do multiple competencies build advocates' brand names, but they also allow advocates to pitch more and varied ideas.

When developing multiple competencies, advocates face up to their personal strengths and weaknesses. We talked about this earlier as an aspect of figuring out your brand name. Most people can easily list their strengths — accounting, or engineering, or speaking extemporaneously — but identifying weaknesses can prove difficult. What do you do poorly? What are you not good at? Advocates' perceived weaknesses affect their reputation as much as, or even more than, their perceived strengths. You should pitch proposals that match your perceived strengths. It is hard to pitch proposals that will require you to do things that others see you as unable to do well.

9. *Master the effortful/effortless principle.* Have you ever felt that others don't appreciate your contributions? That you work hard and nobody notices? This may happen because you don't grasp the effortful/effortless principle: people should experience your work effortlessly, but they should understand the effort you expended. Manufacturers have long grasped this principle. They encourage customers to take factory tours. After walking

through a busy factory, customers come to appreciate the work that goes into making a product and are more likely to purchase it and less likely to complain about price than if they just saw the finished product on display.

People translate perceived effort into commitment and dedication. And the more effort they see, the more difficult it is for them to say no. When audience members believe that presenters have spent a good deal of time preparing their presentations, they evaluate those presentations more positively than they do presentations that they believe were just whipped up. The presentations are the same. The only difference is the audience's gauge of preparation time.[27]

Make sure that decision makers can *see* you work. This doesn't mean that everyone has to watch you labor all day long. Nor does it mean that you should copy everyone on every email—which is annoying. What it means instead is that you help decision makers understand the effort that goes into your projects. Rather than sending decision makers an electronic attachment of a detailed eighty-page proposal, give them bound copies. With a solid eighty pages in their hands, they can appreciate the work involved in producing its contents.

10. *Understand that appearance counts.* Your mother was right: first impressions matter. And first impressions are often formed by how you look. Good-looking people are judged more positively. In the courtroom, attractive defendants fare better than their unattractive counterparts. The same is true in school, in jobs—and when pitching ideas.[28] How do you bolster your appearance? First, dress professionally, so people take you seriously. Here is a test. You are at work and a senior leader needs someone to join her at a meeting with members of the board. Are you dressed in a way that allows you to accompany her to that meeting? Second, dress conservatively. You can always take off the jacket, but if you don't have one, you might regret it. Third, dress just slightly better than others at meetings. If everyone wears jeans, wear khakis. If everyone sports khakis, wear slacks. Finally, dress for the setting. In most high-tech firms wearing a suit would be as inappropriate as wearing jeans at the White House.

Successful Advocates Are Trustworthy

Integrity is power, as former presidential advisor Bryce Harlow used to say. When proponents are deeply trusted, decision makers are more receptive to, and less critical of, what they are hearing or reading.[29] Abraham Lincoln once said, "If you would win a man to your cause, first convince him that you are his sincere friend." Trust precedes successful advocacy. Trust has four components: honesty, consistency, benevolence, and vulnerability.[30]

Honesty. When championing causes, advocates know their word is their currency. If people discover that you haven't told the truth, they discount everything else you say. Your word isn't golden anymore. How can you, as a proponent, demonstrate honesty?

First, be honest—especially when you don't need to be. Robert Miller, a turnaround specialist who has served as CEO of Waste Management and Federal-Mogul, the auto-parts supplier, told the *Wall Street Journal,* "The only thing you've got to sell is your own personal credibility. . . . People will believe you if you have been honest with them when things aren't what they want to hear. . . . Good or bad, tell them exactly the way it is. . . . Tell everyone the truth. . . . Play it straight."[31] Reuben Mark, CEO of Colgate-Palmolive, played it straight in 2000 when he called Herb Baum, CEO of a competitor company, Dial, and told him that a former Dial salesperson had given him a diskette containing Dial's entire marketing plan for the year. Mark told Baum that he hadn't looked at it and was mailing it back immediately.[32] Don't you think everyone in that industry trusted Mark after this?

Playing it straight is difficult when you have been wrong. Mayor Ed Koch of New York once spent hundreds of thousands of dollars painting bike lanes onto the city's streets. The bike lanes messed up traffic, caused bicyclists to run into pedestrians, and created all sorts of havoc. At a press conference during Koch's reelection campaign a reporter raised the issue of the bike lanes, anticipating that Koch would defend them. He didn't. In fact, he said that funding the lanes was one of the stupidest moves he had ever made as mayor. He fessed up and in the process bolstered his trustworthiness.[33]

Playing it straight is also difficult when, say, decision makers are 100 percent behind your proposal but—this is a big but—you know that your proposal involves serious risks. If you are honest, what do you do? You tell them about those risks, of course, even if it jeopardizes the adoption of your idea. Don't hide important information. Address the tough issues directly.

Second, argue against what others would presume you'd be in favor of.[34] Experienced waiters occasionally suggest to customers that a menu choice isn't that delicious. Doing this makes them more trustworthy. Diners expect the waiter to endorse the entire menu, yet here one is dissuading them from a choice. How can he not be trusted when he later recommends another menu item?

Arguing against your presumed position enhances not only your trust-worthiness but also your influence. For instance, prosecutors are more persuasive when they argue against giving courts more power (which we would assume that prosecutors want) than when they advocate accruing power to the courts. Equally, criminals are viewed as more persuasive when they make the case for a more powerful judicial system. Who would expect that plea from a convicted felon?[35]

The same inverse logic holds in the political sphere. When the Asbestos Alliance — a group of asbestos-related businesses that lobbies Congress about lawsuits tied to asbestos-related injuries — wanted attention for a study that laid out the enormous costs of litigation, it chose a consulting firm called Sebago Associates to hawk the study. Three well-known and well-respected Democrats who had held senior economic posts during the Clinton administration led Sebago Associates. The Asbestos Alliance understood that a report from sources (presumably Democrats) thought to oppose it would get more attention than a report from sources that most people saw as partisan. (Also, by having these three Democrats as spokespeople, Democratic colleagues found it harder to challenge the results.) Jean Monnet also understood that proponents can build trust by arguing against their pre-sumed self-interest. In the midst of tough negotiations over the Schuman Treaty (which created the European Coal and Steel Community), Monnet took positions clearly unfavorable to his home country of France. Other nations' representatives initially wondered whether Monnet might be using a negotiating trick. Once they became convinced that he wasn't — that Monnet really was more concerned about Europe than any individual country, including his own — his trustworthiness was established.[36]

Third, be seen as objective. If patients were to discover that physicians who recommended a particular drug were paid by its manufacturer, they wouldn't trust the physicians' recommendations as much as they would the same advice coming from doctors with no financial stake in promoting the medication. Smart advocates make sure people believe their decision to pitch an idea is free and independent. They want it to be clear that no one forced them to make a case and that they chose evidence from unimpeach-able sources. They let decision makers know the opinions of people these decision makers trust, even if the opinions don't match their own. During the first few years of Clinton's presidency, when Robert Rubin served as head of the National Economic Council, all his colleagues trusted him, in part because they knew that when he met with the president, even privately, he represented their viewpoints both accurately and thoroughly — even when he personally disagreed with them.

Fourth, deal immediately with misunderstandings and violations of trust. In most cases, it is appropriate to openly raise issues about trust when you sense that trust has been threatened. For example, in proposing to merge five units of a bank, one advocate knew that a colleague thought he had cooked the numbers. So he met with this colleague to clarify how the numbers were calculated. When the colleague still seemed suspicious after the discussion, the proponent directly raised the issue of trust. The colleague admitted some distrust, opening the door to a frank discussion that eventually rebuilt trust.

Consistency. Do you know people who are unpredictable, even random, in their behavior? A colleague carpools with you and promises to pick you up at 8 a.m. Sometimes he is on time, sometimes he arrives early, and once in a while he is late or even forgets to pick you up. You lose trust in him. He has never lied; he is just unreliable. People lose trust in others who are inconsistent. How do you shape perceptions of reliability? There are several ways.

First, be punctual. It is a first cousin of reliability. If you are late for meetings, people wonder about your dependability. People often infer how you would handle larger, more important issues from how you treat little things.

Second, master the follow-up. Trusted people return calls promptly and answer e-mails without delay. They finish what they start. They are known for their ability to execute their ideas. Decision makers learn to ignore people who spout idea after idea but never follow up on them.

Third, keep your small commitments. Others don't really expect that you will follow up on small commitments. "Sure," a colleague says, "I'll send you that clipping that I mentioned at lunch." Few people expect the clipping to appear on their desk after that conversation. But savvy advocates send the clipping right away. In today's competitive world, people must keep their big commitments to survive, so keeping them is nothing special. Keeping every small commitment gets you noticed.

Finally, avoid being seen as a flip-flopper. "Weathervanes" — people who regularly change their opinions depending on the way the wind is blowing — are seldom trusted. People can and do change their feelings and opinions, of course. When the facts change, opinions may, too. But if that happens to you, frame your change of opinion as a case of being open to new information (e.g., "I have long believed we should do X. Now, after looking at the research and hearing the many wise arguments by our scientists, I have to admit that my opinion has changed").

Benevolence. Years ago, when door-to-door salesmen called on customers in a farming community, they often spent part of a day helping farmers clear land or fix their homes before pitching a product. The salesmen understood that working together built trust. Only after trust was established could a sale proceed.[37] People trust others who they perceive to be considerate, conscientious, and unselfish — who seem to care. So how do you craft a reputation for benevolence?

First, spend time with people in non-task-related discussions. Build relationships before moving toward persuasion. Talk with decision makers about shared interests — families, sport events. If the only time you talk with them is when you want to sell them something, you can be perceived as manipulative. If you have a positive history with them long before you ask for anything, then you are someone they can trust.

Second, never step on someone else's turf. If your idea requires work from some other unit, get buy-in from that unit before making your pitch. If multiple bosses are involved, let each know the choices you have made and why you made them. Don't let supervisors feel blindsided. Doing so ensures fewer misunderstandings and greater trust. Although Jean Monnet was more responsible than anyone else for creating what we know as the European Union, he never held elective office. He always advised his staff to "never take another fellow's place"; he didn't want anyone on his team to be seen as being in competition with elected officials. He didn't want decision makers to think he wanted anything for himself. That way, decision makers trusted him.

Third, engage in positive discretionary behaviors. These are behaviors that go beyond what you are expected to do in a situation. It is polite to hold the door for a burdened colleague when you follow her into a building. You are supposed to do that. A positive discretionary behavior (call it being nice) would be rushing out into the rain to help her lug boxes into the building from her car. You didn't need to offer that extra help, but you did. When people go beyond expectations in helping others, they gain our trust. Check out any CEO's bio. There is always a last paragraph describing all of the charities they support, their religious activities, their children. We assume that if they are nice people with families, they can be trusted.

Finally, communicate principles and act on principles. Decision makers respect principled people. This does not mean being rigid and overbearing. Instead, people should feel that you uphold good values. They should be able to predict how you will react to a proposal because they understand your values. When you argue against an idea that you believe violates important principles, they expect you to be upright. Don't be afraid to connect your principles to your ideas.

Vulnerability. People trust advocates who have something to lose when pitching their idea. How might you demonstrate your vulnerability?

First, be seen as willing to give up valuable things to get your ideas adopted. If you tout an idea to reduce head count and it is clear that your proposal will result in your unit losing people, people will trust your motives more than if you would lose nothing were the idea adopted.

Second, willingly disclose shortcomings and mistakes. As Chris Matthews, the television commentator, once wrote, smart people always "hang lanterns" on their problems.[38] If you make a mistake, be the first to announce it. What gets most politicians in trouble are not mistakes they have made but their attempts to cover up those mistakes. There is an added benefit to speaking up when something goes wrong: executives are more likely to let you take risks when you have a reputation for highlighting mistakes. No one trusts someone who is known for hiding problems.

Third, let people know you have something to lose if your ideas falter. Decision makers trust advocates who are willing to risk status or money, be publicly embarrassed, and even lose their position if their ideas fail.

Successful Advocates Are Passionate and Tenacious

In the end, which wins in a rocky stream — the water or the rocks? Like the water that slowly wears away stones, determination and resolve distinguish successful proponents from the rest. Passion is seductive. It is hard for decision makers to turn down people who believe strongly in their ideas and persist in supporting them.

Regrettably, decision makers sometimes fail to realize how brilliant some ideas are when they are first introduced. Western Union, the predominant communications company of much of the nineteenth century, dismissed Alexander Graham Bell's proposal to sell the company his patent for the telephone, saying, "The telephone has too many shortcomings to be seriously considered as a means of communication. The device is inherently of no value to us." Robert Fulton's steamboat was called Fulton's Folly by dismissive critics.[39] A Michigan banker advised Henry Ford's lawyer not to invest in the automobile: "The horse is here to stay but the automobile is only a novelty—a fad." Advocates need to steel themselves not to take rejection personally. Instead, they need to became even more tenacious in the face of opposition. Some examples may be inspiring.

Kurt Semm, a famous German gynecologist, spent years developing the minimally invasive surgical techniques that are now clustered under the rubric of laparoscopic surgery. At first, his colleagues attacked him. Some said he was unethical. In one meeting, a person went so far as to unplug Semm's projector so he couldn't show slides demonstrating his work. Some even insisted that he have a brain scan because his ideas were so strange. Nonetheless, he persevered. And today his techniques for laparoscopic surgery are used throughout the world.

Richard Drew invented masking tape. His boss, the CEO of 3M, William McKnight, had directly ordered him to stop working on the project. Drew continued. When he finally figured out how to make the tape, he triumphantly went to McKnight for funds to build the machine to manufacture the product. Again, McKnight was a brick wall. And again, Drew persevered. He was allowed to approve spending up to $100 of company money without formal permission from senior executives. So he authorized a slew of purchase orders, each for $99, to complete his machine. Only after the machine was built and masking tape was selling well did Drew tell McKnight what he had done. Drew's tenacity created an entire industry.

As a post office employee, Robert Moon spent twenty years touting number codes for geographic areas of the United States. His original proposal for a three-number code, made in 1944, was ignored. He relentlessly lobbied for the idea. Finally, in 1962, the U.S. Postal Service adopted ZIP codes.[40]

In September 2002, the pharmaceutical giant Eli Lilly paid $325 million to purchase the rights to a new drug for diabetes. A Veterans Administration endocrinologist named John Eng had derived the drug from the venom of the Gila monster a decade earlier. He had tried to convince his bosses that his compound, named exendin-4, had merit, but the agency dismissed it because it was not immediately useful in treating veterans. So Eng spent two years acquiring the patent himself. Then, taking vacation time, he traveled from drug company to drug company to sell it. His persistence paid off. A small biotech start-up, Amylin Pharmaceuticals, bought the rights to what is likely to be a billion-dollar drug and later convinced Lilly to partner in the project.[41]

IBM's Bernie Meyerson also understood the importance of tenacity and persistence. For years he pitched the idea of combining silicon and germanium on a single chip, sure that it would create a much faster processor. His campaign met with rejection, cynicism, and anger. Worse, even after he had proved that the technology worked, IBM discontinued his program. His team's head count dropped from 100 to 3. Undeterred, he sought funding from customers.[42] In the end, IBM adopted his idea and has found extraordinary success with it. Ten percent of IBM's chip revenue came from Meyerson's hybrid chip by 2001. Meyerson told *Red Herring* magazine, "When someone gives you the answer 'No,' you take it as a suggestion or a test of your belief in your idea."[43]

An added benefit of tenacity is that all the extra work required to get an idea adopted by decision makers may actually improve the idea. At Google, researchers found that ideas developed without much support from leadership actually had more impact than those backed by management from the beginning.[44]

Tenacity doesn't mean constantly banging your head against a brick wall, although many successful advocates will tell you that it helps to have at least a bit of masochism if you hope to emerge victorious. In describing the late Richard Holbrooke, the indefatigable U.S. diplomat who brokered the peace deal in the former Yugoslavia in 1995, former secretary of state Henry Kissinger once said, "If Richard calls you and asks you for something, just say yes. If you say no, you'll eventually get to yes, but the journey will be very painful."[45]

Persistence matters if you want to have your ideas adopted. But be careful. Advocates can overdo passion, becoming so intense, so dramatic, that their credibility suffers. Decision makers must sense that you care about your notions, that you will be tenacious in seeking support for them, but they don't want to work with people who scream, yell, or cry.

There is a fine line between being assertive and being aggressive. You don't want to end up like Salomon de Caus, the Frenchman who may have been one of the first people ever to imagine the steam engine. As the perhaps apocryphal story goes, he was so persistent that Cardinal Richelieu had de Caus placed in an asylum for the mad. Seasoned proponents care, but they also know when to stop pushing their ideas; they can identify a brick wall when they have banged their heads against it a few times.

Failure to achieve adoption of an idea may have nothing to do with the quality of the idea. Maybe, instead, it is not the right time to pursue the idea, or the right audience to pitch it to, or the right setting to pitch it in. As the top-level negotiator Dennis Ross says, "Never become desperate for an agreement. A good opponent will see that you want the deal more than they do. They'll then resist taking steps necessary for a deal. Those most able to succeed are those most willing to walk away from the table. . . . So act cool."[46]

5

Form Alliances

The bird a nest, the spider a web, man friendship.

WILLIAM BLAKE

At Data General, a mini-computer company, a successful team "not only had to invent their new computer but also had to struggle for the resources to build it. Resources meant, among other things, the active cooperation [of other units in the organization]. You had to persuade such groups that your idea had merit and would get out the door, or else you wouldn't get much help — and then your machine almost certainly wouldn't get out the door."[1] What was true at Data General is true everywhere: enterprising advocates find allies. They seek support from anyone who might aid their advocacy efforts — from influential senior leaders, from colleagues, from people who are uncommitted, from opinion leaders, and from unlikely allies — even from customers, suppliers, and the media.

Build Coalitions with Influential People

An acquaintance of the wealthy Baron de Rothschild once asked for a loan. The baron replied, "I won't give you the loan myself; but I will walk arm-in-arm with you across the floor of the Stock Exchange, and you shall have willing lenders to spare."[2] The baron understood that advocates must win the support of at least one well-respected person early on. New ideas find champions or else they die. Reflecting this truth are the results of a poll in which project managers were quizzed about the crucial factors involved in promoting buy-in for projects. More than two-thirds said that one factor was having executives champion their ideas.[3] Champions and sponsors are senior people in the organization who believe in the idea and informally rally support for it. They give the project legitimacy, offer access to critical resources, navigate the hierarchies of the organization, help cut unnecessary corners, and willingly take risks in support of the idea.[4]

Early in the development of PARC, Xerox's famous R&D organization, Xerox's board of directors considered closing the center. Fortunately, PARC had a sponsor in John Bardeen, a Nobel Prize winner who served on Xerox's board. Bardeen told his colleagues that the center was the "most promising thing you've got. Keep it." His sponsorship saved PARC from the budget cutters' knives.[5] Similarly, when Honda's Michimasa Fujino came up with the idea of creating a revolutionary small jet plane with engines placed above the wings, most people at Honda thought the notion was silly. One executive said that Fujino was the "stupidest engineer I've ever met in my life." Luckily for Fujino, Honda's president, Nobuhiko Kawamoto, thought the idea interesting and offered support.[6] Soon wealthy travelers will be able to buy Fujino's "Civic of the sky." Without Kawamoto's sponsorship, the idea would have died a quiet death. Who do advocates seek as sponsors? Individuals who believe in them and their ideas, who are influential, who have the time and the political savvy to help them, and who are respected by their peers and by senior leaders. Ideally, the committed champion will show support for the idea and its progenitor in symbolic, behavioral, and public ways.

Senior sponsors often show *symbolic* commitment to ideas by publicly supporting their proponents. Andrew Marshall was a major defense theorist in the Pentagon for more than forty years. From the mid-1980s on, he pitched a transformation of the military. Instead of preparing for another Second World War, he argued, the military ought to plan to engage in much more technologically based warfare. Under the Clinton administration, Marshall didn't get much traction for his ideas. Military leaders ignored him. But when George W. Bush became president, Marshall became an important voice for change. One reason why his credibility skyrocketed was that Donald Rumsfeld, the new secretary of defense, dined with Marshall in the SecDef Mess. All sorts of top Defense Department leaders saw the two huddled together. The symbolic message was clear. Marshall now had a major ally. His ideas mattered.[7]

Sometimes sponsors show their commitment *behaviorally* by adopting the advocate's idea. IBM executive Linda Sanford was charged with creating the internal version of electronic business-on-demand for the company. She understood that to get buy-in from the IBM rank and file, she had to convince them that IBM executives believed in the initiative. In a meeting about how IBM was planning to turn its intranet into a knowledge reservoir filled with "expertise locators" and other useful resources and resource finders, Sam Palmisano, IBM's CEO, expressed concern about the magnitude of the task. In response, Sanford asked Palmisano and his leadership team to lead by example. Their assignment was to list their areas of expertise on the company's intranet.[8] The company leaders did just that, and when people saw that Palmisano was publicly allied with Sanford's project, the project gained widespread support within IBM. Sanford had won employees over to the idea by asking their boss to behaviorally commit to her proposal.

Talented advocates sometimes enlist support by persuading sponsors to make *public declarations* of their commitment. They might ask leaders to sit at the head table when they pitch their idea. Or they may ask their bosses to present the proposals themselves. Hyman Rickover created what today is known as the nuclear navy. Until his successful advocacy for nuclear-powered submarines, U.S. Navy vessels were powered by conventional means — gasoline, oil, and coal for the most part. Rickover knew a nuclear navy would let the fleet stay out at sea much longer without refueling. Although his boss, Admiral Earle Mills, wasn't enamored of Rickover's vision of nuclear-powered vessels, over time Rickover convinced Mills that his notion had potential. Rickover sealed the deal when he persuaded Mills to make the case for nuclear submarines to the Atomic Energy Commission. In doing this, not only did Mills offer a public commitment to the submarine initiative, but members of the commission saw that a senior navy leader — and implicitly the navy — supported Rickover's idea.[9]

Advocates can gain senior people's support in other ways, too. Sundar Pichai, a Google manager working on social networking ideas, was scheduled to pitch an idea to CEO Eric Schmidt. The day before the meeting, Pichai met with his boss, Marissa Mayer, and told her, "It's important you pregame Eric or it will be a disaster." "I know, I know," Mayer responded. "I will call him or write an email." She did, and the next day, Schmidt, after meeting with Pichai, approved the idea.[10] Mayer's intervention mattered.

When top management at Toshiba initially rejected Tetsuya Mizoguchi's idea for the laptop computer, Mizoguchi, undeterred, went underground. He secretly moved budget money around and quietly transferred a few engineers, creating a lab in an Ome factory where a prototype was developed. But it wasn't until the head of Toshiba marketing for Europe, Atsutoshi Nishida, saw the prototype and said he wanted to sell the equipment in Europe that Mizoguchi succeeded.[11] Nishida was Mizoguchi's unexpected ally, and his request was critical in having Mizoguchi's idea adopted.

In some cases, layers of bureaucracy keep advocates from meeting with key leaders. So they find sponsors — people with access to those leaders — to pitch their ideas for them. As a U.S. Air Force officer, Bradford Parkinson developed the design for a navigational system using satellite signals. The air force rejected his idea three times, even after he had shown its effectiveness. Luckily, Ivan Getting, president of Aerospace Corporation, a major R&D organization, saw the merit of Parkinson's idea. "He was a powerful advocate," says Parkinson. "He could get to the higher levels at the Department of Defense, or he could haul me in and let me talk." Thanks to Getting's involvement, the air force finally bought Parkinson's notion and we have GPS — Global Positioning System — devices in our cars today.[12]

Advocates sometimes work around their opposition to gain allies at the top. William Sims was a young U.S. naval officer at the start of the twentieth century. A major problem for the fleet in those days was accurately sighting and firing rounds while the ship was being tossed about on the sea. In fleet exercises in 1898, the navy had five ships fire at a hulk for five minutes. Only two of the many shots fired actually found their target — a terrible embarrassment for the fleet. Sims had discovered during time spent with the British navy that British gunners had solved the problem. Sims recommended their solution to the navy's ordinance and target-practice leadership, only to have them dismiss it. But Sims, a relentless advocate, wrote another report and then another. Finally, after much pressure from Sims and other line officers, the leadership agreed to test the notion. When the tests were completed, the leadership again pronounced his solution unworkable. Sims was astonished but found, upon investigation, that the testing procedures were faulty. Rather than firing guns from a moving ship, the navy had used a stationary gun and the wrong calculations. In exasperation, Sims made a final, risky move. Years before, he had met Theodore Roosevelt, who was now president. He wrote directly to him, summarizing his observations and decrying the poor response from the leadership of the ordnance and target-practice group in the navy. Intrigued, Roosevelt, who liked Sims, encouraged the navy to redo the tests with Sims in charge of the ordinance team. This time the tests were successful, the navy adopted Sims's recommendations and target accuracy zoomed. Sims's advocacy for his idea did not ruin his career. He ended up a senior admiral in charge of the naval forces in Europe during the First World War.[13]

Advocates must be cautious about going around their bosses. Early in his career, Pixar CEO John Lasseter lost his job at Disney because he had sidestepped his immediate bosses when trying to get the okay for an animated film. They retaliated by undermining his idea with a top boss even before he pitched it. Soon thereafter, his immediate boss said, "Well, since it's not going to be made, your project at Disney is now complete. Your position is terminated, and your employment with Disney is now ended."[14] Lasseter won in the end. He went on to head Pixar, and in 2006, Disney bought the company and made Lasseter the head of all animation.

Find Support from Peers and Gatekeepers

If advocates can't persuade units within their organization to support an idea, it will go nowhere, no matter how wonderful an idea it is. Successful advocates continually promote their notions to colleagues in their own department, to people in different departments, to anyone in the company who could offer any sort of support. If executives ask how relevant units that might be affected feel about the proposal, advocates should be able to say that people in those units are behind the idea.

Advocates search out gatekeepers, too — people who control access to decision makers. When Art Fry wanted 3M to adopt his idea of Post-it Notes, he distributed prototypes to secretaries of top executives. They loved the notes and promoted them to their bosses, which was crucial to the idea's success. Gatekeepers may be personal assistants, speechwriters, or secretaries. Because they spend far more time with the decision makers than most other people on the company, they generally enjoy the decision makers' trust. Not only can gatekeepers arrange for advocates to meet with decision makers, but they themselves can raise the advocates' ideas with the decision makers. And since they know the decision makers' moods and the pressures facing them, gatekeepers can also offer advice about when and how to pitch them the ideas.

Seek Out the Uncommitted

For advocates to spend lots of time courting people who strongly oppose their ideas is as pointless as banging one's head against that brick wall. Proponents would do better to assemble coalitions of those who support, or at least share the goals of, the proposals being pushed. Advocates may want to pay special attention to the uncommitted — people with no strong feelings, pro or con, about an idea. It is easier to motivate apathetic people than to convince skeptics. Here is an important caution: Just because people *appear* uncommitted doesn't mean they are. Some seemingly apathetic people are intensely neutral — strongly committed to not making a decision. Some of these "neutrals" refuse to decide. Others are risk averse. Whatever the reason, people who are adamantly neutral are as difficult to build alliances with as passionate naysayers are. So experienced advocates ally themselves with supporters and the truly apathetic while avoiding arch-skeptics and ardently neutral people.

Discover Opinion Leaders

One the first people approached by Thomas Edison to try electric lighting in his home was J. P. Morgan, one of the richest tycoons of nineteenth-century America. Why? Edison understood that other business leaders respected Morgan. If Morgan adopted his idea, others would follow, perhaps even as investors. Morgan was an opinion leader — an individual to whom others turn for advice. Voters often turn to opinion leaders at election time, for example — to people who regularly keep up with the news and engage in political discussions. There are opinion leaders on virtually any subject. Sometimes they are respected as generally knowledgeable or successful, and sometimes they are real experts in a particular field. If you are considering buying a new computer, you might ask the fellow who installs computers in your company which one to buy. If you are contemplating investments, you might query a colleague with a reputation for picking bullish stocks. These people are your opinion leaders.

Wise advocates sell their ideas to opinion leaders who, in turn, will promote those ideas to others. How do you discover opinion leaders in an organization? Although there are different opinion leaders for different issues, most opinion leaders share similar profiles.

First, they are viewed as *experts* about the issue for which they are opinion leaders. Ask colleagues to name the team member who is most knowledge-able about computers, and most will identify the same person. That individ-ual is probably the team's opinion leader on technology. When advocacy groups wanted to reduce swordfish fishing around the world, they created a campaign targeting leading chefs. They felt that these chefs were opinion leaders when it came to food. If chefs publicly opposed catching swordfish, restaurant patrons would listen.

Second, opinion leaders are perceived to be *similar* in most respects to the people who turn to them for advice. If two people have equal competency on some topic, we tend to choose the one who is more like us in other ways. Inexperienced advocates sometimes mistakenly think that compe-tency alone makes an opinion leader. It doesn't. Instead, opinion leaders are viewed as both more competent than others on an issue and similar in attitudes, values, and beliefs to those who ask for advice.

Third, opinion leaders are typically the *first to adopt* new ideas and prod-ucts in their areas of expertise. They are thoughtful trendsetters. They keep up with innovations by browsing magazines, attending conferences, and scanning the Web for promising notions. They willingly prescreen, perhaps by signing on for pilot projects, and enjoy discovering flaws and fixing them. If they like your idea, they will jump aboard early on and help you work out the kinks. Opinion leaders are also often "lead users." Lead users like to tinker with existing products to accomplish new goals. They talk openly about what innovations they want, and help inventors figure out how to create them. They tolerate failures in new products because they know that experimentation entails mistakes and wrong turns. Once con-vinced of the value of an innovation, lead users are often your best internal marketers.

Fourth, opinion leaders often have slightly *higher social status* than others in the organization. They are informal leaders. Pharmaceutical companies often seek out "thought leaders" to promote their medications. They iden-tify respected, well-known physicians in local medical communities and ask them to speak about the merits of a drug. It works. The adoption of tetra-cycline by physicians was enhanced after respected physicians — opinion leaders, if you will — adopted the drug.[15] Walk down the hallway with an opinion leader, and they seem to recognize everyone. Ask opinion leaders for recent gossip, and they can tell you more than you want to know. When they go to lunch, they seldom eat alone. They are the go-to people in the firm. Do you want information about leadership changes, training opportunities, extra funding sources? Opinion leaders are in the know.

Make Friends with the Enemies of Your Enemies

In June 2010, the organization that controls Web addresses created a dot.xxx suffix for sex-related sites. There was strong opposition from a strange alliance of conservative religious groups and well-established pornography Web sites. The religious groups feared that people would look for the dot.xxx sites. The adult-entertainment industry feared increasing regulation and censorship. Two disparate groups with a common interest allied to try to stop a new initiative. The enemy of my enemy can be my friend. In the 1950s the Time-Life magazine empire was pro–air force and anti-navy. When Captain Hyman Rickover pitched his idea of a nuclear submarine, he worked hard to win the endorsement of magazines like *Time*. He succeeded when the editors came to believe that supporting nuclear submarines would doom the aircraft carrier (which challenged the need for an air force).[16] Although Rickover, a navy man, didn't dislike carriers, he understood that his love for submarines and the love of Time-Life for the air force might engender a helpful alliance in the zero-sum game of budgeting in the navy.

Politicians are masters of bifurcation—us against them. After the 9/11 attack, President George W. Bush's goal was to stop terrorism. He had to marshal worldwide support for his cause. A favorite technique was to create two classes of people: good folks and "evil-doers." He told the United Nations in 2003 that people have a choice "between those who seek order and those who spread chaos; between those who work for peaceful change and those who adopt the methods of gangsters; between those who honor the rights of man and those who deliberately take the lives of men, women, and children without mercy or shame." Bush was certainly not the first president to demonize the opposition. Franklin Roosevelt made the same move in the midst of the Great Depression, calling his opponents "economic royalists" and tying them to images of wealthy kings and queens who didn't grasp the perilous state of the working person.[17] Ronald Reagan slyly split the world into two groups: people who believed in democracy and people who supported the "evil empire" of the Soviet Union. What all these presidents knew was that sometimes a simple "us" versus "them" works. Allies on their side of an issue are good; people on the other side are bad.

In organizations the "us vs. them" bifurcation sometimes involves competitors. Adopt this idea because our competitor is doing something that may threaten us. In 1958, John Koss invented the high-fidelity headset in his garage. He believed that there was a great market for his device. But he couldn't persuade major companies to redesign record players to include the now familiar jack that permits us to plug in headphones. Koss knew how competitive the CEOs of the major manufacturers were. So he told the president of one record-player manufacturer that the competition was going to install jacks, and then he told the competitor's CEO the same story. Soon both companies were installing jacks, since neither wanted the other to have an advantage. Other companies joined in, and sales of headsets took off.[18] Koss was partly lucky, of course. If the CEOs had found out about his manipulative move, or if his product had been a giant flop, his credibility in the industry would have been shattered.

Create Surprising Alliances with People Outside the Organization

Being a prophet in one's own land has its challenges, so advocates sometimes build alliances with unexpected allies — consultants, customers, the media, anyone outside the firm who can influence decision makers. It isn't unusual for advocates to pitch their notions to company consultants, especially when executives might value what an expensive consultancy recommends over what employees might recommend.

They can also enlist customers' support. In 2010, a number of PC companies started incorporating WiDi (wireless display) — a technology created by Intel engineer Gary Martz — into their laptops. The technology lets users beam videos they are watching on a small computer to a giant television. Intel executives tried to kill Martz's notion. Other engineers "literally laughed me out of the room," says Martz. So Martz tried an end run. He pitched his idea to PC makers in Asia and to retailers such as Best Buy. The positive feedback from these companies led Intel to change its mind and fund Martz's project.[19]

Some advocates use the media to make their case, hoping that decision makers will react positively when they see the public attention that an idea receives. Charles Momsen invented a breathing apparatus — the Momsen lung — that allowed sailors stuck in submarines to escape. When he took the apparatus to the navy, senior officers dismissed it. But they were forced to seriously consider testing and adopting the device after he demonstrated it in front of members of the press.[20] When the founder of the Salvation Army, William Booth, set his mind to eliminating phossy jaw — industrial poisoning caused by white phosphorus — he visited the homes of sufferers, accompanied by members of the media. After he dimmed the lights, the jaws of people who suffered from the disease started to glow. The ensuing publicity led to the introduction, in the 1890s, of a much safer red phosphorous substance, especially in matches, and in less than twenty years, phossy jaw virtually disappeared as a malady.[21]

Advocates may occasionally create alliances with people who are not obvious partners. For instance, so many Sony executives dismissed the idea of the PlayStation that finally its creator, Ken Kutaragi, was moved out of Sony's corporate offices at Gotanda into a small suburban office in Aoyama, where Sony Music executives had their offices. At Gotanda, his views had been crushed. When he moved to Aoyama, he and his team prospered because people on the music side of the business listened to the idea and later sponsored it. In fact, the PlayStation was developed not within Sony but within Sony Music Entertainment.[22]

Advocates may even seek the buy-in of people who might be expected to oppose their ideas. A converted naysayer is a compelling advocate. Thomas Edison sought and received significant financial support for his electric light from William Vanderbilt, who also owned an enormous amount of stock in natural-gas companies, even though Edison was seeking to replace gaslight with electric light. Vanderbilt invested in Edison's idea as a hedge, but people saw his investment as a public commitment — a commitment amplified when he kept his investment in Edison's invention even after the first electric lights installed in Vanderbilt's mansion almost destroyed it by fire.

Sometimes, too, advocates find a sponsor who is simply someone with political clout. When the children's television show *Sesame Street* was proposed, its creators wisely won Harold Howe, then the U.S. commissioner of education, to their side. Howe greased the bureaucratic wheels to fund the project, and equally important, as head of the federal government's national education agency, he offered the advocates a way around state departments of education. If the planners had had to seek the approval of every state education department, *Sesame Street* would never have become what it is today.[23]

Understand People's Basic Needs

A brief story: In fourth grade I had a teacher named Mrs. Larainne. She was great at teaching everything except fractions. Why except fractions? Well, she taught fractions by asking us to imagine a pie. "Divide a pie into six pieces," she would say, "and then take one out. What do you have left?" Often she offered rich descriptions: "Imagine you have a hot steaming apple pie with apples bursting through the crust," or "You have an ice-cold lemon meringue pie, the meringue stacked tall." The problem was that she taught arithmetic immediately before lunch. Even worse, the school kitchen was located next door. Here I sat smelling fresh baked food and hearing rich descriptions of food! To this day, I have trouble with fractions, but I am here for you when it comes to pie. In school, my need for food overwhelmed my need for arithmetic. The moral? People have basic needs, and when those needs aren't met, they may interpret everything they hear in terms of those unmet needs. Like it or not, advocates must ensure that decision makers' needs are met before expecting their help. How do advocates build positive relationships by addressing people's needs? There are an infinite number of ways, but most techniques can be organized in terms of people's four basic psychological needs:

- inclusion
- control
- efficacy
- affection

Inclusion Matters

If you have ever been excluded from a meeting that you felt you should have been invited to, you understand the importance of inclusion.[24] Leaving people out means that for days, if not weeks, everything you say to them may be interpreted in terms of being excluded.

Why should I support you if you didn't include me in formulating the idea? Scientists and engineers, eager to solve technical issues, often mistakenly exclude marketing, sales, and other meet-the-customer units. The results are sterile products that falter in the marketplace. Even among technologists there are often inclusion challenges. Howard Stringer, CEO of Sony, confessed to the *Wall Street Journal* that one reason some Sony products fail in the marketplace, despite being technologically sophisticated, is that software engineers who create the applications for the products (e.g., operating systems, games) aren't brought into the hardware development process soon enough.[25] Why do would-be advocates exclude people as they create new ideas? Part of it is ego. John Seely Brown, looking back at his career at Xerox, says, "When I started out running PARC, I thought 99% of the work was creating the innovation, and throwing it over the transom for dumb marketers to figure out how to market it. And now I realize that there is at least as much creativity in finding ways to take the idea to market as in coming up with the idea in the first place. I would have spent my time differently had I figured this out early on."[26]

Smart product champions know that they are more likely to get their ideas adopted and to market when key players along the whole development, production, and sales process are included from the start.[27] At a minimum, product designers need people who think in terms of business results. One innovation team in a food company devised a new product. People in marketing gave them a bit of wisdom that helped immensely when the product hit the market: put a window on the packaging so that consumers could see what was inside. The scientists who devised the product had been more interested in such technical issues as taste, portion, and shelf stability. Consultation works both ways: salespeople make big mistakes pitching ideas to customers without including those at their company responsible for creating, packaging, and distributing promised products or services.

Many companies have formalized the inclusion process used in product development. At the General Electric global research center, there are program managers who know the different businesses that the center serves. In addition, a few times each year marketers from a business and scientists from the center meet for what is called a Session T (T stands for technology). They exchange ideas and discover ways to create innovations that will generate new products that customers need.[28] GE's approach has value. When people responsible for different organizational functions communicate frequently on new products, the time and costs of new-product development declines, the quality of new products improves, and the products perform better in the marketplace.[29] One reason that William Campbell and his colleagues were so successful in pitching the idea of creating a drug within Merck that could cure river blindness was that the animal health business had long worked closely with Merck's research groups that were studying human parasitic diseases. That relationship, in Campbell's words, "primed the discovery" of the human use of Mectizan.[30]

Sometimes inclusion is a *political* necessity — people must be included even though they have little or nothing substantive to contribute. When, in 1941, General Brehon Somervell wanted to construct the Pentagon directly below Arlington Cemetery, he made a crucial mistake when he excluded some politically vital people from his planning. In the week that it took him to propose the idea and gain congressional approval, Somervell never talked with Gilmore Clarke, head of the U.S. Commission of Fine Arts, because the commission was purely advisory. Even worse, Somervell ignored the National Capital Park and Planning Commission. Big mistake! The head of the commission was Frederic Delano, President Roosevelt's dear uncle. Clarke and Delano both disapproved of the location for the Pentagon. They complained loudly to the president and to leading members of Congress about aesthetics as well as potential traffic problems. A few days later, Roosevelt forced Somervell to relocate the proposed building to where it now stands — at that time a swampy storage site named Hell's Bottom.[31] We will never know what would have happened if Somervell had included Clarke and Delano from the start. Although neither had legal standing, both were politically important.

Often the move to include people is mostly *symbolic*. Craig Venter is the scientist more responsible than anyone else for discovering ways to rapidly decode human DNA. When he wanted to buy more DNA sequencers (machines that slice DNA into pieces suitable for analysis) for his lab at the National Institutes of Health, he approached his boss, Ernst Freese, with his request. Freese, a perceptive bureaucratic politician, knew that other scientists at the institute would be jealous were Venter to be allocated so much money. So Freese insisted that Venter rename his lab the National Institute of Neurological Disorders and Strokes DNA Sequencing Facility. The equipment that Venter was buying with his new funds could be used, hypothetically, by any of his colleagues within the institute. Of course, almost no one at the institute was doing sequencing work. So Venter got what he wanted, and by symbolically including other scientists, Freese took a step toward alleviating any potential jealousy within the institute.[32]

Some adroit advocates go beyond political or symbolic inclusion to be as comprehensive as possible, including customers, especially lead users, in the design of ideas in the hope that their ideas will better fit real needs.[33]

Xerox developed what it calls "dreaming with the customer": technologists brainstorm with customers who know the problems they have encountered with photocopiers. The product creators spend time with the customers, who visit the company's research centers, and sometimes, like anthropologists, take a week or two to stay with customers to see the problems they experience. The goal is to make sure Xerox creates products that will sell. In the past, Xerox scientists created major marketing challenges when they proceeded on the assumption that they knew what customers wanted and it turned out they didn't.[34]

Too much inclusion, though, can create problems. While too little communication among team members about an idea is bad, too much can be just as bad — creative thoughts are muzzled or constrained by too much input.[35] We have all heard the joke about the elephant: it must have been created by a committee. Similarly, having major customers involved in new-product design may actually reduce product quality, especially when a new product is radically different.[36] Customers, being creatures of habit, seldom want radical changes in what they buy. They know how to use what they already have. Also, marketers and salespeople generally prefer incremental changes in products and services, since their world revolves around what has already made them successful. Why risk that with something radically different?

The fear of disruptive change may be one reason why Xerox took so long to enter the small-copier business. Xerox's major customers were big print shops that preferred continual improvements in their sophisticated large copiers. What would motivate these firms or Xerox's own sales and marketing people — who depended upon the large copiers for their salaries — to support a move to smaller, slower machines with lower sales commissions? Salespeople also rebelled when 3Com founder Robert Metcalfe began creating radically new technologies for his company, and some even quit in disgust when he dismissed their argument that customers wanted only slight improvements in existing products. In the end, the new products were best sellers. The salespeople and many established customers focused on what they needed right now, whereas Metcalfe had his eye on future customers.[37]

Xerox and 3Com aren't alone. When researchers at Monsanto devised innovative ways to create light-emitting diodes (LEDs) in colors other than red, Monsanto's marketing team claimed that customers wanted only the red version. In those days, the LEDs used today in digital displays, traffic lights, and giant outdoor television screens were mostly used in calculators, and red was the standard color. The marketing folks were partly right. Existing customers were quite happy with red. The problem was that the marketers couldn't see potentially new business opportunities beyond their current customers.

Whoever the source, effective advocates don't ignore input. Instead, they assess when in the development cycle inclusion is optimal. If an idea represents an incremental change, they may include everyone in the value chain early on; but if the notion is radical or potentially disruptive, they may be careful about including, at the start, people who might reject it out of hand because it threatens their interests. The innovation lab responsible for Motorola's enormously successful Razr cell phone didn't involve customers or regional managers during the design process. This violated a Motorola tradition, whereby new projects typically received early approval from regional managers. Gary Weiss, senior director of mechanical engineering for the product, said: "We did not want to be distracted by the normal inputs we get. It would not have allowed us to be as innovative."[38] Roger Jellicoe, who led the team, explained, "Anytime you've got something radically different, there will be people who feel that we should be putting our resources on other stuff."[39]

Don't forget the home team. Advocates know it is crucial to make sure they have the continued support of their home team — the team of people who do all the basic work on the idea. Not including these people as the idea progresses through the organization may make them feel ignored and create a sense, accurate or not, of internal discord. If decision makers ask you, "How do your people feel about this idea?" and you cannot answer positively, you will have trouble winning support. In particular, successful advocates enlist support among the people most affected by their ideas. For example, before a senior bank executive pitched an idea to the board of directors that radically changed bank operations, she assured herself that the branch managers — the people most affected — endorsed it. When decision makers sense a lack of consensus among the people who should be supportive of an idea, they often hold back their support.

Include people who have been excluded. Suppose members of a group invite you to join them, but you feel as though the group has ignored you up to now. If you join, will you make a stronger or a weaker contribution than if you had not been ignored in the first place? People who feel they have been initially excluded from a team actually tend to work harder than they would have had they been included from the start.[40] What is the message for advocates? Find people who feel they have been excluded from previous initiatives and include them in your project. They will work especially hard for you. In fact, effective advocates sometimes use people's need for inclusion as a way of winning support. Since even the threat of exclusion can lead people to go along with decisions they might normally argue against, advocates hint, "If you don't go along, you won't be on the team!"[41]

Let people think the idea is theirs. Give them some credit even when they may not deserve it. Inclusion brings psychic rewards. Abraham Lincoln understood this. He used plural personal pronouns eighteen times in ten sentences in the Gettysburg Address. Barack Obama, in his 2009 inaugural address, used nearly 150 plural personal pronouns in a speech lasting only eighteen minutes. Both Lincoln and Obama knew that if people feel included, the ideas expressed are no longer just the president's ideas but also people's own ideas.

How do advocates generate the sense of "we"? Sometimes they work behind the proverbial curtain, understanding that they may not take a bow when their ideas are adopted. Most people have forgotten that besides being a founder of the famed Marshall Plan, which resurrected Europe after the Second World War, George Marshall also served as chief of staff of the U.S. Army during the war. In that capacity, he hired Generals Douglas MacArthur and Dwight Eisenhower, who went on to lead the Allies during the war. Marshall used to say that it's amazing how much you get done when you let others take credit for it.

Advocates sometimes surrender some of the credit by adding others' names to their proposals. In the 1930s, Franklin Roosevelt created what we know today as the Social Security system. To pass the Social Security Act, he depended upon Congressman David Lewis and Senator Robert Wagner. Lewis had spent his entire career arguing for social security, and Wagner had pushed the idea for years. However, Roosevelt decided that the act should be named after Senator Pat Harrison and Congressman Robert "Farmer Bob" Doughton. Although these two individuals were not responsible for the hard work behind the bill, they did chair the Senate's Finance Committee and the House of Representative's Ways and Means Committee, respectively. And the support of these two committees was crucial if the act were to be passed. Naming the legislation the Harrison-Doughton Act ensured the bill would have their vital support.[42] Some advocates go further. The U.S. Navy traditionally named submarines after fish. That was until Admiral Hyman Rickover decided to gin up support in Congress for the submarine service by naming submarines after highly respected members of that body. There was the *L. Mendel Rivers* (named after the chair of the House Armed Services Committee), the *William Bates* (named after the representative who served on the Joint Committee on Atomic Energy), the *Richard Russell* (named after the chair of the Senate Armed Services Committee). You can't be negative about a product or project named after you or your friends.

Sometimes crafty advocates create public pressure to generate a sense of "we." Take, for example, the typical State of the Union speech. The president stands and addresses the nation in the chamber of the House of Representatives filled with members of Congress, the Senate, the Supreme Court, the cabinet, and a rich assortment of other national leaders. Over the president's right shoulder, the audience sees the vice president. Over the president's left shoulder sits the Speaker of the House of Representatives. Every State of the Union address is punctuated with loud applause from the president's party and mild, measured applause from the opposition. In 1997, President Bill Clinton proposed in his address that the budget surplus resulting from his administration's elimination of the federal deficit be dedicated to saving Social Security. Journalist Joe Klein describes what happened as the president made the proposal: "The Democrats were out of their seats with a roar. Newt Gingrich, who sat behind the President in the Speaker's chair, was applauding, too, but reluctantly, and he was still seated. Slowly, Gingrich seemed to understand . . . that the nation would see Democrats vigorously supporting the most popular Federal program, Social Security, while the Republicans were still seated, glumly — and he hauled himself to his feet and joined in a standing ovation for the President."[43]

People Want a Sense of Control

People want control over their lives. When it comes to advocacy, if decision makers feel they have little say over what's being pitched, they may interpret the proposal as having to do with control and power. Since decision makers almost always find a way to show they have power — not necessarily a way that will help advocates get their ideas adopted — successful idea proponents make sure decision makers retain a sense of control.

Let others contribute. As Sinclair Stockman, formally chief scientist at BT Global, once told the *Financial Times*, if you want to persuade people to buy your idea, "you need to get them to think it's their idea. Then it's easy."[44] Sometimes, rather than proposing ideas themselves, advocates plant ideas in a boss's mind. They may do this by raising a problem without directly offering a solution (see chapter 4), by hinting at what other firms are doing, by listing numerous options in a proposal. Then they will help the idea blossom by bringing up small things that encourage the boss to think more about it. Sometimes advocates bolster the commitment of others by letting them construct a personal case for an idea. John Paul Stevens, senior associate justice of the U.S. Supreme Court for many years, often decided who would write the Court's opinion about a case. Sometimes he wrote opinions himself, but when he sensed that one of his colleagues was wavering, he sometimes asked that justice to write it. "In all candor," Stevens said, "if you think somebody might not be solidly behind the decision, it might be wiser to let that person write the opinion." Why? Because when people create arguments in favor of an idea, they tend to solidify their support.[45] If you give people who sort of support your proposal some control over part of the decision, they will feel more committed to it.

Know the difference between "must," "should," and "wouldn't it be nice." It would be convenient if imaginative ideas were adopted without compromise. But that seldom happens. Successful advocates know that they will often have to give way on some, if not many, aspects of their proposals. What they give way on should be based on their understanding of the musts, shoulds, and wouldn't-it-be-nice aspects of their ideas. Some aspects of any idea are *must* issues. They are critical. Without them, the idea won't succeed. *Should* issues, though important, aren't crucial. *Wouldn't-it-be-nice* issues add value but aren't vital. For cars, must items include wheels, an engine, and brakes. Should items include radios and side airbags. Wouldn't-it-be-nice items might be heated leather seats and fancy CD stereo systems. Smart advocates insist on the musts. But they will grudgingly surrender on shoulds and willingly cede on wouldn't-it-be-nice issues. Ronald Reagan once said, "Anytime I can get 70% of what I am asking for out of a hostile legislative body, I'll take it. I figure it will work well enough for me to go back later and get a little more of it here and a little more of it there."[46] The 70 percent were often Reagan's musts.

Offer alternatives. When Anthony Fadell proposed the design of the now-famous iPod to the mercurial CEO of Apple, Steve Jobs, he faced a make-or-break moment. Jobs, he knew, liked to be in charge. If Fadell came across as too pushy, Jobs could reject his notion. So, even though Fadell had an excellent prototype ready to go, he didn't initially pitch that model. Instead, he presented a complicated model, which Jobs immediately dismissed. Then

Fadell demonstrated a second model, a cheap one that wouldn't store songs if the battery died. Jobs hated that one, too. Finally, Fadell pitched his preferred version — one that closely resembled the iPod today. Jobs loved it. And Fadell ended up leading the project.[47] Fadell understood the value of letting decision makers feel that they have choices when presented with ideas.

Decision makers are both more committed and more satisfied with what they themselves choose.[48] Thus, whenever possible, shrewd advocates offer them options. Rather than arguing, "We should do X," advocates might, like Fadell, give decision makers a sense of control by saying, "We could do X, Y, or Z. Which do you prefer?" Not only will the decision makers feel more in control, but they will also typically choose among the options presented. New parents often mistakenly ask children, "What kind of ice cream do you want?" And kids often respond with requests that are impossible ("I want blueberry ice cream with oranges and raisins inside"). Savvier parents ask, "Do you want chocolate or vanilla?" That way, the kids believe that they control the decision because they chose. In reality, parents have the real control.

Augustus, emperor of ancient Rome, understood the value of choices. When Rome's senators rebelled at his idea of a 5 percent death tax, he asked them what they would like instead. They said anything. Augustus said, "Okay, choose either the death tax or a tax on property." The senate, which was composed of wealthy landholders, quickly chose the death tax.[49] Centuries later, in France, Anne Lauvergeon, the CEO of the nuclear-reprocessing company Cogema (now Areva NC), regularly dealt with environmentalists opposed to nuclear power. Often her response was to ask them which they preferred: nuclear power or such major environmental problems as global climate changes brought on by high oil consumption.[50] At another large technology company, this one in the United States, people charged with conducting Six Sigma projects to identify and eliminate process problems were often seen as threatening decision makers' authority. Long arguments ensued. So crafty Six Sigma experts began generating lists of potential projects and asking decision makers to choose which projects they wanted their units to work on. The experts' power lay in their ability to come up with lists that included only projects they thought doable and valuable. Decision makers felt they kept their authority because they got to choose. And the advocates won in another way: they had an opportunity to demonstrate their deep knowledge of the many challenges the company faced.

When people make choices, they are committed to them. In an intriguing study, office workers on Long Island were offered the chance to purchase lottery tickets costing a dollar. After agreeing to buy a ticket, they were either handed a ticket or asked to pick one from a box. On the morning of the lottery drawing, buyers were told that although the supply of tickets was exhausted, an individual still wanted to buy a ticket. Would a purchaser be willing to sell his or her ticket and, if so, for how much? If the person had been handed a ticket, the average amount he or she wanted for it was about two dollars; but if the ticket holder had pulled the ticket from the box (in other words, had seemingly made a choice), he or she wanted, on average, almost nine dollars. Moral: Choice, even just the perception of choice, makes the thing chosen seem more valuable.[51]

Offering alternatives is a powerful way for advocates to encourage people to adopt their ideas. To use this technique successfully, advocates should heed two basic rules.

1. Offer meaningfully different and substantively relevant choices.
2. Don't offer too many choices.

The first rule is self-evident. Don't offer people silly or meaningless choices — for instance, "You have two choices: coffee with cream and sugar or coffee with sugar and cream." That is no choice at all, as decision makers will realize.

The second rule makes sense if you imagine strolling into a fancy grocery store that sells tasty jams. One day a table is laden with twenty-four jams to sample; another day, only six are available for tasting. On which day is more jam sold? Psychologists Sheena Iyengar and Mark Lepper conducted just such a study and discovered that the store sold more jam in the latter case. Fewer choices led consumers to buy more. In another study, they found that students were more likely to write extra-credit papers when they had six topics to choose from than when given thirty topics. In fact, not only were they more likely to write essays when choices were limited, but the papers they did write were of better quality.[52] By reducing the number of varieties of Head & Shoulders shampoo, Procter & Gamble ended up increasing sales of the shampoo. An array of too many varieties confuses customers. Not only do they find it difficult to distinguish among alternatives, but the possibility that they will later regret the purchase also increases ("I wonder if choosing X would have been better"). People faced with many choices often become risk averse and just opt for the status quo.[53] What is the message? Give decision makers a few viable choices and let them decide among them.

One concern that people raise about presenting alternatives to decision makers is, "What will decision makers think if I don't make a straightforward recommendation?" In other words, shouldn't you be confident enough about your ideas to tell people what they should do? In many cases, advocates do exactly that: boldly propose a solution. How an advocate proceeds should depend at least in part on the decision maker's preference. If you know decision makers prefer a straightforward recommendation, make it.

People Want to Matter: Show the Impact of the Idea

The philosopher John Dewey once observed that "the deepest urge in human nature is the desire to be important." He is right. Everyone wants to feel important. In fact, we want to be more than important. We want to feel that we are doing something vital, that we are making critical contributions to our organization, our community, our industry. When people feel that their need to matter is not being met, they grow cynical and unhappy.

Advocates know the importance of focusing on this need for efficacy. They convince decision makers that the proposed product or action is essential and that by adopting it, the decision makers will have done something consequential. When the Merck parasitologist William Campbell discovered that his powerful drug could eliminate river blindness, he approached Roy Vagelos, then head of Merck research, with the idea that Merck should invest in creating the medicine. Vagelos supported the drug's development despite knowing that the company would never make money with it. One reason he went along with the idea was because rejecting it would demoralize Merck scientists. Refusing to create a drug that could make an enormous difference in many people's lives would eat away at their sense of making a contribution to the world. After all, Merck's corporate mission was to improve human health.[54]

Be proud of what you tout. How advocates talk and act about their ideas shapes how others respond. Successful advocates demonstrate strong personal and public commitment to their ideas. They don't blithely say, "It's not a big deal." They have spent time and energy and staked their own reputation on their ideas and, without being egotistical, need to proudly communicate how important those ideas are to them and to the world. It is difficult to turn down someone who clearly believes that what she or he is proposing matters.

Let others feel indispensable to the success of the idea. When the entertainer and social advocate Bono touted his case for debt relief for some of the poorest countries in the world, he approached Larry Summers, then U.S. secretary of the Treasury, for help. Summers dismissed Bono's appeal, saying that debt relief was not up to the United States alone. Finance ministers in other countries, he said, had to agree to the move. Bono replied, "I've been all over the world. I've met with all the finance ministers. They've all said, if I can get Larry Summers, this can get done. So don't tell me this can't get done, because I know it can."[55] Bono understood that when decision makers feel that they are indispensable to the success of a proposal, that without them an idea will falter, they are more likely to lend support.

Sell the vision. In 1983, Steve Jobs felt that Apple needed to hire someone with big-company management skills. He approached the CEO of Pepsi, John Sculley, who demurred. Why leave a top company for a risky venture like Apple? Jobs, a master of persuasion, sold Sculley when he asked him, "Do you want to spend the rest of your life selling sugared water to children, or do you want a chance to change the world?" All of us want to change the world. (Of course, Sculley didn't work out and Jobs came back and did change the world.)

When Bono was pitching the idea of debt relief, he also visited Gene Sperling, a top White House advisor to President Clinton. Clinton was scheduled to give a speech to the World Bank in a few days. As Sperling tells it, "I had a two-foot-high stack of paper by my side. Bono comes in and says, 'Gene, I know your heart's in the right place. I'm looking at that stack and imagining that everything in this stack is more urgent than debt relief. But I want you to ask yourself, ten years from now, is there anything in this stack you'll feel as good about as getting debt relief for the world's poorest countries?"[56] Bono's pitch worked. He convinced Sperling that debt relief mattered more for the entire world than the other issues that Sperling was grappling with. Sperling persuaded Clinton to make the case: to cancel debts owed to the United States by more than thirty nations. Bono understood that advocates must show decision makers how consequential an idea is.

An old fund-raising story goes like this: One fund-raiser approaches a potential donor and says his non-profit health-care organization needs $50 million to build a building. Another fund-raiser greets the same donor and says he needs $50 million to cure cancer. Which one gets the money?

People Need to Feel Liked

People buy ideas from people they like. In sales, customers are more likely to buy from salespeople who seem to like them.[57] People liked by their bosses are more influential. Bosses also better remember what people they like say in meetings.[58] We have all encountered people who think that they can be annoying and alienating yet still successfully champion ideas. Not true! Ford engineers came up with the concept of the minivan. But the engineers and their leadership couldn't get buy-in from top decision makers. Why? Many believe it was because CEO Henry Ford Jr. simply didn't like Hal Sperlich, the fellow who led the minivan project.[59]

Show involvement. Enterprising servers in restaurants greet customers cheerfully, introduce themselves, write thank-you notes, draw happy faces on checks, smile freely, squat when talking to customers so they are at eye level, repeat their customers' orders word for word, spontaneously offer diners candy after their meals, and casually touch customers when handing them the check.[60] All of these are markers of involvement, and servers who master these techniques are rewarded with big tips.

Successful advocates do similar things. When decision makers talk, advocates listen attentively and nod appreciatively; they show that they contemplate feedback from decision makers; they publicly incorporate decision makers' thoughts into their proposals. Successful advocates are like the F. Scott Fitzgerald character Jay Gatsby, in *The Great Gatsby*, who, when meeting people, "smiled understandingly — much more than understandingly. It was one of those rare smiles with a quality of eternal reassurance in it, that you may come across four or five times in life. It . . . concentrated on you with an irresistible prejudice in your favor. It understood you just so far as you wanted to be understood, believed in you as you would like to believe in yourself, and assured you that it had precisely the impression of you that, at your best, you hoped to convey."

When people are busy, they often forget how important showing interest and understanding is. When Steve Ballmer, CEO of Microsoft, was asked what challenges him as a leader, he said, "My brain races too much, so even if I've listened to everything somebody said, unless you show that you've digested it, people don't think they are being heard. . . . If you really want to get the best out of people, you have to really hear them and they need to feel like they've been really heard."[61] Can you go too far and be ingratiating? Of course. Nevertheless, people love being praised, and when they are praised, they think more highly of the person praising them even when they sense that the flatterer has something to gain from them.[62]

Feigning praise is insufficient. Nelson Mandela faced a problem when jailed in South Africa's Pollsmoor prison. The food, paltry as it was, was never warm. He wanted a hotplate. The officer in charge of Mandela's wing, a Major Van Sittert, did not like him. But the officer did love rugby. So Mandela became a rugby fan. After studying up on the sport, Mandela chatted about rugby with the major every time he ran into him, in the officer's language of Afrikaner. Those conversations changed their relationship. Soon the officer was ordering his guards to bring Mandela a hotplate. The lesson: People want to help you when you are interested in what they are interested in.[63]

Notice and remember little things about people. Many successful advocates make it a point to notice things that matter to people they interact with. When they spy baby pictures on someone's wall, they celebrate the baby's cuteness. When someone has a new haircut, they offer a compliment. Many highly respected advocates hone their ability to remember people's names. It is a small but important skill. Remembering names takes practice, but it has its rewards. Salespeople who remember and use others' names are both better liked and more effective.[64] We like people who pay attention to us, and all else being equal, we will be more likely to support their ideas.

Be positive and optimistic. Successful advocates approach their task with affability and optimism. Not only do they believe their ideas are important, but they also believe they will succeed, and they communicate that optimism to everyone. Optimism is catching. When decision makers feel optimistic, they are more agreeable, less defensive, and more open to new ideas, especially risky ones, than when they are feeling negative about life.[65] How do advocates communicate optimism? They are enthusiastic about their ideas. That enthusiasm translates into confidence and commitment. They highlight the positives when proposing an idea: it has an 80 percent likelihood of success as opposed to a 20 percent chance of failure.

Do favors. Reciprocity is basic to humans: I smile, you smile. I yawn, you yawn. If I do something for you, you will feel a need to reciprocate. When advocates have a history of doing favors and publicly supporting others, they are likely to garner support from the people for whom they did favors and offered public support. Celebrate special events with people, thank them often, make them look good in front of others, share successes with them, support their ideas when they pitch them, ally with them in difficult decisions, and show warm regard for them and the people who matter to them, and you will win an ally when you present an idea of your own.

Highlight similarities. When Ireland sought its independence from Great Britain in the 1920s, Winston Churchill was negotiating for Great Britain. One evening he met with the Irish leader, Michael Collins. In the midst of tense discussions, Collins complained that Great Britain had put a bounty on his head. Churchill stood up, grabbed a framed document from his wall, and said, "Wait a minute. You're not the only one!" It was a piece of paper from the Boer War announcing a reward for Churchill "dead or alive."[66] Collins and Churchill now had something in common, and soon a treaty was signed giving Ireland dominion status. Churchill understood how vital it was to find commonality with an opposing party.

Decision makers are more likely to approve ideas offered by advocates who are perceived to share their values, appreciate what they appreciate, and hold the same goals. In one study, students seeking donations to a charity collected two times the amount of money on campus when they prefaced their request for money with the phrase "I'm a student here, too."[67] Indeed, people are more likely to comply with requests from people who are like them than from people who aren't, even when the similarity is entirely incidental — if they dress the same way or share the same first name or a birthday.[68] That is why advocates, in meetings with decision makers, highlight their similar commitment to the organization ("All of us who've worked here for any number of years know . . ."), their similar attitudes ("Every one of us in this room is committed to excellence . . ."), or their similar backgrounds ("As we engineers know . . ."). Even when advocates have little in common with decision makers in terms of background or experiences, they wisely highlight overarching principles that they may share with decision makers ("We're all here because we want to do what's best for . . . ," or "This issue is important to our future together").[69]

Be sensitive to personal dignity, or face. Face is a critically important concept for advocacy. Face refers to those things we want to be known and respected for. We are emotionally invested in our face-related needs. If people disrespect our face-related concerns, if they assault our sense of self-worth, we have immediate, strongly negative reactions.

Most of us have two basic face-related concerns: autonomy and approval.

The need for autonomy or independence prompts us to do whatever someone tells us that we can't do, just to prove that we can. Tell an unhappy child
that she isn't allowed to smile, that if she smiles she's in big trouble, and she
will often burst into a smile. Our second basic face-related need is to be
liked and respected, approved of, and accepted. If you sense that someone
dislikes you, it bothers you. In addition to these two core face-related issues,
we all have individual face-related concerns. Perhaps we wish to be seen as
smart, important, reliable, or creative.

Advocates walk through minefields of face-related issues whenever they
pitch proposals. Sometimes, without even knowing it, they make a disparaging or disapproving remark that is unforgettable and unforgivable.[70]
People remember such remarks for years. Often, given a chance, they will
try to get even. Ask anyone with experience in an organization whether
grudges are being played out in their firm, and they will nod knowingly.
Stepping on someone's face, so to speak, is a prime way to provoke a grudge.
In one government agency, a senior manager quietly but assertively refused
to help a colleague move forward with a proposal. When asked why, he said,
"Fifteen years ago she embarrassed me in front of my staff when I was
making a presentation. It wasn't necessary. She just wanted to make points.
I've never been able to forget it. She knew it would embarrass me and she
still did it. Why should I help her now?"

How do advocates ensure that they don't dent others' dignity? People
often let advocates know indirectly when the advocates are starting to tread
on face-related issues — by making excuses, showing irritation, or changing
the subject. Advocates who persist in ignoring the warning signs evoke a
negative reaction. Sometimes people who feel disparaged seethe quietly.
Sometimes they lash out in anger, even storm out of a meeting. They might
adamantly resist an idea, even when all the evidence establishes its bril-
liance. When Robert Moses, the master urban planner of New York City,
proposed taking land from a number of rich New Yorkers for city parks, he
needed the New York governor, Alfred Smith, to sign the appropriations
legislation. The landowners wanted Smith to quash Moses' plan. Horace
Havemeyer was one of those who met with the governor. Nicknamed the
Sultan of Sugar because of the source of his wealth, Havemeyer told Smith
that creating parks would lead to his and his friends' property being "over-
run with rabble from the city." As Robert Caro reports: "Smith looked up at
him. The blue eyes were steel. . . . 'Rabble? That's *me* you're talking about.'
Smith had grown up as 'rabble' and still thought of himself as one. Smith

reached out a hand and seized the appropriation form. Trying desperately to turn his remark into a joke, Havemeyer said quickly, 'Why, where's a poor millionaire to go nowadays if he wants to be alone?' 'Try the Harlem River Hospital,' Smith said. The Harlem River Hospital was an insane asylum. As Havemeyer flushed, the Governor signed the form."[71] Havemeyer's appeal was rejected because he had stepped on Smith's face.

To avoid stepping on face, advocates must figure out decision makers' face-related issues. How to do that? One way is to walk into their offices. If an executive's walls are covered with diplomas, education is an issue — so you know not to make jokes that schooling doesn't matter. In many a politician's office you will see an "I love me" wall dotted with grip-and-grin photographs of the politician consorting with famous people. She doubtless prides herself on being well connected, on knowing everyone — which you need to know.

Another way to discover people's face-related issues is to listen to what they complain about in others. If someone constantly complains about how ineptly people interpret data and how stupid they are not to use data, he is telling you that he is careful and data driven. If you ever sense that he has misinterpreted some data, you would be wise to tread lightly.

Don't misunderstand. Some issues must be raised even if they are face-related issues. How do advocates raise issues in face-sensitive ways?

First, respect everyone in the room. A successful executive at a large telecommunications company was once asked the secret to his success. He replied that early in his career he learned to "never discount anybody at the table. Treat them with respect; you never know where they'll be in ten years." A well-respected advocate said that he learned early on that the CEO's executive assistant's sense of self-worth was tied to her belief that she ran her boss's life. So he spent time chatting up the secretary and even asked her advice. Not surprisingly, whenever he needed quick access to the CEO, the door was open.

Second, avoid making an issue personal. When Lyndon Johnson was running for president of the United States in 1964, there were whispers that perhaps Attorney General Robert Kennedy, the late president's brother, might seek the vice presidential nomination. In fact, Kennedy was scheduled to deliver a moving memorial to his assassinated brother at the Democratic Party's Atlantic City convention. Johnson didn't want Bobby Kennedy on his ticket. Nor did he want an emotionally charged convention to nominate him. So, rather than publicly saying no to Kennedy (and stepping on his face), Johnson announced that no member of the cabinet would be considered for the nomination. Johnson's real aim was to ensure that Bobby Kennedy couldn't run, and he accomplished it. Even though Kennedy, and other professional politicians, understood the implication of Johnson's decision, by including everyone in the cabinet Johnson made it appear that there was nothing personal in his decision.[72]

Third, communicate in ways that allow people to save face. This is especially true when dealing with people in face-sensitive cultures like those of China and Japan. There, people may speak indirectly, or couch comments delicately or ambiguously or as though they themselves may be at fault. A Westerner, seeing confusion on the face of a listener in a conversation might say, "Do you understand?" A Chinese person might diplomatically ask, "Am I being clear?"[73]

Even within a culture, perceptive people communicate in face-sensitive ways. Ronald Reagan once visited a school for handicapped children, some of whom asked him questions. At one point, a child with a severe speech impediment asked a question that no one could understand. Reagan asked him to repeat it. The child did, but again, no one in the room could understand him. Reagan, rightly nicknamed the Great Communicator, saved the child's face. He told the child that sometimes his hearing aid failed, making it difficult for him to understand what people were saying, so he was going to ask one of his staff members to walk over to the child and write the child's question down so that he, Reagan, could answer it. That piece of quick thinking saved the child from an embarrassment he would have had to live with for years.[74]

When people are intensely involved in a meeting, they may say things that later they wish they could take back. So advocates are especially careful in meetings. They ask questions rather than make judgments. They raise difficult issues in private rather than in public. When a speaker makes a mistake, wise advocates blame the circumstances and not the person. They never make others feel like losers in negotiations.

Fourth, avoid being negative about the past. There is seldom a need for advocates to trash the past. And there is never a need to attack individuals who made previous decisions. In many cases, an organization's leaders achieved their current positions precisely because of their past decisions. Those decisions created their successes. So when an advocate attacks those decisions, the attack can seem needlessly personal. Even when prior decisions were clearly wrong, personal attacks often backfire. In 1847, when many women died from infections incurred after childbirth, the Austrian physician Ignaz Semmelweis specifically recommended that physicians and nurses wash their hands prior to delivering babies. That now-obvious recommendation was a radical one, and colleagues ignored Semmelweis partly because of how he attacked them. He denounced one, for instance, as a murderer and suggested to another that he return to school to learn basic logic.[75]

Rather than attacking the past, a wise advocate shows how the future requires alternative approaches or different ideas. Niall FitzGerald, the highly respected former cochair of the global giant Unilever and chair of Reuters, said that in introducing change, "I try to make very clear that change is no criticism of the past. It's not that what you did in the past was rubbish. It wasn't. It was absolutely relevant to the past and worked beautifully.... But the future's going to be different and we need to equip ourselves for the future."[76]

There is another side to the idea of face. Adroit champions of ideas also leverage face as a positive force when advocating. They do this by astutely tying their ideas to decision makers' face-related issues. If decision makers pride themselves on being data driven, advocates highlight their ideas as data based; if decision makers think themselves sophisticated users of technology, advocates allude to the place of technology in their pitch. When the Pakistani lawyer Raza Kazim needed to convince the president of Pakistan, Pervez Musharraf, to overturn a ruling forbidding banks from charging interest, he knew that Musharraf wouldn't understand all the technical details, so he opted to appeal to Musharraf's ego as a military leader. "I doubted,' he said, 'that he [Musharraf] would follow the technical argument, so I decided to pitch it to him on his image of himself as the brave Army commander. I said I realize what I am suggesting is a bold strategy that requires nerve. He said he had plenty of nerve." Not surprisingly, Kazim got buy-in for his proposal.[77]

Perhaps he learned about advocacy from Winston Churchill. Churchill faced a challenge in January 1941, when Franklin Roosevelt's most trusted advisor, Harry Hopkins, visited London. Churchill, who needed to get Hopkins on his side, sensed that Hopkins had deep reservations about what the British government wanted from the United States. So on the day that Hopkins arrived in England, Churchill gave a speech in which he effusively praised Roosevelt. He said that the president was a "famous statesman, long versed and experienced in the work of government and administration, in whose heart there burns the fire of resistance to aggression and oppression, and whose sympathies and nature make him the sincere and undoubted champion of justice and of freedom, and of the victims of wrongdoing wherever they may dwell." According to Jon Meacham, who wrote a book about the Churchill-Roosevelt relationship, this speech turned Hopkins around. "Flattery worked . . . there was a kind of thaw. Face is important: People like to think the people they are dealing with respect and like them; that tends to keep the waters smooth and tempers cool."[78]

6

Your Idea Is Only as Good as Its Story

Tell me a fact and I'll learn. Tell me the truth
and I'll believe. But tell me a story and it
will live in my heart forever.

INDIAN PROVERB

In the late 1970s, Sony's cofounder and chairman of its board, Akio Morita, faced a crucial advocacy challenge. Although he believed that his company should create and sell what today we know as the Sony Walkman, his engineers and marketers couldn't imagine why people would want a portable audio cassette player with headphones. "Everybody gave me a hard time . . . nobody liked the idea," he recalled.[1] Indeed, had Sony conducted customer-opinion surveys, most respondents probably wouldn't have seen the value of a portable music player either. So Morita famously made his case by relating a brief story: Two shoe salesmen were assigned to an isolated territory. The first salesperson wrote back to headquarters, "Get me out of here. No one wears shoes here—no market!" The second salesperson wired back, "No one here wears shoes—incredible opportunity. Send as many shoes as possible!" Sometimes you need to discover untapped opportunities and excite people about those opportunities. A simple tale like Morita's can be an extraordinarily persuasive tool.

Stories define us. "We tell ourselves stories in order to live," says author

Joan Didion. We are hardwired to think narratively. Throughout history, people have depended upon storytellers to remember ideas, events, and people. These tale-tellers were repositories of their community's historical legacies. The stories they told and retold defined their cultures.[2]

The value of stories can be seen everywhere. Families are, at their best, collections of narratives. Often far more precious than inherited money or land are those verbal heirlooms that we call family stories. These tales ground families in their histories. They offer both continuity and identity. Parents link past to present by relating stories of ancestors' quirks and virtues. Decades after parents have passed on, their children still sit together relating tales of their childhood. Once a few childhood anecdotes are exchanged, the siblings will have renewed and enriched their connections. What are many holiday get-togethers or family reunions if not extended storytelling sessions? True or not, tales told at those events cement relationships and create family history.

Like cultures and families, organizations are collections of stories. Newcomers to teams often feel awkward when old hands tell stories of their past together. Though officially part of the group, they are, in truth, outsiders, because they aren't part of the tales. At lunch, when a yarn is told and everyone else laughs uproariously, the new person meekly smiles, knowing he doesn't really belong yet. A person becomes a true member of a unit only after sharing its stories. To create cohesion, team leaders often manufacture common narratives — the equivalent of the silly and strange stories that emerge from the familiar college road trip, when a bunch of friends spend days packed like sardines in a car. It is the stories that make the trip memorable and create long-lasting bonds among the travelers.

Stories create and maintain organizations' identities.[3] Dell employees know by heart the tale of Michael Dell selling computers out of the trunk of his car while in college. Microsoft employees are informally taught the story of a college dropout with an idea. HP celebrates the narrative of a company founded in a garage. At 3M, there are stories of how Scotchgard was discovered by mistake (a scientist spilled chemicals on her tennis shoes). Sony has the story of Shizuo Takashino, an executive deputy president at the firm, who was informed by engineers in 1994 that it was impossible to make a video camera any smaller than the one they had already created. Oh, really? Takashino suggested that the engineers put the camera in a bucket of water and see if any air bubbles emerged. If they did, there was still space that could be eliminated.[4]

Why Stories Influence People

Not surprisingly, stories are extraordinarily valuable for advocates.[5] As Abraham Lincoln, an advocate of the first order, noted, "They say I tell a great many stories. I reckon I do; but I have learned from long experience that plain people . . . are more easily influenced through the medium of a broad and humorous illustration than in any other way."[6]

There are five reasons why adroit advocates' stories are so influential. First, compelling stories are *engrossing*. They entertain and engage. They grab our attention. When someone says, "Let me tell you a story," we perk up and lean close, eager to absorb good stuff. Our minds don't wander. Listening feels effortless. It is hardly a fluke that movies with engrossing narratives are more likely than other films to win major awards.[7]

Second, people often *understand* what's being proposed when a story is told. Good narrative makes abstract concepts real to people. They put a human face on ideas and tap into decision makers' emotions in far more memorable ways than bullet points on PowerPoint slides.[8]

Here's a personal story. When I was a child, my father and I often took evening walks. Their high point was the ice cream, purchased at a Baskin-Robbins 31 Flavors in Arlington, Virginia. Next to the store stood an empty building that soon housed a restaurant called the Wild Onion. At nine, I thought the name hilarious. My mother often cooked with onions, and one of my chores was to peel the pungent things. "Think of the smell, Dad!" I regularly said. "People must be crying every time they leave the place."

The next summer, my family made our annual weeklong expedition to the beach. After returning home, my dad and I took our usual stroll. I walked over to the restaurant, ice cream in hand, and read a big white sign on its door.

"Dad," I said, laughing. "Come look! The sign says they're bankrupt; they're out of business! Isn't that great? No more onions, no more tears, the smell is gone!" He didn't share my glee. I asked him why. He asked me if I knew what "bankruptcy" meant. I said, "It means they have no money."

He said, "It means a lot more than that. It probably means that a couple, maybe a single person, saved money for years. They didn't go to the beach as we did; they didn't buy nice clothes for their children like you have on. Instead, they saved up their money. And last year, when they opened this restaurant, it was probably the proudest moment of their life. When the tablecloths were perfectly pressed, the crystal sparkled, and the silverware shined, they beamed at what they had created. And now all those dreams are shattered and gone. Why laugh at such sadness?"

To this day, I drive my family and friends crazy when we travel. Given a choice between a chain restaurant and a mom-and-pop place, I always choose the latter. Do you understand why I make the choice I do? Wasn't the story more compelling than a PowerPoint slide that said one of my core beliefs was "entrepreneurship"?

What made Lyndon Johnson, a man from the South, an advocate for civil rights? He claimed it was a story that Gene Wilson, husband of his maid, told him when Johnson asked him to drive his car and his dog back to Texas. "Well Senator, it's tough enough to get all the way from Washington to Texas. We drive for hours and hours. We get hungry. But there's no place on the road we can stop and go in and eat. We drive some more. It gets pretty hot. We want to wash up. But the only bathroom we're allowed in is usually miles off the main highway. We keep goin' 'til night comes — 'til we get so tired we can't stay awake anymore. We're ready to pull in. But it takes another hour or so to find a place to sleep. You see what I'm saying is that a colored man's got enough trouble getting across the South on his own, without having a dog along."[9] Johnson didn't think it was right that any man (and strikingly one working for the president of the United States) should have to go through such an experience.

Presidents, the ultimately successful politicians, have always understood the persuasive potential of stories. When a Virginian suggested that Abraham Lincoln surrender some of his military posts in the South, he responded that doing so would be unwise, and offered one of Aesop's fables to make his point. "A lion was very much in love with a woodman's daughter. The fair maid referred him to her father and the lion applied for the girl. The father replied: 'Your teeth are too long.' So the lion went to a dentist and had them extracted. Returning, he asked for his bride. 'No,' said the woodman, 'your claws are too long.' Going back to the dentist, he had them drawn. The he returned to claim his bride, and the woodman, seeing that he was unarmed, beat out his brains."[10] Lincoln's point was simple: If he were to surrender positions in the South one by one, the Union would become progressively weaker, just like the lion, until, at some point, it would be crushed.

The third reason that stories matter in advocacy is that they *synthesize* ideas. With a good story, an advocate can boil a complex idea down into a coherent whole that makes sense to a decision maker. In 2007, Stephen Epstein directed the Pentagon's ethics office. To teach employees what is ethically appropriate, Epstein produced an "Encyclopedia of Ethical Failure." The volume is filled with stories of people violating ethical rules. They are often titled in memorable ways. An article entitled "Don't let your activities as a 'fore' star keep you from becoming a four-star" relates the story of a three-star admiral who hosted a golf tournament on government time and persuaded defense contractors to pony up prizes. He never was never awarded his fourth star! Such stories communicate far better than dry statutes about what is acceptable and what is not.[11]

You can appreciate the synthesizing power of narrative in courtroom trials. There is often too much information in trials for the average juror to understand and remember. To provide an organizational framework for all this information effective attorneys begin their cases with compelling, well-structured stories. As trials progress, jurors interpret new information in terms of those narratives. If evidence matches the stories that the jurors have absorbed, it sticks in their minds. If it fails to fit, it is ignored or forgotten. Evidence presented in story form typically is more influential than evidence presented in more traditional issue-by-issue formats.[12]

Fourth, decision makers vividly *remember* narratives and the messages that derive from them. History is a collection of well-told stories. What and who we remember is, in large part, a function of the stories we are exposed to about events and people. Take the story of Sir Alexander Fleming's serendipitous discovery of the effectiveness of *Penicillium* mold in killing bacteria. While cleaning culture plates in his laboratory, Fleming noticed that bacteria were absent around the mold. Why? he wondered. The rest is history. This story, often told in schools, reminds budding scientists to notice everything, however seemingly trivial. It also made Fleming legendary. Far fewer people know that by 1932, Fleming had stopped studying *Penicillium*. He couldn't figure out how to purify it and, at the same time, preserve its potency. Not until ten years after Fleming stopped studying the mold did Cambridge University's Howard Florey demonstrate the enormous medical value of *Penicillium*. Without Florey's numerous studies, Fleming's opportune observation could have been lost to history. Why, then, is Fleming remembered and Florey (who was a cowinner with Fleming of the Nobel Prize) forgotten? In part because Florey's diligent laboratory work, summarized in a series of technical articles, offers a far less intriguing narrative of discovery.[13]

Fifth and finally, stories are effective for advocacy because people find it *difficult to disagree* with their persuasive content.[14] Well-told stories transport listeners into mental states where deep counterarguing is difficult.[15] Even when people do argue against what a story proposes, their arguments are less intense and less critical than if the same proposal were made another way.[16] Listeners don't like to disrupt the flow of a story to argue against it. So they are prone to wait until the end, giving the storyteller the opportunity to explain the idea at stake.[17] Equally, decision makers can disagree with data and arguments, they can't say that a personal story is untrue, for, at the very least, it presents the teller's truth.

Epitomizing all of the reasons that advocates use narrative is a pitch made by Bob Marcell, a senior engineer at Chrysler, in 1990. Chrysler, then under the leadership of Lee Iacocca, was debating whether to compete against Japanese car companies by making a small, inexpensive auto. Many people at the company thought any such attempt foolish. Marcell disagreed. At the final decision meeting, he eschewed the traditional financial speech and instead talked about his boyhood town in northern Michigan. Using a slide projector, he flashed a photograph of the town on the screen and began:

> This is Iron River. It's a little town in the western end of the Upper Peninsula. A hell of a good place to grow up, with a lot of blue skies and fresh air. Back in the forties and fifties, every day about three o'clock and eleven o'clock, the pictures all shook in the houses, the ground rumbled, the windows rattled, and everybody smiled. Because that meant the iron mines were blasting. There were jobs for everybody. There was no unemployment. And there was good pay. And snowmobiles, new cars, cottages, and boats. A lot of first- and second-generation Europeans had found a little bit of heaven. But there was trouble brewing. Iron ore was coming in from Brazil and from Canada. There was a lot of competition, foreign and domestic. This happens to be the Hiawatha No. 2 [mine]. My dad was the last person out of this mine. He pulled up the pumps and let the deepest iron mine in the world flood. And we shipped the pumps to Africa and South America, because we couldn't compete.

Marcell then flashed more slides, each showing a once-vibrant community now abandoned. As each slide appeared on the screen, he said, "Couldn't compete." He finished his presentation by saying, "Chernobyl was a nuclear disaster, and you can't live there anymore. My home town had an economic disaster — every bit as devastating, a lot more insidious — and you can't live there anymore, either." Obviously he was, by analogy, talking about the auto industry through his description of Iron River. He finished his presentation by asking the assembled group of executives:

> So, what the hell are we going to do? Not come to work scared every day. We can roll in with a counterattack, and that's what this is all about. Because we can reestablish a beachhead in small cars. We can reverse the long downhill slide. And prove to the world that we're not soft, we're not lazy, we're not dumb, and, damn, we can compete.

The room was quiet. Marcell's story had made his point eloquently. And he was successful. Eight months later, Chrysler made a commitment to develop the small car that Marcell was spearheading.[18] That car, the Chrysler Neon, was a success.

How to Tell a Story

Influential Stories Make Points

Powerful stories — ones that are remembered and taken to heart — make clear and compelling points. Weak stories may be interesting and entertaining, but if their points are unclear, the stories are only distracting. Advocates should know specifically what they want decision makers to feel, do, and remember from their narratives. Ideally, the main points of their stories are obvious — and so persuasive as to be virtually impossible to argue against.

In December 2010, President Barack Obama signed into law legislation that henceforth allows gays and lesbians to openly serve in the military. Here is what the president said at the signing, after a brief greeting and thank-you:

> Sixty-six years ago, in the dense, snow-covered forests of Western Europe, Allied Forces were beating back a massive assault in what would become known as the Battle of the Bulge. And in the final days of fighting, a regiment in the 80th Division of Patton's Third Army came under fire. The men were traveling along a narrow trail. They were exposed and they were vulnerable. Hundreds of soldiers were cut down by the enemy.
>
> And during the firefight, a private named Lloyd Corwin tumbled 40 feet down the deep side of a ravine. And dazed and trapped, he was as good as dead. But one soldier, a friend, turned back. And with shells landing around him, amid smoke and chaos and the screams of wounded men, this soldier, this friend, scaled down the icy slope, risking his own life to bring Private Corwin to safer ground.

For the rest of his years, Lloyd credited this soldier, this friend, named Andy Lee, with saving his life, knowing he would never have made it out alone. It was a full four decades after the war, when the two friends reunited in their golden years, that Lloyd learned that the man who saved his life, his friend Andy, was gay. He had no idea. And he didn't much care. Lloyd knew what mattered. He knew what had kept him alive; what made it possible for him to come home and start a family and live the rest of his life. It was his friend.

And Lloyd's son is with us today. And he knew that valor and sacrifice are no more limited by sexual orientation than they are by race or by gender or by religion or by creed; that what made it possible for him to survive the battlefields of Europe is the reason that we are here today. That's the reason we are here today.

So this morning, I am proud to sign a law that will bring an end to "Don't Ask, Don't Tell." It is a law—this law I'm about to sign will strengthen our national security and uphold the ideals that our fighting men and women risk their lives to defend.

No longer will our country be denied the service of thousands of patriotic Americans who were forced to leave the military—regardless of their skills, no matter their bravery or their zeal, no matter their years of exemplary performance—because they happen to be gay. No longer will tens of thousands of Americans in uniform be asked to live a lie, or look over their shoulder, in order to serve the country that they love.

As Admiral Mike Mullen has said, "Our people sacrifice a lot for their country, including their lives. None of them should have to sacrifice their integrity as well." That's why I believe this is the right thing to do for our military. That's why I believe it is the right thing to do, period.[19]

Obama's story, told at the start of his speech, makes the point of the new law obvious. If he had not included the story, his presentation would have been far less compelling.

Or consider this story told by a safety director to persuade her organization to invest in preventive safety.

A friend of mine recently vacationed in Greece. At one point she spied an old monastery atop a nearby mountain. As far as she could tell, there wasn't anyway to get to it—no road, no pathway, no stairs. So in the village below the mountain, she asked some people how she might visit the monastery. They told her that she'd need to make arrangements at the village chapel. Then a burly monk would come down from the monastery in a basket using a rope and pulley. And that is indeed what happened.

The monk invited her into the basket and once she was aboard, he started tugging on the rope. Soon they were up in the air. It was then that my friend noticed the rope looked frayed. Concerned, she turned to the monk and asked, "When do you change the rope?" He looked at the frayed line, shrugged, and said, "Whenever it breaks."[20]

After the manager's audience stopped laughing, she said, "That won't be the philosophy here. We fix things *before* they break!" Her story made the point.

Often it is important to nail home the point of stories. If advocates finish stories without summarizing what they want decision makers to leave with, they run the risk that the decision makers will make their own interpretations. Kofi Annan, former secretary general of the United Nations, spent his college years at Macalister College in Minnesota. He tells the story of arriving there and seeing people wearing earmuffs. Never, he told himself, would he put on something so ugly. But he changed his tune as winter progressed and temperatures sank below zero. In fact, he bought the biggest earmuffs he could find. The lesson, he told students in a commencement address at his alma mater years later, was, "Never think you know more than the natives do."[21] Interpretation matters.

Influential Stories Are Well Told

Even the best tale can be ruined if it is poorly delivered. Influential narratives are short, fresh, easily understood, and engaging, and they arouse curiosity.

They are *short* because anecdotes that ramble on are boring. People stop listening. Notice that every story in this chapter takes no more than a few paragraphs to relate.

Influential stories are also *fresh*. The decision makers being addressed haven't heard them before. There are exceptions. Many of us enjoy viewing favorite old films every so often, and we love to rehear a delightful joke. But most stories, like most films, have brief shelf lives. When advocates talk with the same group of decision makers more than once, they must be careful about telling the same stories (including the same jokes). The second time you face a group you might simply allude to an earlier story. If some listeners have heard it and others haven't, you might say, "Some of you've probably heard me talk about . . ." and then go on to tell the tale.

Besides being short and fresh, a good story is *easily understood*. If I relate a story about a subject completely foreign to you, I shouldn't be surprised if you fail to be affected by it. Understandable stories are often personally relevant. If you have ever struggled late into the night trying to solve a knotty problem, if you have ever suffered repeated rejections, if you have ever endured a tough election, or if you have ever stared out a dark window waiting nervously for a child to arrive home, then you probably can identify with stories about such experiences. Good stories don't need to be about shared experiences, of course, but they do need to be about imaginable experiences.

If you are an advocate, deliver your story with passion. A story is *engaging* in part because listeners sense that the storyteller cares about both the story itself and its underlying theme. Gripping stories include us emotionally. We can identify with the characters, sense what they are feeling, and imagine being there with them. The speaker's voice communicates her passion. She may use exaggerated verbal and nonverbal behaviors to highlight what is happening. Her intonation, volume, accent, and timing may change as she talks about one character and then moves to another character. Emotions must be heard. Indeed, in many stories exaggerated emotions, well placed, catch the attention of listeners. A pause intrigues, words that tumble forth indicate passion, and tones of anger, happiness, surprise, and disappointment highlight the lesson to be learned. Visual details and colorful words create indelible images in listeners' minds. One important tip: However well told a story, the telling has to seem unrehearsed.

Perhaps something unexpected or novel happens in the story, or maybe there are multiple ways the story may resolve itself. An influential story generates a feeling of suspense as it unfolds; it *arouses curiosity*. Think of the stories you read in the past few pages. At some point in each one you may have wondered where it was going, what the point was.

One important caveat: sometimes stories aren't appropriate. In highly technical discussions, in meetings where time is short, or in certain settings — interviews, for example — where people are simply seeking information, telling stories is often inadvisable. Stories may also not translate well across cultures. Equally, advocates don't want their stories to overwhelm the substance of their talk. Some managers have reputations as great storytellers. But their stories are all that people recollect after meetings. Their business messages are diluted or forgotten in favor of the entertaining tales. The accompaniment to persuasive stories should be strong data and logical arguments, especially when decision makers are listening deeply or otherwise involved. If the available data contradict the narrative of a story, involved decision makers will often dismiss the tale. The proponent's credibility suffers as a result.

Influential Stories Reflect Values

Powerful stories have what psychologists call "emotional resonance" — they tap into our basic values, beliefs, and experiences.[22] At their best, stories convey deep moral wisdom. Some of the greatest stories told are religious parables, which communicate core values in easily understood ways. But secular parables can be equally effective. Consider this story that circulated on the Web.

> A little girl had a ferocious temper. Her mother gave her a bag of nails and told her that every time she lost her temper, she must hammer one nail into the back of a fence. The first day she drove 26 nails into that fence. As the girl learned to control her anger, the number of nails she hammered each day gradually dwindled. It was easier to hold her temper than to drive those nails into the fence. Finally the day arrived when the girl did not lose her temper once. Her mother then said that every day she successfully controlled her anger, she should pull one nail from the fence. Weeks later the young girl told her mother that all the nails were out. The mother walked her daughter to the fence. She said, "You've done well but look at the holes in the fence! The fence will never be the same. When you say angry things, they leave scars just like these holes.[23]

The value taught by this story is clear: Anger has consequences.

Advocates often come up with emotionally resonant tales by thinking of values they cherish. If you believe in honesty, it is probably because you once vividly experienced the pain of dishonesty or saw the wonder of honesty. After a series of corporate scandals, one managing director at a financial firm felt that it was important to tell his employees how much he valued ethical behavior. In a staff meeting, after covering the corporate policies on ethics, he paused and then said that nothing mattered more to him than honesty. He talked of one summer day in his childhood when he ran to a newspaper machine, put a quarter in the slot, and then gleefully took two papers instead of one. His father, when he found out, walked him back to the machine, told his son to dig a quarter — his allowance — out of his pocket, put it in the machine, and place the second newspaper back in the stack. "Honesty, even about the small things," his father said, "is what makes a man." To this day, the executive told his group, honesty matters to him. The small sacrifice of his allowance taught him a far richer value.

To discover stories tied to values, consider questions such as these:

What are my values?
Can one of those values be tied to my idea?
Why does that value matter to me?
Where did I learn the value, and when did I discover its importance?
What was a pivotal experience in my life that might relate to the idea?

Consider a story told by former Microsoft executive Ray Ozzie. As an engineering student at the University of Illinois in the early 1970s, he often passed a building on the Urbana campus that had a "strange orange glow emanating from the windows." Inside, he discovered people sitting at computer terminals using a system called Plato. Intrigued, he eventually became a programmer for the system. By 1974, Plato terminals were connected across campus and the world.

Ozzie often worked with a faceless programmer whom he had never met. To communicate, the two of them used software similar to today's Instant Messenger. His partner had terrible spelling and slow typing skills. One day they met face-to-face, and Ozzie discovered that the fellow was a quadriplegic who typed via a stick clamped in his teeth. Ozzie said, "I realized at that moment that the computer was a medium that enabled communication with people mind-to-mind, regardless of their physical well-being. You can work with someone without prejudice, and their true talents will be shown. And, from then on, I started to focus on how computers could help people work more effectively. After graduation, I said to myself 'By hook or crook, I am going to recreate the interactive environment I'd used with Plato.'" And he did. Ozzie created Lotus Notes, eventually used by millions of people worldwide.[24] When you hear this story, you have to believe that a commitment to help people underlies Ozzie's work on computers.

Influential Stories Make Sense

Stories need to sound real; they must make sense. People instinctively judge narratives in terms of their coherence. Good stories aren't riddled with contradictions. They hang together. There is a beginning, a middle filled with various events and twists, and a conclusive ending. Typically, stories have only a few major components: a *setting* (where and when the story happens), vivid *characters* with *goals*, and some *predicament* — a problem, obstacle, or complication that one or more of the characters confronts. This predicament leads to an action that either succeeds or fails. A story becomes intriguing when we want to know what happens next. There is a surprise, a conflict, frustration, or failure, that the protagonist must deal with.

In advocacy stories, the predicament offers decision makers the reason for hearing a proposal. The problem is *resolved*, and the resolution has a consequence — an *outcome*.[25] Often, stories end with a *lesson or moral*. It is at this point that advocates present their *proposal*: "What we learned from this is that we should . . ." or "In the end, these events convinced us to recommend that we . . ." An example of an advocacy story following this structure is in box 2.

BOX 2. A STORY WITH STRUCTURE

Mikhail wanted to change the way his government agency handled services to citizens. Rather than starting his pitch to leaders with a statistical summary of complaints and a process map, he began with this story:

A very old woman named Natasha came into the bureau yesterday [*character and setting*]. It was her fourth trip to the bureau to discover how she could receive prescriptions for her bedridden husband [*goal*]. Each time, she was told that she needed to schedule an appointment, or fill out a form, or bring in some other document [*obstacle*]. This time, with forms and documents in hand, she politely waited for an hour for her turn at the counter that she had been to three times before. She is of the generation where queues are expected. When she finally reached the counter and began to explain her problem, the clerk, a longtime civil servant, said she was in the wrong line; she would need to go to another line [*obstacle*]. She thanked him and went to the back of the assigned line. She waited another hour or so [*obstacle*]. Now remember, this is an eighty-four-year-old great-grandmother. As she approached the new counter, the clerk told her it was now time for the lunch break, so Natasha would need to wait at least one hour before the office reopened [*obstacle*].

"Where to wait?" Natasha asked.

"Outside," the clerk suggested. Yesterday, as you know, was one of the coldest days so far this year. Almost in tears, Natasha asked if she might wait inside where it was warm. "It's against the rules," the clerk responded [*obstacle*].

So Natasha hesitantly went outside. As she stood by the door wrapped in an old coat, Alex, one of our newest employees, happened to walk out. Seeing her age and discomfort, he asked whether she needed anything. She explained her problem to him. Without knowing the rules, Alex reopened the office and sat with Natasha until the clerks returned from lunch. Then he went over and talked to the supervisor about Natasha's problem. The supervisor shrugged and said, "If you want to take care of her problem, you can." Fifteen minutes later, after hugging Alex and saying his mother should be very proud of him, Natasha left the office with the prescriptions [*resolution*].

Natasha, I am sure, has sung the praises of Alex to her husband, children, and neighbors. She now believes that somebody in the government cares about her [*consequence*]. What should we learn from this story? That we make it too hard for our older citizens to get what they need. We have employees with poor attitudes. Why, I wonder, did Natasha have to visit the office four times? Why, I wonder, does every employee not show the responsibility that Alex demonstrated? [*lesson learned*]. What I want to do is develop a system that lets our citizens receive what they need the first time they visit. I want your permission to hire and train more people like Alex. I want us to give citizens the service they deserve. With your permission, I propose . . . [*proposal*].

This common structure for stories is one in which suspense builds, and we wait to discover what happens. Some stories have an alternative structure, however. They start with the outcome, and then come the setting, characters, goals, complications, and resolution. That structure elicits curiosity. We know the outcome but want to know how it came about.[26]

Whatever the structure, effective stories are plausible and complete. Does this mean that a story should perfectly recapitulate what actually happened? Of course not. As Alfred Hitchcock said, "Drama is life with the boring parts left out." The average two-hour film comprises only forty to fifty scenes. Since not everything can be told in a movie, each scene must contribute to the story's theme. In fact, too many details get in the way of communicating the central story. Good storytellers know when to leave things out and when to highlight other things. Some details are emphasized to ensure that listeners can identify with the story; others are downplayed. "By telling a story, I don't mean story as in make things up," says Robert Metcalfe, the retired founder of 3Com Corporation. "I have told the story of 3Com a thousand different ways. You make it dramatic. You select facts. You add drama. You wink. You smile. You leave out unimportant things that might weaken your point. It is all part of the gentle art of persuasion. But, one of my rules is: Never lie."[27]

Influential Stories Are Personal

Although there are thousands of stories in print and on Web pages that advocates can draw on, the best ones are their own. Borrowing stories from others is risky. If advocates pretend that a story is theirs and people discover the deception, the advocates' credibility is shot. If people have heard a story before, its impact is blunted. So shrewd advocates come up with their own stories — ones drawn from their personal experiences.

Every experience offers possible stories. You may be saying, at this point, "Well, maybe for you, but I don't live a life filled with dramatic stories." Wrong! Everybody has amusing or potentially important things happen to them. You just have to start treating seemingly insignificant events as inspiration for rich narratives.

Years ago, I was consulting for a manufacturing company. The firm had plants spread across North America. The company boss, a man in his sixties, insisted that he travel with me to each plant. On our trip to the first site, I noticed him doing something curious. At the airport, after buying a newspaper, he took his change and placed it, piece by piece, in the coin-return boxes of pay phones. My first thought was that he wanted to avoid setting off the metal detectors at the security gate. But we were already beyond security. So, I noted, he had an interesting quirk.

A week later, we were traveling together again. This time we were waiting for a delayed flight at Chicago O'Hare International Airport. My companion went into a shop near our gate and bought a newspaper. Returning, he strolled past a bank of pay phones and again dropped his change into the coin-return boxes — a quarter in one, a penny in another, a nickel in a third. Once he sat down, I asked him why he did this. "Watch the phones," he said.

With nothing better to do, I stared at the bank of phones. Minutes later a couple walked by the phones with a three- or four-year-old girl between

Table 1. Generating Stories

	Situation	Characters	Goals	Obstacles	Action	Result	Lesson
Teamwork							
Research Project							
New Policy							
Change Initiative							
Other							

them. The child looked exhausted. She suddenly sat down almost in tears. The father headed off in search of a treat while the mother soothed her. Soon the little girl spied the phones. What does any child do with pay phones? Of course, she reached up and started checking their coin-return boxes. In the first, she found a nickel, in the next, a penny, in the third, a quarter. In less than a minute, she went from a cranky, whiny youngster to a child wreathed in smiles. I turned to my friend and said, "That's really nice."

And he replied, "Yeah, it doesn't cost much to make a person happy."

To this day, every time I pass one of the few remaining pay phones in airports, I think of his simple generosity.

This isn't a world-shaking story. But it tells about an experience of mine, and I have turned it into a tale that I tell when making the point about how easy it is to be generous. It meets all the criteria of a story. And it's personal.

How do you come up with personal stories? One way has already been mentioned: consider your values and why you have them. A second way is to ground your notions in specifics: What specific event or person convinced you that your idea was important? What bothered you (specifically) about the current state of affairs? A third way is to create a matrix that prompts you to think of stories.

To create a matrix, list some issues or topics that you might need to address in the future—teamwork, a change, a process or procedure, a policy, your idea (table 1). Across the top of the page, list *situation* (setting, challenge), *characters*, *goals*, *obstacles*, *action*, *result*, and *lesson*. For each issue spend time thinking about a time that you learned something valuable. Who else was involved? What was the predicament? What did you do? What did you hope to accomplish? What happened? What did you learn? If you are really stuck, say something like "I know teamwork is important. For example . . ." If you end statements with the phrase "for example," you force yourself to think narratively.

Factoids to the Rescue

What if advocates can't come up with a story to buttress their arguments? Then they have the option of using fascinating factoids—little known facts that address the idea being raised. A cleverly used factoid can communicate a point as well as a story can, as many successful advocates have demonstrated. Here are some examples.

The financier Alexander Sachs had a goal in October 1939: to convince his friend President Franklin Roosevelt to consider Albert Einstein's worry that Germany was creating an atomic weapon. Sachs was not keeping Roosevelt's attention when they met, so Sachs related a little historical fact—that Napoleon had rejected out of hand Robert Fulton's proposal to build a fleet of steamships for France. If Napoleon had listened to Fulton, he might have successfully invaded England, making the world as we know it today very different. (Ships with sails could not easily proceed from France to England against the wind; steam-powered ships could have.) Sachs told the president that the current meeting was about something as monumental a technological breakthrough as steamships were in the time of sail.[28] That factoid and Sachs's tie-in pricked Roosevelt's attention. Soon thereafter, he ordered his administration to start work on nuclear weapons. Sachs did what successful advocates often do—use their knowledge of little known but striking facts to strengthen their arguments and, simultaneously, build their credibility.

A health-care executive who led a large organizational change used a fascinating medical factoid when telling other leaders how she believed that change initiatives should be conducted. She said that bandaged wounds heal two to five times faster than uncovered wounds. The same is true in the midst of major changes: wise leaders give employees a little protection; that is, they provide some stability and avoid changing every-thing too quickly. On another occasion, she told someone that she had learned, as a change leader, that it is better to have people within an organization create and manage changes. The mistake too many firms make is to use outsiders, such as consultants, to lead change. She said making changes is like transplanting skin or organs. Transplants from one person to another often experience rejection, whereas transplants from one part of a person's body to another, such as skin grafts, mostly take. She used that factoid to make her point that consultant-led changes often don't take. Outsiders, like consultants, have more difficulty creating and sustaining change than people who are from the inside and under-stand organizational culture.

An executive with a small financial firm used another factoid effectively when he was explaining to a room of potential employees how important teamwork was in his organization. Rather than simply saying "Teamwork matters," he asked them if they knew about the giant sequoia tree. People nodded.

"What makes it unusual?" he asked.

One person replied, "It's enormous; it is one of the tallest trees in the world."

Another volunteered that the tree grows from a tiny seed that is re-leased during forest fires.

The executive agreed with these observations but said that what really makes the sequoia so interesting is its root structure. For its size, the tree has one of the shallowest root structures of any tree in the world. The roots seldom go deeper than ten feet. The question that immediately comes to mind, he said, is, "How, with shallow roots, does the tree stay up?" The executive paused while people tried to come up with responses. The answer, the executive offered, is that the roots of a single sequoia can reach out across sometimes more than an acre, and they interlace with the roots of other trees in the grove. Each tree stays up in part because the other trees support it. You can't see this support from above the ground. It is hidden.

Then the executive brought home the point: "That's like our firm. We have brokers, traders, analysts, computer folks, and every other sort of person you need. While they all look different, they all need each other to survive. Each person in this firm holds up every other person." People nodded, and the executive continued: "Think of this: If one tree gets ill, what happens to all the other trees if the roots are interlaced? They get sick too. That's also like this firm. We are only as good as our weakest member. That's why we spend so much time hiring the best people in the industry."

The executive could have simply said, "We're a team, we support one another, and we are careful about choosing only the best." Instead, he opted to use the factoid about the sequoia tree. Which do you think had more impact on listeners?

Factoids like these are part of successful advocates' arsenal of influence. Factoids can be very persuasive. The rules of effective storytelling apply equally to factoids. Effective factoids are interesting. They make a relevant point. They should be true. To some degree, they should be familiar, and so on. But while stories are especially helpful persuading people who are *somewhat involved* in the underlying issues, factoids are often quite successful when pitching a proposal to those who are *deeply involved* in issues related to the proposal.

Where do advocates find factoids? Virtually anywhere. Everyday experiences offer factoids that can be used to explain ideas and influence others. When Jonathan Miller took over as CEO of AOL in 2002, many executives in the parent firm, Time Warner, were upset about all of the problems that AOL had experienced in the past. At his first meeting with the disgruntled executives, Miller said that when your car gets towed in New York City and you want it back, "You have to wait in a long line, and when you finally get to the clerk, you are ready to take his head off. But there's a sign in the clerk's window that says, 'The people here didn't tow your car and they're here to help you get it back.'" Miller said his goal was to get AOL back in order, just as these clerks want to help you get your car back.[29] That brief factoid made Miller's point in a way all the executives could readily identify with. The current team at AOL had nothing to do with the company's past but nonetheless needed to get AOL moving again.

In most cases, the best factoids come from an advocate's personal reservoir of knowledge. It is not surprising that many highly influential people devour biographies and are constantly intrigued by new information about the world. They are voracious learners, always struck by facts they didn't know. History is replete with interesting and applicable facts. A. G. Lafley, when he was the new CEO of Procter & Gamble, was sitting at a table in Greece with his marketing team after a daylong meeting when the team surprised him with a present—a book on Alexander the Great. The play on

Lafley's first two initials (A. G.) was amusing, but the team was also expressing its belief that Lafley was going to build a successful future for the company. Afterward, Lafley said that Alexander might not have been the best example of a leader. Why? Because after Alexander's death, there was massive and brutal infighting among his generals. "That's not what I want to happen here," Lafley told his team. "What I am trying to build into this organization is something that will last long after I'm gone. This is a company that aspires to be around for 1,000 years."[30]

A favorite trick of politicians is to discover historical events and notable birthdays that occurred on the days they deliver speeches. Then they link their ideas to those events. History is only one source. Another might be an advocate's area of professional expertise. One scientist was explaining that coordinating activities in her lab was often difficult, but it was crucial for the success of her research program. To make her point, she related the fact that for a standing person to stay balanced requires up to three hundred muscles. "We've all learned to balance using all of those muscles and so we must coordinate and stay balanced when it comes to this challenge," she told her team.

Wherever advocates find their factoids, once they have a collection, they can use them in many different advocacy settings. Let's say a tour guide tells you a curious fact about the seabird called a puffin: When it is born, its parents stuff it with food. Before long, it becomes larger than either parent, and because of its inflated size, it cannot immediately leave the cave it was born in. Why all this stuffing? It allows the parents to fly off for food, knowing their baby is safe from wandering off and encountering predators. By the time the baby puffin can fit through the cave entrance, it is ready to fly. That's the factoid. How might you use it? One Canadian manager used it by saying that his job was to protect his new employees until they are ready to do "battle" in his company. Another manager used the same factoid to suggest that smart leaders create safe environments for inventions.

Good factoids always make a point. If they don't make a point, they can be both annoying and distracting. Do you remember the character on the television show *Cheers* — Cliff Clavin — who punctuated his conversation with often-pointless factoids, which he spouted just for the fun of it? They were goofy, often uninteresting, and seldom germane.[31] So, just because a factoid is a curiosity doesn't mean that it is worth sharing. Smart advocates don't want to be like Cliff. Instead, their factoids add value to the argument they are making.

7

Who's Making the Decision?

Know the enemy and know yourself, and in a
hundred battles, you will never be defeated.

SUN TZU

The more you know about your customers, the better your sales. That is axiomatic. It is also true that the more you know about your decision makers, the more effective your advocacy will be. Advocates must figure out as much as they can about the decision makers who support or dismiss an idea: Who will like the idea? Who won't? Who's going to sit on the fence? Who can kill the idea with a shake of the head? Who might make the idea look infantile or ill thought through? Who might whisper, "We tried this before, it cost a lot of money, and it never worked. Let's quash it!" In this chapter we look at what proponents should consider about decision makers when preparing their pitches.

Understanding Decision Makers

Successful advocates have a knack for divining whose opinions count — who matters, who makes the final decision, who influences decision makers' judgments, and who might block attempts to persuade people to adopt their ideas. Sometimes people with the *money*, *authority*, and *need* are obvious — it is the boss or the boss's boss who matters. But sometimes the real clout lies elsewhere. When Dean Witter and Morgan Stanley merged in the late 1990s, Phil Purcell, who came from Dean Witter, insisted on being CEO. The Morgan Stanley leadership team acquiesced, calculating that Purcell was "some hick from Chicago who they'd blow away in six months." Purcell began working with the board of directors of the merged company, letting the Morgan Stanley leadership team run the company on a day-to-day basis. Over time, Purcell made sure that his own people were appointed to the board. His biggest internal competitor was John Mack, from the Morgan Stanley side of the business, who had actively lobbied for the CEO position. But the board members, given their allegiance to Purcell, kept turning Mack down. Mack finally moved on, leaving Purcell in charge. As John McCoy, former head of Bank One, says, "Phil outsmarted the best dealmakers on Wall Street. He figured out how to play the game, and he won."[1] He knew the real decision makers were the board members, so he focused on them. (Years later, Purcell's Machiavellian moves caught up to him. He was forced to retire from Morgan Stanley, and John Mack returned as CEO — you can win battles and still lose wars!)

Since it isn't always obvious who the real decision makers are, canny advocates map out strategies early on for getting buy-in from everyone who might have some say over their idea (box 3). They worry about winning support from the assistant who controls access to top people; from the financial guy who everyone listens to, even when his knowledge is mostly irrelevant; from just about anyone. When managing Coca-Cola in central Europe, Neville Isdell proposed creating a single large bottler for all of Europe. To do this he would have had to give partial ownership of this large bottler to each of 116 small bottlers. Other executives brought his plan to a halt. Why? Isdell says that he "underestimated . . . the degree to which there were multiple constituencies that needed to be covered to ensure that the back-door, old relationships that some of the bottlers had built could not stop us. Phone calls came in to headquarters from bottlers around the world, asking, 'What does this mean to me?' I had not thought that through well enough." He learned that "you have to look outside the narrow view you have of where the areas of influence exist. Be sure you have them all covered. Now I think in a different way about where objections might come from."[2]

[handwritten notes in top margin: EXERCISE — LIST IN YOUR ORG WHO QUALIFIES FOR EACH CATEGORY FOR 2 QUESTIONS]

BOX 3. DO YOU KNOW YOUR DECISION MAKERS?

Imagine that you have a great idea to advocate. See if you can answer the following questions about the decision makers you need to pitch the idea to.

[handwritten notes in right margin: 1) HIRING A PERSON 2) CHANGING A POLICY IN YOUR DEPT THAT EXPEDITES A SPECIFIC PROCESS BY USING AN EXCEL SPREADSHEET]

Are you selling to the *right people*? Who are the real decision makers? Are you addressing people who make the decision or who influence the decision? Who has informal influence?

Which decision makers are likely to be *friendly* to the proposal? Which are likely to be persuadable?

What *kind of evidence* do the decision makers prefer? Do they like examples, stories, theories, historical anecdotes, data, or testimonials? How can the proposal be adapted to accommodate their preferences? What do they expect in arguments or presentations?

How *open* are they to change? — Are they more comfortable with the status quo, or are they intrigued by change? What are the incentives or disincentives for them to adopt your proposal? How much experience do they have introducing new ideas into their organizations?

Where in the *organization* do the decision makers come from? Some units of the organization may be more open to new ideas than other units.

How strong are the decision makers' current *beliefs* about the issue? Are they positive, uncommitted, doubtful, or strenuously opposed?

Who are likely to be the *naysayers*? What is the best way of responding to their negativity? Why do naysayers believe what they do? Who is so adamantly opposed to the idea that there is no way they will change?

Who can say no even though they can't say yes? Who *oppose* the idea even though they have no official say? Their whining can stop a proposal from being adopted.

Will those *at the top* of the organization support the idea? Will people who make the decision respond more positively if they know that the top people like the notion?

Who might serve as *champions or sponsors* for the notion? Who, at senior levels, will help you get the resources you need? What senior people can remove blocks that could stop your proposal from being adopted?

How will your immediate *boss* react to your idea? How will your colleagues, peers, and subordinates respond?

Who are *affected* by your idea? How will they be affected? Who have a stake in your idea? Who might lose something if your idea is adopted?

Types of Decision Makers: The Knowing-Feeling Matrix

Decision makers' reactions to ideas fall along two continuums. The first has to do with what they *know* and understand about a proposal. At one end of this continuum are decision makers who are experts about what is being proposed. They know as much about it as the advocates themselves — and sometimes even more. At the other end are people who know little or nothing about it. The second continuum references how decision makers *feel* about the idea. At one end are people who love it. At the other end are people who despise it as unnecessary, dangerous, or stupid. Combining these two dimensions — knowledge and feelings — gives us figure 4. How you pitch an idea depends upon where each of the decision makers falls in this matrix.

As the figure indicates, advocates face five sorts of people when proposing ideas. *Cynics* are resolutely against an idea even though they may know little, if anything, about it. They aren't interested in it, and they don't want to

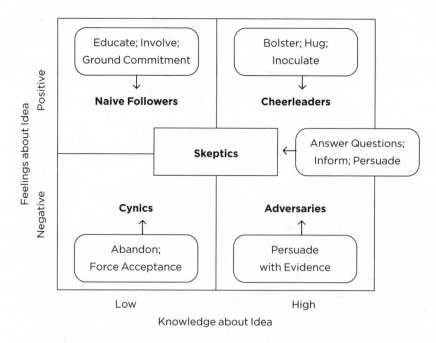

Figure 4. The Knowledge-Feeling Matrix
How you pitch an idea depends upon where each decision maker falls in this
knowledge-feeling matrix.

learn anything about it, either. You can argue with cynics for hours, but they will never change their minds. In fact, arguing with them is like being stuck in quicksand: the harder you struggle, the more quickly you sink. So what should proponents do with these incorrigible naysayers? Try to neutralize them. How? Either ignore them, or work around them. When Honda engineer Michimasa Fujino found himself facing cynics in corporate headquarters about his idea to build and market a small plane with jet engines over the wings, he finally decided that they weren't ever going to change their minds. So he ignored them and chose to work with people who liked his idea. His tactic worked, and the project moved forward.[3] If ignoring or working around cynics proves impossible, advocates recruit senior executives to force acceptance ("The boss mandated this"). Anyone who has been a parent of a teenager understands the occasional necessity of this approach. When the teenager says, "I don't want to go on this trip with you, no matter where you are going!" parents may say, "Get in the car right now!"

Next on the matrix are *naive followers*. They love the idea, but they don't really understand it. They are faddists; they crave the newest, trendiest idea, regardless of whether it works or offers value. At first glance, naive followers seem useful to have on your side, at least for the head count. But since they are easily swayed by competing ideas, you need to ground their commitment by teaching them why they should like your idea. Naive followers need to be educated, not persuaded. A challenge with naive followers is that they may be hesitant to make a final decision because even though they like an idea, they sense that they don't understand it well enough to risk being associated with it. Many years ago, Intel's leadership proposed purchasing Fore Systems, a firm involved in networks and telecommunication. Before the board meeting, company executives were sure the purchase was a sound idea. Yet, by the end of the session, the proposal was rejected "because no one understood networking or telecom well enough to even know what questions to ask."[4] Telecom and networking sounded like good business opportunities, but when pushed, the decision makers lacked enough information to confidently decide. In this case, the lack of persuasiveness was not the problem. What management needed to do was educate the board about the industry generally and Fore Systems specifically before pitching the proposal.

Then there are *cheerleaders*. These people really understand and appreciate your idea. Advocates cultivate cheerleaders not only because they support their proposal but also because they can become missionaries, helping to persuade others of its wisdom. In politics the number one rule is to solidify your base. Cheerleaders are a politician's base. Members of the base consistently vote for the politician, donate money, walk the streets handing out the politician's brochures, work the phones, and do many other mundane yet critical tasks that win elections. Politicians risk losing elections when they distance themselves from their base. Corporate CEOs understand that their base is the board of directors. Experienced advocates keep the board happy. Inexperienced advocates sometimes make the fatal mistake of taking their cheerleaders for granted and instead spend fruitless time arguing with cynics. Savvy champions continually express their appreciation for their cheerleaders, shore up their support, and welcome their help as "inoculants" in resisting counterarguments.

Adversaries, the next category in the matrix, understand the proposal yet sincerely disagree with it. Compelling information, fair and accurate data, and logical arguments matter for adversaries. Bringing them around to another view often entails an extended campaign. The renowned physicist Stephen Hawking argued with his colleague Don Page for years about a basic scientific question: whether information escapes from black holes. Eventually, the preponderance of the data convinced Hawking that he was wrong, and in April 2007 he publicly conceded that Page was right.[5] With an adversary, proponents must show that they thoroughly grasp not only the issues but also the adversaries' grounds for opposition. Wise advocates also temper their enthusiasm and avoid directly disagreeing with adversaries. Instead, they begin their campaign of persuasion by emphasizing points of agreement, at least in terms of principles, and then follow up with evidence. There is a payoff to having adversaries: the arguments that advocates must make to sway them can sharpen the advocates' thinking about their own ideas.

Finally, there are *skeptics*. They are ambivalent. They understand the proposal somewhat but are unsure of its merits. Advocates must energize skeptics, since their uncertainty makes them hesitant to take action. In one American firm an advocate was pitching the idea of offering a different product mix in some non-U.S. markets. Decision makers were uncomfortable about the idea. Though not adamantly opposed to it, they didn't really understand or like the notion of modifying a product mix that was a best seller in the United States. The champion for the idea turned them into cheerleaders by creating an educational campaign. First, she showed them videos of focus groups of customers discussing both the current product mix and the proposed one. Then she invited decision makers to visit the prospective non-U.S. markets to experience the business environment there firsthand. Equally important, she convinced them of the business case by highlighting the value of establishing a stronger brand name through the different mix of products abroad before competitors did, and gaining, as a consequence, significant market share quickly.

Notice that each group of decision makers requires a different set of moves from the advocate. You ignore or use power to outwit cynics, you educate naive followers, you cheer and support your cheerleaders, you argue logically and offer compelling evidence with adversaries, and you both teach and persuade skeptics.

Decision Makers' Degree of Involvement

Most people believe that the quality of a proponent's argument is directly tied to its success. Surely proposals that are logical, thoroughly researched, and filled with compelling evidence will win out over more specious notions. Surprisingly, that isn't always true. Decision makers sometimes adopt ideas supported by fallacious logic and inadequate research. Why don't logical arguments and compelling data always win out?

What makes a good argument depends upon the audience's level of involvement.[6] When decision makers are highly involved, they will thoughtfully consider proposals. In meetings they will listen attentively, offer counterarguments, ask penetrating questions, look for weak logic, and vet the evidence. Their scrutiny is often an obstacle to acceptance. Even before they have heard or read a proposal, they have started crafting counterarguments. In fact, the more they consider an idea, the more counterarguments they generate. Your task with these demanding people is to neutralize their counterarguments with excellent evidence, impeccable reasoning, and well-planned arguments. Don't try to seduce them with emotional appeals, fancy graphics, or energetic humor.

Stuart Card, a researcher at Xerox's PARC, was responsible for creating a computer mouse that worked easily with a PC. When he pitched his idea, many of his engineering colleagues had reservations about it. So he offered cogent arguments based on research.

> As I presented the results of the experiment, . . . the engineers picked away at the conditions and the control of the experiment and just about everything. Then I went through why the results were like they were, which came from the theoretical model. They began to see that there was an organized reason explaining why the results came out the way they did. It

was not likely that there was an artifact in the experiment causing these results. Rather, the theory showed that there was a coherent story of causes. It was logical that the results should come out this way. As they understood this, the engineers fell silent.[7]

These highly involved engineers were persuaded by data and good thinking. Similarly, John Spencer hoped to convince his colleagues at Gore-Tex to directly market the non-shred dental floss ("Glide") that his team had developed. Many in the company opposed his idea because the firm had always marketed through other companies. More important, in the medical field, Gore-Tex had always offered highly sophisticated products, not items typically found on drugstore shelves. To change the minds of his opponents, Spencer created the equivalent of clinical trials found in medicine. He asked customers to try Gore-Tex floss and compare it to the floss they currently used. Only after his colleagues saw compelling evidence that consumers preferred Gore-Tex's floss did they adopt his proposal.[8]

Uninvolved people process proposals differently. They are often easily distracted when listening to a pitch. They nod their heads in agreement even when they don't understand the point. For uninvolved people, if you have many arguments, however lightweight, you will be more persuasive than if you have just one or two strong arguments. Editors of popular magazines understand this. On their covers they run come-ons like "47 secrets to a happier relationship" or "29 ways to make a better speech." By the same token, if you repeat an argument several times, uninvolved decision makers are more likely to accept it. Uninvolved people are swayed by the apparent expertise or credibility of the advocate. Indeed, the strong credibility of an advocate can actually inhibit uninvolved decision makers' critical thinking: the decision makers tend to accept the idea on the basis of the advocate's credibility and not examine it closely. Proponents who are likable, attractive, and humorous tend to win over the uninvolved. Uninvolved decision makers are also likely to go along with an idea when they sense consensus among their colleagues. For them, even a catchy label makes an idea persuasive.

What if proponents have unimpeachable data and forceful arguments that unequivocally justify their proposals but they sense that decision makers are not involved in considering them? Then, before they attempt to persuade, they need to increase decision makers' involvement using a variety of techniques:[9]

Create a strong desire on the part of decision makers to make the correct decision. (You could say, for example, "We need to make sure we are completely correct about this decision. Are we all sure we have the necessary data to make a correct decision?")

Make the issue personally relevant to them (e.g., "This issue is one that will affect all of us for years to come. If we don't make the right decision, we'll all lose a lot of money, and our safety record might drop precipitously").

Put the proposal in writing. People are more likely to carefully consider what they read, assuming they do read it.

Convince them that the issue is important (e.g., "This decision will affect all of us").

Make the decision one that they feel responsible and accountable for (e.g., "Each of us will need to sign off on this proposal before it goes to the CEO. Whatever we decide, our names will be associated with it").

Generate suspicion about the issue or about the motives of people involved in the issue. When people are suspicious, they pay attention (e.g., "You have to wonder what they're trying to get us to do").

Remind them that they already know a lot about the issue (e.g., "All of you are experts about this. The issue is one you have heard about for years").

Raise their uncertainty about the issue by introducing an intriguing ambiguity (e.g., "All of us know this is an important decision, but all of us, I think, are unsure, right now, about which way to go. What do you think?").

Ask rhetorical questions (e.g., "Wouldn't you agree that. . . ?" "Doesn't this show. . . ?" "Don't you think. . . ?").[10]

Surprise them with unexpected information. People perk up and pay attention when an idea or a fact is counter to what they expect.

Create some fear (e.g., "Terrible things will happen if . . .").[11]

Make them angry. Angry people are more sensitive to the quality of arguments than people who are not angry.[12] Be careful before using this tactic!

Give them bad news. People in a bad mood are more likely to become involved in an issue and process ideas in analytic and skeptical ways.[13]

Those are all proven ways to encourage involvement. Now consider the opposite situation: you are dealing with highly involved decision makers, and your arguments may not be compelling. Here, distractions might help. When people are distracted, they don't process information as thoughtfully as they do when their attention is uninterrupted. Loud noises in the hallway or an interesting and highly emotional story may force listeners to split their attention between what you are proposing and the distraction. Because their attention is no longer focused solely on your message, they are less likely to generate good counterarguments to your idea. The value of distraction is why salespeople like meeting clients in crowded restaurants or at street-side cafés. An advocate who wants less scrutiny for an idea might also try to catch decision makers at other times when they are less thoughtful—when they are rushed, when they are experiencing information overload, or when they are likely to dismiss an idea as unimportant or irrelevant to them.

Managing Decision Makers' Core Concerns

In pitching any idea, proponents face resistance. People will talk about why proposals won't work or why they are too expensive or too difficult. They will tie up proposals in bureaucratic procedures, sentence potentially lucrative ideas to endless, futile debates, magnify small flaws in otherwise brilliant notions, and raise frivolous issues as a stalling tactic. These complaints often reflect people's fear of change. Robert Kahn, who was primarily responsible for inventing the concept of packet switching, a foundational aspect of the Internet, found that people didn't readily adopt his idea. "Packet switching," Kahn said, "did not get adopted right away because it was too challenging or too threatening or so counter-culture that nobody was basically able to make a decision to use the technology. I think this is a generic problem with most innovations: The more serious the innovation, the more likely there will be resistance to its acceptance. . . . It's as if the system has antibodies."[14]

Even before pitching ideas, seasoned advocates contemplate why decision makers might be hesitant about their proposals. Try this the next time you plan to promote an idea. First, list all the decision makers. Next to each name jot down why that person might resist your proposal. Maybe one person worries that your idea will rob him of power. Perhaps another worries that if your idea gets adopted, hers won't. When Jeffrey Brewer, the man who created CitySearch on the Web, discovered that his son suffered from juvenile diabetes, he began campaigning to create software-driven

BOX 4. WHAT DECISION MAKERS MAY FEAR

You are stepping on their turf.

Your proposal will threaten the comfortable status quo.

Your idea will challenge who and what they are in the organization.

They might lose status, position, power, or reputation.

You might succeed, and they dislike you or have a bad history with you.

Your proposal is risky, and failure might have serious consequences.

Current customers won't like the idea.

Implementing the idea will be difficult or will require more work on their part.

They might become burned out — there have been too many recent changes.

Your idea will eclipse their own.

Resources are insufficient to support the proposal.

Their unit will lose budget, people, or space.

equipment that would constantly monitor glucose levels and deliver insulin, only to discover that various decision makers had very different reasons to not create the software. Manufacturers worried about liability, researchers wanted to wait until every detail was perfected, and the Food and Drug Administration worried about computers making decisions that could kill a person.[15] To sell his idea, he had to deal with each of these parties and their different objections. Box 4 lists a number of reasons why people resist ideas. Reflecting on the possibilities is an important step in discovering ways to assuage decision makers' concerns.

People sometimes resist new ideas to protect their investment in their organizations. A new product or service might alter their firm's priorities and make their long years of work irrelevant. Years ago, some of the first working quartz watches were created by a Swiss watch industry consortium. After assessing the new watches, the Swiss watch companies decided not to go forward with them. Why? One reason was the massive infrastructure already established in Switzerland around mechanical watches — and the fear that customers would buy the new watches at the expense of the old. A Japanese company, Seiko, with far less investment in mechanical timepieces, quickly began producing watches using the new technology. The Swiss industry's hesitancy to adopt the quartz watch, which they themselves developed, cost them dearly. Before the Second World War, the Swiss watch industry controlled the vast majority of the watch market. They control far less now.

The fear of cannibalization — of selling a new product that eats away at the sales of an established product — is exceedingly common. It may have been one of the reasons Ford didn't initially introduce a minivan even through Ford engineers came up with the idea of a van called the Carousel in 1973. At that time, Ford was also producing a money-making station wagon called the Country Squire. Ford executives worried that the Carousel might challenge the Country Squire in the marketplace. Had Ford introduced the Carousel, it would have had a six- to seven-year lead in the minivan marketplace. Instead, Chrysler established its presence with a minivan of its own, and Ford played catch-up.

Advocates take people's reservations seriously, even those that seem nonsensical. Simply saying that an idea will not threaten what someone values isn't helpful. If the person *thinks* the idea poses a threat, it poses a threat, even if the threat is not specified. Sometimes people will say that they oppose an idea for one reason, but another reason underlies their explanation. A colleague might raise objections to the cost of a proposal, but what she is really saying is that she fears losing control of her budget. If you sense hidden reasons, address them. If you think the true reason for certain people's resistance to your proposal is their fear that they will be required to do more work, be sure your proposal requires little or no work on their part.

Anticipate Objections

Consider a meeting at which an inarticulate proponent touts his idea. He fumbles the answer to a question. Then, floundering, he fails to rebut a pointed objection. In response to the next question, a hostile one, our now-despondent champion offers an embarrassingly weak answer. What typically happens at this point? Other listeners rip into the speaker like sharks going after a blood-soaked towel. Contrast this to when a more adroit advocate pitches a proposal and, under questioning, proves unflappable. She offers more than ample answers and parries objections brilliantly. What happens here? Listeners lean back thinking to themselves, "This person knows her stuff."

The true measure of advocates' competency is not how they present their ideas. It is how well they handle what follows. With proper preparation, nearly anyone can make a presentation. What distinguishes successful proponents is their masterly ability to answer questions and objections.[16] In fact, in today's busy world, many decision makers don't even want formal presentations. They simply want their questions answered. Steve Ballmer, CEO of Microsoft, told the *New York Times* in 2009 that how he likes people to pitch ideas to him has changed. In the past, he sat through presentations. No longer. Instead, "I decided that's not what I want to do anymore. . . . So most meetings nowadays, you send me the materials and I read them in advance. And I can come in and say: 'I've got the following four questions. Please don't present the deck.'"[17]

So how do successful idea champions handle questions, objections, and concerns? For a start, they spend at least as much time contemplating how they will handle questions as they do scripting their pitches. Many naive advocates mistakenly spend all their time preparing their pitches. They craft slides, spin out arguments, and wordsmith their presentations. They need to remember that people might disagree with their proposals, that there might be pushback, that what is obvious to them might not be obvious to others. Little wonder that after presenting a proposal they often suffer humiliation as they flub answers and fumble objections. Before becoming chief justice of the U.S. Supreme Court, John Roberts was legendary for the legal arguments that he made as an attorney presenting cases before that Court. There, each side's attorney has just thirty minutes to present his or her arguments. But the thirty minutes is mostly spent responding to questions and objections from the nine Justices. Roberts was known for brilliantly handling these challenges. He was so successful because he over-prepared, sometimes spending five weeks preparing for a single thirty-minute presentation.[18] He would come up with hundreds of potential questions and then practice his responses whenever he had a few seconds. If he stumbled over a word, he chose a different word that he could readily pronounce.[19]

Advocates prepare *objection worksheets* to organize their thoughts (table 2). To create your own worksheet, jot down possible objections in one column. In the adjacent column, write potential responses to each one. For example, if a likely objection concerns cost, you might demonstrate that your proposal actually saves money compared to current offerings. Or you might show how much profits will accrue once the idea is implemented.

Table 2. Objection Worksheet

Possible Objection	Good Response	Follow-Up Objection	Effective Response to Follow-Up Objection
We don't have the money.			
Where will we get the talent?			
The idea won't get the return you say it will.			
Other			

Wise proponents go further than just planning responses to initial objections. They imagine possible follow-up questions and devise effective responses to those as well. The mark of true expertise doesn't lie in your ability to respond to the first question. It lies in your skill at answering follow-up questions.

In planning for objections, sophisticated advocates know that critics sometimes try to kill ideas by raising concerns about minor, sometimes even irrelevant, aspects of a proposal. So they are prepared to respond to questions about even the smallest details. Colonel John Boyd was a legendary master of advocacy for fighter tactics in the U.S. Air Force. At one briefing, when proposing to change the way the air force flew planes in combat, he was challenged by a senior officer who said to Boyd, then a major, "All of this work, this so-called theory of yours, has been done before . . . and it has all been proven wrong."

Boyd responded, "Colonel, show me the source document that says this has been done before."

"It was done at Edwards [Air Force base] and disproved."

"Do you have the name of the person at Edwards who did the work? . . . If you'll give me his name and show me that he did this work, I'll walk away from this project today."

"Rutowski."

"In the index of my briefing I refer to a 1954 article by E. S. Rutowski entitled 'Energy Approach to the General Aircraft Performance Problem.' Is that the same Rutowski?"

"It is."

"He developed what we know as the 'Rutowski Curve,' which is an optimization theory about the quickest way to reach an assigned altitude . . . but I don't believe it has anything to do with fighter aircraft, with pulling Gs, with maneuvering against an opponent. If I've overlooked something, Colonel, I'd be glad to hear about it."

Boyd clearly knew his stuff—even minor stuff. The colonel shut up and was not invited back to the next briefing by the general who had been present when Boyd responded so knowledgeably to the objection—and to the follow-up objections.[20]

Smart advocates also prepare for questions and objections through practice meetings. They ask trusted colleagues to role-play decision makers and to raise the most challenging questions imaginable. This kind of practice helps advocates hone their responses. In the military, officers who daily brief the chairman of the Joint Chiefs of Staff typically practice their presentation at least three times—once at 5:30 a.m. with colleagues, again at 6:30 a.m. with other colleagues, and then again at 7:30 a.m., this time with two generals. Called the Murder Boards, these sessions are filled with pointed questions and objections. Having gone through three Murder Boards, these officers have compelling answers ready for their upcoming briefing to the chairman.[21]

Proponents sometimes build their pitches around possible objections by incorporating answers to major objections in their presentations. They think about all the noes that might be forthcoming and build their argument on them. That way, they have dealt with the issues up front. Although preempting objections can be an excellent way to prepare presentations, superb advocates also know that one way to display their competency in front of decision makers is by letting listeners raise objections and then responding competently to them, seemingly extemporaneously. Whether or not they respond to every objection in an oral presentation, if they are wise, they make sure to respond to each important objection in the accompanying written materials. Often written material is distributed after meetings to people who couldn't attend, and no advocate wants those people to believe that there are glaring holes in the proposal. Some advocates include, as a last slide in a PowerPoint presentation, a "Frequently Asked Question" list, where they present potential objections and questions and offer incisive answers.

Here are some ground rules for preparing effective responses to objections.

Provide more information than people expect. While a simple yes or no may suffice, a more detailed explanation can bolster listeners' perceptions of your knowledge. A wiser answer might be, "Yes, and let me tell you why." Remember, an objection is an opportunity to further your case.

Turn questions and objections into positives. The mascot for the Democratic Party is the donkey. Its origins as a mascot may lie in the election of 1828, when opponents of candidate Andrew Jackson called him a jackass. Jackson smartly turned the insult into a positive by using a donkey on his campaign posters and telling his supporters that the donkey represented his stubbornness in refusing to bow to Big Business.

Flipping objections into positives is an old sales technique. When customers complained about how plain the instrument boards were on early mass-manufactured Ford automobiles, salespeople were coached to turn that complaint into a positive: "Just note the simplicity of that instrument board. Simple, plain, neat. Not one of those complex boards cluttered with instruments to watch and to fuss with."[22] Another way to turn negative comments into positive ones is by accepting the comments as astute and offering follow-through on the issue. When asked why shipments are so slow, a wise proponent might answer by saying, "You're right. It's essential that we speed up shipments. Let me tell you how we are going to do this."

Wise advocates also turn to general positive principles when challenged. Meg Whitman, the former CEO of eBay, ran for governor of California in the Republican primary of 2010. A moderate on social issues, she responded to questions on immigration, unions, and gay rights by saying, "I am happy to tell people where I stand on social issues, but I think, as Republicans and Californians, we have to lead with the things that will make the most difference in the near term. I don't want to exclude anyone from my campaign. I want everyone to be part of this. But let's rally around what we can mostly agree upon."[23]

Stay on message. Questions and objections can distract poorly prepared advocates. If someone raises a concern, the advocate may, in answering, start talking about issues unrelated to the concern. Shrewd proponents stay on message. They answer the question and bring the discussion back to what they want to discuss.

Avoid disagreeing directly. Rather than disagreeing, especially when concerns are relatively unimportant, advocates sometimes accept objections. If a suggestion doesn't change the core concept, why not go along with it? Even if an objection focuses on something crucial to the idea, perceptive advocates understand that direct refutations can backfire. So rather than saying, "No, you're wrong. It won't work," they might equivocate: "That's an interesting idea. We should certainly consider it."[24] By making a receptive but ambiguous comment, advocates aren't stuck either holding a publicly untenable position or giving in when they don't want to. Consider:

For years, whenever American diplomats were asked about the U.S. position on "two Chinas," China and Taiwan, they answered by saying that the United States had grave concerns about the relationship. What did "grave concerns" mean?

When Israeli spokespeople were asked about nuclear weapons, they traditionally answered by saying that their nation would not be the first to "introduce" nuclear weapons into the region. What does "introduce" really mean?

Alan Greenspan, the former head of the Federal Reserve, could be a master of equivocation. When he didn't want to directly answer a question from the media, he engaged in what he called constructive ambiguity: "I'll just say a little bit this way and a little bit that way, and I'll completely confuse them so there'll be no story."[25]

Be pleasant when answering objections. Treat each question as if it were a sincere request, and treat every objection as a real and deeply considered concern. More than one observer has suggested that Al Gore lost votes in his campaign to be president of the United States when he was seen rolling his eyes and sighing loudly during his first debate with George Bush in 2000. Gore wasn't alone in disrespecting the question-and-answer process. George Bush Sr. made the blunder of looking at his watch in the middle of being asked a question during an electoral debate with Bill Clinton in 1992.

When inexperienced advocates face a fusillade of challenges, they often get flustered and offer emotion-tinged responses that damage their credibility. Decision makers see emotional responses to questions as a signal that respondents are insecure.[26] Wise idea champions remain calm; they thank the questioner for raising a concern, then they answer the objection. One way to assure decision makers that their concerns are understood is to repeat and rephrase their questions before answering them. Not only does this signal that you grasp the issues, but it also gives you time to contemplate answers. It can also slow down the momentum of objections.

Don't gracelessly muddle through. When you don't have good answers, it doesn't help your case to offer inadequate and perhaps evasive responses to questions. If the person objecting is absolutely correct, don't get defensive; don't flounder about for answers. Just agree. Agreement disarms people who are expecting a spirited rebuttal. When the head of the famed Marshall Plan, Paul Hoffman, faced an objection when testifying to a congressional committee, he didn't fight. Instead, he would slap his knee and say, "Senator, you're entirely right. You've hit the nail on the head." Soon after that, the entire committee was working together trying to help Hoffman solve a problem they had just challenged him on.[27]

If the question is one that you don't have a good answer for, say so and promise to quickly get back to the questioner with an answer. Make sure you keep that promise. Bear in mind, too, that following up with someone provides an excellent opportunity to continue discussion of an idea.

If objections challenge important aspects of your proposal, and postponing the discussion isn't possible, advocates might reference principles underlying their proposal. In one meeting with private-sector executives, an advocate was pushing for increased funding for his charity. When challenged about where the money would come from, he offered a number of possibilities. But knowing that people might argue with his suggestions, he raised bigger issues, like the importance of doing what's right, being moral, being charitable. Even when decision makers disliked his suggestions about funding sources, they found themselves agreeing on the principles.

In the same way, when George W. Bush was questioned about how he reacted to so many people disagreeing with his decisions about Iraq, he often said that what is wonderful about the United States was that everyone has a right to an opinion. Notice that he didn't really answer the implied question — why people disagreed — but instead highlighted a principle that no one could disagree with.

What if there is no good answer to a question? Smart proponents sometimes turn to gentle humor. When President George H. W. Bush was accused by some in the media of having been born wealthy, he responded happily, "I couldn't help where I was born, I just wanted to be near my mother at the time."[28]

Avoid having a continuing debate with one person. There are various ways to respond to the problem questioner. If someone constantly challenges you during a meeting, you might suggest continuing the discussion after the meeting so that "in all fairness, everyone else will have the chance to hear the remainder of the presentation [or: ask questions, too]." Now, if the person raises another question, he or she is not being fair to colleagues. If you face relentless objections to your proposal, you might respond, "I'm confident this idea will work, but let me ask you a question: What would make you confident enough to support it?" Smart advocates sometimes even respond to continuing objections from someone by asking, "What would you do?" The question switches the burden to the person who is raising the concerns. When reporters like James Reston came into the Oval Office and critiqued Lyndon Johnson's management of the Vietnam War, Johnson sometimes took a yellow notepad and suggested that they sit down and write out the orders for tomorrow. They couldn't.[29] With that ploy Johnson taught them how difficult his decisions were. Finally, you might raise the stakes by conceding that there is truth to the objection and then asking, "If I can resolve this issue, is there anything that would stop us from adopting the proposal?"

Get senior people to support your position when you are attacked. In defusing attacks it is sometimes crucial to get senior leaders — perhaps a sponsor — involved in publicly supporting your idea. (As we saw, this may be the only way to deal with cynics.) In the late 1940s, for example, the United States began the monumental aid program for Europe called the Marshall Plan. Millions and millions of dollars of aid was shipped to destitute nations suffering in the aftermath of the Second World War. One of the administrators of the plan was Paul Nitze. Nitze was called to the U.S. House of Representatives Appropriations Committee to testify about the program. In preparing for the session, Nitze and his assistants created detailed summaries of every spending initiative and packaged those summaries in brown books. The chair of the committee was Congressman John Taber, who strongly disliked the Marshall Plan.

At the start of the hearing, Taber insisted that Nitze not refer to the brown books. Then he began quizzing Nitze about the plan's budget, knowing that Nitze couldn't answer every question about an appropriations bill filled with thousands and thousands of items. Nitze's background was finance, but rather than focusing on Nitze's strength, Taber raised questions about agricultural aid (e.g., why the United States was sending 25,000 tons of pulse to Austria when Austrian farmers ought to be able to grow legumes themselves). Nitze asked if he might let the individual in charge of agriculture funding respond. Taber said no. Nitze was at a loss to explain the specific issue of the pulse. Then Taber attacked another minor item (tractors), and when Nitze couldn't offer a detailed explanation, Taber left the hearing and called Nitze's boss, Robert Lovett, the undersecretary of state, to complain. What did Lovett do?

Lovett said to Taber, "You know, I could ask you a question that you couldn't answer. For example, how many rivets are there in a B-28 wing?"

Taber replied, "You would know that better than I because you were the Assistant Secretary of War for Air in World War II."

"Well," Lovett said, "that's just the point. Some people are more knowledgeable about certain matters than other people. So why don't you let Nitze have his experts answer those technical questions?" Then before Taber could even answer, Lovett threw out another question: "If it takes eight yards of pink crepe paper to go around an elephant's leg, how long does it take to kill a fly with a flyswatter?"

Taber replied, "That's a nonsensical question."

Lovett said, "Of course! Now why don't you stop asking Nitze nonsensical questions?"[30]

After that conversation, Taber stopping raising minor objections, and, in the end, Congress approved the budget for the Marshall Plan. It took senior-level involvement from Lovett to convince Taber to stop his draconian questioning.

Figure out the real objection. Often what people object to isn't their real concern. Shrewd advocates listen astutely to questions and objections and figure out the underlying real concerns (see box 4). As a general rule, people believe they have good reasons for opposing new ideas. For instance, a high-flying petroleum company engineer was asked to examine why a piece of field equipment kept breaking. After studying the problem, he arrived at an ingenious solution and then was flabbergasted when field managers didn't immediately adopt it. In fact, they created a far more costly and less effective short-term solution. What he later discovered was that because he was seen as a "fast tracker," field managers saw him as a threat. If his idea had been adopted, executives at the company headquarters might have used his innovation to justify taking power away from the field managers.

Great opportunities are lost because decision makers feel committed to another product or service. In the early 1980s, Paul Mercer, one of the major designers of software for many Apple products, found a way to get Macintosh software to run on a hand-held computer. As Mercer admits, his understanding of corporate politics was not nearly as good as his software. Apple's CEO at that time, John Sculley, told him that since Apple had signed an agreement with Sharp Electronics to create what became the Newton PDA, the company didn't want to make a product that competed with it. So Mercer's idea went nowhere.[31] The same was true at Xerox's PARC when engineers in Palo Alto attempted to convince Xerox's leadership to bring to market the Alto, the personal computer they had created. They faced strong political resistance from Xerox's office-machine group headquartered in Dallas because Dallas could not make its sales goals if the machine was introduced. The Dallas group "had to sandbag the Alto because with it they wouldn't make their numbers and therefore wouldn't get their bonuses," says John Ellenby, who was in charge of producing the Alto.[32]

Sometimes people object to an idea for symbolic or political reasons. In the Washington, D.C., area, the Metro system is run by a board of directors composed of representatives from the different regions that the subway serves (District of Columbia, Maryland, and Virginia). When general manager John Catoe proposed raising subway and parking fares in 2007, he faced an avalanche of objections from board members. Although the representatives must have grasped the need for fee increases, they also understood the political value of publicly raising objections and, as a former board member says, making it "look like they [board members] are looking after the riders."[33] Serious discussions about fares could begin only after everyone publicly challenged the proposal.

Act surprised only when you are not surprised. Every good advocate is a bit of an actor. When a question comes out of left field, smart proponents act as though they expected that particular question. For an advocate to act prepared reassures people that the advocate is prepared. Being totally mystified by a question indicates less than thorough research. On the other hand, canny advocates sometimes feign surprise when a softball question is lobbed their way. For the proponent to act surprised makes the questioner feel better and gives the proponent a chance to seem contemplative about an issue he or she already knows how to address.

Have one or more contingency plans ready. In case you are surprised by a bevy of complaints from different people about your proposals, have at least one backup plan. Having a Plan B is one hallmark of successful advocates. They never assume that their proposal is an either-or proposition. They know that there are always compromise positions that can get them part of what they want. You might propose seeking customer feedback on the idea, or conducting a pilot project, instead of simply surrendering. Moves like these encourage objectors to work with you rather than challenge you.

Think about Implementation

Inventing the electric light bulb took years, but consider what else was required before it could ever be used: wiring, outlets, generating stations, standards, and so on. Implementing even seemingly simple ideas can be incredibly complicated.

Opponents often quash proposals by raising implementation concerns. The fatal question may be as simple as "Who has the time to take this on?" or "Who has the budget to support the proposal?" When no one volunteers time or money, the idea fades from the discussion. Or opponents may insist that advocates lay out every last step necessary to accomplish a project. Each step requires work, and the more work there is, the less open people are to taking that first step. When implementation issues are unpacked, people believe that projects will take much longer than perhaps they actually will.[34]

Because implementation is such a difficult hurdle on the way to winning approval for a proposal, smart proponents cobble together ways to assure people that implementation is possible. Before pitching any ideas, they grapple with questions like these: Who will be responsible for implementation? Where will the money come from? What obstacles will we have to overcome to make this idea a reality? They contemplate how every group along the value chain affects, and is affected by, their ideas; they know that changes in one part of an organization may create all sorts of problems elsewhere. Marketing may propose a product that R&D knows will take years to develop; R&D may design a product that people in distribution know will be a nightmare to get out the door; salespeople may promise follow-through that customer support knows is impossible. When questioned about the how of an idea, wise advocates will have devised compelling answers.

Handle Negativity Bias

Let's say you are presenting an idea in a meeting. Admittedly, there are some flaws in the notion, but they aren't that important, and the positives clearly outweigh the negatives. Yet everything brought up about your idea emphasizes the negatives. Minor problems are magnified, and many of the idea's impressive strengths never get mentioned. You are experiencing what is known as the negativity bias: giving negatives too much weight when making judgments.[35] Not only do negatives have a bigger effect on how people judge ideas than positive or neutral data do, but people remember negatives longer as well.[36]

The negativity bias plays out in many ways. For instance, when a decision maker has a bad experience with something that is being proposed — even a minor bad experience — he may reject the entire notion out of hand. When Xerox PARC scientists were trying to persuade the company to have a mouse on the Star computer, one marketing executive fought the idea. Charles Irby, then director of the company's Advanced Development group, recalls: "The first time he'd ever used a mouse he'd had a bad experience — apparently he'd used a dirty one that didn't track right. So for two years he was against our using it, while we spent all of our time on user studies and tests to show him it was the right thing. We spent at least $1 million of Xerox resources proving that it was better than a cursor button or touch screen, which is what he wanted. Finally we presented all these findings to him at a meeting — and he still wouldn't go for it!" Irby ended up screaming, "We're going to use the mouse!" and left the meeting. The marketing fellow gave in.[37]

Enterprising proponents can exploit the negativity bias. For instance, they can highlight the terrible consequences of not adopting their proposals.[38] They can hint about the regret that decision makers will feel if they reject their proposals.[39] When people consider how they will hate themselves later for not adopting an idea, they are more prone to buy into it.[40] Enterprising advocates can also make their ideas seem like safer alternatives than the status quo.[41] They can reassure decision makers that what is being proposed isn't too different from the conventional ideas that the decision makers feel comfortable with. At the very least, savvy proponents understand that if they can make every other alternative look worse, their notions may get adopted.

Push (or Don't Push) Hot Buttons

A person's hot buttons are the things that make him or her figuratively explode. If you walk into a meeting and make a sexist joke, you have probably pushed someone's hot button. If you tease a colleague about a moment of humiliation, you have pushed her hot button. If you propose adding a team member who your boss despises, you have pushed his hot button. Hitting a decision maker's hot button means, at best, that she will stop listening to your idea. At worst, she becomes adamantly opposed to it.

Anything can be a hot-button issue. In one part of a large technology company, decision makers prefer crisp PowerPoint presentations — anything less sparks suspicions of sloppiness. In another part of the same organization, decision makers pride themselves on consensus building: ideas, and decisions about ideas, emerge from conversations. They would be alienated by a sparkling prepackaged slide show.

When promoting ideas, you should know and avoid decision makers' hot buttons. Sometimes, though, hitting a hot button is unavoidable. When that happens, advocates frame their pitches before raising the hot-button issue. They might forewarn people that they are going to be talking about something that may prove upsetting. They might save the hot-button issue until the decision makers are comfortable with the general idea they are raising.

Sometimes, however, advocates push hot buttons strategically. Terrence Murray, the successful CEO of Fleet Financial, grew his business by acquiring competitors. In 1986 he purchased Norstar Bancorp of Albany. When Connecticut bank regulators found out, they demanded that he divest a Fleet subsidiary in their state. Murray didn't want to, so he hatched a clever plan. Knowing that Japanese firms were then aggressively buying banks, Murray found four local Asian citizens and publicly walked with them around downtown Hartford. He told local politicians, "They're interested in our bank here. . . . I'm sorry I can't disclose more." Almost overnight, the politicians, fearful of a possible Japanese purchase, passed a new law allowing Murray to keep his subsidiary. What Murray did was tap a hot button of local politicians.[42]

How do you discover people's hot buttons? Listen to how people react when things come up in meetings. Watch their nonverbals. When in doubt, be careful. Don't raise issues unrelated to your notions that are often hot buttons (e.g., risqué humor, politics, religion).

One last piece of advice: know your own hot buttons and learn to control your emotional reactions when those hot buttons are pressed in meetings. In one organization, a senior manager had an uncanny ability to figure out his peers' hot buttons. Immediately before or at important meetings, he would sometimes provoke a colleague with his or her hot-button issue. The colleague often lost his or her cool and ended up looking bad in the session. The colleague's credibility would suffer as she or he stuttered or stammered, got defensive, or seemed overemotional. Savvy people know their hot buttons and monitor their reactions carefully. They never give away how upset they are.

Working within the Organizational Context

Advocates must grasp the unwritten rules of their organization. Who matters isn't always obvious, as we have seen. In service-related organizations, marketing people often hold sway; in manufacturing firms, factory and distribution people often have a large say in decisions. These are not formal rules, but everyone understands that is the way things are. In some organizations you must get the buy-in of lower-level people before you address decision makers. On Capitol Hill in Washington, staff members often block efforts of lobbyists who sneak around them and pitch ideas directly to their bosses. So wise lobbyists secure staff support first. The chain of command matters in many firms. You must marshal the support of your immediate management before making a proposal to higher-level management. In other firms, the chain of command may be less relevant, but there are still unofficial rules. For instance, it may be important to get the okay from units affected by an idea before promoting it more broadly within the organization. Thus, a marketing proposal may require the sales organization's approval before top management buys it, since marketing-related notions, while easy and fun to imagine, often are fraught with difficulties when it comes to implementation. Similarly, R&D might seek marketing's early acceptance of ideas because of marketers' better sense about what sells. In other firms, advocates don't need to get the buy-in of other units before pitching ideas. They seek forgiveness rather than permission.

Approaches to Innovation

The ways organizations approach innovation shape how advocates pitch their notions. If a firm views innovations warily, advocates propose ideas differently than they would in a firm that celebrates innovation. Generally, organizations fall into one of four categories based on their approach to innovation. They are:

- prospectors
- analyzers
- defenders
- reactors

Some organizations pride themselves on being first in the marketplace with new products and services. We can call organizations in this category *prospectors*. They seek out and exploit new and often radical opportunities. Viewing themselves as change leaders, they feel that their reputation rides on innovation. They calibrate their success using such metrics as the percentage of profits and sales generated from new products. While recognizing that being first in the market with a new product or service is dicey, they nonetheless find the potential of innovative ideas worth the risk. Prospectors continually scan the world for ideas that might lead to imaginative new products and services. They often have decentralized decision making, respond quickly to market changes, and have marketing and R&D people in dominant roles in their leadership.[43] In the early twenty-first century, companies like Apple and Google might be considered prospectors.

Firms in the second category are *analyzers*. They avoid being on the cutting edge of new ideas, since they don't want the risks that prospectors face. But when prospectors' innovations succeed, analyzers quickly latch onto them, enhancing them to make them profitable additions to their own arsenals. They prefer ideas that fit nicely with their strategy. If prospectors are pioneers, then analyzers are settlers. For instance, Acer, the Taiwanese computer company, is an analyzer. Its chairman, J. T. Wang, says, "We can be No. 2. It's O.K. with us." As *Business Week* reports, Acer let its rival Asustek come up with the first netbook. After Asustek proved that the technology would sell, Acer quickly entered the market and took over the number one spot.[44]

Defenders compose a third category. Defenders seek stable, secure, and profitable niches and protect them through quality, service, and price. They pass on new opportunities outside their business domain, relying instead on traditionally successful products and services. They won't invest in innovations that don't directly and significantly enhance their current operations. They celebrate operational efficiencies and being customer-driven. They adopt what are essentially extensions of current offerings. Often run by people involved in production or financial operations, defenders spend significantly less money on marketing and R&D than prospectors do.[45] What would be a good example of a defender company in the United States in the early twenty-first century — Southwest Airlines? It was a prospector years ago. But today, not much radically new emerges from Southwest.

Finally, there are *reactor* companies. They respond to new ideas only when the marketplace forces them to. New and innovative ideas are the furthest things from their minds. They react quickly when they have to, but they often lack any strategic rationale for the changes they make. Reactors are like the Whack-a-Mole arcade game. A mole randomly pops out of one of numerous holes, and the player pounds it back down; another mole pops out, and the player whacks that one. Which companies have reactor cultures today? Maybe the legacy airlines, perhaps many law firms.

In large firms, separate units may fall into each of these four categories. The finance team might consist of analyzers, the marketers might be prospectors, the legal people might be reactors, and the operations team members might be defenders. Smart advocates strategically adapt how they pitch their ideas to fit the culture of innovation. Boasting that a notion is a radical leap forward may resonate with prospectors and perhaps analyzers but not with defenders. Referencing what competitor companies are doing will probably excite analyzers and defenders far more than prospectors.[46] Suggesting that crucial long-term customers like an idea might engage defender and reactor firms, but using terms like "breakthrough technology" and "cutting edge" wouldn't be helpful. You will want to call your idea innovative with prospectors and proven with analyzers. You will want to talk about customer demand with defenders and crises with reactors.

When Tim Berners-Lee sought support from CERN management for what became the World Wide Web, he pitched it as a way to create a documentation system instead of what it really was — a hypertext system.[47] He knew CERN's culture well enough to realize that a radical proposal would never sell. What he proposed would extend what CERN already had. And even when pitching his idea as a documentation system, he was conservative about what he promised the system could do. While privately imagining a technology that integrated all CERN documents (what we know as the World Wide Web today), he knew that past tries at integration had failed miserably. That meant that the management would probably reject another attempt. So he touted his idea as one that could store CERN's telephone directory, which the defender-type decision makers saw as eminently doable and valuable.[48]

Tollgates

Many organizations have onerous formal reviews (often called stage-gates or decision points) that ideas must pass to get adopted. The purpose of these reviews is admirable: to stop bad ideas from moving forward and to trigger alarms when projects stray off course. Common screening criteria include the potential market for an idea, competitors, product superiority and uniqueness, compatibility with company resources and offerings, barriers to market entry, market needs, innovativeness, expected profitability, development risks, talent availability, and the strategic and cultural fit of the idea to the organization.[49]

Advocates must pass through their firms' tollgates if their ideas are ever to see the light of day. Jeffrey Immelt, early in his tenure as CEO of General Electric (GE), decided to increase research spending. But he mandated that researchers submit proposals. Out of the two thousand or so proposals, GE chose just twenty. The criteria for getting a green light were straightforward. The ideas had to concern "big areas, important technologies" that fit within GE's chosen markets. Researchers were quizzed about whether their idea fell within a business area that the company understood, whether people at the company were interested in the idea, and whether the idea addressed a growing industry.[50] Similarly, at Gore-Tex, new ideas were checked over the course of years in a process called Real, Win, Worth. Along the way questions like these were asked: "Is the opportunity real? Is there really somebody out there that will buy this? Can we win? What do the economics look like? Can we make money doing this? Is it unique and valuable? Can we have a sustained advantage (e.g., patent)?"[51]

Although seasoned advocates know what it takes to successfully pass through internal tollgates in their companies, they also understand that they must sometimes go around them. Sometimes the guardians at the established tollgates can thwart the adoption of creative and potentially valuable ideas. Maybe an idea is too radical or risky. Maybe it doesn't fit established categories of business. It is when proponents work around or even ignore management's mandates to stop work on a project that they take career risks. Sony's PlayStation would never exist if its advocate had stopped working on the project after it failed to pass initial reviews. Nor would we have Post-it Notes if Art Fry had not circumvented the established decision-making process within 3M, where many of Fry's immediate bosses saw little value in selling scraps of paper.

8

Network!

I don't consider I have power.
I have relationships.

LEW WASSERMAN

Organizations have many forms of capital. They have financial capital—money on hand. They have human capital—people who make products, sell to customers, manage the books, and handle all the other tasks that keep an organization alive. They have intellectual capital, political capital, and resource capital. Most important for advocacy is *social capital*—the priceless interaction of people working together within the firm. Things get done and ideas get adopted when people connect with one another. "The oil of politics is personal relationships," says former U.S. Senator Alan Simpson, and the same is true in organizations. Capable advocates champion ideas through networks of people. They use their social capital.[1]

Too often, networking is viewed merely as a way to further careers—to gain jobs and promotions. It is true that networking yields both. Many people find positions through their networks, and well-networked people are promoted earlier and more often than poorly networked people. Nonetheless, in today's world, networking has other valuable uses besides locating jobs. It contributes to creativity, personal success, and, most important for this book, influence.

Ask yourself, What portion of your work do you accomplish all by yourself? The amount may be quite small: 5–10 percent. Two generations ago, most people's estimates would have been much larger. Expertise today is more about gleaning knowledge from others. In other words, it is not so much what you know but who you know who knows what you need to know that counts.

In flea markets and bazaars around the world, it is difficult to gather accurate information about what to buy, who to buy from, and how much to pay. The secret to finding good deals is to have a large and astute network among the people who work in the marketplace. They can tell you who has the freshest fruit or the best-quality rugs. They can whisper who cheats and who is honest. More formal organizations aren't that different from these marketplaces. Every firm has a massive amount of unpublished knowledge. People with well-developed networks get the scoop first — secrets, informal cautions, and the newest gossip. They learn who is in and who is out, which bosses count and which don't, when the best time to pitch ideas is, what hidden traps might doom advocacy moves, which ways to frame arguments and promote ideas with different people. As Connie Duckworth, a former partner at Goldman Sachs and the founder of ARZU, a social entrepreneurship organization, said, "Networking is the glue of all business — it's the foundation of how business gets done. Your relationships drive how successful you will be."[2] She is right. Well-networked people get larger raises and are more influential than people with poor networks.[3] Teams with well-networked managers are more effective.[4] And employees are more satisfied when they believe the people they associate with, like their bosses, can influence organizational decisions.[5]

Well-networked people also produce higher-quality ideas that perform better in the marketplace.[6] The psychologist Dean Keith Simonton conducted a comprehensive historical analysis of the lives of more than two thousand famous scientists and inventors and found that the myth of the lone genius was just that, a myth. In fact, successful innovators were surrounded by smart people with whom they talked and collaborated.[7] In a world where money for research is always important, scientists with better networks attract more resources.[8] Even at the earliest stages of devising new products, the more frequent and thorough the communication among various people with expertise relevant to the nascent ideas, the more likely those products will succeed.

Informal networks are crucial for diffusing new ideas, and ideas are more likely to be adopted when diverse networks of people inside the firm support them.[9] So savvy champions constantly refine their networks. Knowing that people are the source of the best information, they spend more time soliciting ideas from others than they do searching for ideas in written documents.[10] They rely on their networks to accomplish what the formal structure of their firm doesn't allow. A DuPont scientist wanted to create a new biodegradable material. To prove that it could be fabricated, he utilized his informal relationship with people in manufacturing to produce sample material. Later, he asked his network of potential customers to raise the idea with his senior managers.[11] In many innovative industrial companies, researchers often use their informal networks with plant managers to surreptitiously complete prototypes, sometimes despite direct orders not to spend plant time producing them; and salespeople sweet-talk researchers into creating nifty innovations that customers want despite what management sometimes thinks best.

Your Network Today

How many people do you have at least a nodding acquaintance with? "Nodding" means that you and the other person would, minimally, recognize each other. You may not remember his or her name or what she or he does, but you could comfortably nod in recognition as you passed in a hallway or at the mall. Most people who consider this question arrive at a number between 500 and 600. Many people calculate over a thousand. This little mind exercise proves a basic fact: you already have a large network.

How many times have you met a stranger and, in the midst of a conversation, discovered that you two know someone in common? In 1967 two psychologists, Jeffrey Travers and Stanley Milgram, hoping to quantify the odds of this happening, asked people in Omaha, Nebraska, to get a letter to a stranger living in Boston. The Omaha participants could forward the letter only to people they knew on a first-name basis and who might, in turn, know someone who knew the Boston resident. Amazingly, the median number of hand-offs (Person A sends the letter to Person B is one hand-off; Person B passes it on to Person C is a second hand-off) was between five and six. This result led Travers and Milgram to famously suggest that we are connected to everyone else by "six degrees of separation."[12]

More recent studies suggest the number has fallen to even fewer hand-offs. Are you skeptical of this number? Then imagine that tomorrow, as you are walking down a street, a man collapses in front of you. When you bend down to help him, he whispers a secret so important that you must find a way to meet with the president of the United States within ten days. You can't reveal the secret to anyone else. If you achieve a meeting with the president through your network, you save the world. If you can't, the world implodes. Can you do it? When most people think about this scenario for a while, they discover a way. They begin to think, "Well, I know somebody who is married to someone who knows someone . . ."

The maxim "It's who you know that matters" is true, then, to some degree. But what's far more important is who knows *you!* Knowing lots of people doesn't mean much unless those people also know you. And they know what you know. Will they return your calls and promptly answer your e-mails? Will they think of you immediately when opportunities arise? You must make yourself memorable in positive ways. Smart networkers carry business cards with them, and when meeting people, they say or do something that helps others remember them (e.g., they use a memorable tagline, they tell funny stories, they dress distinctively). Beyond being sociable, advocates engage in a variety of actions that help them not only to stay memorable but also to build support for their ideas. Those actions are what the rest of this chapter is about.

Becoming a Network Entrepreneur

Stay Nearby

Thomas Edison, America's greatest inventor (he has more patents to his name than anyone else), placed all his workers in a single big laboratory in Menlo Park, New Jersey. When a worker had a eureka moment, everyone else instantly knew it. Menlo Park's proximity to New York offered Edison a marketing advantage, too. Reporters could visit and hear about his newest brainstorm.[13] Edison understood that out of sight means out of mind. The likelihood of two people talking with each other is determined, in large part, by the physical distance between them. If someone sits right next to you, you can easily talk with her; if she is in another building, or downstairs, or even just seventy-five feet away, your likelihood of chatting decreases substantially.[14]

Working closely together in an office is only one sort of workplace proximity. When Nobel laureate James Watson became head of the internationally renowned Cold Spring Harbor laboratory, he promptly renovated the cafeteria. Watson believed that some of the most important informal conversations in research organizations happen in cafeterias. So he made the cafeteria a place that invited people to sit down and spend time with one another. He brightened the walls and replaced small tables with larger ones. Larger tables led, he thought, to more informal conversations with more people. From those exchanges he hoped sparks of creativity might emerge that would ignite great discoveries.[15] Knowledge is social.

Advocates understand the benefits of proximity. If your office is located close to decision makers, you have more and better chances of influencing them. That is why senior advisors in the White House wrestle for the right to occupy cubbyholes in the West Wing within yards of the Oval Office rather than huge, high-ceiling offices with fireplaces in the Eisenhower Old Executive Office Building across the street from the West Wing. Henry Kissinger, Nixon's national security advisor, coined the term "rule of proximity." He said, "The security advisor is down the hall from the President. The cabinet members are ten minutes away by car. You wouldn't think that it would make any conceivable difference, because it takes you ten minutes to set up an appointment with the President if you are in the building. But the proximity of the security advisor [to the president] just makes it easier to call him [the national security advisor] in."[16]

The number of ways you can create proximity with decision makers is limited only by your imagination. You can attend meetings that decision makers are attending. California-based software engineer Rick Osterloh was visiting Motorola's headquarters in Chicago. The recently appointed CEO of Motorola, Sanjay Jha, was holding a town meeting that Osterloh just happened to attend. In his speech, Jha mentioned the Android operating system being created by Google. As Jha left the stage, Osterloh ran up, introduced himself, and told Jha that his team was working on an Android-based phone in California. A few days later, Osterloh flew with Jha to San Jose, where he successfully pitched his phone idea to Jha. Motorola soon introduced Osterloh's phone.[17]

If golf is the favorite sport of decision makers in your firm, you can learn to play. Ditto with poker or bridge. You can volunteer for community activities and committees within your organization that place you near decision makers in informal settings. You can show up at the office when you know they will be there, even though it is a holiday or a weekend. You can place yourself in a vital networking location — as Lyndon Johnson did.

In the 1930s the future president moved to Washington, D.C., to work for a Texas congressman. Aiming to have influence on Capitol Hill, Johnson rented a room in the nearby Dodge Hotel, where many congressional aides resided. Each day he visited the communal bathroom numerous times. He brushed his teeth, went to his room, and returned to brush his teeth again. He showered, went to his room, and returned to shower again. His goal was simple: to meet as many of the other staffers as he could, and where better to meet everyone but in the bathroom? The strategy worked. Johnson was quickly elected head of the association of staff assistants.[18] Later on, as a young congressman, Johnson endeared himself to the powerful Speaker of the House of Representatives, Sam Rayburn, a bachelor, by inviting Rayburn to his home every Sunday for a family meal. The meal gave Johnson private time with someone most young members of Congress never got a chance to know. When Johnson was elected to the Senate, he befriended one of the most powerful members of the Senate, Richard Russell. Knowing that Russell loved baseball, Johnson became a baseball fan, spending many afternoons sitting right next to Russell at Washington Senators' games.[19] Johnson understood a maxim of networking: put yourself in the place of most potential.

More and more people are working online, oftentimes far from people they need to connect with. Out of sight often means out of mind. How do effective networkers develop and maintain relationships from a distance? Broadly speaking, they create a symbolic sense of proximity. They are memorable in audio conferences, they volunteer to coordinate the efforts of their dispersed team, they use their name when speaking in audio conferences ("This is John. What I have been hearing . . ."), they are impressively responsive to e-mails, they appear professional in video conferences, they generously adapt to others time zones, they surprise network colleagues by sometimes unexpectedly showing up at their physical site, and they make it a point to meet up with people on their trips to other company locations.

Stay in Touch

You never know when someone in your network may become a vital connection. When Bob Woodward was a young naval officer in Washington, D.C., in 1970, he was ordered to deliver some papers to the White House. Once there, he found himself sitting next to an older man outside the Situation Room. Woodward started up a conversation, and when he discovered that the man was a senior member of the FBI, Woodward asked his advice about what he should do when he left the navy. Afterward, Woodward kept in touch with the FBI executive, and years later, when Woodward was a young *Washington Post* reporter assigned to cover a seemingly minor burglary at the Watergate Hotel, his relationship with this FBI agent proved invaluable. The FBI agent was Mark Felt, who, under the cover name of Deep Throat, became Woodward's most important source. Without Deep Throat, Woodward probably would not have won the Pulitzer Prize for covering a key moment in the downfall of the Nixon presidency. Staying in touch with Felt mattered.

Most of us regret not keeping in touch with certain old friends. There was that high-school buddy who went to a different college. There was the coworker we lunched with every day for four years until we left the company. There was the neighbor who did little favors for us when we lived next door. Today that high-school friend is a well-known physician, the coworker has moved into a senior position at a prestigious company, and the neighbor was recently elected mayor. In the meantime, your daughter might need medical attention, you might like a job in the company your former coworker runs, and the street you live on might require repaving. If you had stayed in touch with these people, it would be easy to call them. On the other hand, calling them up and saying, "Hi, you may not remember me, but . . ." is awkward and normally unprofitable. The smart networker stays in touch with people. We never know who might help us down the road.

Staying in touch isn't a big deal. As an adult, you need to be in touch only once every few years to keep people's memories of you fresh. How do you arrange that? One advocate uses the address book that his e-mail program automatically creates. Every six months or so he scans the names and considers whether he has been in touch with each person. If he hasn't, he makes it a priority to do so. You don't need a significant reason to write or call. One idea champion calls people in his network at the start of each new year and says, "I made it my New Year's resolution to get back in touch with people I haven't seen for a while. When can we have lunch?" Another sends Valentine's Day cards to friends.

Savvy networkers find ways to continue their exchanges with people they meet. Writing a thank-you note after a meeting brings your name back to mind. When you run into people, spend a few minutes rehashing old times and talking about what is happening now in both of your lives. A consummate salesperson easily turns a twenty-minute meeting into four different conversations. Let's say our salesperson has a face-to-face meeting with a client scheduled for tomorrow. Today our salesperson calls the client to confirm the meeting and e-mails documents in preparation for tomorrow's meeting. The next day, during the meeting, our enterprising salesperson promises to send certain information to the client. Sure enough, the next morning the client receives an express-mail envelope. The day after, our salesperson calls to ensure that the promised information arrived and to plan a second meeting. One meeting has resulted in four exchanges, and as any salesperson knows, the frequency of your interactions with clients matters at least as much as their duration.

These days people often stay in touch using such social media as Facebook and LinkedIn. These Internet sites are excellent places for discovering interconnections among people and for staying in touch with what is happening in people's lives. But simply having a connection doesn't guarantee that the connection is meaningful. Even in today's wired world, face-to-face networking is still the paramount way of staying in touch with people that matter.

One last point: When you need friends, it is too late to make them. So be in touch before you need others' help.

Keep Building Your Network

Good advocates constantly expand their networks. They seize opportunities to meet new people. They implicitly understand Metcalfe's Law, named after the technology pioneer Robert Metcalfe. The law states that the value of a network is proportional to the square of the number of its users. Although Metcalfe was counting Ethernet purchases and connections, the maxim has a social meaning as well: every time you add another person to your network, your potential influence grows exponentially.[20]

There are numerous ways to continually build networks. Make it a point to meet a new person every day. Look for community activities that link people. Join professional associations. Volunteer to become part of the membership committee. Pass out name tags at events, which ensures that you meet everyone attending. Meet people who know people, and let them introduce you to others. When Barack Obama first moved to Chicago in the 1980s, he was befriended by Abner Mivka, an old and well-connected Windy City politician. Mikva says Obama knew how you network. "I remember our first few meetings. He would say, 'Do you know So-and so?' and I'd say yes. 'How well do you know him? I'd really like to meet him.' I would set up some lunches."[21]

A couple of cautions. First, there are people you may not want to get to know — for example, someone with a terrible reputation or someone who will take unfair advantage of you. Second, it is easy to become overbearing and obtrusive, garnering a reputation that encourages people to run when they see you coming. That will happen if you become a network stalker, viewing every event or meeting as a networking opportunity, if you walk into every reception and frantically try to shake everyone's hand and leave business cards with anyone who will take them. Finally, it is worth reminding yourself that networking is about getting to know people. One mistake that eager networkers make is trying to meet as many people as they can without ever really developing more than superficial relationships with them. People see that kind of networking as opportunistic. That networker isn't winning friends.

Become the Parent of Relationships

Bill Gates was, according to some people, discovered by IBM through the efforts of his mother, Mary Gates, who sat on the board of directors of the United Way with a senior IBM executive. The connection gave Gates the link he needed to convince IBM that they should consider his software. Gates's mother was the parent of Gates's relationship with IBM.

Mary Gates may have understood that a nifty way of networking is to connect people who are disconnected.[22] In a roomful of married people, ask how many met their spouses through third parties. Some hands will shoot up. Ask these people who that third party was, and with no hesitation, they will mention a name. Ask them if they owe that person and, to the degree that they are still happily married, they will nod. The introducers played a vital networking role. Successful salespeople are often masters of creating new relationships for their customers. A salesperson has a client who bemoans her inability to find a good vendor for some equipment. The salesperson has another client whose firm offers exactly what the first person needs. The salesperson suggests to both of them, "Why don't I get you two together for lunch?" If the two hit it off, both of them owe the salesperson. This sort of networking can pay off for everyone. Network brokers are more likely to get promoted and are far more influential within their organizations than are nonbrokers.[23] (There are always risks. Perhaps you introduce two people to one another and later one of them causes trouble for the other.)

Good networkers may create environments in which people can interact. For instance, a senior member of Congress was famous for stocking his office with food. When Congress was in session late into the night, members would wander in looking for a snack. Their presence in the office gave the congressman (and his staff) the opportunity to chat with them informally. The technician with the Indonesian coffee in her office, like the salesman with an always-full candy bowl on his desk, has opportunities to network that others miss.

Focus on Power, Not Position

Successful advocates wisely develop strong networks with powerful decision makers long before they pitch their ideas. They also build sturdy ties with people who can influence decision makers.[24] They never ignore the gatekeepers — the mid-level staff members, administrative assistants, and schedulers who control access to the decision makers — because they often have enormous influence on decision makers. As one executive said, "Keep my admin happy and I'm happy!" The father of the European Union, Jean Monnet, was extraordinarily talented at crafting networks of bureaucrats in governments throughout Europe who supported his ideas. As one of his biographers writes, "He was adept at locating unknowns behind the government façade, irrespective of their age, status, or experience, who exercised influence over [those with] crucial power, provided a route to them, or simply conveyed important information. He had no snobbery. A useful contact would be cultivated as carefully as a prime minister or president, and with the same respect."[25]

Eddie Jacobson was a traveling salesman in the middle of the twentieth century. Raised mostly in Kansas City, he served in the U.S. Army as an enlisted man during the First World War. While in the army Jacobson befriended another soldier. Together they created a regimental canteen that was so successful that the other soldier was promoted. Later, using winnings from some poker games, the partners created a men's clothing store in downtown Kansas City. In a tough economy, the store failed after a little more than two years. The two went their own ways but stayed in touch. By 1945, Jacobson's old pal was president of the United States — Harry Truman.

When the nation of Israel was being created in the late 1940s, Truman was besieged by phone calls, letters, telegrams, and visits from members of the Jewish community. Relentlessly, people hammered away at how vital U.S. support for an Israeli state was. Some shouted, others even threatened. Annoyed and exasperated, Truman told his aides that he wanted no more visits on the issue. Indeed, he was leaning against supporting Israel. Advo-

cates for Israel thought that the world-renowned chemist Chaim Weizmann (he invented acetone), then president of the World Zionist Organization, might persuade Truman. But how to get Truman to see him? A Jewish
leader in Boston knew Eddie Jacobson. He called Jacobson and convinced
him to visit Truman.

Jacobson, one of the few people who could walk into Truman's office
anytime he wanted, came to Washington from Missouri. When he walked
in, Truman, said, "Eddie, I know why you are here and the answer is 'no.'"
Jacobson was undeterred. He scanned Truman's office and saw a bust of
Truman's hero, Andrew Jackson. He said to the president, "Harry, all your
life you have had a hero. You are probably the best read man in America on
the life of Andrew Jackson. . . . Well, Harry, I too have a hero. . . . I am
talking about Chaim Weizmann. He is a very sick man, almost broken in
health, but he traveled thousands and thousands of miles just to see you and
plead the cause of my People. Now you refuse to see him because you were
insulted by some of our American Jewish leaders. . . . It doesn't sound like
you, Harry, because I thought that you could take this stuff they have been
handing out to you." Truman drummed his fingers on the desk, stared out a
window, and finally said to his best friend, "You win, you baldheaded son-
of-a-bitch. I will see him."

It worked. At the meeting with Weizmann, Truman made a commitment
that when Israel became a state, the United States would be the first country
to recognize it.[26] Israel might not be a nation today were it not for Eddie
Jacobson, who had no official position in the government. All he had was
the power of being the president's best friend.

Befriend Those Without Friends

At any social event someone is hanging around the periphery not talking
with anyone. You have a new assignment at these affairs: Walk over to those
solitary people. Chat them up. If they don't know anyone at the event,
introduce them to people you know. Why? Besides doing what a nice person should do, by helping people who have no friends you are making
friends. Think back to the first people who befriended you at your current
job, or the first person who talked with you when you entered a school
where you knew no one. You probably still remember those people even if
they are not now close friends. If they called and said they were in town
visiting, you would want to meet. If they needed a favor, you would want to
oblige. Without doubt, some people are ignored at social gatherings for

good reasons. And some solitary people will really be uninterested in talking with you. Otherwise, befriending those alone is a good deed, and you never know how it might benefit you in the future.

Keep Records

We have all had the experience of running into someone we know and suddenly failing to remember anything about them. Effective advocates don't trust important information about people to memory. Instead, they jot down that information so they can refer to it later. Any good networker knows that what is important is not only who you know or who knows you. It is also what you know about who you know. Few things account more for many advocates' success than their Rolodex—a piece of equipment created in 1956 by Hildaur Neilsen and found in some form in every executive's office. David Rockefeller, former chair of Chase Manhattan Bank, had a Rolodex with 100,000 names filed by name as well as geography. His Rolodex resembled a miniature Ferris wheel. The people in it ranged from prime ministers to doormen at prestigious hotels throughout the world. What was on those little cards represented Rockefeller's network. They contained information about meetings he had had with these people and favors done and received. Indeed, he mightily impressed former president of Mexico Miguel de la Madrid Hurtado when he once "easily" recalled nine previous meetings they had had over the course of thirty years.[27] Not surprisingly, Rockefeller was renowned for generating business for Chase Manhattan and for drumming up financial support for the charities he supported. Rockefeller wasn't alone in keeping a massive Rolodex. Even as a young man, Bill Clinton wrote down on index cards the names of people he met, their phone numbers, and the subject of their conversation. By 1980, twelve years before he became president, he already had over 10,000 of these cards, all stored in cardboard boxes. He regularly updated the cards, noting when he had last written the person and what the person had done for him (e.g., donations, introductions).

Nowadays, most people keep their contact list on a computer or phone or other electronic device. Just be sure it is reliably backed up. If your Rolodex is on your office computer and you are laid off, you have lost your entire contact list. If you lose your phone, know that losing the phone itself isn't that big a deal; losing the numbers is a huge problem.

What should you write down about people in your contact file? Names, phone numbers, and addresses are only a start. Sophisticated networkers discover things about each person that make him or her special. This *indi-*

viduating information consists of such things as a favorite sport, the college she or he attended, a fondly remembered trip, or a preferred wine. It might be as simple as the names of the spouse and children. How do you gather individuating information? Listen to what people say about themselves. Observe what is on their office walls. Notice what they order for meals. Procure their business cards. After your meeting with someone, jot down the special things that you learned on the back of his or her card.

Edward Kennedy, the late senator from Massachusetts, had his staff compose lists of people he needed to call each evening. Next to each person's name and number, staff members also noted the name of each person's partner.[28] Why? If I am calling my friend Mary, which sounds better when her husband answers: "Hi, this is John Daly." or "Hi, Jack [Mary's husband], this is John Daly." Ted Kennedy may have learned this technique from his brother President John Kennedy, who, when he was campaigning for the presidency, had an aide right behind him with a notebook whenever he worked a crowd. As soon as Kennedy shook somebody's hand, the aide asked for the person's name and address, as well as something personal about him or her. A few days later, the person would receive a personal note from Kennedy expressing how much he had enjoyed meeting him or her. The letter included a personal comment to distinguish it from the usual form letter.[29]

Remembering seemingly small details about a decision maker, such as a hobby or a partner's name, can be as important as any argument you are making when pitching your idea. If you recall that my daughter is a fine swimmer, you can walk into the meeting, say in greeting, "How's that swimmer of yours doing?" and I can't help but smile.

Work on Your Weak Ties

John Stuart Mill once said, "It is hardly possible to overrate the value . . . of placing human beings in contact with persons dissimilar to themselves and with modes of thought and action unlike those with which they are familiar." You might not have a strong relationship with those people who are utterly different, but the relationship might still be important. A sociologist, Mark Granovetter, established that when he explored how engineers in New England found their current jobs. Not surprisingly, most discovered their positions through personal networks. They turned to people who knew people who knew about possible jobs. But when probing the connections, Granovetter discovered that he had to distinguish between people's *strong ties* and their *weak ties*.[30] Strong ties were the tight connections with people they worked with every day, people they lived with, people who shared the same knowledge and even the same friends. Weak ties represented less intense connections — with people, for instance, whom they vaguely knew who, in turn, knew others who had information the original people needed. An acquaintance who knows the manager of a plant in another country who is willing to introduce you to his local executive — that is an instance of a weak tie. For many of the engineers in Granovetter's study, weak ties mattered more than strong ties in finding jobs. Why? Because the people with whom they had strong ties added few connections to the ones they already had.

Our networks are mostly composed of others like ourselves — people who value what we value, readily understand what we talk about, and generally agree with us. These networks are comfortable and easy. As Mills observed, though, there is often great profit in networking with people quite unlike us. We learn and come to think differently when exposed to others who value different things, who see the world in dissimilar ways, and who know people we don't. Weak ties matter immensely in advocacy. The more weak ties people have, the sooner they get promoted and the greater their mobility.[31] Teams composed of people with many weak ties perform more effectively and more quickly than teams composed of people with only strong ties.[32] New ideas emerge when people are surrounded by others who know things they don't know.[33] Highly productive scientists have more weak ties with other scientists than their less productive counterparts do.[34] Similarly, new ideas are more likely to be adopted when an organization's leaders have many weak ties.[35] And the more diverse the customer base involved in creating new products, the more successful the products are in the marketplace.[36] As Ronald Burt, a researcher at the University of Chicago, says, "People who live in the intersection of social worlds are at a higher risk of having good ideas." Or, as Michael Erard concludes, homogeneity deadens creativity.[37] So it isn't surprising that organizations that integrate many work specialties (i.e., combine weak ties) are more innovative and creative than those that isolate work specialties. And it isn't surprising that innovative firms actively search for unfamiliar ideas by sending their talented people to conferences worldwide, inviting academic experts to give presentations, and studying what organizations outside their industry are doing.

Successful products are often created when innovators develop new networks around their innovative ideas rather than using established networks. Established networks bring with them history and biases that may not exist in new networks. People with whom you have worked for years may hold grudges, suffer from petty jealousies, and remember bad moments. People who serve as your weak ties probably don't have that much experience with you. Historically, in the realm of public advocacy, successful advocates often have their greatest impact through their weak ties. Clair Patterson, the geophysicist at the California Institute of Technology (Caltech) who successfully convinced the world that leaded gasoline is bad for people and the environment, urgently wanted the state of California to create air quality standards. When he wrote to Governor Edmund Brown, he didn't receive an answer. Only after an acquaintance of Patterson's who also knew Brown vouched for the scientist's credibility did the governor consider his notion. Soon the state of California established air quality standards.[38] Patterson's weak tie with the acquaintance made the difference.

Cultivating weak ties doesn't mean ignoring strong ties. Although weak ties are important in garnering influence, strong ties have their own value. People with whom you have strong ties are invested in their relationships with you. They can be your cheering squad. They will trust you, understand what you are proposing, and work with you to sculpt your ideas into successful initiatives. In fact, knowledge is communicated more quickly and effectively among people who have close ties than among people with looser ones.[39] Smart advocates often turn weak ties into stronger ones by spending time with others socially or on projects. Discovering common interests or creating new joint interests can be a step on the way to an expanded, strengthened network.

Put Yourself in Places Where Networking Happens

Good networkers find places where they can connect with others. Every organization has spots where people just sit around and chat — the cafeteria or coffee room, in the lobby or by the elevator. Networking may happen during happy hour or at the seemingly spontaneous "Want to go for lunch?" moment (go!). Any profession or group has known networking locales. Figure out where they are, and spend time there.

You need to be present at networking sites and on networking occasions to be heard in an organization. Ruth Ann Marshall spent the first eighteen years of her career at IBM (she later served as president of MasterCard North America.) Early on at IBM she felt that she "was doing all the right things to stay connected with the decision makers. I'd leave the office on Friday thinking I had everything well in hand, only to be greeted on

Monday morning with decisions that had been made mysteriously over the
weekend. After a bit of digging, I learned that many of the decision makers
(most of them men) were spending hours together on a local golf course on
Friday afternoons. I bought some clubs and starting swinging at a local
driving range. In no time, I found myself in the group where decisions were
being made."[40] Marshall discovered a way to participate in the informal
world where the action was.

Golf is a networking sport. Playing it can bring about informal meetings
with decision makers, but it can also pay off in other ways. Art Fry, the 3M
engineer who created Post-it Notes, first heard about the glue that he later
used to craft his innovation on a St. Paul golf course while playing with an
engineer from a different part of 3M.[41] The networking sport doesn't have
to be golf, of course; the networking locale doesn't have to be a sport field
or arena. Networking takes place in any setting where decision makers
congregate informally outside work — children's events, church functions,
community activities.

The Commerce of Networking

Do Favors

A key to doing business in China is *guanxi*. Loosely translated, the word
means "connection." But *guanxi* means far more than that. It refers to a
relationship marked by reciprocity and mutual obligation grounded in trust
and shared experience. Guanxi are created and maintained by *renqing*, or
interpersonal debt: favors given and received.[42] Renqing is important outside China as well.

Favors, freely given, lubricate relationships. Smart advocates are like the
proverbial mouse that pulls the thorn from the lion's paw. By doing favors,
even small ones, they earn the support of other people. The recipients owe
them. Charities find that people are more likely to donate money when
donation requests are accompanied by small gifts. They give you something
— a pencil, a nickel, some return address labels — and you feel the need to
reciprocate. Sally Greene is the chief executive of the Old Vic Theatre, a
major site for live performances of classical plays in Britain. When pitching
a funding idea to an important decision maker, Greene sent him flowers.
"That always works with men," she says.[43] Favors demand a response — in
this case, a donation.

Proactive is the key word when it comes to doing favors. Sure, if people ask you for help and you aid them, you strengthen your relationship. But offering people favors even before they ask makes a stronger statement. When Michael Faraday was young and impoverished and working in a London book bindery, he attended some lectures by Humphry Davy, then England's leading scientist. Faraday took copious notes and turned those notes into a book containing Davy's lectures. Binding the book in fine leather, he sent it to Davy even though he had never met him. Davy was so impressed by the small gift that he offered Faraday an opportunity to be his assistant. Working with Davy, Faraday moved from serving essentially as a personal valet to being one of greatest scientists of the nineteenth century.[44] An unexpected favor got Faraday in the door.

Here is an assignment for you in the coming year: Once a week, do a proactive favor for someone. Each week choose a different person to help; include people you don't think you will ever need anything from. (You never know what the future holds, after all.) At the end of a year, you will have strengthened fifty-two different relationships. The favors needn't be large. Next time you see someone going out for lunch and you think it might rain, toss them your umbrella. "Here," you say, "you might need this." Or if a friend tells you his car is in the garage, offer him a ride to the shop after work. Send someone an article of possible interest. Doing favors that cost you little may gain you a lot, and you should do them before they are requested.

Ask for Favors: Get People to Invest in You

In 1736, Benjamin Franklin served as clerk of the General Assembly in Pennsylvania. After one year, he had to be renominated. Although many assembly members liked Franklin, a new member of the group spoke in favor of another candidate. After Franklin was selected by the assembly, he decided to try to win over the man who had spoken against him. Here is how he managed:

> I therefore did not like the opposition of this new member, who was a gentleman of fortune and education, with talents that were likely to give him, in time, great influence in the House, which, indeed, afterwards happened. I did not, however, aim at gaining his favour by paying any servile respect to him, but, after some time, took this other method. Having heard that he had in his library a certain very scarce and curious book, I wrote a note to him, expressing my desire of perusing that book, and

requesting he would do me the favour of lending it to me for a few days. He sent it immediately, and I return'd it in about a week with another note, expressing strongly my sense of the favour. When we next met in the House, he spoke to me (which he had never done before), and with great civility; and he ever after manifested a readiness to serve me on all occasions, so that we became great friends, and our friendship continued to his death. This is another instance of the truth of an old maxim I had learned, which says, "He that has once done you a kindness will be more ready to do you another, than he whom you yourself have obliged."[45]

Franklin understood an intriguing principle of networking: when people invest in you, they feel responsible for you. The assembly member, by lending a precious book to Franklin, was investing in Franklin.

If I ask you for a favor and you generously grant it, and later on, I ask for another favor and again you willingly grant it, who owes whom? Clearly, I owe you. You did some favors for me, and I should reciprocate. Counterintuitively, though, you also owe me. In fact, the more favors you do me, the more you will owe me. Why? Because every time you do me a favor, you are investing in me, and at some point you have made so many investments in me that you won't let me fail. Think about it this way: You decide to run for public office. Karen donates $5 to your campaign; Lauren gives you $1,000. The day before the election you need money for a final media push. Which of the two people will you turn to first? Lauren. She has made a substantial investment in your campaign, which she will lose if you aren't elected. She has invested in you.

A general principle of advocacy is that you are generally as successful as other people want you to be. Successful people are adopted by others. They get adopted, in part, by asking for favors. There are numerous ways to do this. One is to ask people to make introductions for you. When people introduce you to their friends, they are vouching for you. Another way is to seek other peoples' advice. A biographer summarizes Benjamin Franklin's thinking on this point: To win friends one should "always play to their pride and vanity by constantly seeking their opinion and advice, and they will admire you for your judgment and wisdom."[46]

Lyndon Johnson was enormously successful as a senator partly because he mastered Franklin's advice as a young member of the Senate. Here is how his biographer, Robert Caro, said this move worked: " 'I want your counsel on something,' he [Johnson] would say to one of the Old Bulls. 'I *need* your counsel.' And when the counsel was given — and of course it was given: who could resist so earnest an entreaty? — it was appreciated, with a gratitude rare in its intensity. He would pay another visit to the senator's office to tell him how he had followed his advice, and how well it had worked. 'Thank you for your counsel,' he would say to one senator. 'I *needed* that counsel.' 'Thank you for giving me just a little of your wisdom,' he would say to another senator. 'I just don't know what I would have done without it.' "[47]

In 1990, George Stephanopoulos was being recruited by several presidential candidates, among them Senator Bob Kerry of Nebraska and Governor Bill Clinton of Arkansas. What attracted Stephanopoulos to Clinton was that Clinton, rather than quizzing him or talking about himself, spent his time seeking Stephanopoulos's advice.[48] Clinton, like Franklin and Johnson, knew the wisdom of seeking counsel.

Building an advice network isn't hard. Next time you have to ask someone a question, rephrase your query from "I have a question" to "I need your advice." Ask someone to look over your proposal and give input. If you want real commitment, ask for help in figuring out the best way to pitch your proposal.

Like everything else in this book, asking for favors and seeking advice as an influence technique can easily be overdone. If you run around asking everyone for help and advice about everything, you will look both ignorant and ingratiating. Use discretion. Further, you should appreciate favors, and you should take advice seriously. If you are always asking for favors and advice and never do anything with them, people will notice, and your credibility will suffer.

Make People Who Are Important to Others Important to You

Suppose that this coming week you are at a crowded reception. You spy one of your best friends from work standing with her husband, somebody you have never met. Soon your colleague is tied up talking with people, leaving her husband standing alone, looking a tad uncomfortable. What should you do? Go up and chat with him. Maybe when they are driving home, he will remark that you are a great person. Moreover, she will think better of you because you made him — someone who is important to her — important to you. To strengthen your network, never ignore people's partners, friends, or children.

When you make people's family members, friends, assistants, and colleagues important to you, that person will be inclined to like you and support your ideas. Jack Valenti was the enormously successful former chief lobbyist in Washington, D.C., for the film industry. Once, when a number of members of Congress and their families attended a movie screening at Valenti's home, the grandsons of North Carolina's senator Jesse Helms couldn't find a place to sit. Valenti saw the problem and had the children sit with him. He spent the next hour talking with the kids about movies, sports, and whatever else came up and he didn't get around to chatting with any of the visiting dignitaries. The next day, after thanking Valenti for his kindness to his grandchildren, Helms, one of the most powerful members of the Senate at that time, said, "You have my marker."[49] Valenti understood that if he made himself important to important people in Helms's life, he become important to him, too.

Keep Things Positive

Lyndon Johnson used to tell his aides, "When you get into a political fight and you are on the verge of winning, always let your opponent depart the field with his dignity intact. Remember, your opponent today may well have to be your ally tomorrow. Never burn any personal bridges."[50] Johnson understood that poor networkers burn bridges by unintentionally or intentionally alienating people. To their chagrin, these poor networkers may find that they later need the help of the same people. We have all seen people leave organizations in bitter, vengeful, accusatory, or dismissive ways that ensure that they will never get a chance to come back. We have also seen people who depart in such generous, appreciative, regretful ways that their organizations would welcome them back with open arms. These folks didn't burn bridges on their way out.

There are myriad ways to burn bridges. You can give an insult, make a point unnecessarily, or ignore someone. You can disrespect the chain of command by going over someone's head. You can step on someone's toes or violate someone's turf. You can embarrass someone by pointing out a minor, unimportant error. You can utter negative comments about a person or something or someone that person holds dear. You would serve yourself better by being positive and leaving the bridge intact.

Manage Your Disclosures

Revealing personal details about yourself may bond you with others. With such a disclosure, people might come to appreciate why your idea is so important to you. But we have all been the recipients of too many personal details; people have told us things we didn't need (or want) to know, things too intimate given the nature of our relationship. If a friend divulges the abuse and betrayal in his marriage, if a colleague confides sexual exploits over a long weekend, if an assistant tells about stealing money at a prior job or cheating on an important test, we can't help but remember. Once we know such things, they will color our relationships. Work is a professional setting, not a public confessional. So don't disclose things that people don't or won't need to know — and avoid hearing them, too.

Be Nice or Be Silent

Remember Thumper, the rabbit in Walt Disney's *Bambi?* Whenever Bambi started to say something mean about another character, Thumper pounded his hind foot and said: "If there's nothing nice to say, don't say nothing at all!" We live in a small world, and when we say something negative about someone, our comments are likely to make their way back to her or him.

In June 2010, General Stanley McChrystal, the U.S. Army leader in Afghanistan, resigned his command. McChrystal and some of his subordinates had made disparaging remarks about President Obama, Vice President Joe Biden, and other leaders in a magazine article. McChrystal apologized. But his effectiveness as an advocate for his cause was gone. Remember, you are one sentence away from destroying your career.

Sometimes this rule is violated in ways no one could anticipate. On a plane a few years ago, two young consultants were gossiping loudly and negatively about a client. They complained about how "old-fashioned" the company was, how weak the leadership was, and how "sexy" some of the "babes" were in the firm. When the plane landed, a distinguished-looking gentleman sitting across from them handed them his business card and told them that they should be more circumspect on a plane. "You never know who is sitting nearby," he said. It turned out that he was an executive in the company that they had been disparaging. Needless to say, the two young men were soon pulled off the account. To this day, the relationship between the consultancy and the company has been tetchy. Here is a simple way of understanding this rule of networking: If you wouldn't say something to the person's face, don't say it to anyone. This rule applies to e-mail, Facebook, and other social media, too.

9

Timing Is Everything

If nothing is as powerful as an idea whose time has
come, then few things can be as tiresome as
an idea whose time has gone.

ROSALIND MILES

In ancient Greece there were two words for time. *Chronis* was chronological time. *Kairos* was the right or opportune time. Advocates need to know about kairos. For every idea, there is, as Machiavelli tells us, an opportune time to make a move. Being too early or too late can make an idea worthless. Timing is everything.

Create Urgency

Decision makers listen when ideas address pressing concerns. As BT's chief technology officer, Sinclair Stockman, said, advocates must "create an impatience in the business, an impatience to get on and improve things, to realize the vision."[1]

Monique arrives home one night to discover that her roommate has unexpectedly moved out. A few days later she learns that the IRS is auditing her. The next evening she senses that her partner is standoffish. Four days later she walks out of her apartment to discover a big dent in her new car. Feeling somewhat depressed, she visits a local counselor. One of the first questions her counselor may ask is, "Why today? What made you decide today was the day you needed to see me?" Monique's answer offers the counselor insight into what physicians call the presenting problem. If the answer is the car dent, the counselor may offer different advice than if it is her partner's distancing, or the roommate's departure.

Advocates must answer the "Why now?" question when pitching their ideas. Why should decision makers adopt their notions *now?* Why not wait? Why didn't we do it a year ago? The answer to the question is core to an advocate's pitch. As Ed Gillespie, one of Washington's most successful lobbyists, said, "Any lobbyist or trade association can make the case that their cause is right, but the real question in policy-making is, why now?"[2]

SWOT Analysis

The "Why now?" question can be answered in many ways. One way is to conduct a SWOT analysis. SWOT stands for *s*trengths, *w*eaknesses, *o*pportunities, and *t*hreats. Marketers often use SWOT analyses when deciding to enter new markets. They tie the decision to the strengths and weaknesses of their firm and the opportunities and threats that exist in that market. Reviewing strengths and weaknesses is a way to highlight *internal* issues that an organization faces. Reviewing opportunities and threats is a way to focus on *external* issues.

Like marketers, advocates conduct SWOT analyses when formulating their pitches. First, they determine what particular *strengths* of their firm justify their idea. They might say, "We should consider this idea now, since we're leaders in our industry, and innovation is part of our DNA." Possible strengths include extraordinarily talented employees, a new discovery, a patented process, the firm's sterling reputation, a reduction in costs, economies of scales, production capability, and abundant financial resources, to name a few.

The second question is, What *weaknesses* within the organization mandate the proposal? For example, "We should consider this idea now because we're not at the forefront of new technologies. If we don't move quickly, we'll lose any advantage we have." Weaknesses include outdated technologies or products, old facilities, inadequate cash reserves, an increase in costs, and limited distribution channels.

The third question is, What external *opportunities* make this the right time to adopt the idea? For instance: "We should adopt the proposal now because interest rates are low." Opportunities might be anything — a booming economy, the demise of a competitor, new product uses, global opportunities, preemption of potential competition, and market deregulation.

The fourth question is, What external *threats* make this the optimal time to adopt the idea? For example: "We should consider this idea now, since competitors are exploring the same concepts. Whoever gets there first, wins." There are many possible threats—new competitors, new government regulations, changes in customers' preferences, resource shortages, poor performance by suppliers, and the introduction of substitutes.

A SWOT analysis helps us understand why ideas are adopted at one time while at other times they would have been rejected. Ivory Soap became a big success in the late nineteenth century because of a strength that matched an opportunity—it floated. That may not be an important aspect of soap today. But years ago, when many people bathed in rivers or big water-filled casks, soap that sank was a problem.

Let's go more deeply into SWOT analysis by considering the case of threats. Advocates commonly use threats when planning advocacy campaigns. They highlight problems that their ideas resolve. Problems have four features:

- magnitude
- predictability
- complexity
- affected parties

Magnitude. When problems are hugely expensive or create massive difficulties, when they kill, injure, or ruin people's lives, they invite more attention than when they have negligible effects. This truth helps explain how Kirk Huang of the New York State Thruway Authority successfully sold the idea of using infrared beams to detect trucks that were too tall to pass under the Hungry Hollow Bridge. Before his innovation was adopted, trucks annually slammed into the underside of the bridge, causing traffic jams and requiring very costly repairs.[3] Had crashes caused only minor problems, he probably would not have been successful in pitching his idea.

Predictability. A problem can be *regular, cyclical,* or *random.* Which problems immediately get decision makers' attention? Random ones! It's difficult to prepare for or cope with problems that can pop up anytime, whereas you can plan for constant or constantly recurring events. Although hurricanes are scary, they aren't as worrisome as earthquakes. We can predict to some degree when and where a hurricane will hit once it is sighted. No one can predict earthquakes to the same degree of accuracy.

Complexity. Some problems are easy to resolve; others are wickedly complex. Decision makers dislike complex problems, which take more time and competencies to solve.[4] Thus, proposals that address easy problems are more likely to be adopted quickly.

Affected parties. When problems create suffering for important or powerful people, decision makers view them as crucial problems to resolve. So proposals that make the lives of top executives measurably easier are heard over proposals addressing issues unimportant to powerful people. Other affected parties have priority, too, not just powerful people. Proposals that resolve threats to young children or pregnant women often get more attention than problems affecting grown men.

Which of two problems will decision makers turn to first? Problem A has been a challenge for years, has very limited consequences for the business, is complex to resolve, and affects very few people — and those that it affects are not influential. Problem B recurs unpredictably, affects powerful people in serious, even life-threatening ways, and has an easy solution. Obviously, problem B is the first to be addressed. This is why, for example, traffic problems in cities like Mexico City will probably never be resolved: rush-hour traffic is so slow that people are rarely badly hurt; the traffic jams are predictable; solving the problem is almost impossible, since buildings are built close to the streets, and construction of multilevel highways would create potentially bigger problems because of earthquakes; and rich people can avoid driving during rush hours, live close to work, or even take helicopters.

Six Ways to Make the Case for Immediacy

Besides using SWOT analyses to make the case for immediately adopting a proposal, advocates typically cite any of six reasons to create a sense of urgency:

1. Market demand
2. Consequences of not acting
3. Time pressure
4. Crises: competition, disasters and near disasters, failures of other initiatives, external crises
5. Changes that mandate new ideas
6. Powerful individuals

1. *Market demand.* When customers cry out for an idea or when rival organizations change the competitive landscape in ways that require innovation,

it is amazing how nimbly some organizations can respond.[5] Smart advocates leverage customer surveys, market research, and competitive intelligence to make cases for the urgency of their ideas.

In addition to the demands of customers and competitors, many other sorts of demands might create urgency. In the 1920s the New York parks commissioner Robert Moses and Governor Al Smith wanted the state legislature to create parks throughout the state, along with highways to create access to those parks. Facing strong opposition from wealthy people who feared losing their land and privacy (and who contributed mightily to the election campaigns of members of the legislature), Moses and Smith perfectly timed their pitch for acquiring the necessary land. They waited until the middle of a sweltering summer to call a special session of the state legislature to consider their proposal. Citizens stuck in urban ovens such as New York City loudly applauded the idea of open parks filled with trees and fresh air, giving the legislature no choice but to vote yes. Had Smith and Moses touted the idea in the middle of an icy winter, who knows what would have happened?[6]

In 1995 members of Greenpeace, the environmental advocacy group, took over Shell's 14,500-ton Brent Spar oil-storage platform in the North Sea. Greenpeace activists believed that the toxic residue in the oil tanks would pollute the North Sea if, as Shell planned, the tanks were sunk. Key to Greenpeace's move was its timing — members took over the platform just one month before the European Union was scheduled to meet to discuss pollution in the North Sea. Greenpeace understood that at that moment, environmental issues were at the top of the agenda in many European minds. Greenpeace won — the Brent Spar platform was towed to land, where it was dismantled.

Alternatively, great ideas sometimes get ignored when decision makers question whether market demand justifies investing time and money in them. It is difficult to persuade pharmaceutical companies to develop and market "orphan" drugs, which help only the small numbers of people who suffer from relatively rare maladies. Other ideas falter when they might cut into sales. Bayer initially dismissed the idea of aspirin tablets in 1898, for example, in part because the company had recently devised a wonder drug called heroin, and executives feared that introducing aspirin might cannibalize sales of heroin.[7]

2. *Consequences of not acting.* In the 1920s the North East Electric Company of Rochester, New York, created a motor to power Remington Com-

pany's early version of the electric typewriter. After the first batch of Remington typewriters sold out, North East Electric executives approached Remington and asked if Remington wanted to order more motors. Remington executives hesitated. They were busy negotiating a merger. So North East Electric made its own typewriter, the Electromatic. IBM later bought North East's typewriter business, turning the Electromatic into its Model 01, and IBM's typewriter business blossomed. Had Remington executives sensed North East Electric Company's urgency, Remington might have become the dominant player in the typewriter industry and, perhaps, later in the word-processing and PC business.[8]

Successful champions often frame their issues in terms of rapidly closing windows of opportunity: "If our idea isn't adopted immediately, we will regret our inaction." "We'll lose enormous sums of money if we don't adopt the idea now." "Our market position will suffer if we miss out."

One way advocates pitch ideas is by convincing decision makers that someone else, often a prime competitor, may benefit if the decision makers don't make a move.[9] The first time the U.S. Congress considered admitting Texas to the United States, the idea was rejected. The next time the issue came up, Congress voted to make Texas part of the United States. Why? Partly because the newly established Republic of Texas had initiated discussions with Great Britain about joining the British Empire in annexing the west coast of North America. That threat provoked deep concern in Washington. Congress thought of what might be lost by adhering to the status quo. Inaction has consequences!

Advocates can also highlight the consequences of not acting by demonstrating how painful continuing with the status quo might be. When the cost of inaction is too high, organizations take action. In 2003, Senator Blanche Lincoln wanted the Bush administration to pay attention to the many American women and children being held against their will in Saudi Arabia. The administration did nothing about Lincoln's concern until she blocked the Senate's approval of James Oberwetter as ambassador to Saudi Arabia. That pricked the State Department's attention, and the U.S. secretary of state wrote to Lincoln telling her that her issue was now a top priority. (Oberwetter's nomination was approved.)[10]

3. *Time pressure.* Each January the president of United States delivers a State of the Union speech to a joint session of Congress. Because that speech gets so much attention, every White House aide wants to shoehorn his or her ideas into it, which leads to endless debates. But deadlines force

decisions. At some point before the cameras roll, what's in is in, and there is no more time to tinker. In negotiations, as time grows shorter, people often make concessions.

In 1951 the U.S. Air Force disseminated a request for proposals for a plane capable of doing many things — carrying soldiers as well as bulldozers, trucks, and other equipment; operating on short runways; having a rear ramp for easy loading; and flying, if necessary, with one inoperative engine. The Lockheed Company gave the assignment to an engineer, Willis Hawkins. Eventually, Hawkins created a design that met all the specifications. But one decision maker at Lockheed, aghast at the design's "ugliness," said that submitting it would "destroy" the company. But when Hawkins said, "The Air Force expects us to submit a proposal. We told them we would, and we have to get it in the mail *today*," the bid went in. The air force approved it, and the C-130 Hercules plane that Hawkins designed is still flying today. The deadline forced Lockheed to adopt Hawkins's proposal.[11]

4. *Crises.* Crises are the mothers of innovations. They compel organizations to focus on important issues and offer opportunities for advocates to pitch their ideas.[12] Jack Welch, the former CEO of GE, puts it well: "It's in the worst of times that things get fixed."[13] Not only do things get fixed but, as A. G. Lafley, the former CEO of Procter & Gamble, says, "In a crisis, people accept change faster."[14]

History is filled with stories of political leaders who used crises to get buy-in for their ideas. When a few rebels attacked and burned the Roman port town of Ostia in 68 BCE, politicians used the attack to justify radical changes in the way Rome was governed. Panicked citizens surrendered the treasury of Rome and, in the end, their independence.[15] Similarly, Adolf Hitler used the Reichstag fire in February 1933, when the building where the German parliament met was set ablaze, ostensibly by communists, to justify the Reichstag fire decree, which gave the Nazis effective control of the German government.

In the midst of crises, decision makers are especially interested in ideas that will resolve those crises. Hyman Rickover's extraordinary advocacy of nuclear-powered ships culminated in the launch of America's first nuclear submarine in 1954. The timing of the launch was politically perfect — the Soviet Union had recently created an atomic bomb, stories of spies filled newspapers, and Senator Joe McCarthy was fulminating against the threat posed by communists. Crises were everywhere. The launch let the United States celebrate its technological genius as well as the ability of the private and public sectors to cooperate to keep the country strong in a dangerous time.

For advocates, four major sorts of crises open doors to new ideas:

- competition
- disasters and near disasters
- failures of other initiatives
- external crises

Charles Darwin published his epic work on evolution only after discovering that Alfred Russel Wallace planned to publish a paper making claims that Darwin believed he himself had discovered much earlier. When a competitor was ready to launch, Darwin responded. To stop the search for perfection and move forward is a typical response when faced with *competition*. Pharmaceutical companies know that a major motive for physicians to adopt new drugs is their informal competition with other doctors—if a physician down the street begins to prescribe a new drug, then maybe they should, too.[16]

In successful organizations, when decision makers sense that competitors are vigorously working on new initiatives, they are more open to ideas related to those issues than if no change were on the horizon.[17] Competitors motivate innovations. When Tesla Corporation introduced an electric car in 2008 that could go from zero to sixty miles per hour in less than four seconds and travel for more than 240 miles without recharging, Bob Lutz, then the vice chair of General Motors, said, "All the geniuses here at General Motors kept saying lithium-ion technology is ten years away, and Toyota agrees with us—and boom, along comes Tesla. So I said, 'How come some teeny little California start-up run by guys who know nothing about the car business can do this and we can't?' That was the crowbar that helped break up the logjam" that had prevented creation of an electric car at GM.[18]

A change in competitors also creates opportunities to promote ideas. When new competitors enter the market, everyone else starts worrying about what the new kids on the block will do. This can provide a golden moment to propose a product or service that might differentiate your firm from others. In the 1940s the typical rollout of a new Procter & Gamble product took two to three years. Procter & Gamble had a logical, well-defined process that it methodically applied to every innovation. But when some company scientists created Tide and wanted to speed up the rollout of that innovative detergent, they urged executives to eschew the established process because competitors like Lever and Colgate would soon enter the same marketspace, and any advantage for Procter & Gamble would be lost. That argument won the day, and the company speedily took Tide to market.[19]

Lyndon Johnson famously advised that you should never give a man a present when he is feeling good. Instead, wait until he feels bad, when he will treasure the gift. Johnson was right. New ideas get traction after bad news or failure, after *disaster or near disaster*.[20] Here are a few examples.

Benjamin Franklin invented the lightning rod. But after enjoying some early success, the idea that you could prevent fires by sticking a piece of metal to the top of a building and stringing the metal to the ground fell on tough times. In fact, some people believed these rods would cause earthquakes by putting lightning into the ground. Not until some military munitions buildings blew up (failures) because of lightning strikes did governments around the world adopt Franklin's technology.[21]

In the nineteenth century, waste from all over London poured into the Thames River. Over the years more than 130 different waste-disposal systems were proposed, and every one of them was voted down. But in 1858 the odor from the pollution was so bad that Parliament contemplated leaving town. In less than eighteen days, a new sewer system costing more than $3 billion (in today's value) was approved. It took the crisis of the Great Stink to prompt action.

Not until late 1937 was methyl mercaptan added to natural gas to make it malodorous. Why was it added? Because on March 18, 1937, a natural gas leak sparked an explosion that killed more than three hundred students and teachers in New London, Texas — the single worst disaster to happen in a school in U.S. history. Adding the bad smell to the odorless gas allows leaks to be detected.

More than one hundred people died in 1937 from Elixir Sulfanilamide — a concoction that included diethylene glycol, a chemical found in antifreeze. The deaths prompted Congress to pass the Food, Drug, and Cosmetic Act, which mandated that pharmaceutical companies prove their products safe before selling them to the public.

Only after Russian MIGs shot down a Korean Airlines flight in 1983 because the plane had inadvertently strayed into Russian airspace did President Ronald Reagan make signals from the U.S. government's global positioning satellites available to private companies.[22] For years, American airline companies and other organizations had been requesting access to the government satellites that provided GPS information. Only after an international crisis was it provided.

On Christmas Day, 2009, a Nigerian man tried to explode a bomb in his underwear while aboard a Northwest Airlines flight from Europe. In the Netherlands, he had gone through airport security, but the technology at Schiphol Airport wasn't sophisticated enough to detect the bomb. This failure created opportunities for companies to pitch expensive, but more effective, screening equipment at airports and for the U.S. government to require far more intrusive body searches at airports.

Environmentalists, who had long argued for restraints on deepwater oil drilling, won wide support after the massive oil spill in the Gulf of Mexico in the summer of 2010.

When one proposal is shot down by decision makers, an advocate can grab the opportunity to pitch an alternative proposal. The *failure of one initiative* may make the need for some action apparent, and its rejection can open the door to other options. Ken Kutaragi's idea of the PlayStation was adopted by Sony only after an anticipated joint venture with Nintendo collapsed. When Nintendo instead chose to work with Philips, Sony's CEO, Norio Ohga, was so miffed that he told Kutaragi to develop the technology previously ignored by Sony.

In 1957 the Russians launched their first Earth-orbiting rocket, *Sputnik 1*. When the U.S. Army missile expert Wernher von Braun heard the news, he begged Secretary of Defense Neil McElroy to let him launch a missile that his team had developed. "We have the hardware on the shelf," Wernher Braun said. "For God's sake, turn us loose and let us do something. We can put up a satellite in 60 days, Mr. McElroy! Just give us the green light and 60 days!" McElroy said no, since the navy was currently working on a missile called the Vanguard. But when the first Vanguard missile was launched, it collapsed into a flaming mess on the launchpad. Newspaper headlines read, "What a Flopnik" and "U.S. Calls It Kaputnik." Members of Congress complained loudly and sarcastically about the military's inability to devise a suitable rocket. That is when Braun got the go-ahead. He needed the failure of the Vanguard to get buy-in for his proposal.[23]

Sometimes advocates pitch their ideas as insurance. In case another initiative fails, then, by supporting the advocate's idea, the organization will still have a product or process to meet its business objectives. This was true at Data General, a mini-computer company, where project manager Tom West pushed his idea for a particular computer even though his company had decided to invest in another initiative. He successfully argued that if something went wrong with the other initiative, his project would provide a valuable hedge for the firm.[24]

Crises not directly tied to an advocate's organization or product can also encourage decision makers to adopt ideas. Wars are examples of *external crises* that almost always provoke innovations. It was the financial problems caused by the First World War that prompted the U.S. War Industries Board to standardize various products as well as reduce their variety. The number of typewriter-ribbon colors dropped from 150 to 6, and automobile tire choices dropped from 287 to 9.[25]

Jasper Kane is one of the unsung heroes in the development of the wonder drug penicillin. During World War II, while working for Pfizer, which was then mostly a manufacturing company supplying the food and beverage industry, Kane devised an innovative method to make massive quantities of the drug. Henry McKinnell, Pfizer's chairman in 2004, recalled that Kane got a "cool reception [from Pfizer executives] because of the risks he was asking Pfizer to take. One executive said that the mold in question was as temperamental as an opera singer, that its yields were forbiddingly low, that its isolation was as difficult as its extraction, and that the purification process itself invited disaster."[26] Kane was able to overcome strenuous objections like these because the United States was at war and thousands of soldiers were dying weekly from infections and infectious disease. Without the crisis of the war, Kane might never have sold his idea to the conservative and careful decision makers that he faced.

The Cold War with the Soviet Union in the mid-twentieth century created crises that justified new ideas in the United States. The decision by the USSR to create nuclear weapons created a golden opportunity for Admiral Rickover to push for the U.S. government to develop a nuclear navy. Likewise, President Eisenhower successfully pitched a national highway system as a way to quickly evacuate civilians and move military supplies across the nation in the event of a war with the Soviet Union.

War is only one external crisis. In 2008, economies around the world collapsed. While many executives hunkered down, wise ones took advantage of the emergent opportunities. Howard Stringer became the first non-Japanese CEO of Sony in 2005. He faced an entrenched bureaucracy and a change-resistant culture. But in the tough economy, Stringer was able to convince his leadership team to modify how Sony did business. "When this crisis [the recession of 2008] came along, for me it was a godsend, because I could reorganize the company without having to battle the forces of the status quo."[27] Advocates can take advantage of other crises, too: a financial crisis in another nation (e.g., banking crises in Portugal, Ireland, Greece, and Spain), a major health scare (e.g., a pandemic), natural disasters (e.g., Hurricane Katrina), a new discovery by a competitor (e.g., a fuel storage cell that powers automobiles for years without a recharge), impending short-ages (e.g., China's withholding of rare earths that are vital to many new technologies), or an accident (e.g., the collapse of a deep-sea oil rig).

Let me say three last things about crises. First, crises are perceived. If people think there is a crisis, then there is a crisis. So advocates sometimes shape the perceptions of decision makers so they view events or issues as crises that mandate approval of the advocates' proposals. Second, in the midst of crises — financial, political, or even personal — decision makers have a laserlike focus on core issues related to those crises. Only proposals that deal directly with the crisis get attention. Other ideas are distractions. After September 11, 2001, the attention paid to terrorism made proposals about the environment, domestic policy, and even other foreign-policy ini-tiatives unimportant. Advocates must make sure their ideas are seen as directly relevant to the crisis. Finally, crises often need to build before they become important enough for decision makers to focus on. Savvy advocates often bide their time knowing that until decision makers see and feel the pressure of crisis, crisis-related proposals won't get attention. President Franklin Roosevelt probably sensed long before most Americans that the United States was going to have to go to war in Europe. But he had to wait until a major crisis — Pearl Harbor — to win the support of most Americans.

5. *Changes that mandate new ideas.* Advocates can create urgency by highlighting impending changes that mandate new ideas. A change might be symbolic — for example, your organization is coming up on its fiftieth anniversary — a perfect time to start a new initiative. A change can also be substantive — for example, the firm is integrating two units, or it is in-troducing a major internal technology change, either of which might sup-port a proposal to reduce the head count or introduce new training. In the early 1960s most tomatoes in California were picked by Mexican la-borers. The decision by the U.S. government in 1964 to end the Bracero program (which allowed cheap non-U.S. labor to work in agriculture) was

an impetus for scientists at the University of California, Davis, to invent the mechanical tomato-picker.

Although government regulations are often seen as a bane by organizations, they can also push organizations into making needed changes. Advocates for the disabled had long argued that buildings should be friendly to people who use wheelchairs, are blind, or have other challenges. But nothing much happened in the United States until the federal government passed legislation requiring that the work environment be broadly accessible. Today street corners have ramps, and elevators have Braille-inscribed buttons. The fuel-injection engine, created in the 1950s, never gained traction until the federal government mandated new emission standards in the 1970s that created a demand for catalytic converters. Regulations often force crises, so shrewd advocates link their ideas to new rules.

Even the possibility of change can spur the marketing of an idea. When Colonel James Burton started advocating for better testing of army equipment like the Bradley fighting vehicle, he met strong resistance from many Pentagon leaders. They didn't like his research, and they disapproved of his advocacy for realistic testing of equipment in the field. Finally, some general officers in the Pentagon who opposed Burton's notions transferred him, with only seven days' notice, from Washington, D.C., to snowy Alaska. Burton used this reassignment (a change) as an opportunity. He made copies of his reports and data and distributed them to any number of colleagues under the guise of sharing information ("I am being transferred and you might end up with this on your plate so I thought you should know"). Burton knew that in the world of Pentagon politics the documents would be leaked. He was right, and very soon questions started flying about his findings and his transfer. The military quickly reassigned him to the Pentagon. And soon thereafter, the Pentagon initiated more realistic testing of new equipment. Burton used a change to garner attention for his idea of live-fire testing.[28]

6. *Powerful individuals.* A good time to pitch an idea is when everyone senses that top people in the organization urgently want it. In 1996, Bill Clinton's White House wanted slow-moving bureaucrats at the U.S. Department of Health and Human Services to adopt a somewhat radical welfare-reform proposal pioneered in Wisconsin. White House staffers pushed the bureaucrats into action by incorporating a statement into Clinton's weekly radio address saying the Wisconsin approach, "one of the boldest yet attempted," had "the markings of a solid welfare-reform plan.

We should get it done." It was difficult for bureaucrats to resist an idea that they felt was being advocated by the president.[29]

Make Your Solution Feasible

A sense of urgency drives decision makers to adopt an idea; knowledge of its feasibility reassures decision makers that implementation is possible.[30] Identifying a problem is often easier than devising feasible solutions. We all occasionally see ingenious proposals that are impractical: they are too expensive, they require unavailable people or technology, or they would create more problems than they solve. Inexperienced advocates are often stopped in their tracks when people say, "It's a great idea, but how are we ever going to do it?" If you can't answer questions like that, be prepared to kiss your idea good-bye. On the other hand, decision makers are more likely to buy your idea when they believe it is both technically and commercially feasible.

There are nine ways to demonstrate the feasibility of an idea:

1. Make the proposal seem eminently doable.
2. Assure decision makers that there is little risk in adopting the new idea.
3. Graft the new idea to other initiatives in the organization.
4. Connect the proposal to trends.
5. Demonstrate the availability of resources: money, talent and knowledge, technology, interdependencies, and time.
6. Show that implementation of the idea is near completion.
7. Make the idea politically easy to adopt.
8. Wait for a necessary change that will make the idea feasible.
9. Demonstrate that the idea is likely to succeed in the marketplace.

Let's take them up one by one.

1. *Make the proposal seem eminently doable.* Decision makers prefer ideas that can be easily implemented, have a good probability of working well, and are sustainable over time and across markets.[31] A good way to demonstrate doability is to show how the idea was successfully implemented in other organizations or business settings. Clinique executive Angela Kapp had a tough time convincing her boss to put a store in the Pittsburgh airport. At that time, cosmetic stores were not common in airports. However, when her boss traveled through Pittsburgh's airport and saw that

various retail stores were succeeding, he adopted her idea.[32] Similarly, when Apple's Steve Jobs took a tour of Xerox's PARC—the research center in Palo Alto that had just created one of the first PCs with graphical user interface—he saw that personal computing was doable. That tour sparked the beginnings of Apple Computers.[33]

Admiral Wayne Meyer pitched the integrated AEGIS shipbuilding program in the early and mid 1970s. Traditionally, weapons, radars, and other equipment were added to warships after they were built. Meyer proposed building a totally integrated combat weapons system that would make it possible, for instance, for sailors in the command and control center of an AEGIS cruiser to integrate data from every available source (e.g., radar, satellites) to track and destroy multiple incoming enemies and weapons. Meyer's philosophy of "build a little, test a little, learn a lot" stressed doability. Each step in the development of his program marked a small victory. And enough victories, even small ones, offered compelling evidence of doability. For example, Meyer knew that to construct the ships he had in mind the U.S. Navy would need to buy equipment in far more integrated ways, not in the piecemeal way that the navy typically purchased equipment. To prove the doability of integrated purchasing, Meyer arranged for the Naval Weapons Support Center in Crane, Indiana, to procure microwave tubes not only for radars but also for fire-control systems. Buying a technology for more than one function at the same time was a new concept in those days. Meyer was shrewd about the small things, too. He insisted that replacement items for his ships' technologies weigh no more than forty pounds. That way, individual sailors could easily lift and replace broken items.

2. *Assure decision makers that there is little risk in adopting the new idea.* There might even be benefits. Phossy jaw, the disfiguring malady caused by inhaling the white phosphorus used in the production of matches, faded from concern for several reasons. First, public health advocates built an emotional case by displaying photographs of the victims. Second, advocates convinced Congress to tax the use of phosphorus. Third, and most compelling, a superior substitute for the white phosphorus, sesquisulfide, was readily available—and the Diamond Match Company, one of the largest producers of matches, owned the rights to it. If match companies started using the new substance, Diamond benefited. Making a change away from white phosphorus was a no-risk proposition for Diamond.

One way to reduce the perceived risk of new initiatives is through pilot projects. Pilots allow ideas to be implemented without all-or-nothing investments. When the creators of Gatorade wanted to test their drink, they persuaded the University of Florida's football coach to let them pilot it with freshmen players. (The scientists weren't allowed to "mess with the varsity," because Gator football is serious business.)[34] Wise advocates often suggest trying their ideas in one unit, or in one region, or with one sort of customer, or on one system and then use the pilot's success as a rationale to make larger introductions. 3M, for example, wasn't convinced of the commercial value of Post-it Notes until the company's sales team blitzed businesses in Boise, Idaho, with samples. The extraordinarily positive reaction of local customers to the product was compelling.

Another way of reducing perceived risk is to break complex initiatives into smaller steps. Only after one step is completed successfully do advocates seek buy-in for the next step. Proceeding by steps has two advantages. First, it reduces the perceived risk: we don't risk much by taking one step at a time. Second, it creates increasing momentum toward the larger idea. Gatorade was first used by Florida's varsity team in a 1965 game against the nationally ranked Louisiana State University Tigers. When Florida won, Gatorade had found a place in sports. "If we had lost, you probably never would have heard of Gatorade again," says James Free, one of the drink's inventors.[35] The success of the beverage in one game opened up opportunities in other games.

A third way of reducing perceived risk is to convince decision makers that proceeding with the idea will add substantial value to the organization even if the idea should fail. In one firm, an executive pitched a new business opportunity that required, among other things, devising new software. He sold his idea in part by persuading decision makers that even if his notion faltered, the software would be extraordinarily valuable to other parts of the firm. In short, there was no real loss in adopting his notion.

3. *Graft the new idea to other initiatives in the organization.* There may well be other projects in the organization or business environment that could accommodate the new idea.[36] Pollution from cars was a major problem forty years ago. In 1971, at the annual meeting of the Society of Automotive Engineers, General Motors president Edward Cole announced that GM cars would stop using leaded gasoline. Why did GM decide to abandon use of leaded gasoline? Because it was beginning to produce autos with catalytic

converters, and leaded gasoline wrecked the converters. The introduction of a new technology — the catalytic converter — made the efforts of proponents to end the use of leaded gasoline much easier.

Grafting ideas to other initiatives makes ideas seem evolutionary rather than revolutionary, new but not radical. Decision makers often resist novel ideas but easily adopt notions that seem comfortably familiar.[37] When Thomas Edison devised the first electric lighting systems, gas had been used to illuminate streets and houses for more than fifty years. So rather than emphasizing how different electric lighting was, Edison highlighted how similar it was to lighting with gas: meters looked the same, electrical lines were placed underground like gas lines, production was centralized just as with gas companies, and even the light was initially as dim as gaslight.[38]

One way to graft a new idea to another initiative is to package it as part of the initiative. If decision makers buy the major initiative, they are more likely to buy the grafted one, too. Car dealers preload cars with many features. Members of Congress have traditionally placed earmarks — appropriations for specific needs in their districts — in the much larger appropriation bills that get up-or-down votes as total packages. William Stewart was the U.S. surgeon general in the 1960s, and when Congress created Medicare for older citizens, he used the new law to force racial integration of hospitals: if they wanted the funds from Medicare, they had to stop discriminating.

If people are prospecting for gold, wise entrepreneurs sell shovels and pans. The same principle is true in advocacy. Every new innovation opens or expands markets. When you buy a new computer, what do you need? Software. When companies construct new buildings, what do they need? Furniture, cables, computers, artwork — the list goes on. In pitching ideas, effective advocates understand and exploit the vast array of interdependencies that accompany new proposals. Until freezers were readily available in America, there was little market for frozen foods. The introduction of the automobile not only made the horse obsolete for transportation but brought with it highway construction, motels, drive-in movies, and virtually every suburb that surrounds a city. It even created entirely new occupations and functioned as a matchmaker for those seeking romance.[39]

Interdependencies can be related to the availability of resources. If a company has some unused resources — an unused plant, an empty lab, an unoccupied office — decision makers are more willing to support proposals that use those slack resources. Another form of interdependence is when a new idea is sold as a vital part of a larger notion. If we are producing X, then idea Y is necessary to make X successful: Every time an electronic toy is created, battery makers are happy. An iPod without iTunes is hard to imagine. A curator at a major museum pitches purchasing a famous piece of art because it fits perfectly with the strengths of the museum's current collection.

Ideas that can't be grafted to current strategic initiatives often falter. For instance, pharmaceutical companies generally focus on a few broad disease categories. One company emphasizes oncology; another dedicates itself to diabetes. Investigators in each company are encouraged to study potential drugs that deal with diseases falling within the interests of the company. Ideas outside those interests seldom gain traction. Similarly, if a company is currently building market share in Asia, ideas having to do with Asia get more positive responses from decision makers than proposals having to do with Africa. Proposals requiring, say, an entire new manufacturing process are less salable than ones that use current tools.[40] Software innovations are more easily adopted when they fit with installed hardware platforms and operating systems.[41] If ideas require too many new activities, processes, or people, they will face resistance.

Crafty advocates may also package their proposals as part of a project or product the firm has already launched successfully: they try to sell their proposals through momentum. Once a company starts down a pathway and experiences successes, it is comparatively easy to get buy-in for ideas that lie along the same route. Management is thinking, "We have been very successful with this sort of product [or: in this kind of marketplace], so why not add this new idea to that list of products [or: businesses]?" If the firm has become a world leader in one sort of software, new ideas in the same realm seem more feasible than those in another realm.

When organizations make new strategic moves, smart advocates align their ideas with those moves. Even when a strategic initiative is not strongly relevant to a proposal, a successful advocate rides the bandwagon of change by hooking the proposal to the new agenda. This works because decision makers prefer investing resources when they see clear links among initiatives. They believe they will get more bang for their buck when new ideas are closely tied to other ideas being pursued by the firm. Efforts exerted to resolve one issue should have positive payoffs for other related issues.[42]

Ideas are more feasible not only when they fit with new strategic moves but also when they match the organization's culture, both national and corporate. In the early 1990s, the Japanese were not as interested in new ideas about electronic mail as U.S. companies. But they were more curious about new fax technologies. Why? They saw a fax as a more formal means of communication than e-mail, and Japan is a more formal culture. Just as important, faxes allowed the Japanese to use kanji, their form of writing, while e-mail in those days couldn't easily adapt to its characters.[43]

Organizations are cultures as well. It is far easier to promote ideas that fit an organization's culture than ones that don't. Xerox missed out on commercializing some amazing innovations created by its engineers in the 1970s and 1980s. Why? Partly because the ideas didn't fit easily within the Xerox culture. How did Xerox make money? On clicks. Every time photocopiers went click, Xerox heard ka-ching. Where is the ka-ching with computers? Another factor was that Xerox product development cycles were traditionally quite long — often four years or more. The shelf lives of computers were far shorter. A third factor was that Xerox liked to develop proprietary technologies. Open-source technologies were more common with high-tech computers.[44]

Wise advocates fight to have their ideas placed in certain units and not others. When an idea is squeezed into a unit that doesn't have a natural affinity for it, rejection is often the result. Where do new ideas about executive compensation fit — HR, the office of the chief executive, or accounting? Where do Six Sigma projects fit — manufacturing, operations, or sales and marketing? Where do customer service ideas fit — sales, marketing, or operations? Radical innovations often falter because they are placed in units that have established ways of doing things and have no desire to change. When setting priorities, implementing the new idea is ranked low.

4. *Connect the proposal to trends* — in the world, in the industry, or in the organization. Companies are trendy. If everyone else is doing something, then they want to, too. Starting in 2006 or so, sustainability issues, environmental consciousness, being green — all started becoming major issues for many firms. Suddenly proposals that included a focus on saving energy or reducing carbon emissions became popular.

The media sometimes make an issue especially salient to decision makers, thereby creating a trend. In 1972, Congresswomen Edith Green and Patsy Mink successfully pushed Title IX through Congress, and now schools were required to give women the same opportunities as men in education-related programs or activities like sports. But the law received little attention until a year later, when a fading male tennis star named Bobby Riggs challenged the leading female tennis professional in the world, Billy Jean King, to a match. In promoting the match, he spouted any number of chauvinistic claims (e.g., "Any half-decent male player could defeat even the best female players"). After King ably beat Riggs in Houston's Astrodome in a match broadcast around the world, Title IX got more attention. All of a sudden women were seen as competitors who could not only play sports but even do better than men.[45]

5. *Demonstrate the availability of resources.* Convince decision makers that their organization has the resources necessary to successfully implement your proposal. When Eric Schmidt joined Google as CEO, the two founders of the firm almost immediately started talking about developing a Web browser. Schmidt strongly disagreed with his new bosses. He believed that Google didn't have the resources in 2001 to compete in the browser marketplace. In 2006, when Google was a very different, and much stronger, company, Schmidt approved the idea, and Google created Chrome.[46] Schmidt understood that the feasibility of an innovation often revolves around resources.

In most organizations, vital resources include:

- money
- talent and knowledge
- technology
- interdependencies
- time

When *money* is tight, organizations are less open to new ideas than when they are flush. Some commentators have suggested that Xerox's inability to focus on the Alto, the world's first PC with a graphical user interface, was partly because the company faced massive legal problems, a poor economy, a downturn in profits, and weakening acquisitions. Without money even great ideas seldom see the light of day. Numerous initiatives get no traction in tough economic times. More than one company quashed plans for technical advances because of the recession of 2008.

Successful advocates often have to find money to make their ideas happen. They look for people within their organizations who have discretionary funds, or they figure out nifty ways to fund projects. T. Y. Lin was both a world-famous engineer and a distinguished professor at the University of California, Berkeley, in the 1980s. When visiting Shanghai, he imagined a bridge across the Huangpu River connecting the city proper to the island of Pudong. Shanghai's leaders said the city lacked the funds to build such a bridge. Lin finally sold his idea by telling the mayor, Jiang Zemin, that the bridge would pay for itself. The city could build the bridge, then sell or lease land on Pudong after the price of real estate on the island had skyrocketed.[47]

In technology companies, advocates sometimes seek out government money to aid in the development of their ideas. Companies like DuPont, GE, IBM, Northrop Grumman, and Xerox have all partnered with DARPA, the U.S. Defense Department's agency responsible for developing radically new innovations. Numerous health-related companies have worked closely with the National Institutes of Health. Some of the original funding for *Sesame Street* came from the U.S. Office of Education.

One easy way to kill ideas in meetings is to say, "It sounds interesting. Who wants to take responsibility for doing it?" When no hands go up, the idea dies. Successful advocates line up *talent* to execute their proposals even before making their pitches. They convince stellar people to join the project early on and market the stars' commitment. Without the right people, even great ideas falter. When asked why Xerox ignored AstraNet, an exciting new technology, created by its employees, that could speed up the transmission of network data, Andy Ludwick said, "None of Xerox's operating divisions was interested in AstraNet because they didn't have the right sales force to sell this system."[48] For want of sales talent, the idea was lost.

Not just any talented project leader will do. Decision makers see ideas as feasible when they sense that the crucial issues are deeply understood by those executing them. You would be hesitant to let technicians work on critical pieces of equipment if you felt that those technicians didn't fully understand how the equipment operated. The same goes with new ideas: project leaders should be *knowledgeable.*

Decision makers must also be reassured that *technologies* vital to an idea are available. If they don't exist or are too expensive, ideas that need those technologies are often viewed as unfeasible. For example, in 1975 the German scientist Harald zur Hausen theorized that cervical cancer was tied to the human papilloma virus (HPV). But until new technologies were created to test his theory, most medical researchers ignored or dismissed it. Indeed, it took thirty years for scientists to create a vaccine, based on zur Hausen's work, to prevent cervical cancer.[49]

One reason that Ford didn't adopt the minivan concept in the early 1970s, despite consumer studies showing that customers loved it, was that the company lacked the infrastructure to produce front-wheel-drive engines. Developing that infrastructure would have cost Ford more than half a billion dollars. When lead designers from Ford were hired away by Chrysler, their pitch to create a minivan won approval because Chrysler had technologies that could be adapted to front-wheel-drive vans.

Decision makers are often concerned about how much an idea *depends upon other parties* for success. If you are championing a new way to clean fabrics, you need to demonstrate that the technique works with different fabrics produced by various manufacturers, that laundry and dry-cleaning companies could easily adopt the new process, and that organizations who make cleaning equipment could comfortably implement important components of the technique.[50] To cover all the bases is a big challenge.

Throughout the development of Kimberly-Clark's most sophisticated diaper product, designers kept in touch with people in manufacturing. As *Fortune* magazine tells it, the researchers had to make sure their new product, "with its curvier lines, could actually be produced at high speed on assembly machines. . . . The technology behind those machines had to match the design advanced, beat for beat. The right materials also had to be available at an appropriate price."[51] Ideas requiring immense coordination among different units within an organization are often less feasible than ideas that affect only one unit. The friction that complex ideas create can quash any possibility of implementation. As a general rule, the fewer organizations, units, people, and so on, that have to accommodate an idea, the more feasible it looks. When advocates must integrate diverse parts of the organization or build alliances with suppliers and other companies, advocates smartly line up those units before pitching their proposal to senior executives.

Feasibility is also a function of what else is happening in the organization. If people are overwhelmed with current assignments they may see another idea as unworkable. In fact, cynics often try to crush ideas by asking, "Who has the *time* to do this?" On the other hand, when nothing special is going on, new ideas may prompt positive responses. As silly as it may seem, many ideas have faltered because their proposers were unable to gauge how busy the decision makers or their organizations were when they proposed their notions.

6. *Show that implementation of the idea is near completion.*[52] People like to get things finished. Today Texas Instruments is one of the world's leaders in creating digital signal processing (DSP) chips used in everything from cell phones to PCs. Amazingly, the genesis of DSP chips lies in a kid's toy. The company engineers who developed Speak & Spell did it for fun, without

management authorization. By the time management discovered the Speak & Spell project, it had been running for nearly eight months and was so close to being a marketable product that management said, "Okay, we can't kill it. What's it going to take to finish it?"[53]

As projects approach completion, they seem more feasible. In fact, decision makers focus more and more on getting a project done and less and less on either its cost or its potential for profit when they think that it is close to being finished.[54] This can be a problem if the project is not a good one. But once it is close to being done, it is likely to be finished regardless.

Because decision makers want to get things done, they often think, "Why invest in something that will take months or years to finish? Why not pick one that is ready to go right now?" In 2009, when the Obama administration sought to stimulate the economy, "shovel-ready" was the word of the day. The chief minister of West Bengal, Siddhartha Shankar Ray, knew the value of this "almost done" strategy. Calcutta, a city in his state, was vying with two other cities for funds for a major metropolitan railroad project. The day before Prime Minister Indira Gandhi visited Calcutta, Ray had city employees dig up the ground along the proposed route for the rail line. Large mounds of dirt were piled everywhere. When Gandhi asked why so much land was dug up, Ray explained that work on the underground portions of the rail line had already begun. Seeing that Calcutta had already made some headway compared to the other two cities, Gandhi gave Ray's city the government funding.[55]

How do advocates give decision makers the sense that an idea is almost done, as opposed to just begun? One way is to do all the hard work before pitching the proposal. Have the due diligence done, and the relevant operational documents completed. Second, if you can't get a lot of the work done prior to pitching a proposal, consider what Ken Kutaragi, creator of Sony's highly successful PlayStation, advised idea champions. He suggested not telling decision makers every step required to successfully hatch a new product; instead, he suggested highlighting a few of the immediate steps, getting approval for them, and executing them, which would build decision makers' confidence and make them inclined to approve the next steps.[56] A third way is to assure decision makers that the benefits of adopting your idea will accrue immediately. People like instant gratification. The attractiveness of a proposal wanes as its benefits seem more and more remote.[57] A fourth technique is to propose ideas that are virtually impossible to reconsider later. Many companies know how important winning the bid for a project is. Even if, later on, the company discovers that it can't do exactly what was promised, rebidding the entire project may be too expensive or time-consuming for the purchasers, so the company would keep the project.

7. *Make the idea politically easy to adopt.* Ideas that encroach on others' turf or threaten decision makers' power or status often falter. Ideas that make current products or processes look outdated or slipshod face myriad objections simply because the people who created them may love their creations. In search of budget cuts, an advocate would be ill advised to propose shutting down the small manufacturing plant where the current CEO began his career and where his father worked for thirty years. Instead, the advocate might propose closing a plant no decision maker has much personal investment in. Some ideas, no matter how logical and no matter what their potential, have no political chance of being adopted unless they are modified to make them palatable to those who decide the menu.

8. *Wait for a necessary change that will make the idea feasible.* In other words, pitch a new idea only when other changes occur that make implementation possible. Kemmons Wilson created the Holiday Inn chain in the 1950s to provide standard and predictable accommodations for travelers driving city to city. One reason that Wilson's notion proved such a success was that America was constructing an interstate highway system at the time. Without major new highways crisscrossing the nation, Wilson's hotels would have had many empty beds.

Many companies sign long-term contracts with unions or vendors. Until the contracts expire, it isn't feasible to pitch ideas that might violate important contract terms. On the other hand, a great time to introduce new ideas about working with unions and vendors is when contracts are up for renegotiation.

Sometimes adoption of an idea requires changes involving cost. In 2009, the cost of shipping goods by sea plummeted. All of a sudden, it became feasible in some firms to push the idea of sending goods from one part of the world to another by ship.

Sometimes advocates wait until there is a change in company strategy before they pitch an idea. Bernie Meyerson's development of silicon germanium chips got traction only when IBM changed its strategy and started selling chips to non-IBM firms. Likewise, public-interest advocacy groups know that it is often wise to wait until after an election to press their case. If the current administration opposes a group's ideas, it can wait until the next crop of administrators is in office. Here is another example of judicious waiting: In 1955 the decision to launch the nuclear submarine *Seawolf* was up in the air. Navy engineers working for Admiral Hyman Rickover wanted the Advisory Committee on Reactor Safety to approve the launch. But Edward Teller, the man responsible for the hydrogen bomb and a leading voice on nuclear power, was on the committee, and he didn't think the sub was ready. When Rickover, always a perceptive advocate, heard that Teller was planning to resign from the committee, he withheld his recommendation to launch the sub until after Teller had stepped down.[58]

Often the best time to pitch an idea is when decision makers are new in their positions. Most executives have brief honeymoon periods; right after assuming a leadership role, they have credibility and funds — and are searching for new ideas that will cement their reputation. That may be the perfect time to make a suggestion.

9. *Demonstrate that the idea is likely to succeed in the marketplace.* An engineering marvel might not be suitable for the marketplace; it might not even be usable. The technologically superior Sony Betamax video technology never flourished because JVC's less technologically sophisticated VHS tape was less expensive, and it could store two hours of material compared to the Betamax's one hour. In fact, entire movies could be stored on a VHS tape but not on a Betamax tape, so Betamax wasn't going to win in the marketplace.

Geoff Nicholson, the product development manager of Post-it Notes, took Joe Ramey, a vice president of 3M, to Richmond, Virginia, where they cold-called to see if the product would sell. It did, and Ramey and 3M was convinced.[59] Sometimes decision makers have to see the reactions of customers to value an idea.

One especially good way of showing the value of an idea is to discover multiple profitable applications. The more different and profitable uses a product or service might have, the more attractive it is to decision makers.

Grab the Right Moment

Adroit proponents know that decision makers are more receptive to ideas at some points than at others. For example, decision makers may not give full attention to new ideas when their plates are full with other challenges. So when advocates want the undivided attention of executives, they find a time when comparatively little is going on. That probably rules out Monday mornings, because many people like to churn through e-mails, phone messages, and all the other news and changes and queries that came up over the weekend. Nor is the day before an important board meeting a good choice. Nor is it productive to waylay a decision maker rushing out the door to catch a flight to Germany. On the other hand, you might find yourself on a plane with the same decision maker: that might be a great time to raise an idea when you want a thorough discussion.

Timing also has to do with the nature of your idea. If your notion promises to resolve a huge problem that people are struggling with right now, then right now is the best time to propose it. If your idea is minor and involves nothing controversial, you might pitch it when bigger issues are clamoring for attention: distracted decision makers may go along without much thought. (You knew this when you were a teenager. When you wanted to borrow the car, you probably waited until your mother was busy fixing dinner, your brothers were fighting on the floor, the dog was barking, and the phone was ringing to ask. Your mother was so busy she said "Go!" and off you went.)

Flush Times

It is far easier to promote most new ideas when money is plentiful. A highly profitable year opens the door for new ideas. One reason that Merck decided to donate millions of dollars' worth of Mectizan (the drug that prevents river blindness) to people in need around the world was that the company was prospering. And the drug, which in another form was used to cure parasitic diseases in animals, was selling extremely well. In the 1980s the version for animals was the world's most profitable veterinary drug.[60]

When times are tough, when, for example, companies are cash poor or downsizing, it is far more difficult to pitch most new ideas.[61] Yet even in challenging times, ideas are occasionally sold successfully. To understand why some ideas are adopted even in very tough times, you must grasp two principles.

The first is that in good times ideas are best pitched as ways of making money or improvements ("This idea has the potential to double our revenues."). In tough times, however, decision makers are more interested in saving money or conserving what they already have ("This idea will keep us from having to spend money on that unit"). Projects that increase efficiency, reduce operating expenses, and lower head counts are often better sold during difficult times. In the world of high finance, brokers are more successful selling stocks (risk) in good economic times and bonds and gold (security) in tough times. So if you are touting the idea of purchasing a new computer system for your company, you could highlight either how the system would contribute to increasing profits (in good times) or how it would make the firm more efficient (in bad times).

Second, decision makers are more conservative when everything is going well. Why should they risk mucking things up? So in good times shrewd advocates skew their proposals toward incremental investments. Ideas promoting radical change are probably not welcome when the status quo is satisfactory. On the other hand, when the economic picture is dismal, when even the possibility of survival is slim, people often embark on very risky ventures. If your football team is winning by one point, twenty seconds is left to play, and the ball is in your hands, what do you do? You hang on to the ball and take a knee! You don't take any risks. But if you are losing by one point in the same situation, what do you do? You are desperate, so you attempt a Hail Mary pass! When pitching ideas that will challenge everything your organization is doing and create enormous risks, wait until decision makers are seeing the bottom fall out of the market. They might listen.

Cycles

At certain times in the business cycle it is more advantageous to seek buy-in for ideas than at other times. One cycle involves the budgets. Often the best time to secure funding for an idea is during the first quarter of a budget year. Decision makers feel rich, rightly or wrongly; they have money to spend. By the second quarter, companies start freezing budgets in anticipation of acquisitions, revenue losses, and so on. At home, budgeting works the same way: kids understand when to ask for money from parents — right after payday, not the day before.

Another good time to seek support for ideas is at the end of a budget year. Some years ago, a friend of mine working in the medical industry called on December 8. "John," he said, "I need you. I'm desperate!" I asked what I could do. He responded, "I have to spend $15,000 on training by the 15th. Can you help?" Why did he want to spend the money? Because if he didn't spend his training allotment by year's end, he would lose it. Even worse, his superiors would reason that if he didn't need the money this year, he wouldn't need it the coming year. To take advantage of such windfalls, wise advocates might consider pitching some of their ideas, especially small, one-time-only notions, at the close of the budget year, when decision makers may have funds to use or lose.

Often the best time to pitch an idea is when a budget is being hammered out. Many of us have approached our bosses with great ideas only to hear, "I wish you'd brought me this idea last month, when we were putting the budget together. Now we'll have to wait another year before we consider it." If we had pitched the idea earlier, it might have been adopted.

A business cycle to consider besides the budget cycle is the marketing cycle. Products expire at some point in time — they becomes stale or outdated. So smart advocates pitch new product ideas when current versions of the products are close to expiration. Don't pitch buying new computers just after the company has invested in computers. Don't propose a new version of a product when the warehouses are still full of the current product. Don't push a sale when the customer has just signed a three-year sole-source contract with a competitor. One reason for the failure of Ford's Edsel was that the automobile was introduced in September. Traditionally, September and October are the months when car dealers try to sell off their inventory of current cars.[62] So the salespeople hawking the Edsel were competing against dealers offering discounts on end-of-year models. In addition, and unluckily for Ford, the 1957 recession struck right when the company was trying to introduce the pricey Edsel. Consumers were in no mood to spend money on fancy cars in a stumbling economy.

A third business cycle for advocates to be aware of is the informal work cycle of an organization. It isn't wise to pitch a major initiative in early August in Europe. Why? Because many Europeans spend August on holiday. No one would be around to discuss it. (If your goal is to make sure there will be little discussion, maybe early August would be the right time after all!) Nor would it be wise to propose an important meeting on Friday in Israel, where Friday is part of the weekend, or on the Fourth of July holiday in the United States. Depending on the organization, at certain times of the year people are also typically overworked. In accounting firms, any proposals made on April 12 aren't going to get a good hearing, because tax work needs to be submitted by the 15th, and everyone in the firm is feverishly working to beat the federal deadline. And no one in retail in the United States will support a new idea during the fourth quarter of a year — too much is at risk in the winter holiday season.

Political cycles are also relevant to advocacy. Politically, newly elected mayors, governors, and even presidents understand the value of the honeymoon phase, when they have a lot of political capital. But the moment they announce that they aren't running for office again, they become lame ducks, and their ability to successfully pitch ideas fades. The same goes for top business leaders. They can accomplish a lot when they first take control, but their effectiveness at pitching ideas wanes as rumors of their retirement grow louder.

The media have cycles, too. Ken Johnson, press secretary for the U.S. House of Representative's Energy and Commerce Committee, told the *New York Times* that when he had to work with fourteen different public relations consultants working for Ford Motor Company and the Bridgestone/Firestone tire company during the crisis about the failure of the Ford Explorer's tires, he intentionally released his statements to the media late in the afternoon. That left little time for the public relations people to respond before the news that he released was broadcast or printed. Being the latest news gave Johnson's statement added weight in the media battleground.[63] Johnson understood the news cycle. Companies as well as government agencies often announce bad news on Friday afternoon, after the deadline for printing it in the Saturday morning paper, which few people read anyway.

A Year from Now

Your boss announces that she can't go to Australia, Hong Kong, and Bali for sales meetings. They are scheduled a week apart, so whoever goes will need to spend two weeks in South Pacific resorts relaxing between meetings —at company expense. She asks whether you might go. The corporate jet will be leaving this very evening. Could you go? Although some people would instantly say, "Sure!" many people would have to say no. They have children in school, tasks that need their attention, responsibilities that can't be shirked. On the other hand, suppose she asked if you could go a year from today? Most people would say, "Of course!" A two-week paid vacation? Why not?

This little mental exercise demonstrates an important principle of timing: It is easier to commit far ahead than for tomorrow. People discount the challenges involved in future projects, believing that they will have more time and often more money than they do now.[64] When they make decisions about far-off projects, they think in terms of the project's attractiveness and ignore some of the less appealing details.[65] They are also overconfident about their ability to do what they commit to.[66] On the other hand, when considering projects that might start tomorrow, they think of more immediate issues, such as feasibility. As the Duke University psychologist John

Lynch wrote, "When we think about a task in the distant future, we focus on the benefits — the good stuff. When we think about doing a task today, we think about the mundane and less interesting details."[67] This is why people will pay more money for the same product when using a credit card than when using cash. A credit card makes the cost of the purchase seem less real or immediate.[68] They will pay for it in the future, not now. This is also why advertisements promise "No payments for six months!" or "No interest charges for a year!" Where, you might wonder, will these people acquire the money in six months or a year?

What does knowledge about now versus a long time later imply for advocacy? If you are pitching a big idea, get decision makers to approve initiating the project in the future, nine months from now, instead of tomorrow. Don't get too specific about the individual moves that will have to be completed. Instead, ask decision makers to adopt the broad notion. Later on, details that are part of the overall agenda can be justified. This is one reason why experienced advocates get decision makers' approval for pilot projects rather than complete initiatives. Once decision makers can see the success of a small commitment, they are likely to be willing to make a larger commitment down the road.

Take Advantage of Changes in Leadership and Structure

Changes in leadership often create opportunities for advocacy. A new leadership team, especially one that comes from outside, may be open to ideas that an entrenched leadership group never saw value in. Take Bernard Meyerson, a senior research leader at IBM. After spending seven years creating computer chips that blended silicon and germanium, a compound that greatly increases processing speed, Meyerson's team hit an advocacy wall. Executives at IBM dismissed the project and broke up the team. Meyerson, though, didn't abandon the idea. He labored at night to refine the process and spent his days convincing customers that his idea was sound. All of his effort would have still gone nowhere except that a new CEO from outside of IBM, Lou Gerstner, came aboard, heard about the project, and saw its merit. He ordered IBM executives to get out of Meyerson's way, and the project took off. Gerstner's joining IBM saved Meyerson's idea.[69] New leadership can also quash established ideas. Support for constructing the superconducting supercollider in Texas faltered when a newly elected Congress balked at the expense of the huge project.

Major changes in the structure of an organization — a reorganization, an acquisition or a merger, even a spin-off — offer opportunities to advocate for ideas. At the start of the twentieth century, turning oil into gasoline was an inefficient process. Along came two scientists, Robert Humphreys and William Burton, who found that by heating oil at high pressure to break the long molecular chains into shorter ones (thermal cracking), they could get high yields. But executives at Rockefeller Trust's Standard Oil weren't interested in adopting the idea. No progress was made until 1911, when the trust was broken up. At that point, executives of Standard of Indiana, one of the successor companies created from the breakup, got interested in the technology.[70] Humphreys and Burton's notion took off.

10

Create Persuasive Messages

Persuasion is often more effectual than force.

AESOP

People have always been interested in discovering ways to be persuasive. In classical Greece, Aristotle and Plato wrote about how to influence others by phrasing ideas with care. In ancient Rome, Cicero and Quintilian advised colleagues how to craft potent messages. In the Renaissance, Niccolò Machiavelli wrote a still-cited manual about influence. In modern times, Dale Carnegie's *How to Win Friends and Influence People* is a perennial best seller. In the 1940s, social scientists began exploring empirically what made certain messages — speeches, brochures, advertisements — more influential than others. In this chapter we will draw on this research to outline how advocates create persuasive messages.

Successful advocacy is almost always a *campaign*. People aren't persuaded to change their opinions overnight; persuasion takes effort over time. In 1937, Franklin Roosevelt understood that the American public, recovering from the Great Depression, wasn't eager to intervene in Europe to stop the rise of Nazism. Most Americans were isolationists. They saw no reason to worry about events overseas. Still, the president wanted to prepare people for what he felt would be America's inevitable involvement in the European conflict. So in speeches he spoke about international lawlessness — an epidemic, he said, that must be "quarantined." Following Germany's invasion of Poland in 1939, he went a step further. He persuaded Congress to adopt a "cash and carry" program. European allies could buy American weapons, provided the weapons were transported on Allied ships. The program allowed the United States to maintain token neutrality while materially aiding its allies. In 1940, Roosevelt took another step. He created the military draft and arranged to give Britain fifty aging destroyers in exchange for bases in the western hemisphere. In early 1941, arguing that the United States must be an "arsenal of democracy," he successfully pitched the Lend-Lease program, whereby the United States lent military equipment to its allies in anticipation of payment later. (The final payment of $83 million from Britain to the United States was made on December 29, 2006.) What Roosevelt was doing was slowly edging America toward the war that he understood was unavoidable.

Politicians are not alone in understanding that persuasion is often a gradual process. Procter & Gamble approached the marketing of Crest toothpaste as a campaign. In the 1950s dentists were skeptical about the vaunted benefits of fluoride. Yet what distinguished Crest from other toothpastes was fluoride. So Procter & Gamble's initial marketing goal was simply to "get to neutral." If dentists could be persuaded to stop saying negative things about fluoride toothpaste, Procter & Gamble would be satisfied. That was slowly accomplished. By 1960, company salespeople were visiting dentists and offering them samples of Crest to pass on to patients. Procter & Gamble was happy when 12 percent of dentists recommended Crest.[1] The campaign to have Crest, and fluoride toothpaste, accepted proceeded slowly but surely, and by the late 1960s, Crest was the nation's leading toothpaste. Persuasion is almost always a campaign. In campaigning, advocates must craft messages that influence decision makers to listen to, and then adopt, their ideas.

When creating persuasive messages for their campaigns advocates employ any of three major techniques: (1) prove the idea by using good evidence, (2) scare the decision makers appropriately, and (3) organize the message for optimal impact.

Prove the Idea by Using Good Evidence

John Snow was an anesthesiologist in Britain in the mid-nineteenth century. Struck by the huge number of people who died during cholera epidemics, he explored what caused the disease. The common theory at that time was that foul air from human and animal waste was responsible. So cities, to reduce the dangers of malodorous air, regularly deposited waste in nearby rivers. Snow had an alternate hypothesis. He suggested, in fact, that dumping waste in rivers led to cholera outbreaks. In early September 1854, when cholera erupted on Broad Street in London's Soho district, Snow got a chance to test his notion. He noticed that some people caught the cholera and others didn't. Why? Using carefully drawn maps and statistical analyses, Snow discovered that many of the victims drew water from one particular water pump on Broad Street. People who procured water elsewhere didn't catch the disease with the same frequency. As it turned out, the culprit pump drew water from part of the Thames River that was polluted with sewage. Snow's careful counts of sick people and where they drew water — his empirical evidence — started the move to cleanse water in London.[2]

Compelling evidence is essential to advocacy. Facts matter. Decision makers want statistics, expert advice, and historical information that justify adopting proposals. So what makes evidence compelling?

- It is understandable.
- It is new.
- It is credible.
- It is pertinent to decision makers.
- It brings home the point.

Good Evidence Is Understandable

Advocates make sure decision makers understand the evidence that is presented to them.[3] Evidence loses its impact when it isn't clearly delivered. Technical jargon and complex findings can easily confuse decision makers. Take this statement: "In the data analysis, the maximum likelihood estimators were non-significant. Thus we should adopt the model." Persuasive? Only if you have a background in statistics.

How do you make sure that evidence is clear? You might ask colleagues with backgrounds similar to the decision makers' to preview your evidence. Ask them what is understandable and what isn't. You might also translate complicated evidence into easy-to-grasp points. You could highlight important numbers, edit out extraneous quotes, and use everyday metaphors.

Sometimes the best evidence is evidence that people can see. In 1881, Louis Pasteur wanted to convince people that his anthrax vaccine was effective. In May of that year he administered his vaccine to thirty-one goats, cows, and sheep at a farm in Pouilly-le-Fort, near Paris. An equal number of animals weren't vaccinated. He then exposed every animal to anthrax. Two weeks later he brought a collection of scientists and journalists to his farm and presented his results (evidence). To their astonishment, almost every unvaccinated animal was dead, and none of the vaccinated animals exhibited any signs of disease. Everyone was persuaded by what they saw.

Good Evidence Is New

Can you quickly repeat what the warning label on a cigarette pack says in the United States? Is it: "Warning: Cigarette smoking may be hazardous to your health"? Wrong! That hasn't been on a pack of cigarettes for years. For the past decade, one of four different warning labels has randomly appeared on packs. And soon those warnings will be replaced by large graphic images of people suffering from smoking. Why? Because the effectiveness of evidence wanes after people see or hear it more than a few times. New evidence is more persuasive than old evidence. Every time a Pfizer drug representative visits a physician to tout products, the company wants that rep to have a new message about its drugs.[4] Pfizer knows that if doctors have already heard about a study, they are probably thinking, "Yeah, yeah, that's old news. Tell me something I don't know." The same is true for television and magazine ads. You see them for only a few weeks before they mostly disappear. Once they become familiar they garner little attention.

Good Evidence Is Credible

Were you to have told people centuries ago that humans would someday fly machines around the world or walk on the moon, you would have been dismissed as a dreamer, if not a heretic. If someone had told you in 1960 that Polaroid, General Motors, and Montgomery Ward would go bankrupt in the future, you would have found those predictions ludicrous. Some scientific claims fare no better today. For example, many people doubt scientists' warnings about the major environmental challenges associated with increasing amounts of greenhouse gases in the atmosphere, despite the preponderance of evidence. Evidence that may be perfectly correct has little impact on decision makers if it seems far-fetched. Evidence must be credible if it is to be persuasive.

First, credible evidence is grounded in decision makers' *personal experiences*. Frances Perkins, who later became the first woman in the U.S. cabinet, was a passionate advocate for New York's working poor in the early twentieth century. One way she convinced state leaders to worry about labor issues was by conducting factory tours. Here is what she later said:

> We [she and her colleagues] used to make it our business to take Al Smith, the East Side boy who later became New York's governor and a presidential candidate, to see the women, thousands of them, coming off the ten-hour shift on the rope walks in Auburn. We made sure [state senator] Robert Wagner personally crawled through the tiny hole in the wall that gave egress to a steep iron ladder covered with ice and ending twelve feet from the ground, which was euphemistically labeled "Fire Escape" in many factories. We saw to it that the austere legislative members of the Commission got up at dawn and drove with us for an unannounced visit to a Cattaraugus County cannery and that they saw with their own eyes the little children, not adolescents, but five-, six-, and seven-year-olds, snipping beans and shelling peas. We made sure that they saw the machinery that would scalp a girl or cut off a man's arm. Hours so long that both men and women were depleted and exhausted became realties to them through seeing for themselves the dirty little factories. These men realized something could be done about it from discussions with New York State employers who had succeeded in remedying adverse working conditions and standards of pay.[5]

Perkins understood how convincing personal experience is. Decision makers left those tours understanding, perhaps for the first time, the horrors of the workplace and the need to pass better laws about safety, child labor, and work hours.

Second, credible evidence is *memorable*. It is often compelling data in the form of statistics or examples.[6] The most persuasive statistics are both dramatic and irrefutable. For example, a call-center executive proposed that her organization increase the number of people answering phones. This advocate's case was particularly powerful because she reported that "in the last three months we've had a 30% increase in calls. More importantly, the number of people who have hung up after waiting more than 8 rings has increased by more than 40%. That means we're losing 12% to 15% of new customers. They can't get to us, so they go elsewhere. And, we lose huge revenues!" She could have said, "We need more people answering calls. We're getting more calls and are not responding quickly enough. In the end, that means we're losing many new customers." The statistical presentation was more compelling.

Donald Wilson devised what is today known as LexisNexis, a computer database of articles and other references that can be quickly searched. When it was introduced to lawyers, many were skeptical that a computer could do searches better or faster than a well-trained legal clerk. So in the early 1970s, Wilson conducted a public experiment at the U.S. Supreme Court. The test was to search and find more relevant legal cases in a set period of time, with his computer software pitted against highly experienced court clerks using traditional manual methods for searching through printed volumes. The computer won, and Wilson used this real-life test as his persuasive case.[7]

Third, credible evidence is *legitimate* — accurate, unbiased, relevant, and up-to-date. Nothing destroys an advocate's credibility more quickly than for decision makers to discover that the advocate's evidence is inaccurate. If you say a process works in a certain way, make sure you are right. Similarly, decision makers who discover that your facts are cherry-picked, and therefore consistently one-sided, are apt to cry, "Fraud!" After weapons of mass destruction were not found in Iraq, President George W. Bush's credibility plummeted because he had used the "evidence" that they were there as a rationale for America's invasion of Iraq in 2003. The administration's biases appeared to have shaped the evidence.

Decision makers want relevant evidence. Decision makers in a small South Carolina–based company will find data drawn from a large corporation in Kazakhstan less compelling than evidence from a same-sized Virginia firm. Decision makers managing a biomedical manufacturing unit will find data from a chemical plant more relevant than data from Nordstrom's. If evidence is seemingly irrelevant, advocates must make the relevancy clear to decision makers. Relevant evidence is also up to date. More than one advocate's appeal has faltered when decision makers notice the age of the evidence and decry it: "That may have been true in 2000, but that was more than a decade ago."

Fourth, credible evidence comes from *credible sources*. If the source of an advocate's evidence is seen as sketchy, decision makers will ignore it even if the actual evidence is valid. On the other hand, a reputable source enhances the impact of evidence. When Crest toothpaste was launched by Procter & Gamble in the 1950s, it wasn't a big seller. But in August 1960, Crest was endorsed by the American Dental Association; it said that the paste was "an important aid in any program of dental hygiene." The endorsement (which no other toothpaste had) was immediately plastered on every tube of Crest. Within the decade, Crest became the dominant toothpaste in America and stayed that way for more than thirty years. The rapid growth is directly attributable not simply to the evidence but also to the credibility of the source of the evidence. What if Crest had cited a market survey conducted by its own researchers? The results would hardly have been the same. Compare the independence of the source of evidence in Crest's case with the story of J. Kenneth Blackwell. In 2004 he served simultaneously as Ohio's secretary of state in charge of, among other things, ensuring the fairness of elections. He was also co-chair of George W. Bush's reelection campaign in Ohio. When he made a case for the accuracy of Ohio's vote in favor of Bush, some wondered about his potential bias.

Shrewd advocates use multiple sources of evidence when making their cases, knowing that it is all too easy for a single source to be viewed as biased. Multiple sources are especially compelling when the sources represent diverse interests. For example, an advocate proposing a new approach to manufacturing a product might cite a recent journal article by a lead engineer at a competitor firm, a Wall Street analyst's comment supporting the notion, and some academic studies, as well as a study done at her own plant. A caution: Too much evidence can be overwhelming. It ends up confusing decision makers. How do you handle this? First, select and summarize representative studies. Second, like scholars in medicine and the social sciences, integrate a number of studies into one cumulative analysis: a meta-analysis.

Finally, here is a little trick: When the source of evidence (who says it) is highly credible, mention that source before summarizing the evidence ("According to the independent Congressional Budget Office . . ."). The source's strong reputation will strengthen the impact of your evidence. Alternatively, when your source may be viewed as biased or unqualified, delay mentioning the source until after you have presented the evidence. There is at least a chance that your evidence will affect decision makers positively before they consider the source. (Obviously, find a highly credible source if you can.) If you yourself have high credibility, put your name at the top of your written proposal; alternatively, if you have low or unknown credibility, put your name at the end of the report.[8]

Good Evidence Is Pertinent to Decision Makers

David Wallerstein, president of a nationwide movie theater chain in the 1970s, sat on the board of directors of McDonald's, the fast food giant. In his theaters, selling large sacks of popcorn had been an incredible success.

People almost always bought the bigger size. So he suggested that McDonald's offer larger servings of french fries. Roy Kroc, McDonald's founder, disagreed. "If people want more fries, they can buy two bags." Wallerstein responded, "But Ray, they don't want to eat two bags — they don't want to look like a glutton."[9] Kroc wasn't convinced. Undeterred, Wallerstein conducted his own research. While spending two days in McDonald's restaurants he noticed that all diners emptied their sacks of fries. Movie popcorn eaters did the same. So Wallerstein again pitched his idea to Kroc. This time he convinced him.[10] Why? Because this time, Wallerstein's evidence had been collected at Kroc's stores.

Two Australian physicians, Robin Warren and Barry Marshall, believed, early in their careers, that the bacterium *Helicobacter pylori* was responsible for certain stomach ulcers. The medical community dismissed their idea: everybody "knew" that stress, spicy foods, and acid caused ulcers. Some scientists even labeled them quacks. Exasperated by their reaction, Marshall mixed some of the bacteria with water to form a gray mush and swallowed it. A few days later his stomach was inflamed. Then he took some antibiotics, and the inflammation dissipated. Did this experiment convince the medical establishment? No. For them, the gold standard, a double-blind experiment, counted far more as evidence. Only after completion of large-scale studies tailored to the expectations of physician-scientists did the medical community accept Marshall and Warren's claim. In 2005 the two scientists were awarded the Nobel Prize in Medicine for their breakthrough. The point here is, know what evidence counts with the decision makers — numbers? testimonials? stories? comparisons? — and provide it.

Good Evidence Brings Home the Point

Ineffective advocates often erroneously assume that decision makers automatically see the point of their evidence. That is often not true. No matter how good the evidence or how obvious the problem being addressed, advocates must be sure to answer the "so what?" question. Inexperienced politicians may promise to improve schools or reduce taxes, but those promises lack the "so what?" They need to tell voters that they "will improve schools *so that your children will get better educations, which will get them better jobs.*" Or they "will reduce taxes so that *you will have more money in your pocket to spend on your family and home. You will be able to buy that new car and afford college for your children.*" Too many PowerPoint slides have headings like "Relationship of Pricing to Sales." So what? A better heading would be "When Prices Go Down, Our Sales Increase!" That gets attention.

There are many ways of bringing home the point of evidence. One is to give decision makers a personal "so what?" — that is, tell them what it would mean for them if they adopted the proposal. Which statement is more likely to convince people to vote against a tax increase: "The tax increase the town is asking for will cost citizens $27 million next year alone" or "The tax increase the town is asking for will cost each of us — you and me — $1,900 next year"?

When numbers are used, the "so what?" question is often persuasively answered through the *multiplier effect*. Here advocates show the impact of their proposal by multiplying the effect over and over again. For instance, a pizza parlor manager wanted to convince his employees of the lifetime value of a customer. Rather than saying the average customer purchases a $20 pizza, he said, "Let's consider Ms. Gorham. She has three children. She bought one $20 pie this week. But she buys a pizza almost every week. That means she's worth at least $1,000 each year. And because her youngest child is only three, she'll probably keep buying pizzas for another twenty years. That makes her worth $20,000. But remember, Ms. Gorham is a well-connected young executive. She may influence the pizza choices that three other people — colleagues, neighbors, or even her company's food-service managers — might buy. That means she's worth perhaps $60,000. So the next time she walks in, treat her as though she's spending $60K with us, because if she decides to go elsewhere, that's what we've lost!"

A second way of bringing home the point is to come up with personal examples or striking analogies. For instance, during the Second World War many U.S. Navy leaders thought that one-cell flashlights attached to life jackets were a needless waste of money. All that changed when one sailor told his father — then a powerful admiral — that the flashlight had saved his life when his ship sank and he found himself drifting in the ocean.[11] You can't argue with the personal testimony of that sort. Sometimes analogies make the evidentiary case. When Akio Morita, the mind behind Sony's Walkman, was challenged by his colleagues about why people would ever want a tape recorder that couldn't record, he disarmed their objections by reminding them that people had car stereos that didn't record. Point made!

Scare the Decision Makers Appropriately

In the early sixteenth century, a young Italian bureaucrat was removed from office when his city's leadership changed. For the remainder of his life, unable to get another municipal job, Niccolò Machiavelli resided on the outskirts of Florence writing plays and books. His most famous work was *The Prince*, which offers an utterly pragmatic, unsentimental portrait of power pursuers and power wielders. Central to Machiavelli's treatise was the effective use of fear. Nothing has changed in five centuries. Fear is still an effective tool of persuasion. Medical advertisements promote healthy living by raising anxieties about all sorts of maladies. Politicians on the campaign trail exploit voters' fears. Teachers threaten poor students with low grades and extra assignments. Parents lay down rules for time-outs and retraction of privileges. Executives threaten layoffs. Fear is a powerful influence technique.

Let us be clear: the fear tactic must be used carefully. Fear appeals can boomerang, increasing resistance to an advocate's notion rather than winning people over. In 1924, the U.S. Congress was debating immigration issues, as it had before and would again. At that time, the House of Representatives set quotas for immigrants from some nations and ruled that people from other nations, including Japan, were to be totally excluded. Recognizing the obvious racism of this push for exclusion, as well as the foreign policy implications, the Senate wasn't as rash in its debates about Japanese immigration. But when the Japanese ambassador to the United States, Masanao Hanihara, threatened "grave consequences" if the Senate passed the bill, his threat led to exactly what he feared. Calling the statement an infringement on the sovereign rights of the United States, the Senate quickly voted to exclude Japanese immigrants.[12]

Done well, though, fear appeals prompt decision makers to attend to, and buy into, ideas. In the 1980s and 1990s, Chinese airlines had woeful safety records. Planes were crashing with frightening regularity. So, in 2000, the Chinese Aviation Ministry declared that no new aircrafts would be delivered to Chinese airlines until every airline had created a comprehensive safety plan.[13] Without new planes, the companies couldn't expand. Airlines focused on safety, and by 2007, Chinese airlines had among the best safety records in the world.

How can you frighten decision makers into accepting your proposal without causing a boomerang effect? There are several ways to use fear effectively:

- Make the threat believable.
- Address significant others.
- Give decision makers a way out.
- Present a novel threat.

Make the Threat Believable

Fear tactics work only when people find the threats credible. That is why Visa advertisements tell consumers how many places accept Visa and do not accept American Express. It is believable that you could be stuck someday where you can't use your credit card. If Visa said that we would starve and die without a Visa card, we would dismiss the threat as unreasonable. How do advocates enhance the believability of their message of fear?

Threats should not be too extreme. Inexperienced advocates sometimes scare decision makers so much that they stop listening out of psychological self-protection. Some well-meaning environmentalists, for example, have painted images of undeterred global warming that are too frightening for people to handle (e.g., pictures of plague-ridden bodies being carted off en masse; predictions of New York City underwater). Rather than listening, people just avoid those sorts of messages.

Threats must be personally relevant. People respond with fear when they feel personally threatened. In Bern, Switzerland, at the boundary of the ancient city, stands the Kindlifresserbrunnen, a fountain featuring a sculpture of an ogre stuffing a naked infant into his mouth while holding a sack of young children. The statue was built centuries ago to make children fearful of venturing beyond that point into dangerous territory. The fear that it engendered in children was real, but adults who understood the fanciful nature of the ogre probably walked right by the statue every day without even a slight tremor.

Experienced high-school principals know that the only threats that snag students' attention are ones that they see as directly relevant. Too often, high schoolers worry about auto safety only after a fellow student has been in an accident. After somebody they know is crippled in a wreck, they grasp that they themselves are potential victims. In 1999 a drunk driver slammed into a car in Austin, Texas. A passenger in the vehicle that was struck, a young woman named Jacqueline Saburido, was terribly burned. Her face got the worst of it. Years later, she bravely made public-service television advertisements about the dangers of drunk driving. The first picture on the screen was Saburido's pretty face before the accident; that picture faded to reveal her now-unrecognizable face, disfigured in the extreme. The message was aimed at young people who might drive drunk — it warned them they could cause equivalent damage to someone just like themselves. A similar advertisement featuring a fifty-year-old victim would probably not have received the same attention from adolescents.

Threats must address something that matters to decision makers. After the First World War, France wanted to purchase the U.S. Navy's powerful Lafayette radio station near Bordeaux. Figuring that it would be too expensive for the United States to tear down, the French offered a paltry sum to the young Franklin Roosevelt, who was then assistant secretary of the navy. Roosevelt dismissed the offer. Later in the same meeting, an aide walked in and handed him a telegram from the secretary of the navy. Roosevelt read the note aloud, "Dismantle and ship station to America. [Signed] Daniels [secretary of the navy]." The French, who really needed the station, quickly offered the 22 million francs that Roosevelt wanted for the station. Roosevelt later told friends that he had written the telegram himself and had arranged for the aide to bring it to him at just the right time.[14] He understood that the station mattered to the French. If they hadn't cared, his ploy would have failed.

Threats must raise immediate concerns. The cancerous impact of smoking is typically many years away. Knowing that most people don't worry much about something that might occur thirty years hence, a shrewd advocate might highlight more immediate effects of smoking — for example, a smoker's breath and clothes stink, the teeth and fingers turn yellow, the voice becomes raspy, and so on. One reason George W. Bush's 2005 campaign to change Social Security gained little traction was that the crisis he forecast seemed to be far in the future. Social Security was working just fine. In fact, there was a surplus. The Social Security deficit that he was warning people about was more than two decades away. Why worry about it now? In studying whether people changed their behavior because of warnings about the 2009 swine flu, British scientists discovered that people were not inclined to take precautions unless they believed that they were likely to catch the flu themselves (an immediate concern) and that the outbreak would continue for a while (another immediate concern).[15]

Threats must be real. If you threaten to resign if your idea isn't adopted, decision makers must believe that you mean it. If you say that the company will go broke if your idea isn't adopted, you should feel certain that financial collapse could really happen. A young investment banker who was pitching an idea in his firm became exasperated by an unruly colleague. He shouted that if this colleague didn't immediately behave, he would make sure the deal never happened. A hush fell over the room, and someone broke into sarcastic laughter. Others joined in. They knew the banker couldn't, on his own, stop a deal from happening. His threat fell flat, as did his credibility.

Address Significant Others

For years, Michelin's advertisements featured a cherubic baby sitting in a tire. The message to any parent was, "If you care about your child, choose a safe tire — choose Michelin." Michelin marketers understood the power of addressing what sociologists call "significant others" — people we care about: our spouse or partner, our children, our parents, our friends.

Appealing to significant others is not a new technique. In the nineteenth century, life-insurance salesmen distributed booklets describing the horrors that families experienced when the bread earners (usually men) died: wives ended up in desperate poverty, and children lost their chance for an education.[16] The message: Buy insurance so that your loved ones will be okay when you pass away.

In the 1950s, when the United States was building its first nuclear submarine, there was a heated debate about how important it was to weld a backing on gaskets holding the bolts on the reactor. Many engineers thought the welds unnecessary. But Captain Hyman Rickover disagreed. He wanted the extra security of welds. So he met with the engineers and asked, "Suppose *your son* were to serve on this submarine, with his life dependent on its safe operation. Would you be willing to let his life depend on the continued integrity of a gasket to hold back every droplet of the highly radioactive water? Or would you rather have a weld backing it up just in case?" There was a long silence, and then the engineers changed their stand. Welds were included in the design.[17]

When Lou Gerstner became CEO of IBM in the 1990s, he visited different IBM locations to motivate his employees. He freely used fear. In one speech he flashed photographs of the CEOs of the company's top competitors. He "read quotes from them belittling IBM, gloating over our fall." He continued his speech and, looking visibly angry, said that IBM's "competitive focus has to be visceral, not cerebral. It's got to be in our guts, not our heads. They're coming into our homes and taking our children's college money."[18] He figured — correctly — that IBM employees who were worried about their children would be strongly motivated.

Give Decision Makers a Way Out

Effective fear appeals don't just frighten people. They also offer ways to avoid or eliminate the fear-provoking concern. Advertisements telling people to practice safer sex don't say, "If you have sex, you die." Instead, they remind people that if they don't use condoms or if they exchange needles, then their chances of becoming HIV-positive increase. But if sex partners are careful, use condoms every time, know their partner, and use new needles, they will probably not become HIV-positive. Similarly, advertisements warning of the hazards of mixing alcohol and driving don't tell people not to drink — that's unrealistic. Instead, they offer people ways to drink and remain safe: use designated drivers, take taxis, and stay at a friend's house overnight instead of heading home under the influence.

Present a Novel Threat

Nathan Zohner was a fourteen-year-old junior-high student in Idaho Falls in 1997. For his science fair project he described the dangers of dihydrogen monoxide (DHMO).[19] DHMO is an industrial solvent, he explained, and is also an additive in junk food. It is regularly dumped into rivers and oceans, it erodes land, it contributes to the greenhouse effect, it is a component of acid rain, and it may, under certain conditions, cause terrible burns. Eighty-six percent of people who saw his presentation favored banning DHMO. How would you have voted? Do you think DHMO ought to be banned? But that would be a big problem, since DHMO is nothing but H_2O — water. A fear appeal is especially effective when it raises a threat that people haven't considered before: Who has ever thought of water as harmful? Zohner's argument, tongue in cheek as it was, gets your attention — it's novel. A new disease — SARS, AIDS, swine flu — gets people's attention more than familiar maladies.

Organize the Message for Optimal Impact

Presenting good evidence and raising fearful concerns are two ways to persuade people. There are, in addition, many ways to organize messages to make them more persuasive.

The Four Steps of Persuasion

The process of persuasion, whether undertaken in a drawn-out campaign or a written report or an informal conversation, can be broken down into four steps:

1. Create a need; create some pain.
2. Offer a solution that resolves the need.

3. Describe benefits accruing from the proposal.
4. Outline difficulties that will emerge if the proposal isn't adopted.

Wise advocates know these steps and take them to convince decision makers of the value of their ideas.

   1. *Create a need; create some pain.* Jeong Kim runs Bell Laboratories, which is renowned for introducing such new technologies as the laser, the transistor, the electronic microphone, and the UNIX operating system for computers. AT&T used to grandly let Bell Labs scientists work on whatever interested them. Today, Bell Labs scientists must create competitive innovations that quickly yield high returns. In explaining which innovations researchers should pursue, Kim classifies ideas as either "vitamins" or "painkillers." Vitamins are cheap but offer few quick returns. They are fun to develop, but the tangible rewards for Bell Labs are minimal. Painkillers, however, meet real and immediate needs. People pay good money for technologies that cure painful problems.[20] So, Kim says, wise innovators create painkillers.

   People seldom adopt new ideas when all systems are working smoothly. Why fool with something that isn't broken? On the other hand, ideas that resolve crucial problems get everyone's attention. If a product isn't working, a process is failing, a major new competitor is creating a challenge in the marketplace, customers aren't buying, senior executives are complaining, then the first step in persuading decision makers to take action is to get them on the edge of their proverbial seats thinking, "Oh gosh, we're so screwed. This is terrible! What can we do?" One advocate in an energy firm began her presentation on improving safety by displaying a graph of the number of accidents on job sites over the past year. The line on the graph sloped sharply upward. And along the line were photographs of each injured person. We have, she said, a major problem. That got people's attention.

   2. *Offer a solution that resolves the need.* After presenting a compelling need, an advocate presents a plan — his or her proposal and what decision makers need to do to make the proposal succeed. Smart advocates yoke features of their proposals to the specific pains of decision makers: show that pain 1 is resolved by features A and B, that pain 2 is handled by features B, C, and D, and so on (table 3). Alternatively, advocates sometimes start with the features of their proposals and, by defining problems with their proposals in mind, yoke features of their proposals to problems that decision makers don't even know they face (see chapter 3).

Table 3. Matching Proposal to Need

	Pain 1	Pain 2	Pain 3	Pain 4	Pain 5	Pain 6	Pain 7
Feature A							
Feature B							
Feature C							
Feature D							
Feature E							
Feature F							

However pains and features are aligned, wise advocates present the pains first. A fatal mistake that inexperienced advocates make is proposing ideas before decision makers feel any pain. These advocates start their pitches with statements like "Here is what I would like to do." Only later do they get around to explaining the problem. That is the wrong sequence. When advocates pitch plans before demonstrating needs, decision makers may challenge the plans before the advocates can explain their rationale. "We can't afford that!" "It will never work!" "It's too complex!" "The media will kill us!" The poor advocate is left pleading, "Just let me explain . . ." But by then the case is often closed. Pain gets people to listen to the plan.

3. *Describe benefits accruing from the proposal.* After pitching their proposals, deft advocates describe potential benefits that will accrue over and above simply resolving specific problems. In some cases, the benefits are easy to see. In other cases, they may be overlooked unless advocates make them explicit. When President Dwight Eisenhower pitched the Interstate Highway System, the obvious beneficiaries included companies and truckers who could whisk products to market. There were also clear benefits for families who wanted to visit loved ones and take vacations. Less obvious were indirect economic benefits. Highway construction is a big-budget infrastructure program. It throws off enormous amounts of money and stimulates the economy by providing jobs. Once built, highways continue to generate money. Salable real estate expands, and new businesses prosper.

Investing in highways, Eisenhower reminded Congress, will make money. He was right. In the 1950s, highway spending was responsible for 31 percent of the increased productivity of the United States. In the 1960s, highways accounted for about 25 percent of national economic growth.[21]

Just as threats must raise immediate concerns to be successful, not long-term ones, proposals must deal prominently with the here and now, not the far-off future. Smart proponents emphasize the immediate benefits of their ideas because, as we saw earlier, most people are more interested in what they are going to get tomorrow, not in a year or two. Like it or not, immediate gratification matters. In fact, people tend to value smaller instant gains more than larger postponed gains. Given a choice, they prefer a $250 lottery prize today to a $410 prize a year later.[22]

4. *Outline difficulties that will emerge if the proposal isn't adopted.* To clinch acceptance of a proposal, an adroit advocate relates what difficulties might occur if the decision makers give it a pass. These difficulties are over and beyond the needs that the proposal is meant to address — the "pains" raised at the start of the pitch. Years ago my wife and I were mulling summer vacation plans. I was thinking of a cool trip to Canada. My wife suggested Disney World.

"Let's do that next year," I suggested.

She responded, "You know, if we don't go this year, the kids may be too old to enjoy everything. Our daughter may not be into princesses next year." So off the family went to a humid Orlando — a classic case of avoiding regret.

People often fear missing out on something even more than they anticipate opportunities. Let decision makers know the cost of not investing (e.g., "If we fail to seize the opportunity, competitors will, and we'll lose out. We won't get a second chance.") As the innovator Guy Kawasaki contends, "If there's anything an investor hates more than a lousy deal, it's not getting in on a good deal."[23]

For many years, every film made in the United States needed to be screened by a committee, which used the Hays Code to rate it. If a film was too provocative, the committee could block its release to theaters. By the 1960s, too many films worldwide were challenging the basic presumptions of the code, and audiences were demanding change as well. The Hays Code was dropped. Jack Valenti, who was running the Motion Picture Association of America, knew that the association had to provide audiences with guidance about films — something akin to the rating system we have today

(G, PG, R, and so on). But Valenti faced resistance from much of Hollywood's leadership. The argument that won the day for him was simple: if we don't do it ourselves, the government will; and what the government does will probably be a lot more unwieldy.[24] By highlighting the possible outcome of failing to accept his proposal, Valenti succeeded in pushing it through. If you remind people of what happens if they don't adopt your idea, you may win the decision makers' approval.

Techniques of Persuasion

Structuring messages for influence is easy if you practice some tried-and-true techniques.

The foot-in-the-door technique. Your doorbell rings. Opening the door, you discover a woman on the porch. She asks if you might donate $5 to an organization whose mission is to assist destitute children. Generously, you reach for your wallet. After you hand her the money, she asks, "Oh, and would you also mind distributing these requests for donations to your neighbors? You just need to give them the requests and then collect them." Will you comply with this follow-up request? You are far more likely to agree if you have already given $5 than if she had made the request without asking for $5 ahead of time.[25] Psychologists call what she did the foot-in-the-door technique: ask for something small, get it, and then ask them for something more. The name for the technique comes from the classic maneuver of the door-to-door salesman. When a homeowner opened the door, the salesman slipped a foot between the door and the doorframe, keeping the door ajar so he could continue the sales pitch even if the homeowner tried to slam the door in his face.

The foot-in-the-door technique works because people like consistency. If you have already donated $5, it is inconsistent to refuse a second request. Once committed, you stay committed. If your mailbox is littered with charitable requests, you understand the technique. If, feeling charitable, you send a charity $15, weeks later you will open another request from the same organization, this time asking for more. And you may well fall for it. Once you start giving to a charity, it is hard to say no to future requests.

In organizations the foot-in-the-door technique is often used when advocates seek start-up funding for ideas. Once decision makers provide a small budget, advocates bid for additional funding for development costs, then for pilot tests, then for more and more. Soon, decision makers find themselves approving major initiatives. When organizations are hesitant about a big initiative, crafty advocates often make small requests that over time amount to big projects or significant changes. Proponents for the famous Hubble space telescope used this method to procure government funding. Even though scientists knew that the total cost of the telescope would be in the billions, they initially sought only $300 million. Once Congress approved the project, they could go back and ask for more.[26]

The door-in-the-face technique. A friend's daughter called home from college one evening to ask her mother for $200. Her mother said no. "But Mom," the daughter pleaded, "I *need* $200."

"No," replied the mother.

"Please!"

"No way."

"Okay, then, how about $50?" the daughter asked.

"Yeah, I suppose I can get that to you right away."

How much money did the daughter want in the first place? Probably about $50. The daughter had mastered the door-in-the face technique.

In organizations the technique works like this: Advocates ask for something quite large — a big investment, a sizable increase in head count. Decision makers promptly turn them down. Then the advocates request something smaller — a minor investment, maybe two additional people — and decision makers accede.[27] You see this at budget time. Managers inflate what they need, knowing they will be rebuffed. Then decision makers offer an amount close to what the managers really wanted in the first place. The second, smaller appeal doesn't seem so big after decision makers have contemplated the much larger first request.

Scaling down. A pizza maker offers you a basic cheese pizza, then tells you that you can add anything you want to that pizza, although each item will cost a bit of money. Meanwhile, a friend of yours is offered a fully loaded pizza and told that he can remove ingredients that he doesn't want. For each item he deletes, the pizza's cost goes down. Who ends up spending more money on a pizza — you or your friend? When this experiment was conducted, researchers discovered that the friend spends more.[28] Why? Because it is hard to give up what you already possess. And because it is relatively easy to say no to things you don't already have. You see this in car sales. When you test-drive a fully loaded model, you are more likely to buy the additional features. If the salesperson had instead presented a basic vehicle and then let you, for a price, add one feature after another, you probably would not have bought some features included in the loaded version.

Savvy advocates exploit this tendency. When pitching proposals, they generously incorporate many features. They present, in effect, complete packages (also called turnkey solutions), easily implemented with available resources. Even though decision makers may knock items off the complete proposals, advocates will get more than they would have if they had presented minimal proposals and then pitched additional items, one by one.

Highlighting points of agreement first. Wise negotiators quickly work through items both parties agree on before negotiating for items on which there are disagreements. If they begin with points of disagreement, they realize, some items that both parties might have originally agreed upon might shift to the category of disagreed-on items.

Advocates do the same. They start discussing issues and ideas that decision makers can readily buy into and hold off on controversial ones that might arouse grumbling. You have heard effective proponents begin pitches with statements implying agreement: "As we all know . . . ," or "We've all been through this . . . ," or "I think we can agree on . . ." Bill Clinton, an astute politician, was a master at highlighting agreements first. In meetings, "he always grabbed on to some point of agreement, while steering the conversation away from larger points of disagreement—leaving his seducee with the distinct impression that they were in total harmony on just about everything."[29] After he churned through the many points of agreement, the disagreements seemed minor. This technique is especially useful when advocates meet with decision makers who may automatically disagree with their ideas. In these cases, wise advocates begin their pitches by highlighting shared experiences, concepts, or principles.

Telling them what you want at the end. People want to believe they are free to make their own choices. When that freedom is threatened, they struggle to show that they can't be controlled. When unsophisticated advocates tell decision makers early on that by the end of a pitch they will be persuaded to buy some notion, decision makers often react by thinking, in the words of Dirty Harry, "Make my day!" Wise advocates don't loudly broadcast their intent to persuade.[30]

On the other hand, once advocates have successfully explained their ideas and seen some nods of agreement, they should end their pitches with specific recommendations.[31] They should close the sale. And they may choose to do so in very specific and unusual ways. In one study, undergraduate students acted as street beggars. When some of them approached people and simply asked for money, 44 percent of passersby gave them money.

When others went up to people and asked for a specific amount of money, 64 percent of passersby gave them money. Interestingly, when the student beggars asked for atypical amounts (e.g., 37 cents rather than a quarter), 75 percent of passersby gave money.[32] Charities often take advantage of this tendency and ask for $13 or $42 instead of $10 or $30.

Presenting both sides of the story. Are you more likely to be successful in winning approval for your proposal if you present only your own side of an issue, or should you present both sides? Naive advocates may at first think, "Just my side. Why tell people the other side?" They may be right if they are speaking to uninterested, inattentive, or stupid people. They may also be right when listeners already agree with them, which is typically the case, for instance, at political conventions, where speakers, reasonably enough, rarely feel the need to articulate both sides of an issue.

Effective advocates know, however, that most of the time their proposals are more likely to win approval if they give both sides of an issue. This is certainly true in advertising, where boldly presenting a comparison of two brands is often a successful strategy.[33] Decision makers know that any issue has another side, so they are probably thinking about alternative perspectives while the advocate is pitching one side. For many decision makers, mitigating risk is all-important. So if there are risks, enumerate them. By candidly presenting some of the potential drawbacks of a proposition, advocates disarm decision makers and preempt their objections by dealing with them before they are brought up.

An even better approach than describing both sides of an issue, however, is to present a *refutational* message.[34] Here advocates describe their perspective on an issue, outline arguments against their idea, and then refute those arguments. By using refutational messages advocates demonstrate their thorough knowledge of the subject and establish themselves as experts. Further, when advocates offer counterarguments to what those opposed to their ideas might say, they help decision makers generate responses to what the opponents are arguing. Let's say a savvy politician gets up and makes her campaign proposals. Then, after a pause, she adds:

> My opponent is going to get up here after me and tell you he'll reduce taxes, increase funding to schools, improve health care, and guarantee inexpensive drugs for every elderly person. All of these are excellent ideas. I wish I could propose all them as glibly as he does. Do me a favor. When he stands up and promises to reduce taxes, applaud loudly. But when he starts talking about spending money for schools, for teachers, for health,

for drugs, ask yourself, over and over again, how is he going to pay for those gifts? How is he going to pay for them? How is he paying for them? Force him to tell you where the money is going to come from. What will he be cutting? How will he reduce taxes and spend more at the same time?

Her opponent faces a tough challenge when it is his turn to address that audience. What the first speaker has done is help the audience develop resistance to the rhetoric of her competitor.

Refutational messages can occur in the context of meetings. Advocates make their pitches; they suggest possible objections or problems that they believe decision makers may hear or consider later and then offer meaty responses to those concerns. Sometimes adroit advocates, after decision makers accept their ideas, spend time leading a discussion about how others in the firm might respond to the now-approved ideas. What objections might others have? What flaws might they see? These advocates are getting decision makers to informally rehearse their own responses to people who might object to the decision.

By improvising answers and having discussions about them, decision makers deepen their commitment to a proposal far more than if the advocates had simply told them how they might respond to others' concerns. When people craft arguments justifying their positions, they become more committed to those positions. And when they come up with arguments against an opponent's position, they are more likely to disagree with the opponent's proposal.[35] Indeed, in the legal environment, smart trial lawyers often raise weaknesses of their own cases and then downplay them rather than letting their opponents introduce those weaknesses.[36] Most of the time, when people reflect on advocacy, they think that their task is to persuade people to adopt their ideas. But that takes them only halfway. After persuading others to commit to your idea, you must ensure that the persuaded stay committed, that they will resist counterproposals and counteroffers. Refutational messages are one way of building resistance to arguments that might weaken their support of your proposal.

11

Make the Idea Matter

> It is not on the generosity of the butcher, brewer,
> or baker that we depend for our dinner,
> but on their self-interest.
>
> ADAM SMITH

Successful advocates package ideas in ways that motivate decision makers to adopt them. They make their ideas matter in three ways. First, they convince decision makers that what they are proposing benefits them. Second, they make their proposals easy to adopt. And third, by linking their proposals to decision makers' beliefs and values they make their ideas valuable and important.

Discover What's In It For Them (WIIFT)

In the eighteenth century, city dwellers around the world regularly fell sick and died because of streets that were little more than open sewers. John Bellers, an early public-health advocate, campaigned to clean London streets. He offered the king of England a seductive argument: "Every Able Industrious Labourer, that is capable to have Children, who so Untimely Dies, may be accounted Two Hundred Pound Loss to the *Kingdom.*"[1] Bellers understood that the king, like any decision maker, would quickly calculate, "What do I gain?" from any proposal. The answer in the king's case was lots — more taxes, more labor.

Before making proposals, advocates, like Bellers, figure out what we will call WIIFTs. WIIFT stands for *What's In It For Them?* WIIFTs are what excite people about an idea. WIIFTs answer questions like "Why should I care?" and "What's in it for me?" Lyndon Johnson had a genius for divining the motivations of the people he worked with. Hubert Humphrey, his vice president, compared him to a psychiatrist: "He didn't stop until he knew how to appeal to every single senator and how to win him over. . . . He knew how to appeal to their vanity, to their needs, to their ambitions."[2] It is an advocate's responsibility to find the right WIIFT for each decision maker.

Next time you plan to pitch an idea, create a simple two-column chart. In one column, list decision makers. In the adjacent column, write down a WIIFT for each of these people. There are an infinite number of potential WIIFTs.

Finances (e.g., saving money, making money, building market share)

Success (e.g., making them more successful; getting them a promotion)

Efficiency (e.g., streamlining data entry, reducing paperwork)

Status (e.g., titles, power, recognition, an enhanced role, "turf" protection)

Social consequence (e.g., doing the right thing, shaping the future)

Peer pressure (e.g., if everyone else does it, we should too)

History (e.g., tradition, alignment with what we have done before)

Affinity (e.g., people will like them; they will be part of the team)

Organization (e.g., enhancing reputation, beating competitors)

Security (e.g., job security, reduced risk, predictability, increased information)

Product (e.g., marketability, technical superiority, feasibility, enhanced speed to market, decreased cost, ability to patent)

Emotional attachment (e.g., link to their past successes, to their alma maters)

Good WIIFTs help decision makers justify their choices. When people contemplate adopting an idea, they mentally calculate what they will gain from the proposal compared to what it will cost to adopt it. If the ratio is positive, they buy in; if it is neutral or negative, they hesitate.[3] Back in 1983, when Walmart executive Glenn Habern proposed creating a $24 million private satellite system, CEO Sam Walton balked. It was expensive. Besides, Walton wasn't particularly enamored with technology. But he *was* passionate about personally spending time communicating with employees in stores. And he was fanatical about data. As the company grew, it became increasingly hard for him to make the visits he wanted, and the telephones in Bentonville had difficulty handling all the incoming calls with data. What convinced Walton to take the gamble was that the satellite system would let him regularly talk with employees and handily collect data. As David Glass, former CEO of Walmart, says, Walton "was a merchant first and foremost. He loved the idea of being able to talk to all the associates."[4] That was Walton's WIIFT. That was what sold him on the proposal. The benefit of communicating mattered more than the cost of the technology.

Politicians are masters of WIIFTs. In 1956 the White House needed to convince members of Congress to support the original national Interstate Highway System. One move that the White House made was to ask the U.S. Bureau of Public Works to produce a booklet. Titled *The General Location of National System of Interstate Highways Including All Additional Routes at Urban Areas*, it was bright yellow and contained ninety-seven pages of maps displaying the proposed highway system, which would cross major cities in forty-three states. The message? A vote for the highway system meant construction jobs, new highways, and money for members' districts (three big WIIFTs for any representative). The pitch was successful: every representative whose city was included in the booklet voted for the bill (all save one — and he wasn't reelected).[5]

Boris Johnson, London's mayor in 2011, took a similar approach. A bright fellow with an irreverent sense of humor, he has sometimes gone too far. He once promised voters that "voting Tory [Johnson's party] will cause your wife to have bigger breasts and increase your chances of owning a BMW M3." Johnson understood the value of WIIFTs — and who knows?

Your WIIFTs aren't necessarily their WIIFTs. Wise advocates never assume that what excites them about ideas will excite others. One of Thomas Edison's first inventions was a machine that could tabulate votes in state legislatures. When he pitched the invention to a member of the Massachusetts legislature, he was stunned when the man vehemently opposed his fancy new technology. The legislator told Edison that he wanted *delays* in voting — delays let people haggle, switch votes, and engage in all sorts of politicking. Speed was not what he wanted. In creating his machine, Edison had not grasped that a legislator's WIIFT might be diametrically different from his. The lesson stuck. Edison later wrote, "Never waste time inventing things that people would not want to buy."[6] Edison's next major invention was an alphanumeric ticker tape machine that quickly communicated changes in stock market prices. Speed was again the selling point. But this time, Edison's invention was immediately adopted. Wall Street's WIIFT was speed. Not matching WIIFTs to decision makers' interests reduces your effectiveness as an advocate.

Robert Taylor, a leader of Xerox PARC's efforts to build an early personal computer, ran headlong into the WIIFT issue when his team demonstrated its first PC to Xerox executives in Boca Raton. At the end of the demonstration, Taylor's team made the technology — a PC, the Ethernet, a laser printer — available for audience members to try. The wives of the Xerox executives — some of them former secretaries — immediately understood why the innovations were exciting. The executives themselves, in those days almost entirely men, couldn't imagine why they would want to use the newfangled machines. Taylor later said, "I came to realize that the wives had jobs in offices dealing with the document-preparation steps that our systems addressed. The husbands were high-level managers and thought it was beneath them. . . . Copying was still making them a lot of money and they were successful. They said, 'Why should we be interested in this other stuff?' "[7] The wives saw WIIFTs in the new technologies; the executives didn't. Consequently, Xerox missed an incredible opportunity.

Different decision makers have different WIIFTs. Advocates must recognize that within an organization, different decision makers will have their own WIIFTs about the same idea. So savvy advocates simultaneously address a variety of WIIFTs. Given the cyclical nature of the toy industry, Mattel Canada's warehouses were often filled with surplus products, so employees at one location proposed creating an outlet store in their warehouse. The notion got little traction until its advocates presented a multiplicity of WIIFTs — the sales organization would make money, smaller inventories would free up capital, and product distribution would be easier.[8]

Different times also mandate different WIIFTs. The economic recession of 2007–2010 required many proponents to highlight savings more than profits when pitching their ideas. A project's developmental stage also affects what WIIFTs matter. At the early stages of product development, when ideas are being screened, feasibility issues and the market potential of ideas are vital. Later on, such business metrics as projected sales are more important. Still later, as products are being made and sold, issues of performance and quality, as well as budget, matter most.[9]

Sometimes people's WIIFTs aren't obvious. Really savvy advocates figure them out. John Mack faced a major challenge when he was CEO of Credit Suisse First Boston during the down years of 2001–2003. The company's income stream was smaller than anticipated. Nonetheless, the firm's prior management had agreed to pay some senior executives enormous bonuses. Mack needed these people to give back almost $50 million of that money, so he appealed to their sense of justice and their love of the firm. He told one group of executives, for example, that if they were unwilling to give back money, many young associates were not going to get bonuses. "It's about fairness and building a great firm." One executive told Mack that, sure, he was willing to forgo his substantial bonus. Mack nodded and thanked him. This executive was surprised that Mack's acknowledgment wasn't more effusive. After all, the executive was walking away from a lot of money. An hour later, the executive's phone rang. Mike Krzyzewski, the famed coach of the Duke University basketball team, was on the line. Coach K told the executive — a huge fan of the team — that Mack was his best friend and had just confided to him what this executive had generously done. Krzyzewski went on to compare the executive to one of Duke's best players, a young man known for his selflessness. By the end of the call, the executive was left feeling deeply touched by Mack's gesture. Mack had understood that this sort of thank-you would mean much more to him than anything Mack himself could do or say.[10]

How do you figure out likely WIIFTs? Obviously, the more you know about people, the easier it is to determine their WIIFTs. Sometimes people tell you directly what matters. But mostly, successful advocates look for tacit cues. They notice what appears in decision makers' offices and what decision makers read. They listen to decision makers' complaints, their jokes. They think about what and whom the decision makers criticize. They consider the questions they ask, knowing that questions are often statements about what matters to them. In fact, finding out WIIFTs is much like finding out face-related matters, as discussed in chapter 5.

A challenge for advocates is dealing with groups of people who might have very different, even conflicting WIIFTs. Successful advocates will sometimes be blunt, highlighting legitimate WIIFTs that accrue from their proposals and honestly addressing conflicting WIIFTs. Wise advocates also create proposals that effectively address the WIIFTs of seemingly opposed parties. For example, Richard Sandor, one of the intellectual founders of the notion of carbon trading, successfully created a highly profitable business in trading carbon credits. That business pleased investors — they could make gobs of money trading these credits (money was their WIIFT). At the same time, environmentalists were happy. If carbon trading was to work, caps on carbon credits would, in the long run, reduce pollution — a WIIFT for them.[11] Sometimes savvy advocates move to general WIIFTs that integrate conflicting WIIFTs. When Barack Obama traveled to the Middle East in his first year as president, he raised the issue of freedom when discussing the Israel-Palestine dispute. But he focused on freedom from fear — something important to all.

WIIFTs can be features, functions, or benefits. Here is a quick exercise: describe a bottle of water you recently bought. You might say the bottle was clear plastic, held twelve ounces or 355 milliliters, was cylindrical, and had a catchy label and a twist-off top. These are the bottle's features. But are any of these features the reason you purchased the bottle? Do you really care whether it was made of plastic or glass? Does it matter that it holds twelve ounces rather than fourteen? Probably not. You purchased the bottle because you were thirsty. You wanted the benefit of quenching your thirst in a portable way.

In advocacy, features, functions, and benefits need to be distinguished from one another. *Features* are characteristics of products or ideas, *functions* are what those features do, and *benefits* are what the functions offer us. Because the bottle is cylindrical (feature), it is easy for us to hold (function), which means that we can carry it as we walk and talk (benefit).

Inexperienced advocates often spend too much time trying to sell the features of their ideas before pitching their benefits. They might hold up a bottle of water and say, "I am proposing to create a twelve-ounce clear-plastic molded container in a cylindrical form that will hold liquid. It will have a paper label attached to it, along with a twist-off top." No one will buy that idea. Instead, advocates should begin with benefits. "How many of you are thirsty right now? Would you like to quench that thirst in a refreshing way? In a way that you can take with you anywhere?" Benefits are a form of WIIFTs. They seduce people into buying an idea.

James Boswell, in his classic 1792 biography of the life of Samuel Johnson, related Johnson's ability to sell benefits. When given a brewery to sell, Johnson's pitch was, "We are not here to sell a parcel of boilers and vats, but the potentiality of growing rich beyond the dreams of avarice."[12] The features were boilers and vats. The benefit to buyers was wealth.

During the Great Depression, Lilly-Tulip introduced small paper cups that restaurants could use for serving condiments. Sales were dismal. Restaurant owners saw no reason to spend money on a seemingly needless new product. Frank Dosher, who later headed the company, overcame their hesitancies by suggesting that the cups offered perfect portion control. And what did that mean? Less waste, more profits.[13] The feature, a paper cup that served the function of holding portions, gave restaurant owners the benefit of greater returns.

My favorite example: Charles Revson, founder of the almost eponymous cosmetics company, said that he didn't sell cosmetics. He sold hope.

How much advocates focus on features or benefits depends on how much decision makers care about what's being proposed. Decision makers who aren't particularly involved in the idea being pitched care mostly about benefits. By contrast, highly involved decision makers want both benefits and features. Think about a typical car commercial on television: A car traverses dusty desert highways, snow-covered mountain roads, and muddy streams. In the last scene, the car is perfectly, amazingly clean. That is because people watching television advertisements aren't typically involved in what they view. Consequently, they care mostly about benefits. It is when they decide to purchase cars that they care more about features — the costs, miles per gallon, repair history.

Within an organization people care, to varying degrees, about any new idea. As an advocate, you should highlight the benefits of initiatives that don't affect a person very much. On the other hand, if proposals will significantly impact that person, you had better be prepared to discuss features along with benefits. Suppose you and your immediate boss are pitching an idea to senior decision makers. These top people are probably mostly interested in the benefits of your idea — its financial return, its PR value, its fit with corporate strategy. You needn't spend much time describing the features of your proposal. But as you walk from the meeting after gaining their okay, your immediate boss may ask, "Okay, how are we going to do this?" (She will probably ask before the meeting as well.) She wants to know exactly how you will execute the project and what she will have to do. Since she is more involved — her reputation now rests on how this idea turns out — she will want to know more about the idea's features.

Pandering subtracts from credibility. Advocates must be very careful to avoid being seen as pandering to decision makers' interests. There is a thin line between highlighting WIIFTs and being ingratiating and promising every decision maker benefits that the idea being pitched may or may not bring about. Overpromising or faking a benefit destroys advocates' credibility. Equally important, advocates must be sure that what they promise as WIIFTs actually happen after the idea is adopted.

Taking away things that matter to decision makers leads to failure. Tim Berners-Lee, creator of the World Wide Web, knew that at CERN, where he developed the Web concept, prior systems that didn't allow people to use their own personal style and software had been shot down in their infancy. So, to forestall resistance, he proposed systems that ensured that everyone at CERN would be able to keep what they already had.[14] And since CERN employees were familiar with programs that included angle brackets, Berners-Lee used those brackets when he created HTML, thereby subtly increasing users' comfort levels.[15] Not only are people interested in seeing their WIIFTs addressed in a proposal, but they also want to make sure they aren't losing anything they value. One sales manager tempted his team with big bonuses if they worked especially long hours over a few months. His pitch failed. Why? For many of his team, free time mattered more than extra money, and the only way they could achieve the bonus was by working weekends and evenings.

Make the Idea Easy to Adopt

Every idea has competitors, one of which is the status quo: "Why make any change at all? What works now is fine! Why fool with it?" Other competing ideas are other colleagues' proposals and notions being proposed by vendors and suppliers. To get ideas adopted, advocates must win out over competitors in a marketplace of ideas. They do that by successfully answering a series of questions.[16]

1. Does the proposal address something *important and useful?* People don't want to waste time or money dealing with unimportant issues. The perceived usefulness of a new innovation is a major predictor of whether people adopt an idea.[17]

2. Does the idea offer *advantages* over competing ideas? If a new notion is no better than the status quo, why choose it? Potential advantages include enhanced efficiency, big financial wins, gains in status, and good publicity. Decision makers tend to support ideas that they believe will improve on the current state of affairs or work out better than other proposals.

3. Is the idea *distinctive?* Skeptics often nix proposals by saying, "We

Table 4. Idea Assessment

	Your Idea	Status Quo	Alternative Idea 1	Alternative Idea 2
Is it important and useful?				
What are its relative advantages?				
What makes it distinctive?				
What is it compatible with?				
How complex is it?				
What is its history?				
Is it reversible?				

already do this!" They don't see how the new idea is different from what is already being done. So a successful idea will offer something meaningfully different. At the same time, a good idea shouldn't be too novel. An idea's novelty is often inversely related to how quickly it's adopted.[18]

4. How *compatible* is the idea with the organization's culture, capabilities, goals, and structure? The more compatible an idea is, the more likely it is to be adopted.[19] If the idea has an obvious home within the firm, it is more

likely to be adopted. If current customers will easily see its features or benefits, it is more likely to be adopted. Ideas that require companies to enter into entirely new markets will face more resistance than ideas that fit the current markets of firms.

5. How *complex* is the idea? Good ideas are easy to understand and implement. It is far more challenging to promote ideas that must be highly customized in every setting or that will require the entire restructuring of a business. The greater the complexity of a new idea, the more inclined decision makers will be to opt for the status quo.[20] One complaint about the Obama administration's 2010 health-care initiative was how challenging it was for people to understand.

6. What is the idea's *history?* Who backed it in the past? Are those backers respected and liked? Has the idea been hanging around forever? Was it rejected before? How did it fare in pilot testing?

7. Will it be possible to *reverse* the decision? Especially when decisions are consequential, decision makers want to know that there is a way back if the proposal falters.

The next time you are pitching a proposal, you might create a chart listing your idea, its competitors, and answers to these questions (table 4). Discovering unique and positive characteristics of your idea that may differentiate it from others is an important step on the way to successfully pitching it.

Connect to What Decision Makers Value

Smart advocates connect to decision makers' values, particularly their psychological preference for consistency, their emotional attachment to core values, and their beliefs.

Valuing Consistency

My mother used to declare, "You say you want to do well in school, but I never see you open a book!" She was trying to persuade me to read by highlighting an inconsistency between what I said I wanted and what I was doing. Because inconsistency makes people psychologically uncomfortable, they try to resolve the discord by changing their behaviors or their opinions. Advocates leverage this need for consistency by pointing out how doing what they are proposing is aligned with decision makers' values and beliefs. This preference for consistency grows stronger as we grow older, and decision makers usually are not the youngest people in their organizations—which advocates would do well to bear in mind.

In 1972, Miller Brewing faced the challenge of marketing a new low-calorie beer. Previous attempts to interest American consumers in "diet" beer had been abysmal failures. Americans apparently didn't want low-calorie beer. Nonetheless, Miller was confident that consumers would like low-calorie beer if they just tried it. How could they persuade people to try it? Is the typical male beer drinker concerned about his intake of calories? Well, maybe. But weight watching wasn't his first thought when he popped a brew. So Miller's advertising agency didn't highlight weight. Instead, it used athletes like NFL All-Stars Dick Butkus and Bubba Smith to hawk the wonders of "Lite" beer. The football players debated in television advertisements whether Miller Lite "tasted great" or was "less filling." The campaign was a smash. Today more than 44 percent of beer sold in America is low in calories.[21]

Why was Miller's campaign so successful? Because consumers prefer consistency in their beliefs. If we admire an athlete, and see that he or she prefers low-calorie beer, then perhaps we, too, should like that beer. It would be inconsistent to like and admire the athlete and not consider the beer he is drinking.

Miller Brewing isn't alone in using endorsements to build sales. Indeed, 10 to 20 percent of all advertising expenditures in the United States are directed toward paying celebrity endorsers, and many television advertisements use celebrity endorsers.[22] Since at least 1894, when bicyclist Annie Cohen Kopchovsky was paid to carry a sign for Lithia Spring Water on an around-the-world tour, sports figures have lent their names to products. Heavyweight boxer George Foreman made scads of money endorsing "George Foreman grills," made by Salton. Golfer Tiger Woods received over a quarter of a billion dollars just from Nike to endorse its various products.[23]

Use of celebrities to sell products happens worldwide. The British Dairy Association increased milk consumption among children by 12 percent by running an advertisement in which one child is drinking lemonade and another, milk. The lemonade drinker sneers at the milk drinker. In response, the milk drinker says that the famous Welsh soccer star Ian Rush likes milk. If you don't drink milk, he says, you'll end up playing for "Accrington Stanley."

"Who are they?" the lemonade drinker asks.

"Exactly!" says the milk drinker.[24]

The power of people like David Beckham (soccer) to hawk products in Europe, Ronaldinho (Ronaldo de Assis Moreira; soccer) to hawk them in South America, and Yao Ming (basketball) to hawk them in China cannot be underestimated.

Not only athletes make endorsements, of course. Every social cause finds its spokesperson. Actor Danny Glover speaks for anemia, Julia Roberts for Rett syndrome, and Celine Dion for cystic fibrosis. Sometimes their advocacy is heartfelt — for example, Katie Couric's husband died of colon cancer, and she is a strong advocate of colon checkups. At other times, spokespeople are paid by, for instance, the drug companies who produce medications for treating the ailment being showcased.

Using endorsements isn't a new strategy. Endorsements give advocates legitimacy. In 1882, Thomas Edison cajoled financier J. P. Morgan to be one of the first people in New York City to install electric lights in his house. Once the lights were installed, Morgan held a reception for hundreds of his friends to showcase the new technology, which prompted other wealthy New Yorkers to wire their houses. In 1952, Captain Hyman Rickover persuaded President Harry Truman to dedicate the keel of the first nuclear submarine. Truman's implied endorsement generated massive publicity for the submarine and for the idea of a nuclear navy. It also signaled to Rickover's adversaries in the navy that he had presidential support.

Sometimes endorsements are made nonverbally. Anthony Lake was President Bill Clinton's first national security advisor. During the Balkan crisis Lake had to persuade many in the administration to go along with his ideas for negotiating peace. At one point, Lake arranged to have Clinton drop in at a meeting where Lake was discussing his ideas with government agency heads. Clinton's silent yet visible presence was an endorsement of Lake's ideas. It ensured that the others in the meeting got the message.[25]

Not just any endorser will do. Savvy advocates collect endorsements from people who are admired by decision makers within their organizations. They link those people to their ideas. If decision makers don't like or respect a strong supporter of an idea, it would be foolish to use that person's name. Accenture dropped Tiger Woods in 2010 because of his widely reported sexual dalliances.

Advocates also use people's value for consistency to thwart ideas. Proponents for Prohibition gained support for banning the sale and consumption of alcoholic beverages when the United States entered the First World War by linking alcohol (made by brewers, many of whom had German backgrounds) to the enemy—the German kaiser. Americans who wanted to support the troops had to be against drinking.[26] In 2006, a very close presidential election in Mexico may have been decided when Felipe Calderón's campaign ran television advertisements tying his competitor, Andrés Manuel López Obrador, to Hugo Chávez, the controversial socialist president of Venezuela. Chávez was not popular in Mexico. The implication of the advertisements was that a vote for López Obrador meant a vote for Chávez.

Connecting to "Lust" Organizations

In using the consistency appeal, advocates don't necessarily name a person. Sometimes they connect their proposals to organizations that are trusted and admired by people within their firm. Think about it this way: Most organizations have "lust" companies—firms that top executives admire. In today's world they might include, among others, Nordstrom's, Google, Apple, or IBM. If your CEO could invite the head of any company worldwide to speak about how his or her organization operates so successfully, what company head would the boss pick? If a lust company has adopted an idea similar to the one you are proposing, you might remind decision makers about it. In the late 1990s, GE was a much-admired company. It had adopted Six Sigma as a way of doing business. (Six Sigma is an initiative designed to reduce variability in business processes by reducing errors and bolstering efficiency.) So if you were pitching the idea of using Six Sigma in your company, you might have said, "GE does this; we should too." The rate of adoption of new ideas in an industry often depends upon who has already adopted them. When early adopters of ideas have great reputations, other companies follow along.[27]

Using "God" Terms

Organizations have certain sacrosanct values, principles, and initiatives. Years ago, "quality" was such a value. More recently, "transformational," "diversity," "customer experience," "transparency," "globalization," "sustainability," "return on investment [ROI]," "product leadership," and "lean" (not fat) have achieved the status of "god" terms in some companies. You cannot legitimately argue against them because they have acquired the status of unquestionable values.

So what do savvy advocates do? They glue their ideas to current god terms, thus making it virtually impossible for anyone to object to their proposals.[28] In many companies, "safety" is a god term, so when advocates glue their ideas to "safety," decision makers are hard pressed to oppose them. After all, imagine saying that safety isn't important! In health care, "patient-centered care" is often a god term. Who can argue against it? In China, a god term the country's leadership often uses is "harmony." Who doesn't want harmony? As the Second World War ended, Gianni Agnelli, heir to the Fiat fortune in Italy, had the difficult task of convincing the American occupying force to let Fiat stay private. He succeeded. He convinced U.S. decision makers that they were supporting the notion of "free enterprise" by keeping Fiat in private hands.[29] For Americans fearful of communism, "free enterprise" was a powerful god term.

One reason why invoking god terms works so well is that it forces people who disagree with your idea to seem to be also rejecting the values or principles that the god terms represent. If a decision maker is not for the idea (and its associated value), then the decision maker must be against the idea (and the associated value), and who wants to go on record as opposed to diversity, or free enterprise, or harmony? Richard Daley, mayor of Chicago in 2003, wanted to rid the city of Meigs Field, a small airport downtown on Lake Michigan. He faced massive resistance from any number of groups. So late one night he had the city's construction department bulldoze giant Xs into the runway. Special interest groups screamed, pilots of small planes expressed dismay, newspapers called Daley a dictator. When asked why he hadn't let people know ahead of time, Daley said, with a straight face, that he had to move quickly because he was worried that terrorists might be planning to use Meigs for an attack on Chicago. In 2003 "terrorism" was a god term.[30]

Effective god terms take the high ground — "quality," "freedom," "family values," "fairness," and so on. President Lyndon Johnson successfully instituted school desegregation in the South despite strong opposition from many, including Governor George Wallace of Alabama. In trying to get Wallace to accept his plan, Johnson reminded the governor: "You came into office a liberal — you spent your life trying to do things for the poor. Now why are you working on this [school segregation]? . . . Now listen, George, don't think about 1968. Think about 1988. . . . What do you want left after you, when you die? Do you want a great big marble monument that reads 'GEORGE WALLACE — HE BUILT'? Or do you want a little piece of pine board lying across that harsh caliche soil that reads, 'GEORGE WALLACE — HE HATED'?"[31] One or the other, nothing in between. Choose the god term you want to be remembered for.

George Pake, founder of Xerox's Palo Alto Research Center, was challenged by colleagues about the costs of the center and his tendency to hire expensive talent. He replied: "I will hire them for their *competence* and their judgment about how best to do that research, and, until they prove my judgment wrong, I will do my best to provide them with the kind of *first-rate* technical support it is reasonable to expect in Xerox research laboratories. If that is the wrong way to build a *first-rate* corporate research center for Xerox, then I am the wrong man for the job" (italics added).[32] He won the argument, and his operation was not questioned again. To argue against him would have been to argue against both competence and being first-rate.

Similarly, Mohammed Aziz, a Merck physician, made the case for his company donating millions of dollars' worth of Mectizan, the powerful drug that prevents river blindness, by connecting the donation to a godlike principle crafted by founder George Merck years before: that the firm's primary purpose "is for the people, it is not for the profits. The profits follow." The moral argument won.[33]

Carly Fiorina faced tough opposition from some current and former employees of HP when proposing a merger between HP and Compaq. Understanding how much employees treasured the historic legacy of HP innovation, Fiornia used god terms from the history of the company to convince people that the risky move was justified. In one speech she linked HP's history to the changes she wanted to create in the company. "This company's history has always been about being daring. It's been about doing things that others said it was not possible to do."[34] "Daring that leads to innovation" — that was the god term. Who in the high-tech world could oppose being daring or innovative?

All of us have been victims of people using god terms. How do you resist such moves? The obvious way is to unglue the link between the proposal and the god term. A more powerful technique is to counter the proposal with another god term. When somebody argues that their notion will improve profits and build revenues (two possible god terms) the adept advocate might respond, "I absolutely agree that the proposal will enhance revenue and profits. But we have an ethical — indeed, a moral — responsibility ["ethics" and "morality" are god terms] to our stockholders, customers, and employees not to squander our company's reputation." Now the battle is on.

In 2007, Congress was debating the CLEAR Law Enforcement Act. Proponents of the legislation — which would have allowed local and state police officers to be involved in immigration enforcement — constantly reminded people about the importance of "safety" — clearly a god term.

Opponents countered with another god term—the threat of a "police state." The bill died. More recently, the Transportation Security Administration (TSA) initiated "enhancing screening." The public quickly called it "groping" ("don't touch my junk"). The TSA responded by talking about "terrorism" (a god term). At one point, some parents complained that the TSA was doing things to children that would be considered sexual molestation. "Children" in this context was clearly a competing god term. The TSA relented and changed their policy. No longer would children under twelve be hand-searched.

If you don't believe in god terms yet, think back to your teenage years. There was probably at least one conversation where you challenged a parent with "Don't you trust me?" "Trust" is a god term. Savvy parents may have responded with a competing god term: "We love you." Now the battle of god terms was even. You couldn't tell them not to love you.

Making It Personal—but Carefully

Certain ideas matter immensely to their advocates. Advocates believe so much in these "do or die" notions that they're willing to risk their careers to push them. When advocating for those sorts of ideas, advocates can increase their persuasiveness by explicitly making them personal. They can present the ideas in ways that clearly link the ideas with them: rejecting my idea means rejecting me as a person. Even hardened decision makers find it difficult to shoot down notions that advocates say define them. When advocates say, "Ethically I have to stand up for this" or "It represents everything I've worked on for the last ten years—it my entire career we're debating," they are making rejection a hard choice. Of course, advocates must be careful and not draw lines in the sand unless they are willing to live with the consequences.

Sticking to Norms

In a delightful scene in *Monty Python's Life of Brian*, Brian, who everyone believes is the Messiah, tells followers, "You don't need to follow me. You don't need to follow anybody! You've got to think for yourselves. You're all individuals!" After a brief pause, the crowd responds in unison, "Yes, we are all individuals."[35] No one wants to be seen as too different. People are inclined to do what others do.

Years ago, opera singers sometimes hired elegantly dressed people to stand and cheer "Bravo!" after they sang in the hope that the "clackers" would spark mass applause. Opera singers aren't alone in creating cheering squads for themselves. When Wendell Willkie ran in the 1940 presidential primary, he faced an uphill battle at the Republican Party convention. In a quirk of fate, the person responsible for distributing passes to the public galleries at the convention — a man adamantly opposed to Willkie's nomination — suddenly died. One of Willkie's supporters, Sam Pryor, replaced him and put Willkie supporters in every available seat. Consequently, throughout the convention attendees heard loud chants of "We want Willkie!"[36] The acclaim mobilized convention goers to support Willkie, who won the nomination.

Many decades later, investigators empirically tested the strategy of those opera singers and Sam Pryor. They asked students to check out the music at a local bar on one of two nights. Unbeknownst to the students, on one evening some people in the bar were plants. Their job was to respond enthusiastically to the entertainment. On the other evening, the same plants offered tepid responses to the music. Days later, all the undergraduates were asked about the music. Remember, same bar, same music, same everything except for the reactions of the plants. Students who had been in the bar with enthusiastic confederates were far more positive toward the music.[37]

"Norming" is an influencing technique seen everywhere: in the clothes we buy (we don't want to appear too different), in our response to events (the canned laughter on comedy shows prompts us to laugh along), in our behavior (cards placed in hotel rooms urging people to reuse towels as part of energy conservation are especially effective when they report that *most guests* already reuse towels), even in our recollections (people often remember seeing something that never really happened if others remember it).[38]

In recent years a new technique called social norming has been successfully introduced on some campuses to reduce excessive student drinking. Counterintuitively, students are not told not to drink. Instead, they are told how much alcohol their peers consume on average. Students see large posters in dormitories declaring that most students on campus have perhaps four or fewer drinks when they party. Why is this effective? The reasoning goes this way: Raised on movies like *Old School* and *Animal House*, students just out of high school overestimate how much drinking college students do. They imagine campus life as a continual party with lots of binge drinking. And because they want to fit in, they think that since everyone else drinks excessively, they should too. But giving them a different, more accurate norm may make them want to fit in with real students. On campuses using social-norms theory, drinking has been substantially reduced.[39] On the other hand, students who drink less than the "average" student consumes sometimes actually increase their alcohol consumption after being given the norming information — that is how powerful social norms are.[40] The concept of social norming also works in such areas as tax compliance, traffic safety, and sexual behavior.[41] Neurological research has even demonstrated that when we agree with the opinions of others, the pleasure part of our brains lights up.[42]

Norms often influence decision makers' responses to proposals. Advocates often highlight industry "norms" or "standards" to win their approval: "It's what everyone in the industry is doing today." The message is clear: if everyone else is doing it, we should, too.

Lyndon Johnson used to cajole fellow senators to vote his way by talking about the commitments he had already obtained. He would say, "Ah talked to Styles. He's goin' along. Ah talked to John. He's goin' along. Hell, even ol' Wayne's goin' along." As Johnson's biographer Robert Caro says, "Implied, if not stated, was the question: Do you want to be the only member standing in the way of the subcommittee's work?"[43] In recent years, posters in New York City subways, following through on an earlier anti-terrorism campaign, read: "Last year, 1,944 New Yorkers saw something and said something." The idea behind the poster was norming. If other people have reported seeing dangerous people and acts, so should you.

Adding Values or Beliefs

A company offering steam-cleaning of carpets advertised that "our company uses our own employees" — that is, it did not use subcontractors. At first glance, the argument is an odd one. Why should using your own employees matter when cleaning carpets? But in fact the advertisement does something that savvy persuasive advocates do: it creates a new, and perhaps unexpected, issue that decision makers (potential customers) might never have considered before.

Many scholars of influence consider a person's *attitude* to be a function of his or her beliefs. *Beliefs* are, in turn, composed of expectancies and values. *Expectancies* are subjective probabilities — how likely something is to happen, or how strongly related one thing seems to be to something else. *Values* refer to how good or bad that something is.

Suppose you are trying to convince a decision maker to approve of a

Table 5. Calculation of Attitude toward a New Process

Belief	Expectancy	Value	Product (= Attitude)
New process will speed up shipping	0.5	+2	+1.0
New process will increase efficiency	0.4	+1	+0.4
New process will be more costly	0.8	−2	−1.6
Sum of products			−0.2

new process. First, you might ask him what beliefs he has about the new process—for example, the process might speed up shipping, might make tasks more efficient, and might be costly. Next you might have him rate how likely it is that the new process will result in greater speed, enhanced efficiency, and increased costs. Use a rating scale that ranges from 1 to 0, where 1 means absolutely, without doubt, and 0 means never. These ratings are his *expectancies*. Then you might ask him to rate the *value* of greater speed, enhanced efficiency, and more costs. This time, use a scale ranging from +3 (wonderful) to −3 (terrible). (I made up some numbers as a demonstration in table 5.) After collecting the numbers, if you multiply each expectancy by its associated value, then add the products, the sum signifies a person's current attitude toward the new process.

Suppose you want to persuade the decision maker to be more positive about the new process. How might you do that? First, you might get him to change an expectancy. Right now he thinks the likelihood that your process will introduce greater efficiency isn't that high (0.4). So convince him that greater efficiency is more likely than he thinks. Much persuasion revolves around likelihoods—children assure parents they won't get hurt climbing trees, airlines tell passengers about on-time arrivals, engineers say the chances of an apparatus failing are small. In our example, if you persuade the decision maker to adjust the expectation that the new process will be more efficient up to 0.7, then the sum of the products would be +0.1. He now has an overall positive attitude toward the new process.

Alternatively, you could work on the decision maker's feelings about the value associated with each belief. Let's assume that the decision maker sees the value of efficiency as +1. What if you could persuade him of the huge importance of efficiency and he raises his rating to +3? Then the sum of products would be a +0.6. Persuasion is often about getting people to change their feelings — good or bad — about some aspects of an idea.

"It isn't that bad," says a child to her parents after getting a mediocre report card. They respond, "Yes, it is!"

"Arriving late is not that big a deal!" says an airline employee. "It's huge! If I miss the meeting, I lose the deal!" replies the passenger.

Getting people to modify their expectancies or their values is what most advocates do when pitching ideas. There is, however, another, more creative, way to change the sum of products and thus people's attitudes: you can add a new belief. Suppose you suggest to the decision maker of our example that the new process will bolster the brand name with customers. That may be a belief he has never considered. Adding a new element to the persuasive mix changes the overall calculation. Let's say you convince the decision maker that there is some likelihood that the process change will affect the brand name (0.6) and that it will be a plus to do so (+2). Now the sum of the products is +1.0 (table 6). Bingo, you have won approval.

Decision makers often have well-established beliefs about many aspects of any ideas being pitched; they have mentally calculated the advantages of the ideas and the potential problems, such as cost and time. Rather than trying to tear apart current beliefs, creative advocates generate novel beliefs about their ideas. As we just saw, adding a new way to think about an idea to the presentation may make the difference between success and failure.

Ralph Reed was, for many years, the public voice of the Christian Coalition, an umbrella advocacy organization for a number of conservative Christian groups. Reed later became a lobbyist for some major American companies. When Boeing, one of his clients, sought his help to build support for a more open trade policy with countries like China, Reed created an organization called the Alliance of Christian Ministries in China. The alliance made the case, in advertisements, that more free trade with China would bolster opportunities for more missionary work in atheist China. Typically, members of Congress, especially from conservative districts, would vote

Table 6. Calculation of Attitude after Adding a Belief

Belief	Expectancy	Value	Product (= Attitude)
New process will speed things up	0.5	+2	+1.0
New process will increase efficiency	0.4	+1	+0.4
New process will be more costly	0.8	−2	−1.6
New process will improve brand name	0.6	+2	+1.2
Sum of Products			+1.0

against any policy that would encourage trade with atheist China, but in this case Reed created a new belief that helped sell the idea.[44]

The music industry tried to derail Internet services that allowed people to download and share music. Because the industry knew that everyone had already heard the common arguments (e.g., "It's illegal") and had also already decided whether the issue mattered personally, it came up with a fresh argument linking the Internet services to the distribution of child pornography. It argued that users of the services could easily exchange pornography, and children, some of the primary users, ought to be protected from pornographers by having the services legally banned.

In June 2010 the Japanese Ministry of Finance raised a new and unexpected belief to persuade people to buy government bonds (JGBs). It ran advertisements showing attractive women saying things like "Men who hold JGBs are popular with women" and "Women have a thing for men who own JGBs!!!" What men had previously considered investing in government bonds to make them more attractive?

Consumers buy goods on eBay because of the bargains and the variety found on the Web site. In 2010 the company pitched a new reason for shopping on eBay: to help save the environment by buying used goods. eBay went so far as to have a consultancy calculate how much carbon a shopper would save by buying various products, such as a leather handbag, on eBay rather than purchasing them new. It turns out that one purchase of a previously used bag on eBay saves as much carbon as a person would expend in a flight from London to Paris.[45] Chocolate manufacturers have done the same thing in creating a new criterion for buyers: Is the chocolate certified by an organization such as Fair Trade USA or the Rainforest Alliance, which assures that products aren't made by factories that use child labor or squander water resources?

Sometimes inventive advocates recognize that their organization's toll-gates won't let their ideas move forward. So they convince decision makers to consider alternative criteria for their projects. For instance, in many biomedical firms, one criterion for new oncology drugs is that they reduce tumor size. But some new drugs approach cancer differently: rather than shrinking tumors, they stop them from growing. In pushing a drug that inhibits growth, a researcher would be stymied if the criterion was reducing tumor size. She might argue that a valid alternative criterion might be "Does it hold tumors at their current size?"

Politicians constantly scan the landscape for issues that people haven't yet considered. Bill Clinton came up with all sorts of small issues that resonated with voters — issues that typically weren't even the province of presidents. For instance, he made a passionate case for requiring school uniforms. School uniforms?

George W. Bush latched onto estate taxes (he relabeled them "death taxes") in the South Carolina primary during his first presidential campaign. Realistically, estate taxes are a financial nonissue to most people, since most people aren't rich. Indeed, when Bush campaigned against the tax, only the top 2 percent of estate holders had to worry about it. In fact, half of the country's entire estate tax was paid by only 3,300 estates, and a full quarter of the tax was paid by just 467 estates, each worth more than $20 million.[46] Not surprisingly, most people had never even heard about the tax. But Bush shrewdly made this nonissue into a major one: he created an issue that people had never thought about before.

Likewise, George H. W. Bush, in his race against Michael Dukakis, introduced late in the campaign an advertisement highlighting the fact that prisoners were given furloughs. That commercial, often called the "Willie Horton ad" after one of the individuals referred to in it, showed prisoners leaving jail on furloughs while the voice-over told viewers that during Dukakis's term as governor of Massachusetts, some furloughed prisoners had robbed people and even raped women. What the advertisement did, in other words, was introduce into the election campaign an issue that most voters were unaware of—prison furloughs. Voters had already assessed each candidate on many well-established issues, such as the environment, taxes, and national defense, but few had ever considered prison furloughs. (Nor did the advertisement mention that the Massachusetts furlough program was introduced by a Republican governor in 1967.)

Make a Memorable Case

There are no days in life so memorable as those
which vibrated to some stroke of the imagination.
LAWRENCE DURRELL

Stroll along a crowded city street. What do you notice? Actually, not much when you consider how much could grab your attention. Eventually, though, something sparks your interest. Why? What makes that thing more conspicuous than anything else? When you are advocating, it is useful to imagine decision makers as pedestrians winding their way along avenues of ideas. Successful advocates get decision makers to notice their proposals among the clutter of ideas. How they strike sparks of interest is what this chapter is about. You can make your own ideas memorable if you use the same techniques: (1) make ideas vivid; (2) anchor arguments; (3) apply unforgettable labels; (4) use striking images; and (5) come up with convincing figures of speech.

Make Ideas Vivid

You are contemplating buying a new computer. Let's say *Consumer Reports* has a comprehensive, unbiased, empirical evaluation comparing the X-900 computer against many competing models, including one called the Castillion. According to the magazine, the X-900 has outsold the Castillion by a factor of ten and has far fewer problems than the alternatives. The X-900 sounds like just the ticket. As you check it out at the store, the fellow next to you asks if you are thinking about buying the computer. You nod. He leans over and whispers, "It's the worst computer I've owned!" He details a myriad of problems he has experienced. "Take my advice — buy the Castillion instead," he urges. "Two of my friends brought Castillions and love them. I just ordered one myself." What do you do at this point? Do you buy the X-900? Or do you start wondering about the wisdom of purchasing the X-900 despite the *Consumer Reports* summary? If you are like most people, the vivid description of one man's problems sways you more than all the statistical information.[1] We are biased toward vivid information: an example, a story, a striking detail.

Vivid examples make memorable and powerful points when an advocate is pitching an idea. As Mark Twain once quipped, few things are harder to put up with than the annoyance of a good example. In 2003 the German economy was suffering. Many Germans were complaining that some people were receiving excessive and undeserved welfare money from the government. In the midst of the uproar, the *Bild Zeitung* reported the case of Rolf John, a German citizen who had lived for more than twenty years in a gated community in Florida. Each month the German government sent him a $2,200 unemployment check for rent, living expenses, and a housekeeper. The story struck a nerve. It sparked public outrage. Germany's chancellor said that Mr. John's stipend was unacceptable. The head of Germany's health and social security agency agreed, telling reporters, "There won't be any more welfare under palm trees."[2] Mr. John's vivid case affected the government's entire policy on welfare.

People are persuaded by vivid examples, even if they are unrepresentative. They are more likely to buy flood insurance immediately after a flood has been in the news; they overestimate the likelihood of succumbing to unusual but colorful ways of dying (sharks kill fewer people each year than mosquitoes or elephants, but try to convince people of this after they watch *Jaws*). Successful proponents know the value of a memorable example. They talk about successful pilot runs of their ideas or raise the names of well-respected companies that have already adopted an idea. When opposing issues, advocates mention failures (e.g., "When this was in the lab, the entire apparatus blew up — knocked a giant hole right through the wall"; "This reminds me of last year's biggest and most embarrassing flop. We can't let that happen again.").

Sometimes advocates even wait to acquire a vivid example before they pitch their proposals. Clair Patterson, the Caltech professor who convinced the world that leaded gasoline was dangerous, conducted numerous scientific studies, but all of them received limited public attention until the sociologist S. Colum Gilfillan garnered worldwide media attention in 1996 by claiming that lead in water pipes caused the downfall of the great Roman Empire. The vivid example of one of history's most powerful states being brought to its knees by lead poisoning attracted public attention to Patterson's scholarship.[3]

Good stories are persuasive because they are vivid. Think about those hour-long television "news" programs that present compelling narratives of people being injured — physically, psychologically, or financially. Most viewers quickly and mindlessly generalize from those single horrendous events to the entire world. They seldom ask how typical the events they viewed are. Do they occur often? To many people? Data are marginalized in favor of vividness.

Striking details are as persuasive as stories. Suppose you devise a new method to kill dust mites, those almost invisible creatures that lurk in every corner of our homes. Your first step in pitching your idea might be to make people aware that dust mites live in their homes and are likely to nest in mattresses. Alternatively, you might report that the weight of the average mattress can double in a decade as it gets filled with dust mites and their excrement.[4] Which statement has a bigger impact?

Numbers can be striking details, too. But straightforward quantitative information is often mind-numbingly boring. People can get lost in figures. As Oliver Wendell Holmes said, "Most people reason dramatically, not quantitatively." So when wise advocates use numbers, they incorporate vivid equivalencies for those numbers that make them both interesting and real.

The Centers for Disease Control and Prevention (CDC) urges people to wash their hands regularly to avoid colds and flu. How long should you scrub? Twenty seconds, says the CDC, adding that twenty seconds is the equivalent of singing two choruses of "Happy Birthday to You."

The space shuttle zipped through space at 17,500 miles per hour. That speed sounds impressive, but you don't really comprehend it until you are told that astronauts saw a sunrise and sunset every forty-five minutes. Now *that* is fast!

In 1981, President Ronald Reagan complained about the "incomprehensible" size of the national debt, then at $1 trillion, by saying: "If you had a stack of $1,000 bills in your hand only four inches high, you'd be a millionaire. A trillion dollars would be a stack of $1,000 bills 67 miles high."[5]

In every example, the number is brought home by a vivid equivalency. Vivid equivalencies make advocates' pitches especially compelling. Consider these examples:

When proponents of planting and protecting trees in New York City sought to build public support for conserving trees, they reported that just 322 street trees kept 143 tons of pollution from the lungs of New Yorkers.[6] If you want clean lungs, support trees — the message is crystal-clear.

In 2009, U.S. energy secretary and Nobel Prize winner Steven Chu said that if the roofs of about two-thirds of the buildings in one hundred large cities in tropical and temperate areas worldwide were painted white, we would gain the same climate benefit as we would by taking all the world's cars off the road for ten years.[7] Get painting!

The average office desk has 20,961 germs per square inch. The *Wall Street Journal* told readers that the number of germs on a desk was four hundred times greater than the number found on the average toilet seat.[8] Who funded the study? Clorox, the maker of disinfecting products.

The Center for Science in the Public Interest has mastered the use of vivid number equivalencies. To convince us to reduce our consumption of desserts, the center came up with some hard-to-ignore, hard-to-forget comparisons: a Cinnabon Roll (670 calories; 34 grams of fat) is equal to a McDonald's Big Mac plus an entire hot fudge sundae. Cheesecake Factory's "The Original" cheesecake (710 calories; 49 grams of fat) is equal to a Pizza Hut Personal Pan Pepperoni Pizza plus two Dairy Queen banana splits.[9] Which has a bigger impact — the number of calories and grams of fat or the equivalencies?

The center later made other tasty items less palatable through vivid equivalencies. For example, a bucket of movie popcorn has the same amount of fat as 6 Kentucky Fried Chicken drumsticks, or 42 pounds of jellybeans, or 500 carrots. Eating one dish of fettuccine Alfredo is equivalent, in terms of fat content, to eating thirty-one pieces of pan-fried bacon.[10] Carrot, anyone?

You might think that vividness affects only nonexperts, people who don't deeply understand an issue. Not true. Even people with enormous expertise can be swayed by vivid examples. For example, doctors may read excellent studies that conclude that a particular medication is appropriate for treating a disease. But they may ignore the advice because one patient, years ago, had a life-threatening response to that treatment.[11]

Anchor Arguments

The kitchen store Williams-Sonoma discovered that if it placed its priciest, $429 bread maker next to its $275 model in stores and catalogs, it doubled sales of the less expensive model.[12] Why? The expensive one established a mental *anchor* that made the less expensive one seem quite reasonable. If people had seen only the $275 machine, they might have thought the price exorbitant. But the higher-priced item anchored the consumers' perception of the price of bread makers.

Anchoring is a powerful technique that advocates use when pitching their ideas. Savvy salespeople use anchoring every day. After finding a Persian rug you like, you ask the salesman, "How much?" He flips over a corner of the rug showing the price tag. Seeing your crestfallen face, the salesman smiles and says, "How about I drop the price by 10 percent? You're my first customer of the day!" You perk up and start negotiating. Minutes later, you walk out of the store smiling because you got such a great deal — 30 percent off the list price. Sure you did! Were you to walk back in the store, you might see the rug salesman gloating. He had overpriced the rug by 80 percent. The price tag served as the anchor.

Even professionals can be biased by anchors. When experienced real-estate agents are shown a house and asked to estimate its value, they are biased by the listed price. The higher the listed price, the higher the agents' estimates of the value of the house. The listed price establishes an anchor.[13]

Successful leaders use anchoring when they are persuading people and changing corporate cultures. In the 1980s, Coca-Cola was the dominant player in the cola market. Roberto Goizueta, CEO of Coca-Cola, convinced the company that it needed a new anchor to assess business success. Instead of talking about its market share of cola sales, Goizueta mandated using a different anchor, which he called "share of the stomach." Now the anchor was the company's market share of beverages. While Coca-Cola clearly had big numbers when it came to its market share of cola, it had quite small numbers when all beverages were added together (e.g., juice, water, tea). Changing the anchor made it possible to think again in terms of big growth. During Goizueta's sixteen-year term as CEO the company's total return on stock grew almost 7,100 percent.

A less positive example of how anchoring is used to influence decisions is the tendency of some companies, when setting executive compensation, to anchor salaries to the salaries of companies that pay executives more than average. For example, the *Wall Street Journal* reported that Tootsie Roll Industries (sales of about $500 million) used Kraft Foods (sales of over $40 billion) as a peer when setting executive compensation in 2008. By using Kraft as an anchor, Tootsie Roll could justify high pay for its executives even though Tootsie Roll is much smaller and has much lower revenues than Kraft.[14]

How do advocates use anchoring in pitching the ideas?

Advocates understand decision makers' anchors. What are decision makers' points of reference when judging your ideas? What criteria do they use? What are they used to? At first, 3M had little interest in Art Fry's Post-it Notes. According to formal market research within 3M, there was little demand for his innovation. Fry felt differently. Early on, he kept track of how many Post-it Note pads people in his unit used. He found that his colleagues were using between seven and twenty pads per year. The same people were using only one roll of Scotch Magic Tape (a very popular 3M product) per year. Yet Magic Tape was one of the company's cash cows. Anchoring potential sales of Post-it Notes to sales of the tape made the sticky notes look like a money spinner.[15]

Advocates create new anchors for decision makers. Is benchmarking politics or data gathering? It is both. Politically, an adroit advocate in HR who wants to make the case that people in her department are underpaid might benchmark against three firms that pay employees more. On the other hand, if she felt that her employees were overpaid, she might seek data from three companies that pay theirs less. Savvy consultants benchmark potential client companies against best-in-class companies to justify the cost of their consultancy. If consultants benchmarked potential clients against weaker firms, the potential clients would see no reason to hire them. When the *New York Times* interviewed Kim Jeffery, CEO of Nestlé Waters, one of the largest bottled-water companies in the world, about the environmental effects of bottled water ("Can you really justify using all that plastic?"), Jeffery responded, "We use less packaging than sodas or other convenience beverages. . . . The bottles for carbonated beverages are twice as heavy and Gatorade bottles are three times heavier."[16] He didn't answer the question about using plastic. Instead, he offered a comparison with other sorts of drinks, making his product look good.

Advocates ask for more than they want. Smart negotiators, like the rug salesman, know that an opening offer anchors what follows.[17] In budget meetings, savvy political infighters always ask for more than they need. In all likelihood, some of what they are requesting will get lopped off. But the larger number they request anchors decision makers' attitude toward their request.

Apply Unforgettable Labels

"What's in a name?" Shakespeare wrote. "That which we call a rose by any other name would smell as sweet." He was wrong. In truth, labels matter immensely. As the three-time Pulitzer Prize winner Thomas Friedman says, "In the world of ideas, to name something is to own it."[18]

Advocates know the value and potential power of catchy labels and taglines. Consider the group People for the Ethical Treatment of Animals (PETA). Who can be against ethical treatment? Or think of the abortion issue, with "pro-choice" and "pro-life" sides. Who can be opposed to life or to choice? Contemplate Las Vegas. Which is the reason for your trip — gambling or gaming? Think about oil. Which does an American oil company do — drill for oil or explore for energy independence? Look at medicine. Would you be more afraid of contracting Creutzfeldt-Jakob Disease or Mad Cow Disease? They are the same thing, but the scary new name, Mad Cow Disease, makes people avoid eating beef.[19]

Political activists understand that what you call something really matters: 42 percent of Americans think the country spends too much on "welfare," whereas only 7 percent feel the nation spends too much on "assistance to the poor."[20] No wonder the U.S. House of Representatives has a Ways and Means Committee rather than a Committee on Raising Taxes. And consider the significance of another word choice and the difference it has made: Thomas Jefferson's decision, when editing a draft of the Declaration of Independence, to replace the word "subjects" with "citizens."

Let's move from politics to commerce. The Patagonian toothfish once populated Pacific waters extensively. In the late 1990s the marketer Lee Lantz relabeled the toothfish. With the name changed to "Chilean sea bass," the popularity of the fish exploded; in fact, it is now threatened with extinction. Same fish, different label, different result.[21]

The New Zealand fruit exporter Turners and Growers understood the political difficulty of selling Chinese gooseberries to Americans during the Cold War, when the United States and China were at odds. So the exporter changed the name to kiwi fruit—and sales took off. Which do you prefer: prunes or dried plums? Same fruit. Many people have happily bought a Mongolian desert rat for a house pet, but only under its new name: gerbil. There are many more examples of labels that make a difference. And there are many ways that labels can be used.

The Many Uses of Labels

Labels can make things seem more or less valuable. When entrepreneur Tim Blixseth was a young man, he bought three donkeys for $25 each, hoping to sell them for a profit. Seeing an advertisement that read "Pack mules for sale $75" gave him an idea. His advertisement read, "Three pack mules, $75 each." The phone rang off the wall. "All we did," Blixseth says, " is relabel the donkeys into pack mules" and their value skyrocketed.[22] Labels sell.

In Urbana, Illinois, some diners at a place called the Spice Box were offered a free glass of wine from a bottle labeled "California Cabernet Sauvignon from Noah's Vineyard" (in the United States, California wines are considered top-class). Others were offered a glass of wine from a bottle labeled "North Dakota Cabernet Sauvignon from Noah's Vineyard." The California wine drinkers ate 11 percent more food during their meals and lingered at their tables ten minutes longer than the people served North Dakota wine. Yet both sets of diners drank the same wine—a cheap $2 wine called Two Buck Chuck. The only difference was the label.[23] The California label inspired a sense of class and ambience that the North Dakota label didn't. That sense translated into leisurely dining and extra consumption. Associating the word "sale" with a product increases demand by up to 50 percent even when the price remains unchanged.[24] Used cars are more valued when they're called pre-owned.

Politicians use imaginative taglines to promote their ideas. Franklin Roosevelt offered America the "New Deal." Ronald Reagan labeled the USSR the "evil empire," and he called a particularly deadly missile the "Peacekeeper." In the 1990s, Republicans offered the country a "Contract with America."

Effective labels not only provide compelling taglines for ideas but create disincentives for opposing those ideas. Forty-five days after the devastating terrorist attacks on the Pentagon and the World Trade Center in 2001, the House of Representatives and the Senate passed a bill officially titled "Uniting and Strengthening America by Providing Appropriate Tools Required to Intercept and Obstruct Terrorism," but they presented the bill to the public as the "USA Patriot Act." Who in Congress could vote against patriotism at that time?

In 2009 the Obama administration called its huge spending initiatives "investments." Few people want the government to *spend* money, but *investing* in health care, infrastructure, and so on, is fine.

Roger Smith headed the Indian Head Division of the Naval Surface Warfare Center near Washington, D.C., in the 1990s. With budget cuts occurring throughout the government, Smith worried that his organization might be on the chopping block. So, without official approval, he renamed his organization the National Center for Energetics. He created the word "energetics" to describe his group's research on explosives. Smith even created signs with the name and added it to business cards and letterhead. Why? He knew that it would be easy for the navy to close a division of the Naval Surface Warfare Center, but not so easy to close a National Center. Smith's creative solution worked, and the center stayed open.[25]

A well-chosen label can sell even a bad idea. Ulysses S. Grant was a young general when the Civil War began. At one point he disobeyed orders. Instead of simply showing the flag to a massive Confederate force, as he had been told to do, he attacked. His move failed miserably, and Grant and his men barely escaped. Showing an impressive grasp of the power of labels, Grant insisted that his foray was a raid, not an attack. That is, his soldiers had not been repulsed in an attack. Rather, his raid — a quick in and out — was a daring success.[26]

Advocacy is sometimes about stopping or hindering ideas rather than promoting them. So advocates understand that creative labels can be used to undermine ideas. Think of how the label "death panels" changed the health-care debate in 2009. Thomas Edison was an energetic proponent of direct current (DC) electricity. He adamantly opposed George Westinghouse's competing notion of alternating current (AC). So when New York State began using an electric chair powered by alternating current to execute criminals, Edison promptly called alternating current the executioner's current and told people that it was good for only one thing — killing people.[27] Following through on that description, some of his employees suggested that criminals facing death were being "condemned to the 'Westinghouse.' "[28] Earlier, Edison had used labels to sell his inventions in another way. Whenever he talked about electric lighting, he labeled gas-based lighting "old-time lighting" and his technology "modern."[29]

Edison may have been unsuccessful in stopping alternating current, but history is filled with examples of how labels extinguish ideas. For example, a proposal to allow individual drivers to use high-occupancy-vehicle lanes (normally restricted to cars with two or more passengers) after paying hefty tolls faltered in northern Virginia when opponents labeled the lanes "Lexus lanes" after a luxury car.[30] What elected official can support a proposal favoring the wealthy? Opponents of genetically modified foods attacked companies selling such food for using "terminator technology" to create "Frankenfood." Evoking death and a mad scientist's monster could put off diners' appetites.

Persuasive politicians attack foes through labels. Richard Nixon's opponents dubbed him "Tricky Dick." Bill Clinton was called "Slick Willie." Political name-calling is seen everywhere. In the 2006 presidential election in Mexico, candidate Andrés Manuel López Obrador called incumbent president Vicente Fox a "chachalaca" — a bird that incessantly makes noise. Translation? Fox was all noise and no substance. Sometimes labels effectively strip opponents of their ability to even pitch their ideas. For instance, President Bill Clinton often successfully argued against Republican proposals by labeling those proposals "partisan," suggesting that their arguments were merely political. Similarly, when Vice President Al Gore questioned details of George W. Bush's economic plan, Bush made all the analytic work done by Gore's team irrelevant when he labeled it "fuzzy math."

Although critics may create labels to undercut others' ideas, sometimes proponents of notions unwittingly create labels that sabotage their own ideas. Steve Sasson was a young engineer at Kodak in 1975, when he devised the world's first workable digital camera. Did Kodak commercialize Sasson's invention? No. One reason, Sasson said ruefully, may have been his label: when discussing his idea in internal meetings filled with people whose careers revolved around film, he labeled his device a "filmless camera." "Talk about warming up an audience," said Sasson later.[31]

How to Create a Label That Sells Your Idea

Companies have long used internal code names for projects. Savvy advocates understand that since any idea gets called something, why not choose a striking name? Great labels insinuate themselves into people's minds, automatically and unconsciously creating instantaneous reactions, good or bad. As Microsoft product manager Michael Burk says, "If it's named properly, you get a little chill up your back" when you hear the name.[32] Equally important, when a label is used every day, people begin to believe that the notion behind the label is real. That makes it difficult to stifle the idea behind the label.

Memorable labels can be invented (e.g., Dasani, Exxon), or they can be drawn from real words (e.g., SoHo, for south of Houston Street in New York City) or people (e.g., Marriott). Wherever they come from, effective labels for ideas have a number of things in common.

Effective labels have substance behind them. A label by itself is not enough to generate consistent sales. When people ask advocates about their catchphrases, the advocates must be able to thoroughly explain the ideas behind them. The best labels communicate the substance. Think Weedwacker — the name says it all.

Effective labels are brief. Long labels aren't as effective as short ones. To increase the effectiveness of a necessarily long label, an advocate may turn it into a memorable abbreviation. People could stroll into the ophthalmologist's office and request "laser-assisted in situ keratomileusis," but they will probably simply say they want LASIK surgery.

Effective labels sound snappy. They should have a ring to them that gets people's attention. They should be easily pronounced.[33] Think of many best-selling alliterative brand names — for example, Coca-Cola and Bed Bath & Beyond. Both are easy to say, recognize, and remember. Ideas with hard-to-pronounce labels are seen as less inviting and riskier.[34] Companies with easily pronounceable names also generate higher financial returns in the stock market than those with more complex names.[35]

Amazon.com started off as Cadabra, Inc. But its founder, Jeff Bezos, had second thoughts and renamed it. Why? First, "Amazon" starts with the letter *A*. Just as AAA Plumbing gets first billing in the Yellow Pages, Web addresses often appear alphabetically when listed in magazines and newspapers. Second, the Amazon River is enormous, and Bezos had big dreams, so why not let the company's name shout size?

Snappy labels strike sparks. Think of Intel, for *int*elligent and *e*lectronics; Qualcomm, for *qual*ity and *comm*unication. Viagra was originally known within Pfizer as UK-92,480 or sildenafil — not names to conjure with. The new name, Viagra, implies vigor and rhymes with "Niagara," the waterfall. Harley Davidson switched its stock ticker name from HDI to HOG.

Effective labels communicate value. One unit in a military R&D organization was named Quality Assurance. Each year the unit's funding was cut. Recognizing that the label was both stale and uncommunicative, the unit's leaders renamed their program Mission Assurance. What matters most to the military? The mission! Funding cuts stopped.

When the civil-rights leader James Farmer proposed to President Lyndon Johnson that the federal government help disadvantaged black Americans gain increased access to opportunities, Farmer offered a program he called "compensatory preferential treatment." Johnson liked the program but not the name. Always a deft strategist, he relabeled it "affirmative action." Not only was that label more palatable, but it also communicated better what Farmer had in mind.

Effective labels make ideas look good. Great labels put the opposition in an awkward, often indefensible position. In 2009 some representatives in the U.S. Congress sought to mandate reductions in greenhouse emissions. They labeled their piece of legislation American Clean Energy and Security Act of 2009 — so opponents would have to vote against both clean air and security. An urban planning move is labeled "smart growth" — so opponents would have to support — what? — dumb growth? If voters oppose "energy independence," what are they for — energy dependence? Lots of labels make programs hard to oppose: "no child left behind" (who wants to leave children behind?), "clean air legislation" (are you for dirty air?), "family values" (are you against families? against values? against both?).

Effective labels are matched to trends. In the 1990s, simply changing the name of a company to include the ".com" significantly increased its stock price and its trading activity.[36] Even today, when mutual funds change the name of funds to match the trend of the day (e.g., changing "Small Cap Equity Fund" to "Small Cap Growth Fund"), the amount of money they collect increases substantially. Everything else stays the same; the only difference is the label.[37] What happens when trends change? You create new labels.

Some savvy advocates name their ideas after important people. In 1610, Galileo scanned the skies using a recently invented telescope. One of his first discoveries was four large moons orbiting Jupiter. Galileo desperately needed patrons for financial and political support — he wasn't rich, and his discoveries were challenging the dogma of the very powerful Roman Catholic Church — so he promptly named the moons after the four Medici brothers who led that wealthy and influential family. His labeling worked.

The Medicis invited him to Florence and gave him money, honors, a home, and a title.

In the late 1980s and early 1990s, Senator Daniel Moynihan pushed Congress to construct a large and expensive government building on Pennsylvania Avenue in Washington, D.C. Moynihan had long hoped that the street linking the Capitol Building to the White House would be filled with impressive buildings. The site that Moynihan had in mind had been an ugly parking lot. Construction proceeded, but massive cost overruns invited investigation. Moynihan was concerned that the Republicans in power in Congress might shut the project down. Luckily, a Republican congresswoman from California (Andrea Seastrand) introduced a bill to name the building for Ronald Reagan, an icon of the Republican Party.[38] Moynihan was relieved. No Republican could vote against a memorial to Reagan. Today, that building, the second largest federal building ever constructed, stands proudly on Pennsylvania Avenue with Reagan's name chiseled into its wall.

Similarly, in the late 1940s, Paul Reuter and Jean Monnet came up with the idea of integrating the French and German coal and steel industries. The two were wise enough to name their proposal the Schuman Declaration. Who was Schuman? The French foreign minister, who had, oddly enough, been born in Germany. Knowing how opposed many of France's leaders would be to any notion of working with archenemy Germany to meld major industries together, Reuter and Monnet figured that naming the plan after the popular minister would give the idea extra political traction.

Harry Truman's popularity as president was low in 1948. Knowing that a Republican congress would reject anything he might propose, he wisely named his administration's proposal to rescue a broken Europe the "Marshall Plan." George Marshall was a hugely popular figure in the United States at the time. He was secretary of state and the former chief of staff for the U.S. Army in the Second World War.

Effective labels are used frequently. Labels can be memorable only if they are seen and heard everywhere. When IBM changed its focus to the Internet, it introduced the term "e-business." The company shrewdly never copyrighted the name. It *wanted* people to use it freely. IBM encouraged its use by highlighting the term in numerous catchy commercials. Meantime, its top executives made "e-business" part of every speech they gave. IBM's strategy was to have the label, now almost synonymous with "IBM," become part of everyday business jargon. The impact of a label correlates with the frequency of its use.[39]

Effective labels don't promise too much. Inexperienced advocates sometimes come up with labels that suggest more substance than is feasible. One Canadian marketing manager, attempting to promote his idea of expanding the sale of company products to the United States, called his initiative "worldwide." Products would have crossed one national border. Suggesting global reach jeopardized his credibility.

Effective labels preclude unfortunate nicknames or meanings. In 2007, Seattle began constructing the South Lake Union Transit system. Pundits quickly turned the first letter of each word into a snicker-worthy acronym: SLUT. Although the city relabeled the project the South Lake Union Streetcar, the old acronym stuck.[40] Here is another unlucky choice of name: LUST. It is found, among other places, in a report entitled "Guidance to Regions for Implementing the LUST Provision of the American Recovery and Reinvestment Act." No, lust is not a government policy. LUST stands for "leaking underground storage tank." Another potential minefield was avoided when the U.S. initiative in Iraq was—so the story goes—almost called Operation Iraqi Liberation, or OIL. Policy makers changed the name to one less likely to backfire: Operation Iraqi Freedom.

Sometimes labels are limp or dull or imply the wrong thing. For example, advocates who want to inspire will avoid labeling an idea with any variant of the word "maintain" in it. And they will propose a "project," not a "program." The first has an end by implication; the second doesn't.

In crafting new labels for international use, be careful about what they might mean in other languages and countries. There are many, often-humorous examples of very different meanings that a label for a product can take on when it crosses a border. Rolls-Royce needed to change the name of its luxury car, the Silver Mist, to the Silver Shadow when it discovered that in German *Mist* means manure.

Even numbers used as labels can backfire. One company introduced a product in Asia with a model number of 44-4. The product fared poorly in China. No one in the company could account for it. Finally, a Hong Kong native told the executives that in Mandarin the word for "four" sounds like the word for death. The company gave the model a new number, 88-8. Eight (*ba*) in Mandarin rhymes with the word for "wealthy" or "prosperous" (*fa*). People and organizations in Hong Kong pay large sums to get telephone numbers or license plates with 8s in them.[41] The Olympics in Beijing started on the 8th day of the 8th month of 2008 at 8 p.m. Not surprisingly, sales for model 88-8 increased substantially.

Use Striking Images

In the early twentieth century, travelers crossed oceans by ship. Just like today, business travelers sought the fastest passage possible, but it was technologically difficult for steamship companies to build speedier ships. So some crafty engineers proposed adding smokestacks. In truth, oceangoing ships needed just one, two, or three funnels to handle the smoke belching from their boilers. But perceptions matter. If there were more funnels, even if they were there only for looks, passengers might think the vessel was faster and more powerful than it was. Famous ships like the *Vaterland*, the *Titanic*, and the *Lusitania* all had at least one faux smokestack. The design was so successful that in 1913 passengers aboard the modern three-funneled ship *Imperator* complained that they had been assigned a sluggish ship after sailing past the four-funneled *Deutschland*, an older, much slower vessel with a fake funnel.[42] Later on, naval architects went further: they angled ships' funnels to increase the perception of speed. Now ships seemed to fly!

The steamship designers understood what every great advocate knows — that image matters. As we discussed in chapter 2, visuals help decision makers comprehend ideas. But powerful images — photographs, models, or even mental images created by picturesque phrases — do far more than aid understanding. They garner attention and make compelling cases for proponents' ideas.

Gerhard Mennen, a druggist in New Jersey, made his fortune selling talc in the late nineteenth century. It was traditional to put a picture of the company's founder on products. He changed this. Mennen instead used a picture of a smiling baby. The image told consumers: "Use this product and look how happy your child will be!"[43]

Modern beer advertisements use images to communicate positive values. You never see advertisements featuring solitary old drunks with scruffy beards throwing up in toilets in seedy bars as they clutch their pint of stale, warm beer. Instead, you see attractive young people in warm, inviting taverns joyfully drinking ice-cold beer together. Message: "You're having fun in good company if you drink this beer."

For images to be persuasive, they must be carefully crafted to have:

- congruence
- vitality
- simplicity
- realism
- solidity

Images must *be congruent* with whatever is being pitched — status, safety, adventure, security. The polo horse image on certain brand-name shirts matches the image of wealth (who but wealthy people play polo?). In marketing electric lights, Thomas Edison added a lampshade. Why? Because his potential customers used shades on their gas lamps, and a familiar shade made his innovative electric lights congruent with their expectations for interior lighting. By the same token, he designed his electric lamps to emit sixteen candlepowers of brightness — just like gas lamps. And to turn on with a key — again, just like gas lamps.[44]

Images should *communicate something vital* about an idea. Think, for example, of insurance companies and the images they create. Prudential uses the Rock of Gibraltar to celebrate its stability, surely a desirable attribute in insurance. Travelers uses an umbrella to tell insured customers that they are "covered."

Images should *be simple*, without surplus details to distract people from the message. They shouldn't be complex. The average billboard is illustrative. Its simplicity helps people get the message in a flash as they whiz past in their cars. In Victorian England, John Sainsbury spent extra money putting tiles and marble on the walls and countertops of his grocery store. Critics claimed that his decorating was a waste of money. But Sainsbury understood his customers. In an age when disease seemed to be everywhere, customers wanted safe food. Shiny smooth tabletops and clean walls communicated cleanliness.[45] Today, more than 125 years later, Sainsbury is still a successful purveyor of food.

Images must *seem realistic* even if they are not completely accurate. Many nineteenth-century frigates carried few, if any, cannons. Nonetheless, many had black portholes painted on their sides. Why? Because from a distance the first thing that potential attackers spied was what they thought to be gun ports — and it was risky for them to ascertain whether the gun ports were real. In demonstrations of new technologies, the models often only approximate the appearance and working of the eventual products to be sold. But they give decision makers a sense of what the technologies will do when fully developed.

Images must *be solid* through and through, so they don't backfire. In political campaigns each side hunts for silly images of opponents. Who can forget the video of presidential candidate John Kerry windsurfing during the election campaign? No politician accused of flip-flopping on issues should ever windsurf. As a Republican strategist, Mark McKinnon, said, the image "perfectly conveyed the message" that Kerry kept changing his mind.[46]

It isn't possible to predict every possible mischance, of course. On July 4, 1996, President Bill Clinton helicoptered to Patuxent, Maryland, to release a bald eagle named Freedom as a way to symbolically celebrate the environmental accomplishments of his administration. The American national bird was soon to be removed from the endangered species list, but Freedom didn't make that any easier. After soaring into the sky, he was promptly attacked by two ospreys. Wounded, the poor bird plummeted into the water. The Coast Guard rescued him, but the damage to the president's message was done.[47]

Come Up with Convincing Figures of Speech

In 1940 most Americans didn't want to get involved in the war in Europe. Nonetheless, President Franklin Roosevelt felt that, like it or not, America needed to play a role. One of his ideas was to lend ships and other military equipment to Britain. But how could he convince the average American that this was a good idea? Roosevelt's solution was to use a striking figure of speech: "Suppose my neighbor's home catches fire, and I have a length of garden hose four or five hundred feet away. If he can take my garden hose and connect it up with his hydrant, I may help him to put out his fire. . . . I don't say to him before that operation, 'Neighbor, my garden hose cost me $15; you have to pay me $15 for it.' . . . I don't want $15 — I want my garden hose back after the fire is over." Americans understood this analogy: Europe was on fire. If it couldn't put out the fire, then the blaze might jump the ocean. The image that Roosevelt evoked helped him win congressional support for the Lend-Lease program. Figures of speech — metaphors, similes, analogies, and other forms of comparison — can be wonderfully persuasive.[48] Showing how an idea is like something else helps make it tangible.

How Figures of Speech Make Ideas Tangible

Well-chosen figures of speech *translate complex or unfamiliar notions* into understandable concepts.[49] They are a way of making the abstract concrete. For example, in explaining why cell-phone manufacturers in Europe were unwilling to adopt a new and improved standard, Lauri Rosendahl, an analyst with Deutsche Bank in Helsinki, said, "Everyone knows that CDMA is technologically superior to the early GSM. . . . But it's like having a railroad built in your country. Say the railroad has three feet between the rails. Someone comes by five years later with a better system, but that system demands four feet between the rails. It's irrational to rip out track that has already been built. It's not practical to replace the one thing with something slightly better. It has to be hugely better."[50]

Effective figures of speech also *provide common ground* between speakers and listeners. They link what advocates are pitching to the experiences of listeners. Lyndon Johnson justified the Vietnam War in terms of the "domino effect." If we don't stop the communists in Vietnam, he argued, democracy will falter there. From Vietnam, communists will conquer the Philippines, then Indonesia, and so on, until we are battling them at our own shores. For anyone who had watched lines of dominos topple one after another, this metaphor for interconnection and inevitability was a familiar referent.

When Abraham Lincoln tired of people criticizing every move he made as president during the Civil War, he responded: "Gentlemen, suppose all the property you were worth was in gold and this you had placed in the hands of [one man] to carry across the Niagara River on a rope. Would you shake the cable and keep shouting at him: 'Stand up a little straighter; stoop a little more, go a little faster, go a little slower, lean a little more to the south?' No, you would hold your breath, as well as your tongue, and keep your hands off until he got safely over. The Government is carrying an enormous weight. Untold treasure is in their hands. Don't badger them. Keep silent and we will conduct you safely across."[51]

One particularly attractive feature of figures of speech is that they give advocates ways of *concisely expressing their ideas*. In fact, great figures of speech can become shorthand for complex concepts. The metaphor of the "information highway" gave people a simple way to describe an often-puzzling new technology otherwise known as the Internet. Similarly, when cautioning the world about the Soviet Union, Winston Churchill said, "An

iron curtain has descended across the Continent." The "iron curtain" metaphor gave everyone a simple way of understanding a complicated foreign
policy issue.

What makes figures of speech so vital for advocacy isn't simply that they
help people understand issues being pitched. They also *garner attention.*
They incite emotional responses. Pithy metaphors help people grasp vis-
cerally what is being described. Rather than saying that an IRS tax audit is
stressful, you might use a simile to win heartfelt winces from friends — for
example, "Going through an in-depth audit by the IRS is like an autopsy
without the benefit of death."

Indeed, compelling figures of speech can change people's opinions about
issues. In 1980, Chrysler was essentially bankrupt. The CEO, Lee Iacocca,
journeyed to Washington, D.C., to seek over a billion dollars of loan guarantees. Congress wasn't interested in giving money away, and Iacocca knew
it. So he framed the loan as a "safety-net." Large numbers of auto workers'
jobs and homes would be saved by the guarantees, he said, and Congress
gave him his guarantee. (In 2008, financial firms used the same metaphor
rather than the more negative image of a bailout.)

Another figure of speech reframed an issue for factory owners in the early
twentieth century. They told the social activist Alice Hamilton that if immi-
grant factory workers didn't like working long hours in unsafe conditions,
they could quit. Hamilton responded, "For an employer to say to his work-
people, 'If you don't like the job, get out,' may be like a captain at sea saying
to his sailors, 'If you don't like the ship, get overboard.' " Just as the sailors
had to stay aboard or drown, the immigrants had to keep their jobs to
survive.[52]

Clinical trials are vital to developing new medical treatments. In these
trials, people suffering from a disease are randomly assigned to receive
either the new drug or procedure that is being tested or standard care.
Persuading people to volunteer to participate in these trials is often a daunting task. Research finds that when physicians use the "right" simile to
explain what random trials are, people are more likely to feel comfortable
enrolling in them. Telling people a trial is like a flip of the coin doesn't work
as well as explaining that a random trial is like determining the sex of a baby.
Having a boy is just as likely as having a girl. Why? Because the coin flip
implies that someone wins or loses, and when you are ill, you don't want to
lose because you were assigned to the wrong experimental group. There is
no winner or loser when it comes to the sex of a child.[53]

Finally, dramatic figures of speech *mobilize people;* they gain support for the proposed idea. Establishing a "war on cancer" and a "war on poverty" brought battalions of people together to fight for the cause. Understanding and support are exactly what advocates want.

How to Craft Striking Figures of Speech

Since it is difficult to generate metaphors, similes, and analogies on the spur of the moment, experienced advocates are constantly collecting and creating them. To make sure the figures of speech are persuasive, they adhere to certain critera. You will recognize some of the criteria, for persuasion requires many of the same attributes — relevance, novelty, and so forth — in its many aspects.

Figures of speech should be relevant.[54] Stephen Friedman, former head of Goldman Sachs, used a striking simile when encouraging his team to look for new business opportunities. He said that many investment bankers focus so narrowly on their goals that they are like coal miners who ignore rich veins of gold in the mine because they are so singularly focused on mining coal.[55] What more relevant image for the financial industry than gold!

Even when figures of speech are apt, decision makers must be able to understand their relevance. In one corporation, an executive described the difficulty of making an acquisition by saying that the leadership of the candidate company was "like a herd of South African sable antelopes." The simile had no impact — no one understood what he meant — even though it captured how alert and defensive the company's leadership was to possible attack from firms they viewed as predatory. (When threatened, sable antelopes form a circle with their antlers facing out, making it almost impossible for predators to snatch a meal.) On the other hand, consider this analogy about the value of preparing for a crisis: "Crises are as inevitable as changes in the weather. Like a rain or snow storm, crises usually show signs before they happen. Just as most of us hate to be caught in the rain without an umbrella or raincoat, people who are good at managing crises have prepared ahead."[56] This analogy makes sense to anyone ever caught in a storm.

Figures of speech should match decision makers' interests. Choosing a wrong figure of speech can have untoward consequences. Bill Clinton's political team knew they had won a second term the evening that the Republican presidential candidate, Bob Dole, delivered his convention speech. In it he suggested that as president, he would offer America a bridge to the past, to a time of tranquility. Clinton countered that he would build a bridge to the future. (His campaign theme song began "Don't stop thinking about to-morrow.") He won. Why? Because American culture is future oriented.

Within organizations it is vital to use the right metaphorical category. For instance, sports metaphors ("teeing up an idea," "pitching a proposal") work well with people who enjoy sports. But when metaphors don't match the interests of decision makers, they may even alienate them.[57] In one company, an executive was legendary for her distaste of sports metaphors. If you used them, there went your chance of selling your ideas. In certain industries, there are commonly understood metaphors that outsiders don't get. In the world of finance, there are, oddly, many penal-related metaphors (e.g., "golden handcuffs," "collar," "lockup"). Even within an industry, companies may have very different metaphorical frames. One firm, for example, may like warlike metaphors ("enemy," "in the trenches," "shot down that idea"); another may prefer culinary ones ("stir the pot," "seasoned").

Figures of speech should be culturally specific. They don't always translate across cultures or languages. Thus, talking about "selling like hotcakes" or "throwing the baby out with the bathwater" might frustrate people not familiar with the English idioms. Talking about "going postal" or "drinking the Kool-Aid" might dumbfound a visitor to the United States. A German might tell you that an executive is living "like a maggot in bacon" — living in luxury because, as the French would say, "his wool sock is well stuffed." In other words, he's got a nice pot of money. But most English speakers wouldn't grasp the meaning immediately.

Figures of speech should be thematic. Avoid mixing them — for example, talking about "storming the gates of the competition" in one sentence and "drowning in data" in the next. Mixing figures of speech confuses and distracts people.[58] Shrewd advocates choose a single theme and weave it deftly through the entire pitch. But an extended comparison, one that every feature of your proposal is forced to fit, can also become laughable. Metaphors, similes, and analogies should fit your argument. Arguments should not be shaped by them. And remember, as soon as figures of speech become predictable or strained, they become tiresome.

Figures of speech should be contextually appropriate. In describing a self-centered person, one pundit said that he reminded her of the boy who murders his parents and then complains that he's an orphan. This might be an excellent analogy, but not for use in a bank that risked massive amounts of capital only to later request a loan from the government. Similarly, figures of speech must match the times. In the nineteenth century, farming was a common occupation, so agrarian metaphors were popular. Today, agricultural metaphors might not get as much traction.

Figures of speech should be accurate. Advocates don't want to make a comparison and then have someone challenge it. An executive was pitching the idea of creating a new line of business. Believing that his company needed to stop ignoring what was happening in the industry, he said, "We have to stop acting like ostriches burying our heads in the sand." One of the firm's leaders retorted, "Get your facts straight . . . ostriches don't put their heads in the sand!" End of argument. The advocate had both used a cliché and blown his credibility.

Many leaders of companies reference basketball or football teams when describing how competitive they are. In fact, most large firms aren't metaphorically similar to either. Instead, they are more akin to swim or track teams. In track meets, numerous events happen simultaneously (as in most big businesses), and most team members have little idea of how other team members are performing in events that are not their own, even though, in the end, the team wins or loses as one.

Figures of speech should create images that the audience can identify with. When Jean Monnet, the advocate for European integration in the mid-twentieth century, wanted to explain why his plans regularly changed even though his goal didn't, he said: "Suppose that you must climb a mountain never climbed before. You do not blindly hold to the course you planned at the mountain's base. Weather or unforeseen obstacles may force you to stop and reconsider at the end of the first day. Then you try a route of ascent not visible when you began your climb. On reaching the next level, you may again find yourself stymied. So, again, you seek an alternate route — perhaps several alternative routes. You can be entirely flexible about the paths you take. But you must be uncompromising about your objective, which is to successfully reach the mountaintop."[59]

Figures of speech should be fresh. The best metaphors, similes, and analogies are new ones. Often-heard figures of speech lose their emotional impact, but of course, some last forever. When Barack Obama pitched a huge spending plan in a speech at Georgetown University in 2009, he framed his initiative biblically. Referencing the parable from the Sermon on the Mount about two men who build houses, one on sand and one on rock, Obama said, "We cannot rebuild this economy on the same pile of sand. We must build our house upon a rock, a foundation that will move us from en era of borrow and spend to one where we save and invest."

A fresher example: During the 2010 congressional campaigns, Obama compared the economy to a car stuck in a ditch. He spoke about the efforts of the Democrats to right it and said about the Republicans:

> These are the folks who were behind the steering wheel and drove the car into the ditch. So we've had to put on our galoshes, we went down there in the mud, we've been pushing, we've been shoving. They've been standing back, watching, say you're not moving fast enough, you ain't doing it right. Why are you doing it that way? You got some mud on the car.
>
> That's all right. We don't need help. We're just going to keep on pushing. We push, we push. The thing is slipping a little bit, but we stay with it. Finally — finally — we get this car out of the ditch, where we're just right there on the blacktop. We're about to start driving forward again. They say, hold on, we want the keys back. You can't have the keys back — you don't know how to drive. . . .
>
> And I do want to point out, when you get in your car, when you go forward, what do you do? You put it in "D." When you want to go back, what do you do? You put it in "R." We don't want to go into reverse back in the ditch. We want to go forwards. We got to put it in "D."[60]

Figures of speech should withstand distortion. A figure of speech that can be turned against you can't be effective. In pitching an idea for spending more time developing a particular sort of software, one technologist said, "Like counting the number of cars in a restaurant parking lot, counting the number of people who use our various products offers a great metric of what we should, as a company, invest in." A person opposing this idea turned the analogy around: "Sure, but the cars that are parked in that lot of yours are old, rusty cars with fat but poor owners. What we should do is create software that attracts new cars with rich drivers, and your idea certainly won't do that!" The Republicans turned Obama's car-in-the-ditch analogy against him when they suggested that the car had a bumper sticker on it reading "Obama/Biden."

Think about figures of speech this way: When Superman was first introduced on the radio, he wasn't just faster, stronger, and more powerful. Instead, he was "faster than a speeding bullet, more powerful than a locomotive, able to leap tall buildings in a single bound!" Proponents make their ideas as memorable as Superman.

13

Demonstrate Confidence

What convinces is conviction.

LYNDON JOHNSON

A colleague of mine often shows his classes a video containing 12 ten-second segments drawn from CNBC, the business network. In each segment, a different speaker discusses a potential investment. After each presentation comes a pause during which students rate the perceived confidence of the preceding speaker. Students watch one speaker and rate that speaker, then watch a second speaker and rate that person, and so on. After all twelve speakers are rated, the video is restarted, and everyone again watches each segment, but this time the students are asked to assess each speaker's competence. What is the correlation between students' ratings of confidence and competence? Very strong. Confident people are perceived as competent, at least when they are unknown to the listeners. Crucial to successful advocacy is the belief, on the part of decision makers, that the advocates are competent. For advocates the corollary is that they must appear confident.

Many years ago a Yale psychologist, Ellen Langer, had pairs of people draw from the top of a card deck. One person in the pair was a confederate. With some subjects, the confederate appeared quite confident and socially skilled. With other subjects, the confederate was socially awkward. After drawing the cards but before looking at them, the subjects bet on whether they held the high card. The results were amazing. Subjects made much higher bets — almost double in size — when the confederate displayed little confidence. What is the message? People don't want to bet against confident people.[1] Why? People who speak confidently are more trusted and are perceived to be more competent and influential.[2] Decision makers are more willing to buy ideas from individuals who appear confident.[3] Tentative speakers, on the other hand, are seen as both less intelligent and less credible.[4] In courtrooms, jurors are far more inclined to believe eyewitnesses who confidently report what they saw. Hesitant witnesses are considered less credible even though there is only a very modest correlation between eyewitness accuracy and eyewitness confidence.[5]

The courtroom scene plays out in business as well. In describing Carly Fiorina, the former head of HP who successfully advocated merging HP and Compaq, a graduate-school colleague said, "Her main secret was confidence. She may not have had a clue about the subject, but she addressed it with such confidence that you would never know."[6] Similarly, Tamotsu Iba, a managing director at Sony, explained that Ken Kutaragi, the champion of PlayStation, was so "self-assertive" and "self-confident" that you just wanted to back him.[7]

Advocates can, of course, be overconfident, even cocky, and that can undermine their influence — and their credibility — as in this dialogue.

> A fellow says to a friend, "Anyone who says they're absolutely positive about something is a fool."
> The friend asks, "Are you sure of that?"
> He replies, "Yep, I'm totally positive!"

The relationship between sounding confident and being influential, when tabulated, looks like an inverted U (fig. 5).[8] Both too little and too much confidence hurts advocates' persuasiveness. If you aren't confident enough, you are a verbal wimp; if you are too confident, you can overpower the decision makers and lose your credibility.

How much confidence advocates should display requires careful calibration, depending upon quite a few factors.

1. The ethnic *cultures* involved need to be considered. Spanish-speaking cultures as well as many Asian cultures value indirectness in conversation. On the other hand, in the United States, being direct is often seen as a sign of credibility. Geographic areas within the country may also play a role; New Yorkers, for example, may be more direct than Alabamans.

2. The *issues* being addressed may require a greater or lesser display of

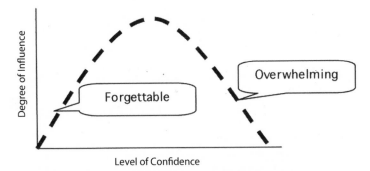

Figure 5. Level of Confidence and Degree of Influence

Decision makers respond positively to confidence — until it amounts to cockiness or unbelievable certainty. They also perceive lack of confidence as lack of competence or lack of conviction. Successful advocates calibrate their level of confident language.

confidence. A physician giving unhappy news to a patient may be more tentative than when chatting with a technician about a diagnostic piece of equipment. Scientific dialogue is often speculative; experts may speak tentatively with peers about recent discoveries. On the other hand, when a science teacher is reviewing a well-understood phenomenon, she may be far more direct.

3. The *preferences* of decision makers may affect the overt display of confidence as well. Some decision makers are dismayed to hear overly powerful language from subordinates. Others approve of very confident people. Astute advocates temper their intensity when pitching ideas to senior leaders until they know their preferences.

4. Advocates' *knowledge* about the organization and the issue should be factored in. Outsiders with little experience with an organization (e.g., newly hired consultants) might tone down their suggestions until they understand the power structure and the organizational culture. Advocates with little knowledge about an issue should also moderate their presentations to avoid being seen as simultaneously overconfident and ignorant, which could shatter their credibility.[9]

5. The *contexts* of the decisions should also affect an advocate's display of confidence. An overwhelmingly strong delivery when counseling someone about a personal crisis can backfire. Sounding hesitant when delivering a motivational speech to an auditorium of eager salespeople is a recipe for failure.

Language

Used carefully, words sell ideas. Used carelessly, words hinder, even stop, the development of brilliant ideas. Here are some keys to choosing the words that will most usefully convey your conviction that your ideas are worth advancing.

- Use simple language.
- Use inclusive language.
- Use vigorous language.
- Avoid tentative language.
- Vary your language.
- Use goal-oriented language.
- Use action-oriented language.
- Include meaningful details.

Use Simple Language

Straightforward, unambiguous terms communicate confidence. Wise advocates treasure short phrases that are instantly clear and shun lengthy sentences, convoluted phrasing, and obscure words. They translate ideas into language that other people, often less knowledgeable about their issues, can easily grasp. As Nobel laureate Günter Blobel says, scientists who can't explain their work to their grandmothers "probably don't understand it themselves."[10] Former prime minister Margaret Thatcher, when describing the experiences that taught her how to advocate on behalf of the Tory Party agenda for Britain, said, "Not only had we worked out a full programme for government; we had also taken apprenticeships in advertising and learnt how to put a complex and sophisticated case in *direct, clear, and simple* language."[11]

Inexperienced advocates often use polysyllabic words and phrase-embedded sentences in the hope perhaps of sounding superior. In both written texts and oral presentations, shorter words are remembered better than longer ones. Keep it simple, or risk losing your audience:

Long-Winded	Simple
Our team performed an analysis of	We analyzed
In regard to	About
In the event that	If
At the present time	Now

If keeping it simple means not showing off with big words when shorter, everyday words suffice, it also means not showing off with convoluted sentences. Instead, stick with straightforward declarations about your ideas.[12] When Martin Luther King Jr. gave his famous "I have a dream" speech on August 28, 1963, near the Washington Monument, he didn't say, "I have a strategic plan that, given the current environment and extrapolating from current trends, will enhance our competitive opportunities, locally and nationally, over the next seven years." King understood the power of simplicity: "I have a dream." By the same token, a great manager will replace the statement "His performance on the project, undertaken on his own initiative and completed in record time, far exceeded the parameters of expected quality" with "He did great! He's the best!"

Simple words and short sentences make it easier for others to grasp ideas. And when advocates' ideas are clearly and simply expressed, the advocates themselves are viewed as more credible, and their ideas are judged more positively.[13]

As with all the other ways of demonstrating self-confidence, being straightforward and simple can be overdone. A public ceremony may be enhanced by eloquent and flowery language; the occasion makes it entirely appropriate. A literary essay requires different word choices than a technical report does. A meeting about grant applications may require complex terminology, and everyone in the room may understand it. Technical conversations are often appropriately laced with jargon and few, if any, strong declarative statements. Conversely, successful advocates may be intentionally vague when clarity and precision can limit their ability to maneuver in dicey conversations. Sometimes advocates don't want to make a straightforward commitment.

Use Inclusive Language

Rather than me-oriented pronouns like "I," "my," or "me," advocates use, when appropriate, us-oriented pronouns like "we" and "our." Implicitly giving others some credit for ideas builds their support. Rather than saying, "I have a problem with the sales department. It never gets orders out on time. So what I want you to do is work around those guys by . . . ," say, "Our sales department has a problem getting orders out. So what we all need to do is . . ." Happily married couples (marriages require constant advocacy!) use more first-person-plural pronouns like "we" than do unhappy couples.[14] Indeed, in one study, spouses that began a conversation with statements like "We're a couple . . ." or "We've been together for a while now . . ." and then followed with a persuasive appeal were more successful at convincing their partners of their reasonableness. Spouses who began with "I" made less progress toward persuasion.[15]

Use Vigorous Language

Words that tap into decision makers' emotions lend power to an appeal. In the original draft of Franklin Roosevelt's famous address to Congress declaring war on Japan after the Pearl Harbor attack, the president used the phrase "Yesterday, December 7, 1941, a date which will live in world history." In editing the speech, Roosevelt scratched out "world history" and replaced it with "infamy" — a much more powerful word. Like Roosevelt, John F. Kennedy was a master of vigorous language. John McConnell, a White House speechwriter for George W. Bush, pointed out features of Kennedy's inaugural address with admiration: "Kennedy said we would 'pay *any* price' to assure the survival of liberty. That we would 'bear *any* burden.' . . . not *some* price, not *a little bit* of burden. *Any* price. *Any* burden. *Any* hardship. Support *any* friend. Oppose *any* foe."[16] The language is simple, and his commitment comes through.

Vigorous language is often intense, even passionate. Which of the following is more persuasive?

a. "Jack's proposal to expand our business into South America isn't bad. It could have some payoff for us at some future point. We should probably adopt it."

b. "Jack's proposal to expand our business into South America is *fantastic!* It'll pay off *extraordinarily well* for us in the future. We *must* adopt it."

Because passion is seductive, it is the second statement that wins attention. Intensity tells decision makers how invested advocates are in ideas. The cues that passion lies behind an idea get attention and often induce buy-in.[17] When Steve Jobs described the iPad tablet computer Apple introduced in 2010, he was enthusiastic: "We have an *incredible* group that does custom silicon at Apple." The chip they created has "everything" in it, "and it *screams.*"[18]

Beyond indicating the speaker's support for an idea, intense language affects how decision makers interpret what is being said. Suppose you witnessed a car accident. An interviewer asks, "How fast were the cars going when they *smashed* into each other?" What is your estimate? Now suppose you are asked, "How fast were the cars going when they *hit* each other?"

What is your estimate now? And if we change "hit" to "contacted"? In a famous study, people who had all watched the same filmed accident reported significantly different speeds depending upon the word used in the question. For "smashed," they estimated forty-one miles per hour; for "hit," thirty-four miles per hour; for "contacted," thirty-two miles per hour. The only difference in the question that affected their estimates was the interviewer's choice of verb. In fact, when asked to describe the accident scene, witnesses who were prompted with the word "smashed" were two times more likely to report broken glass, although there was no broken glass at the accident scene.[19]

For advocates, the use of passionate language should have limits. As Francis Bacon said, "Speaking in perpetual hyperbole is comely in nothing but love." For advocates, the audience determines the limits in part. With deeply involved decision makers — that is, people who are both knowledgeable and concerned about the issue — highly intense language can backfire, especially when the decision makers doubt an advocate's credibility. If a marketer talking to a group of experienced software engineers says, "This is the single best piece of software ever written!" the marketer might be laughed out of the room. On the other hand, when decision makers are less involved, intensity can enhance advocates' credibility.[20] The same marketer might win support if he speaks passionately when chatting with people with no background in computer software who don't particularly care about software. When advocates are perceived as highly credible, they are more persuasive when using intense language. However, when their credibility is suspect, they are wiser to tone down their claims.[21]

Avoid Tentative Language

Tentative language may communicate a lack of confidence. Many poor advocates signal that they are uncertain when they speak or write by using hedges, disclaimers, disfluencies, and tag questions.

Hedges are words or statements that signal uncertainty — for instance, "These data are *sorta* right," or "*Maybe* we should do this." Hedges can sabotage credibility and persuasiveness.[22] Using them implies that you are not confident. And if you are not sure of your idea, why would others want to adopt it? Phrases like "in my opinion" (whose opinion is it otherwise?), "I think" (oh, is this a special moment?), and "to be candid" (you normally aren't?) diminish your arguments. There are obvious exceptions. For instance, hedges accompanying discussions of data can hurt advocates' credibility, but a discussion of limitations in a scientific report can enhance advocates' credibility.[23]

Disclaimers are phrases that weaken or qualify what is being said. For example, a hapless advocate might say, "I may not really be the right person to be proposing this," or "I'm no expert," or "You may think this is stupid." Disclaimers show up in many ways. For example, George W. Bush, at a press conference toward the end of his first term, was asked whether he had made mistakes as president. Caught unprepared, Bush stumbled awkwardly through his answer: "You know, I hope I — I don't want to sound like I've made no mistakes. I'm confident I have — I just haven't — you put me under the spot here and maybe I'm not quick, as quick on my feet as I should be coming up with one . . ."[24] Bush was not communicating confidence.

Disfluencies are breaks and interruptions in the flow of your speech. They include filler words ("like," "you know"), repetitions ("I said . . . I said"), and sounds ("er," "um") that may signal uncertainty. When you say, "The proposal I am making is, *um*, really about, *er* . . ." you may be communicating nervousness, uncertainty, incompetence, or lack of preparation. So be careful of disfluencies, long pauses, and other signs of hesitation. They reduce your credibility and your persuasiveness.[25]

In 2009, Caroline Kennedy was interested in being appointed to the Senate seat that Hillary Clinton had occupied before being appointed U.S. secretary of state. Her chance to become a senator faded when she gave an interview dotted with fillers: in the space of two and a half minutes she said "you know" more than thirty times. Compare that statistic with this one: in all the recorded inaugural speeches by U.S. presidents since 1940 there is not a single "uh" or "um."[26]

Tag questions are statements followed by unnecessary pleas for agreement through questions that reveal self-doubt. For example, a clumsy advocate might end his pitch with "It's a great idea, *isn't it?*" or "Doing this will succeed, *don't you think?*" He would be more effective if he simply said, "It's a great idea!" or "Doing this will succeed!" Be careful not to undercut your authority by sprinkling your discourse with tag questions.[27]

How do experienced advocates eliminate markers of tentativeness? Some people tape themselves speaking and then listen to discover their most common verbal faults. If they make it a habit to listen for those faults every time they talk, they may catch and correct themselves. Other people set up practice sessions and ask friends to clap their hands, tap a table, or snap their fingers every time they hear one of those markers. A tic or habit becomes controllable to some extent once you become conscious of it.

There are times, however, when markers of tentativeness can enhance an advocate's persuasiveness. For example, skilled advocates might use disfluencies to draw attention to a point, since people tend to remember words that immediately follow a disfluency.[28] So if you are trying to get decision makers to focus on a specific term, it might, counterintuitively, be clever to precede the term with a thoughtful "er . . ." or "um . . ."

It is also the case that people's credibility suffers more when they speak with great confidence and then are proven wrong than when they speak more tentatively before they are proven wrong.[29] If you are not sure that your data are perfectly correct, you may want to be a tad tentative. Tentativeness may also be appropriate when conversing with certain people. If you are disagreeing with your boss in public or if your boss is one of those people who must always be right, you would be wise to use a few tentative statements. Rather than saying, "We should consider this," you might add a "perhaps." When dealing with uninvolved decision makers — people who don't really care about your proposal — tag questions such as "Right?" or "Don't you think so?" or "Isn't it?" will invite their attention and get them psychologically involved. Why? Because phrases like these, even though purely rhetorical, call for a mental response.[30]

Vary Your Language

Everyone learns in composition class not to overuse the same words and phrases. The same admonition applies to speech. Advocates are perceived as more competent when they use a varied vocabulary to describe an idea or product.[31] Experts working in high-tech industries use many words to describe computer chips (e.g., "IC," "silicon"). Similarly, smart advocates addressing a problem allude not only to the "problem" but to the "challenge," the "issue," and the "point we are talking about."

Use Goal-Oriented Language

Years ago, undergraduates in New York City were asked, under the guise of measuring their ability to create meaningful sentences, to compose four-word sentences from collections of five words. They might be given this five-word prompt:

they her polite usually see

They were then supposed to craft a meaningful four-word phrase — for example:

They usually see her.

Some people in the study received 30 five-word prompts in which 15 of the combinations contained one word hinting at politeness (e.g., "considerate," "polite," "patient"). Other people received the same 30 prompts, but in their case, the 15 words hinting at politeness were changed to ones suggesting rudeness (e.g., "bother," "disturb," "intrude"). After completing the assignment, the students were asked to bring their written sentences to the experimenter, who was in the hallway outside the classroom. When exiting the room, each student encountered the experimenter chatting with somebody. The question was, How long would these New York City students wait before interrupting the conversation? The results were stunning. Those exposed to polite words when crafting sentences waited more than *double* the time of those who had worked with rude words. The polite or impolite words, which the students didn't really notice in most cases, primed them to behave very differently.[32]

Research has since demonstrated the same priming effect with words about achievement (people exposed to words related to achievement are quicker to complete word problems), cooperation (people exposed to words related to cooperation are more likely to work together on tasks), and age (people exposed to words related to elderly people walk slower).[33] If you label a test "Form A," students will do significantly better than on the same test labeled "Form F."[34] They must unconsciously associate A with a high grade and high expectations and F with failure. And — this is particularly relevant to advocacy — people primed with words suggesting conformity (e.g., "agree," "follow," "obey") are more likely to go along with the opinions of others.[35] The moral? When advocating, use language hinting at your goal. Phrases like "as we've all agreed," "what convinced us," and "we were persuaded by" may prime others to accede to a later request.

Successful advocates also use words highlighting success rather than failure. Rather than saying, "*If* we adopt this plan, the company's profits will soar," they might say, "*When* we adopt this plan . . ." Positively phrased ideas (e.g., "Data show . . .") are both easier to mentally process and more persuasive than negatively phrased ones (e.g., "Data have not shown . . .").[36]

Use Action-Oriented Language

Decision makers perceive advocates who write or speak in action-oriented ways as more powerful than advocates who communicate in more deliberative ways. Compare these alternatives:

a. Let's contemplate doing this.
b. Let's act on this now.

a. We must closely study . . .
b. We must push forward on . . .

a. I want to think this over.
b. I am going to propose . . .

In each case, the *b* phrase communicates action. When speakers or writers use action-oriented phrases, they are seen as more powerful.[37] Powerful people, in short, talk about implementing — about getting things done.

Include Meaningful Details

As Ronald Reagan's speechwriter Peggy Noonan says, details are the soul of credibility — listeners view advocates as more competent when meaningful details are included in what they say. In one study, people were presented with one of two slightly different transcripts of a robbery-murder trial. In one version an eyewitness offered small details about the robbery (e.g., "got a box of Milk Duds and a can of Diet Pepsi"), while in the other transcript the descriptions of the candy and the soda were replaced with the generic phrase "a few store items." People felt that the eyewitness who offered the details was more credible.[38] The message for advocates is to be specific. When describing a report they wrote to justify their idea, advocates might say, "The eighty-page report . . ." rather than "The report . . ." They might say, "To get this to you he traveled from Dallas to Chicago and then to London" rather than "He traveled a long way."

Again, as we discussed in chapter 2, be careful about distracting or irrelevant details. They can hurt an advocate's argument. Details must be pertinent. And remember the inverted-U curve mentioned at the beginning of this chapter. It also describes the relationship between details and effectiveness: just as too few details detract from a point being made, so do too many details.

Voice

Using powerful language is only one way to shape decision makers' perceptions of an advocate's conviction. When making oral presentations, wise advocates also use their voices in memorable ways.[39] They vary their speed of talking, they employ pauses and emphases, they rhyme, and they show enthusiasm.

As Cicero said, monotony is the mother of boredom. Watch Steve Jobs on YouTube as he introduces the iPhone. He begins by speaking slowly and quietly. As he continues, his pace quickens, and his volume builds. When he reaches the key moment and he says, "Today Apple is going to reinvent the phone," he has everyone's rapt attention. Jobs was very persuasive in that 2007 speech. Like any great presenter, he talks fast sometimes and he slows down at other times; he quickly moves through some material and pauses at other points; his voice is sometimes loud and sometimes soft.[40]

Speed. The average speaker of English talks at a rate of about 125–150 words a minute. Yet the average listener of English can comprehend double that—up to 250–300 words a minute. We can process messages faster than the average person talks. Radio and television advertisements are sometime sped up by about 30 percent with no loss of audience comprehension and no change in people's decisions to buy the advertised products.[41] Interestingly, people who talk a trifle faster than normal are seen as more competent and more likable. President John Kennedy was famously a fast talker, often speaking more than 300 words per minute. Fast-talking speakers are more persuasive (as long as they aren't too fast).[42]

The advice to talk a little faster than normal depends on who is being addressed. Talking too fast makes you hard to understand and, in some cases, creates the stereotype of the motormouth. Talking even a little faster works only when you can clearly enunciate your words; if you can't, don't. When meeting with people who are more comfortable in a language different from the one you are speaking, a slower rate of speech is advisable.[43] Even with decision makers who share your language, slowing your speech at certain points commands attention. When you want to highlight a point or a detail, speaking slowly and with great certainty is a good way to draw attention to it.

Wise communicators speed up on easily grasped issues and slow down on ideas that are more complex. Although Kennedy often spoke fast, he knew the impact of slowing down when giving formal speeches and when he wanted to show people how important an issue was to him. Scholars estimate that Abraham Lincoln, when he delivered important speeches, spoke at a slow rate of about 110 words per minute.[44] But that was Lincoln, the great orator. When a speaker talks too slowly *and* the speech is uninteresting, the audience is lost, and advocacy fails.

When people aren't motivated to listen to what's being said, a faster delivery is often more effective than a slow one for three reasons: it gets people's attention, it increases the presenter's credibility, and it encourages people to accept the speaker's arguments without much thought. A fast rate of speech substantially reduces listeners' ability to critically evaluate what is being said. But when decision makers are highly involved in what is being discussed — when they are motivated to listen carefully — a fast delivery is judged negatively.[45] In any case, slow down when making important points. And never sound rushed — it hurts your credibility.

Pauses and emphases. Savvy persuaders also understand the importance of well-timed pauses and vocal emphasis in their oral presentations. When you read a script of a play, the words often don't have that much impact. But when you hear them delivered by a brilliant actor, the same words can stick with you forever. Why? The actor emphasizes words by pausing and "punching" — vocally highlighting words or phrases for emphasis.

What makes former president Bill Clinton such a persuasive speaker? For one thing, he is a master of the pause. When we write, we use commas, dashes, periods, parentheses, and paragraphs to indicate when, where, and how much readers ought to pause. Skillful advocates use pauses to put punctuation marks in their speech, signaling how listeners should interpret what they say by where and how long they pause. Pausing is an important skill in most cultures. Former Indian prime minister Atal Behari Vajpayee was famous for long pauses in his speeches. Listeners sat there enthralled as they waited for his next words (although people started getting annoyed by the pauses as his popularity waned).

Advocates also emphasize what they are pitching by *punching*, or emphasizing, certain words. As you say each of the following sentences, use your voice to emphasize the words in italics.

My idea is one we must immediately adopt [you are making an unemphasized statement].

My idea is one we must immediately adopt [you are talking about yourself].

My *idea* is one we must immediately adopt [the idea is highlighted].

My idea is one *we* must immediately adopt [inclusion is the key].

My idea is one we *must* immediately adopt [this is mandatory].

My idea is one we must *immediately* adopt [do it now!]

Notice how your voice conveys different meanings depending on which word is punched. The emphasis may not be something that listeners consciously notice, but punching does affect how they judge what is being said.[46]

Persuasive advocates combine pausing and punching to enhance their pitches. Rather than saying, "We must get moving on this issue. Otherwise, we'll lose some of our most important customers. And we all know what that means!" a persuasive advocate might say, "*We must* get moving on this issue. Otherwise, [pause] we'll *lose* some of our *most important* customers. And [pause] we all know what *that* means!"

Rhymes. Enterprising advocates come up with striking ways of summarizing their ideas vocally to help people better grasp them. One way is by employing lyrical or rhyming phrases that stick in decision makers' minds. When people read adages phrased as rhymes, they find them more believable. For instance, "Woes unite foes" is seen as more accurate than "Woes unite enemies."[47] This tendency surely helps explain the success of Johnny Cochran's argument about a glove during his legal defense of O. J. Simpson: "If it doesn't fit, you must acquit."

Enthusiasm. Whether or not advocates are fast-talking, punchy, or rhyming, they all should sound enthusiastically committed to their proposals. Being prepared both mentally and physically for the pitch is vital to evincing enthusiasm. One advocate listens to songs from *The Lion King* before important presentations. Another advocate taps into his own conviction and almost physically explodes as he walks into rooms to pitch his ideas. The energy is palpable.

Advocates often have little control over the timbre of their voices. For example, a deeper voice is generally perceived as more pleasant, authoritative, and persuasive.[48] Think of James Earl Jones, Charlton Heston, Barbara Jordan, or Sean Connery. Any of them could creditably supply the voice of God. Most of us would be upset if God's voice turned out to sound like Big Bird's or Pee-wee Herman's. However, unless you want to undergo surgery, changing your voice is difficult. We do know that when people feel nervous, tense, angry, excited or less powerful, their pitch increases, their voice sounds shaky, and their volume decreases, all of which communicates less authority.[49] So if certain words or actions set you off, anticipate them so that you can control your reactions.

All the aspects of advocacy presented in this chapter must be delicately balanced. There are times when you want to sound more formal; at other times, informality wins. Constantly punching words can hurt your credibility as much as never being memorable in your language. Using too many rhyming phrases can make you sound silly. Using none might reduce the impact of your message. Saying "we must" or "we have to" too many times may create a boomerang effect — people will say "we mustn't!"

Behavior

"Radiate confidence. That's the first duty of a top commander," said Field Marshall "Monty" Montgomery. He was right. Adroit advocates communicate their conviction through their body language. They walk into rooms as if they own them and presume comfortable relationships with all.[50] There is not a trace of unease — no fidgeting, no rocking on the balls of their feet, no glancing back and forth nervously. Here is how Robert Caro described President Lyndon Johnson when he persuaded people: "His face spoke, too, expressions chasing themselves across it with astounding rapidity, his huge, mottled hands spoke, too, palms turned up in entreaty or down in dismissal, forefinger or fist punching the air for emphasis, hands and fingers not only punctuating the words but reinforcing them. . . . His whole body spoke, with expressive posture and gestures."[51] It is said that Roger Ailes, when he founded Fox Television, chose hosts for different news and talk shows by looking at audition tapes with the sound turned off. He was watching for energy and mannerisms. He wanted people who *looked* the part, who commanded attention. Try this sometime — watch yourself on a video with the sound turned off.

Numerous academic studies have isolated specific nonverbal signals of power in conversations and meetings. Here is a sampling of what we know:

Gaze: When communicating, confident advocates gaze at decision makers more, break eye contact later, and look at them less when listening than their less confident counterparts do.

Personal space: Powerful advocates move closer to others when talking. They may even invade the space of others, although others respect their space. The boss can walk into your office without invitation, but you stand at the boss's door waiting to be invited in.

Body movement: More dominant people take charge when meeting with others. They move about comfortably, have more relaxed postures, and lean in when speaking (e.g., Bill Clinton literally hugs podiums). Powerful people don't fidget as they talk and listen.

Gestures and touch: Confident persuaders are more likely to gently touch others when talking, initiate touch more quickly (e.g., a handshake), engage in more purposeful mannerisms when making points, and demonstrate less nervous gestures than their less confident counterparts.

One study revealed that when people acted powerful — assuming an open posture, spreading their arms, occupying more space at a table — their feelings of power increased, their testosterone went up, and their stress hormones went down. When people posed in submissive ways (e.g., hunched over, arms close to the body), the opposite happened: their testosterone went down, their stress hormones went up, and their sense of powerlessness increased. Act powerful, and you will feel powerful.[52]

All of these moves are appropriate only in some settings and with some people. If you are the subordinate, it isn't wise to invade the space of your boss regardless of how confident you are about your ideas. If you are working in a culture where touch is a no-no, even reaching out might easily eliminate any possibility of success.

Successful advocates project confidence both verbally and nonverbally. Often how you say something is as important as what you say. Conviction must be communicated. Nearly 150 years ago, the scientist Michael Faraday advised that presentations "depend entirely for their value on the manner in which they are given. It is not the matter, not the subject, so much as the man."[53] Faraday's observation is as true today as it was then.

14

Steer Meetings Your Way

Meetings are indispensable when you
don't want to do anything.
JOHN KENNETH GALBRAITH

When Lloyd Bentsen stepped down as secretary of the Treasury during the
Clinton administration, he was asked what he thought of Clinton's team.
He wryly responded, "This is the meetingest crowd I've ever seen."[1] Most
of us can probably think of people in our own work experience who fit
Bentsen's description. Yet despite our ingrained cynicism about meetings,
in today's world, meetings are the venue where many ideas die or thrive.
Understanding this, sophisticated advocates consciously plot moves and
countermoves to shape the outcomes of meetings.

In a perfect world, solid preparation and compulsive competence on the
part of advocates would mean that they would have at least a fair chance of
achieving their objectives at meetings. Regrettably, the world isn't that fair.
In the face of Machiavellian opposition, even well-prepared advocates can
lose control of meetings and end up with decisions nowhere close to what
they wanted. To be successful as an advocate, preparation and expertise
must be accompanied by a superb understanding of how to strategically
influence meetings.

Selling One-on-One

In Japanese, *nemawashi* technically means "root-binding" — digging around the roots of a tree before replanting it. In Japanese organizations, however, the term has a second meaning. It refers to the consensus-building process that happens prior to formal meetings. Before meetings people presell their notions in one-on-one conversations with colleagues. Slowly, through individual politicking, they get buy-in for their ideas, so that there is little or no opposition when a formal meeting is called. Nemawashi eliminates public conflicts and surprises, ensuring that everyone is onboard with decisions.

Wise advocates everywhere practice forms of nemawashi. They avoid large meetings and instead go door to door, chatting up each decision maker individually. Sometimes they raise the issue when they run into a colleague briefly in the hallway; at other times they schedule private sessions. Alan Greenspan, former head of the U.S. Federal Reserve, understood nemawashi, although he called it bilateral schmoozing. "I know that if you really want to get something done," he said, "you go one-on-one privately but never publicly."[2] One-on-one meetings offer many advantages.

Information gathering. Starting the advocacy process by lobbying one-on-one lets advocates identify allies and foes. In individual meetings, advocates can discover which issues are likely to be sensitive, what matters to different decision makers, and how various interests might be integrated into a compromise that everyone can live with. Indeed, in these private sessions, savvy advocates can sometimes resolve issues that, if raised in a formal meeting, might torpedo success.

One-on-one exchanges also let advocates informally gauge whether now is the best time to pitch their ideas. Alan Greenspan was famous for visiting individual members of the Federal Open Market Committee prior to formal committee meetings to ensure that he had the votes he needed.[3] He chatted with each governor, letting him or her know which way he was leaning on important decisions. In these conversations, Greenspan was counting heads. He wanted to ensure that he had the majority on his side before a formal vote was taken. Like Greenspan, perceptive advocates are good vote counters — they are rarely surprised by the decisions made at meetings. If they lack the votes, they postpone raising their issues until later, after they have done more preselling.

Problem avoidance. Suppose you want to get your colleagues to adopt a new design for your company's logo. You decide your best move is to sell one-on-one. First you visit your colleague Sarah, whose office is next to yours. She says she doesn't care — "I'm too busy to worry about that." Then you stroll down to Sunil's office. He tells you that whatever you want is fine. Walking out of his office, you run into Chantal. She likes the new logo but thinks it ought to be brighter. You ask her if she'd be happy with the logo if you made the change. She says, "Of course." Later you pass Jessica in the hallway, and she smiles when you show her the logo. "It looks great!" she says. Finally, you walk into Geoff's office. He tells you the only thing he'd change is the size. "Our name should be bigger." So you brighten the color and make the logo larger, and you have sold your idea. No meeting necessary.

Now imagine that you pitch your design at a meeting of the group without any preselling. When Chantal proposes a brighter color, Sunil says he prefers a deeper shade. Sarah leans forward and says she always prefers muted colors. When Geoff proposes a larger size, Jessica claims that the logo is already too big, and Chantal worries about whether it should be even larger. After a pause, Sarah raises the question, "Do we even need a new logo?" And off they go, jousting about why and if logos are important. You have lost control.

Notice what happened. Before the meeting, few people cared about the logo, and those who did wanted minor changes. Now, when meeting as a group, all sorts of issues that probably would never have occurred to some attendees become relevant. Most people didn't care about the color until someone proposed a color. Then everyone felt the need to chime in, arguing for personal favorites. Too often, people get highly involved in issues raised at meetings that they cared nothing about beforehand. One-on-one meetings can prevent nonissues from becoming issues.

Openness. Another advantage of one-on-one sessions is that people will often reveal privately thoughts they would never admit before a larger audience. Based on those private remarks, advocates can make their notions more palatable to the group as a whole. In one-on-one meetings people also may reveal information about the group's dynamics. "Jack," one person may say, "is a tough one. He'll push, but in the end, he'll go along. Mary, on the other hand, will sit there saying nothing, but she'll be a negative vote unless costs are addressed."

For sure, one-on-one meetings have a downside. In some firms, early individual politicking is seen as manipulative. Yet even in those organizations, people at the top seldom have formal meetings until preparations are made and the time is deemed right.

Don't misunderstand: formal meetings have many advantages. They can open minds and ward off missteps. Better decisions often happen when groups of people trade ideas. If you tried to presell the logo design and everyone wanted different colors, a meeting would be necessary to hash things out. Some people like formal meetings—they want to be heard by all. Formal meetings also build commitment to ideas—people stick with what they say in public.

In this chapter we will look at moves that advocates make to shape decision making in meetings. These moves are organized around what advocates do (1) before meetings, (2) at meetings, and (3) after meetings. A warning: Some of the moves may seem extreme. You may think you wouldn't want to make this or that move. That's fine. But understanding how others might use moves can make you more effective in resisting them. Some of these suggestions work only in small meetings in any case; some work only when no pushy bosses are present. Context matters. What applies in one setting may be irrelevant in another.

Before the Meeting

In preparing for meetings, advocates need to consider: (1) focus and preparation, (2) logistical concerns, (3) people issues, and (4) agenda management.

Focus and Preparation

Know your objective. Carl von Clausewitz, the famed military strategist, once said: "No one starts a war . . . without first being clear in his mind what he intends to achieve by that war and how he intends to conduct it. . . . This is the governing principle which will set its course, prescribe the scale of means and effort which is required, and make its influence felt down to the smallest operational detail."[4] Clausewitz's observation is true in advocacy. Enterprising advocates know what they want to achieve before meetings begin. And they enter every important meeting with strategies for obtaining their goals. As Admiral Hyman Rickover advised his team: "You're supposed to be going [to meetings] to achieve certain defined objectives. They should be written out in advance. . . . How will you know if you've accomplished what you wanted to if you haven't defined your objectives in advance? You'll end up agreeing to somebody else's objectives without realizing the implications of what you've done."[5] Wise advocates know not only what they want but also what they are willing to concede. Equally, like good negotiators, advocates spend time early on trying to grasp what others at the meeting might want and what they might be willing to give way on.

Be prepared. In the intrigue of meetings, advocates who are better prepared than their adversaries do better. It is surprising how many people go to meetings without reviewing the agenda beforehand. Their lapse gives well-prepared advocates a huge advantage. Before meetings, smart proponents know as much as they can about what they are pitching. They review even insignificant issues that might arise, since those minor issues can blossom into significant ones. And even if minor concerns remain minor, their own credibility is enhanced when others discover how much they know.

Understand the group's norms for meetings. Every organization has certain unwritten rules about how meetings are conducted. Advocates understand and use these norms. For instance, in some firms, it is appropriate for participants to viciously attack one another's ideas; only the strong survive. In such firms, shrewd advocates gird themselves for battle and expect no quarter. In other organizations, people coax one another. You would prepare there for gentle persuasion. Most of the time, advocates adapt to norms. But sometimes they take advantage of a norm by violating it. For instance, in some groups impugning anyone present is a no-no. So a crafty advocate might raise a point that would, if debated, make an attendee look bad. That move cuts off debate and may lead to agreement about the advocate's idea.

Logistics

Where? In today's world many meetings are mediated — they happen over phones, via e-mail, through video-conferencing, or on the Internet. Technologies certainly save time and travel. However, as we saw in chapter 2, it is harder to persuade people in mediated settings, and it is difficult to develop the vital personal relationships that arise in face-to-face encounters. People may be harsher in what they say about a person or a person's ideas when the person is not right in front of them. It is also easier to turn people down in mediated exchanges. No wonder salespeople fight for even brief live sessions with potential customers. For everyday issues, e-mail and telephone calls are often sufficient. But the more important the issue is, and the more difficult the sell will be, the more advocates should try to get face time with decision makers.

Savvy proponents prepare the meeting site so that it works for them. If there is a phone in the room and they don't want distractions, they may unplug it. Rooms with many windows also offer distractions, so if they want people's complete attention, they may draw the shades. They consider the room temperature: If it is too warm, people get sleepy. Brightly lit rooms make people more active and make them less likely to behave dishonestly.[6]

Advocates assess technical equipment to ensure that everything works — nothing ruins a presentation more quickly than technical nightmares. A diminutive engineer, scheduled to make an important presentation, approached the front of the room only to discover that the lectern was taller than she was. She spent three minutes trying to adjust it and, when that proved impossible, moved in front of it and started her presentation, clearly flustered. But her troubles weren't over. The keyboard for the visuals was attached to the lectern, so every time she had to change a slide, she had to rush back to the lectern and disappear briefly. Needless to say, everyone remembered only one thing about her presentation — and it wasn't her proposal.

When? What's the best time of day for a meeting? Which day of the week is optimal? Ultimately, the time and the day are whatever works best for you and the decision makers. If you are a morning person, brimming with enthusiasm at 7 a.m., then morning meetings might be best; if you don't really wake up until after lunch, afternoon sessions are better. How about right after lunch? Most people would say, "No, people are sleepy then." But what's wrong with that? Maybe their lethargy will make them more willing to go along with your proposal. One member of Admiral Rickover's team said, "We knew that Senator Clinton Anderson, chairman of the powerful Joint Committee on Atomic Energy, was taking medication that made him somewhat laid-back in the afternoon and irritable and aggressive in the morning. If we wanted him to get mad about something, we'd bring it up in the morning. If we had bad news and were worried about his reaction, we'd bring it up in the afternoon."[7]

People who control the scheduling of meetings have a decided advantage. Tommaso Soderini, a citizen of Florence in the fifteenth century, often opposed the powerful Lorenzo de' Medici. Once, when a treaty was being debated, Soderini announced a sudden meeting of decision makers. By the time Lorenzo, who was typically a very astute politician, heard about the session, a decision had been reached and the official memo had been dispatched. There was little Lorenzo could do.[8]

When the advocate controls the schedule, the advocate can tinker with all sorts of time-related issues. For instance, if things look dicey for an advocate who controls the meeting schedule — if, say, she finds herself lacking the support she needs — then she can reschedule the meeting to give herself time to regroup. If the meeting itself can't be rescheduled, she can create an agenda for the meeting that ensures that her issue gets only minimal play if that's to her advantage.

People

Who decides? As we have seen in other chapters, it is crucial to know who makes decisions. In meetings, there may be a single formal decision maker, or a few people who decide, or no one who can make the decision, or several informal opinion leaders. At other times, the room may be filled with peers, and everyone will, in the end, have some say.

When advocates have a great deal of control over who is involved in decision making, they can use that control to shape the decision-making process. They might, for instance, change the membership of the decision-making group. In a government agency, an executive felt that an advisory council had too much power over decisions. So, under the guise of needing a continual stream of fresh ideas as well as more representativeness, he created term limits for members of the council. Now they would serve no more than two years and would then rotate off. Only he and a few other leaders of the agency would serve longer. Now the executive had more power.

Who is attending? In medieval times, meetings called *things* were typically called to make military decisions. When people disagreed with a pending decision, they absented themselves from the thing and, as a consequence, were not expected to participate in the forthcoming military action.[9] Today, smart advocates still contemplate whether they ought to attend meetings. And, equally important, they try to shape who does attend meetings. Then their goal is to make sure more allies than opponents are present when they pitch their ideas. Clair Patterson, the Caltech scientist who helped convince the world that leaded gasoline was bad for people's health, claimed that the U.S. Public Health Service knowingly scheduled a vitally important meeting when he was going to be in Antarctica. Whether the agency did this is not known for certain, but it is true most government scientists didn't buy Patterson's notion about leaded gasoline at that time.[10]

If advocates are planning to pitch technical ideas, they would be wise to invite one or two recognized experts who support their proposals to the meeting. Their presence will encourage people to adopt the proposals. If a senior leader loves your idea, invite him. He doesn't need to say much, but when he nods his head as you talk, others in the meeting will notice. Jean Monnet, father of the European Union, understood the value of making sure the right people attended meetings. He advised a colleague that in European government meetings it was always wise to get politically power-ful labor on one's side and make sure representatives of labor attended decision-making meetings. "An industrialist, or politician for that matter," he said, "behaves better when a trade unionist is present, even if the trade unionist never opens his mouth."[11]

Peer pressure is equally effective. In 1967, when *Sesame Street* was still being imagined, there was disagreement about whether it would be best to create a separate organization in New York to produce the show or to have one of the Hollywood studios in charge. Lloyd Morrisett was one of the brains behind the show. One day he invited some of the nation's leading television producers to meet to discuss the idea of *Sesame Street*. Sensing that attendees would opt for an independent organization, he also invited Lou Hausman, a government official who strongly felt that one of the Hollywood studios should be in charge of producing pilots of the show. Hausman was important since the government was a major funder of the show. During the meeting, one participant said that without question a new, independent organization was essential. Others immediately agreed. As Joan Ganz Cooney later said, "Lloyd was so shrewd. One of the reasons he had that meeting was to have Hausman in attendance. Lou [Hausman] respected the producers and when everyone was in favor of creating a new entity, that was the end of the [Hollywood] discussion. It was a turn-ing point. Lou left knowing it wasn't going to go his way, but he came around."[12]

Agenda

Manage the agenda. In virtually every book on effective meetings, readers are told to distribute agendas beforehand. That way participants arrive prepared. The advice is excellent — people's contributions will be more relevant and substantive when they have had a chance to prepare.[13] In some situations, though, shrewd champions avoid distributing agendas beforehand. That way they have an advantage — they are the only ones prepared for the session. Because they are prepared, they can quell dissent with loads of information. Henry Paulson, the U.S. secretary of the Treasury during the market crash of 2008, needed major U.S. banks to free up credit. In mid-October he met with leaders of the nation's nine largest banks. When the bankers walked into the Treasury Department's conference room at 3 p.m. they had no idea what Paulson was going to discuss. They had been told to "just be there." Some thought the meeting would be a briefing about the economy. Instead, each found a single page in front of him laying out an ultimatum: the government was going to give the banks substantial funds in exchange for preferred shares. The banks would use those funds to simulate lending. By 6 p.m. each banker had signed on.[14] Had Paulson distributed his proposal beforehand, the bankers would have had a bevy of pre-meeting meetings to consider Paulson's idea and would have come up with numerous reservations. The entire effort to stimulate the economy that way would have slowed to a crawl. Paulson understood the value of catching people unaware by not distributing an agenda before the meeting.

Savvy proponents understand that whoever creates the agenda has power in meetings. What is placed first or last, who is listed as speaking, and so on, affect how meetings turn out. Here is a question: Where should your idea appear on an eight-item meeting agenda? First or second, midway (perhaps fourth or fifth), or last? The surprising answer is often midway. Why not last? The problem with being last is that the meeting may never reach your item. In many firms, meetings don't end; they just fade away as people, one by one, rush off to another meeting, the airport, or home. Ronald Reagan's chief of staff used to host a weekly meeting with senior White House staff. One staff member was notorious for proposing ideas that no one, especially the chief of staff, felt made much sense. So that person soon found his issues always placed last on the meeting agenda. Meetings often ended before he could raise them.[15]

One time you do want to be placed last is when you don't want the group to take up your issue. Why would that ever happen? One advocate cannily placed his item last on the agenda at three separate meetings. After the third meeting he went to his boss and said, "I've tried my best to get people's okay on this. But we never seem to get around to discussing it." He had, in other words, made a good-faith effort to obtain input. His boss said, "Well, just go ahead then and do it."

Why not first or second on the agenda? Because, in many meetings, whatever issues come up first and second are the victims of speeches that attendees feel they must make. No matter what the first items are, one person will, for example, say that the firm needs to be more cost-conscious, another person will predictably argue for more customer input, and a third individual will be adamant about the central role of sales in decision making. By the time the meetings reach the fourth or fifth item on the agenda, the routine arguments have been made and the speech makers are exhausted. If you don't believe this, notice that in most meetings the first few agenda items almost always take up half the meeting. Additionally, personal conflicts among decision makers are often played out in discussions of the first few items. Their animosities sabotage whatever is at the top of the agenda. One other reason not to go first or second is captured by an old maxim: "The second mouse gets the cheese." By being fourth or fifth on the agenda, you will have a chance to hear the comments that people make about prior issues and will be able to adjust your proposal accordingly. If the person pitching the first item is hassled mercilessly about spending money, and if the second item on the agenda is quashed because of costs, you might wisely revise your pitch to highlight how your idea conserves money.

There are, of course, exceptions to this rule of appearing midway on the agenda. For instance, when advocates want to create a framework for understanding an issue, they may want to go first. That way those who follow must live with the now established frame. Consultants often want to be first to make their pitch. They are promoting a framework for understanding the problems they want to address. Decision makers tend to use whatever item is presented first as an anchor for what they hear afterward.

Have material for people to react to. At the first meeting to discuss the treaty that became the precursor to the European Union, Jean Monnet arrived with a forty-article draft treaty. He knew that his draft would serve as a useful starting point for discussion. Monnet once said: "I never sat down to a table to discuss anything without having a proposal. . . . I must say that our initiatives often won the day for lack of competition."[16] Clever advocates, like Monnet, bring something to meetings that people can react to. What they bring frames the discussion; they establish the terms of the debate. While participants may chip away at what's included in a draft, much will remain the way it was written. Some very crafty influencers go further. They volunteer to do the grunt work prior to a meeting. They prepare reams of materials relevant to the upcoming session and distribute everything as close in time as they can to the start of the meeting. Attendees, faced with piles of documents, often turn to the person who put the materials together and ask, "What should we know?"

Plan several "what if?" scenarios. In meetings, people seldom get exactly what they want. So, rather than betting on a single specific outcome, sophisticated advocates imagine, before a meeting, several prospective scenarios. They might think: "If A were to happen at the meeting, then I would pitch X. On the other hand, if B arises, I would tout X + Y." Shrewd advocates prepare materials for each scenario that they imagine might come up. They have the extra numbers, examples, and recommendations related to each scenario at hand.

Put attendees in a good mood. Amazingly, across twenty-six different stock exchanges worldwide, there is a positive correlation between sunshine in the morning and the daily stock market index. Sunny days bring better stock returns.[17] Why? Perhaps basking in sunshine puts traders in a better mood, so they evaluate business opportunities more positively.

The same basic correlation holds true in meetings. When decision makers are happy, they are more flexible in the ways they approach problems, they are more open to novel ideas, and they are more likely to solve problems in innovative and integrative ways.[18] Happy people pay less attention to the quality of arguments.[19] People in bad moods find negatives more relevant than positives in judging ideas. They make more pessimistic inferences about whatever is being pitched.[20] And they focus more on the details of proposals.[21]

For all these reasons, wise advocates cultivate positive moods at meetings. They may invite attendees to recall happy events or to talk about themselves — people love talking about their families, their hobbies, their successes. They might bring little gifts or snacks to the meeting — people are kinder when they have been fed.[22] In fact, even the sight of food creates a surge of pleasure in the brain that may transfer to listeners' reactions to ideas.[23] Giving people warm beverages makes them see others as more generous and caring than handing the same people cold beverages.[24] People are also more persuadable when they have had caffeine.[25] So lay on chocolate snacks and coffee! And sit them in soft chairs. People who sit on hard chairs are less flexible in negotiations.[26]

At the Meeting

You are thoroughly prepared for the meeting. Now you walk into the meeting room. What should you consider doing during the meeting to influence others? Broadly speaking, you should (1) consider the seating, (2) organize and facilitate, and (3) make verbal and nonverbal power moves.

Consider the Seating

Imagine you are attending a meeting with the big boss. By tradition, he always sits in the seat marked A in figure 6. People will sit in every remaining seat. Where should you sit to maximize your influence?

The answer . . . F. Why? First, who typically sits at B and J? Yes-men, support people, people who don't count. Second, the boss sitting at A can easily see you if you choose seat F. If you selected B or J, you would often be out of view. At Microsoft, when people wanted to be invisible in meetings with CEO Bill Gates, they purportedly sat immediately to his right (J). There they would be in his peripheral vision, and besides, he had a tendency to look left. Those wanting his attention sat either directly across from him (F) or to his left (B), where he could readily see them.[27] The same happens at the White House. In meetings with Barack Obama, the person who is considered the lead on the policy issue being discussed sits directly across from the president.[28]

Studies find that you will perceive whoever sits directly facing you in a meeting as more vital to tasks at hand than other people. People perceive those they face in a conversation to be more influential.[29] Finally, taking the F seat allows you to observe everyone at the meeting. You can gauge attendees' reactions to your contributions, note who's involved, and even see nods of agreement more easily from F than from B or J.

When you want to create a cooperative spirit at the meeting, the place to sit is right next to the person you need to work with. Jean Monnet once said, "If the parties sit on the opposite sides of the table, and proceed from their established positions, they will never come to agreement. However, if the parties sit on the same side of the table — and place the problem on the opposite side — they will see things in an entirely different light and have a chance for success."[30] If you are going to sit next to the decision maker, choose to sit on his or her right-hand side (J) — unless you are at a table with Bill Gates. Oddly enough, people are more likely to agree to requests that are whispered in their right ear than their left ear.[31]

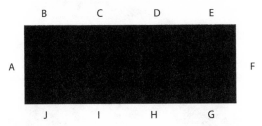

Figure 6. Seating for Advocacy at a Rectangular Table

Sitting directly across from the chief decision maker at a meeting will give the decision maker the impression that you are more vital to tasks at hand than other people are.

Here is another scenario. Imagine no boss is at the meeting. Instead, a group of peers are sitting at a round table. Where should you sit to be influential? The best answer is to sit across from the most talkative person or the person with whom you are most likely to disagree. If you have ever sat next to a person who has never had a quiet thought, you know how difficult it is to get a word in. Moreover, trying to disagree with someone right next to you is awkward.

Now look at figure 7. Where should you sit at a semicircular table if you want influence? If you guessed D, you would be correct. On an American television game show called *The Weakest Link*, contestants were positioned in a semicircle. After each round of questions, the contestants had to vote one person off the show. Person D was far less likely to be voted off even if that person was no more accurate in answering questions than others on the panel. Viewers of the show also thought that person D was more often correct than she or he really was, and they believed that people on the periphery (A, B, F, G) were more often incorrect than they really were.[32]

A myriad of seating arrangements are possible. When people want to bask in media glory (e.g., when photographers are present), they won't choose to sit far away from the decision maker. When individuals want to engage in side conversations with decision makers, they opt to sit next to them as well. The point is that smart advocates think about where to sit instead of just plopping down anywhere.

Smart proponents also attempt to shape where others sit. In 2007, Senator Joseph Lieberman, who wanted to increase bipartisanship, changed the seating arrangement of the Senate Committee on Homeland Security and Government Affairs, which he chaired. In Senate committee meetings, the

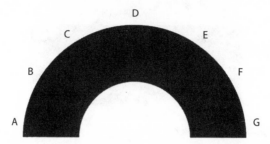

Figure 7. Seating for Advocacy at a Semicircular Table

The person sitting at the center of a semicircle appears to be a stronger, more
integral member of the group than those sitting on the periphery.

members of the minority traditionally sit to the right of the chair, the
majority party members to the left. Lieberman changed that. He had the
senators alternate — one Democrat, one Republican, another Democrat,
another Republican, and so on. He hoped that way to achieve his goal: more
cooperation and less competition.[33] Sales teams understand what Lieberman was doing. If a meeting is likely to be competitive, people from one
company sit on one side of the table and people from the other firm sit on
the other side. But if both companies want cooperation, attendees from the
two companies intermingle.

Management expert Charles Handy was once the warden of St. George
House at Windsor Castle. At one meeting a major decision was to be made.
Handy, who knew what he wanted, "arranged the seating [so] that those
whom I knew would be in favour voted first. When it came to diehard oppos-
ers it was clear to each of them that they would be outvoted, so, to preserve
harmony they went along."[34] Handy created pressure through seating.

Sometimes people get emotionally attached to an opinion. So wise advocates, when facing disagreements, may consider rearranging the seating.
Consider the case of Joel Steinberg, a New York City lawyer who was
prosecuted for killing his adopted daughter. Following closing arguments,
the jury retreated to arrive at a verdict. After a few days of deliberation,
jurors found themselves deadlocked. One juror recalled learning years before that sometimes by changing seats, people get less attached to their
point of view. So the jurors agreed to rearrange themselves, and a short time
later they unanimously found Steinberg guilty of manslaughter.[35] It was as
though their feelings about the case were glued to their chairs. When they
occupied different places, they saw the case differently.

Organize and Facilitate the Meeting

From the moment the first people enter the meeting room — when you should be there to greet them — to the adjournment of the meeting, you can organize and facilitate the discussion in many ways that help establish your influence and promote your ideas. Here are some of the things you can do at the meeting itself.

Host the meeting. Smart advocates host meetings they attend, even if they aren't the official host. They arrive early to welcome people. They help attendees set up computers, bring them coffee, and make everyone feel comfortable. Throughout the meeting they are personable — they use people's names, discover commonalities among participants, and show good-natured humor. They build up participants' egos. And they make all of these moves not simply to be nice but also to create the impression that they are managing the meeting. Sociability generates agreement. People are more likely to accede to an advocate's requests when they have conversed earlier with that advocate — even if just for a minute or two.[36]

Start (and end) the meeting. Most meetings don't begin until the formal leader enters the room. And when that person opts to leave, the meeting is over.[37] When no official leader is present, however, anyone can assume some degree of authority by starting and ending the meeting. Whoever talks first, especially in ambiguous situations like meetings, is often viewed by others as the leader. On juries, the first person to talk in the jury room is commonly chosen as foreperson. Why? That individual seems to know what to do, and others look to him or her for direction. They assume that the first speaker will take some ownership of the process.

Orient and summarize. Wise advocates offer orienting and summarizing statements. Orienting statements tell people what they will be talking about. For example, at the start of the meeting an advocate might say, "We need to talk about three things today: A, B, and C. Why don't we start with A? What does everyone think about A?" The advocate then lets others talk. At some point, he offers a summarizing statement, followed by another orienting statement: "Well, it sounds as though people think A could be resolved by either action 1 or 2. Why don't we decide which would be better?" People then start discussing their preferred option. Influence comes by shaping and summarizing interactions.

Change the topic. Powerful people successfully change topics in meetings by saying, for example, "Why don't we move on to talk about B?" In truth, another attendee may not have finished considering topic A, but since it is awkward to say, "Hey, I'm not done with A yet," that person often goes along with the topic change. Advocates must wait for the right moment to introduce a new topic, perhaps during a lull in the discussion. Further, the topic change must seem relevant to the ongoing discussion. And if they suggest moving on and someone says, "I'm not done!" their graceful response is, "Of course, please continue." They have shown power even then, since they gave this person "permission" to continue.

Take notes on a board. Wise advocates know the power of the board. What is written down on a flip chart, whiteboard, or computer screen matters. What isn't jotted down often gets forgotten. Savvy proponents freely use boards to post summaries of people's contributions, decisions that have been made, and attendees' commitments to action. If you want power in a meeting, consider volunteering to take notes early on. When people say, "That will be great," stand and take notes in front of everyone. Soon, not only are you recording participants' comments, but you are also directing the discussion. You might spy one attendee nodding in agreement to a point that matches your objective. Ask the nodder to enunciate her thoughts, and jot them down, thus reinforcing what has been said.

Find common ground. On controversial issues, advocates often begin by seeking common ground with others. They ask others, who might disagree about their specific proposal, to buy into general principles. When people have agreed with those principles, they will be more open to specific implications that follow from those principles. In the midst of a heated argument, an advocate might say, "Look, all of us agree in principle that we're strongly committed to excellence, that we want to do the right thing for our employees, and that we must be competitive in the marketplace. What this means is that we need to . . ."

Another way to build common ground is to establish early on a general purpose for the meeting that bolsters your agenda. For instance, if you are proposing a method for strengthening inventory management you might say, "We're here today to examine ideas that will make us more efficient. All of us know how much money and time inefficiency is costing us, so . . ." This statement establishes a tone that favors ideas revolving around efficiency.

Use deadlines. Deadlines — real or imagined — often force people to reach closure.[38] They also can discourage people from looking at options and thinking deeply about ideas.[39] So, at the start of a meeting:

Propose a deadline: "A lot of us have another meeting in an hour. Can we agree to try make a decision before then?"

Highlight time pressures: "We made a commitment to get a decision to the CEO by the end of the day."

Hint at how overloaded people are: "I have a report to finish, and I know Josh and Madeline are trying to beat a deadline. Could we try to wrap this up?"

Remind people how long the meeting has gone on: "We've been at this for two hours now. Can we make a decision?"

Observe and listen carefully. Lyndon Johnson once told his assistants, "Watch people's hands, watch their eyes . . . read eyes. No matter what a man is saying to you, it's not as important as what you can read in his eyes. The most important thing a man has to tell you is what he's trying not to say."[40] Like Johnson, sophisticated advocates are astute observers of how people react in meetings. Like poker players, they look for "tells," signals that people make, often unconsciously, to communicate feelings. In one organization, a senior board member had a hot temper. His neck often reddened when he got angry. When the CEO noticed this board member's neck changing colors, he would propose a break. During the break the CEO worked through the troublesome issues with the board member one-on-one, thus avoiding a public blowup. When a break wasn't possible, the CEO switched the topic to a more agreeable one until the board member calmed down.

Good advocates are also good listeners. The next time you are at a meeting, ask yourself: "Are you listening or just waiting to talk?" Tom Daschle served in the U.S. Senate with Barack Obama. In describing Obama, Daschle said: "He's a great listener. We share a common view [that] the best way to persuade is with your ears."[41] When listening to what people say in meetings, advocates try to figure out why people believe what they are saying. One way to proceed is to employ the nifty "feel-felt-found" method of persuasion used by salespeople. When a meeting attendee — let's call him Ed — disagrees about a crucial point, you might say, "Ed, I understand why you *feel* that way." You summarize Ed's feelings. "I *felt* that way too, until I *found* that . . ." Now you explain what you discovered that makes your idea such a good one.

Ask persuasive questions. Excellent questions make an advocate's case. They get decision makers' attention. When Scott Cook, the cofounder of Intuit, first pitched his proposal for what we know today as Quicken and TurboTax to Wall Street investment bankers, he intrigued them with a couple of questions. He began by saying, "Raise your hands if you pay bills." Everyone's hand shot up. "Now keep your hands up if you like paying bills." Hands went down. Cook then presented his idea of software to automate bill paying. Not surprisingly, the often-skeptical decision makers bought his idea.[42] Good questions direct people's attention to core concerns. As an upstart presidential candidate, Barack Obama had to make a strong showing against presumptive candidate Hillary Clinton in the Iowa primary. His campaign manager, David Plouffe, needed his staff to focus. So he asked at every staff meeting, "What did you do to help us win in Iowa?"[43]

A popular method of selling is called SPIN selling.[44] Developed by Neil Rackham, the technique suggests a way for salespeople to get clients to persuade themselves that they need the products or services being offered. This is accomplished through strategic questions. One sort of question used in SPIN selling is the *problem question*. Problem questions create dissatisfaction with the status quo. If you are trying to convince decision makers to adopt a new order-processing system, problem questions might include, "What makes the delay between order and fulfillment so long?" or "Are we getting more complaints from customers about lost orders?" Once people are conscious that there might be a problem, advocates ask *implication questions*. These questions bring home the consequences of the issues raised by problem questions. Implication questions induce pain: "How do delays between order and fulfillment affect customer retention?" "How has this delay hurt profitability?" Then decision makers are asked *need-payoff questions*. The goal of these questions is to prompt decision makers to consider the benefits of adopting a proposal: "How would customers react if we really sped up order fulfillment?" "If the delay between order and fulfillment is significantly reduced, how much more money could we make?" These questions provoke decision makers into contemplating the positive payoffs of adopting your idea. Notice that the salespeople (advocates) have made few, if any, direct persuasive statements. Instead, SPIN questions let decision makers arrive at their own decisions.

Advocates can induce decision makers to reflect on issues by asking questions, getting answers, and then staying quiet. Silence is uncomfortable for many people. If no one is talking, people generally feel the need to talk. In one case, an advocate was pushing to open a sales office in Asia. In the midst of a meeting about the topic, the advocate asked her boss, "What's our biggest challenge in opening an office there?" He responded, "We don't have people who speak the language." She stayed quiet. Soon he thoughtfully said, "But we need more people who think globally. That's where business is going. Let's keep talking about this office idea." She remained silent, and he went on, "The only way we're going to get people who speak the language is to start up something there." Had our advocate immediately responded to his comment about language, the boss might not have reached the conclusion he did.

Effective proponents also ask decision makers questions that prompt positive responses. Let's say you are asked to look at a painting and describe what you like about it. Or you are asked to look at the same painting and describe what you don't like about it. Afterward, you are asked your opinion about the piece. If you listed things you like, you will rate the painting more positively than if you listed things you didn't like.[45] An advocate might suggest in the middle of a meeting, "There are always good and bad aspects of any idea. Why don't we spend some time listing positive aspects?" People may still mention some bad aspects, but subtly emphasizing the positive aspects of a notion can encourage decision makers to buy it. At the start of a meeting, an advocate might ask decision makers, "Shall I tell you why we should adopt this proposal?" or "Can I explain why this will work?" Such questions are difficult to respond to negatively. When someone asks an advocate a negatively framed question in a meeting, the advocate might reframe the question positively. Asked, "Why is your unit behind on the software?" the smart advocate might reply, "So you're asking what our unit can do to get the software out faster?"

Make Verbal and Nonverbal Power Moves

As the meeting proceeds, wise advocates establish their influence by speaking or staying silent, pushing or conceding, and generally using words and actions to augment their influence and win approval for their ideas. Let's review some common power moves to make at meetings.

Talk more. A very consistent finding in the research literature is that people who talk more in meetings are perceived to be more influential in those meetings. Some people go overboard and merely become tiresome, of course. What an advocate contributes ought to have substance. Some advocates believe, incorrectly, that if they say very little, but what they do say is well reasoned and substantive, they will be persuasive. Regrettably, this is not generally true.

Get a word in. High-stakes meetings often resemble political talk shows on television. They are conversationally competitive. Everyone wants maximum airtime. Quick-witted participants grab the floor as soon as someone finishes a thought, or even before. Others have difficulty being heard—someone else starts to talk before they are able to gather their thoughts and jump in. Smart advocates know that the more quickly someone gains the floor, the more influential and credible they are.[46]

How do advocates get a word in quickly? First, they realize that if they wait to think through what they want to say before talking, they will not have a chance to be heard. So they grab the floor and figure out what to say after they open their mouths. One way to start talking while still thinking is to use filler words and phrases like "If I may . . . ," "You know, it all depends . . . ," "As I have been listening, I've started to wonder . . . ," or "I'm glad that point was raised, because it is a very good point for further discussion." Of course, as we saw earlier, wise advocates are careful of using too many filler phrases and being labeled as not having confidence in themselves.

Second, advocates who want to take the floor master turn-taking skills. The next time you watch two friends converse, notice how they take conversational turns effortlessly. They seldom, if ever, talk over one another's comments. A good conversation is like a well-coordinated dance. Person A is talking. At some point, person A signals person B that he is just about done talking, so B should get ready. When A finishes his thought, B begins talking immediately—no interruption, no awkwardly long pause. Studies of conversational turn-taking tell us that when people are speaking to more than one person, they look only briefly at individual listeners. Listeners look at speakers more. But when speakers are almost done talking, they look more at a listener, signaling that it is this listener's turn to talk. In addition, as people complete their turns, a slight drawl—with drawn-out vowels, lengthened tones—signals the other person to get ready to talk.

Interrupt. Although advocates don't want others to interrupt them, they often manage to interrupt others in meetings without sounding pushy or discordant.[47] How do they do this? First, they listen carefully to how the current speaker sounds. They note, for example, how quickly she is speaking and how loud her voice is. Then, when interrupting, they match her speech patterns; the interruption seems like a natural extension of what the speaker is saying. Second, they wait for the current speaker to pause, because at that point their interruption seems less intrusive. Third, once they take the floor, they quickly, yet gently, raise their voice to signal that they are taking over the exchange. Fourth, they "bridge," or tie their initial comments, to what the previous speaker was saying and then weave in their own issue. Consider the following exchange.

JACK: " . . . and, as Mary already knows, the project has been delayed three times in the last month. We need to get over those blocks and get this project out the door. The last delay was because Rudy's group is under-staffed and Celeste's team has a tight — "

SETH (interrupting with a cadence matched to Jack's and with a slightly raised voice): "Jack's right, the delays need to be addressed, and he has hit one of the reasons — Rudy's understaffing. But we should really look for the root cause of the problem. It's structural in this organization. What I propose we do is look at reorganizing. . . ."

Seth found a pause as Jack was talking, won attention by raising his voice, adopted Jack's speech patterns, and bridged by noting what Jack had said. Seth also did something else — he made his own point sound relevant by going to a broader concern: the root cause. Crafty advocates often interrupt with statements like "Well, isn't the real issue . . . ?" or "There's a bigger principle here . . ."

What do advocates do when people try to interrupt them? They might raise their voice slightly and speed up their rate of talking. They should avoid long pauses. And perhaps they could hold their palms up, signaling that they are not done.

Get people physically involved. When people nod their heads while listening to persuasive messages, they are more likely to later agree with what they heard than if they shook their heads while listening to the same messages.[48] Savvy proponents begin meetings by introducing issues that generate head nods — principles, facts, and issues that people already buy into. Initial agreement may prime them to respond positively to the advocates' specific pitches. Further, advocates may nod ever so slightly themselves as they discuss their notions. People have a tendency to nonverbally reciprocate behaviors. And when people raise points supporting their ideas, advocates nod again, creating what amounts to a norm of head nodding when their ideas are discussed. As with everything in this chapter you can go too far — you don't want to look like one of those bobble-head dolls you find in ballparks.

Mimic others' behavior. Effective salespeople have long known that if they subtly mimic the behaviors of clients, they are more likely to make the sale. If a client crosses his legs, you cross yours; if she nods, nod in return; if someone says "You really do this?" say "Yes, I really do this," not just "Yes." Mimicry, as long as it isn't blatant, generates affinity and creates openness to persuasive appeals.[49]

Let others do your talking. People can only talk so much before wearing out their listeners. So advocates encourage others to speak for them in meetings. If others make points that an advocate was planning to make, or if they respond the way the advocate would have to a question, the advocate just nods in agreement. The payoff of letting others do the persuading is twofold. First, when others publicly support an idea, they seldom change their position later.[50] Second, public support by others can bolster the advocate's position. Skeptical decision makers may be swayed when they hear other decision makers support a notion.

Stay quiet. "While the word is yet unspoken, you are master of it; when once it is spoken, it is master of you." As that Arabic saying suggests, there are times when it is better to remain quiet. If an opponent is clearly wrong in what he is saying, stay quiet. Remember Napoleon's advice: "Never interrupt your enemy when he is making a mistake." When he finishes, see if someone else will challenge him.

Staying quiet is especially important once decision makers have approved your proposal. Many inexperienced advocates make a crucial mistake by not taking yes for an answer. They oversell. They keep pressing points even after decision makers have said okay. Stop selling the moment you have agreement. Silence is often your friend. President Calvin Coolidge, well known for being laconic, once advised, "If you keep dead still, they'll run down in three or four minutes. If you even cough or smile they'll start up all over again."[51]

Give in on a prior issue. Reciprocity is a basic principle of human interaction: I do something for you, and you do something for me in return. In meetings, it is useful to let people have their way on an issue as long as they will feel some pressure to give way on your issue later. In fact, sometimes advocates will take an extreme position because they know that people will react extremely. Then they offer to compromise at a midpoint that represents what they really wanted in the first place.

Retreat. Savvy advocates know the value of tactical retreats. If the tone of the meeting is going against them, rather than giving up, they might say, "Why not move on to the next agenda item and discuss this later?" Postponement is better than rejection. And if decision makers seem uncomfortable with postponing a decision, advocates might propose having a subcommittee look further into the issue and come back with a report. And then the advocates try to populate that subcommittee with allies.

Accede without bitterness. Impassioned advocates sometimes risk their credibility by losing control in meetings. When people disagree with them, instead of listening and finding common ground, they respond angrily, alienating the very people whose support they need. Don't be thin-skinned. Don't respond with threats. Don't make scenes. If you are fuming, shut up or propose a break. In tense meetings, be cautious of words that might upset attendees. Avoid "you" and "your" when disagreeing with people (e.g., say "the budget," not "your budget"). Avoid reminding people that they weren't listening (e.g., "As I have already said . . ."). Avoid subtle jabs.

Make sure everyone agrees. At the conclusion of meetings, it is wise to ask the group at large, "What did we agree on?" Surprisingly often, people who have all sat in the same session will answer this question differently. If people leave with different conclusions, advocates face challenges when trying to go further with their ideas. Silence does *not* mean consent. Sometimes when you think you have agreement, you will discover later that you didn't, so make a point of double-checking.

Savvy advocates continually seek new ways to influence decision makers in meetings. They observe successful proponents to discover what works to effectively shape discussions. Years ago I watched a successful lawyer take control of an important meeting. Most of the people attending the session barely knew each other. The meeting was scheduled to begin at 9 a.m. A couple of minutes after nine, the lawyer said: "It's a bit past nine. Why don't we sit down and get started?" Then he said, "We should probably introduce ourselves first. Why don't you start?" he said, pointing to the person to his immediate left. Consider what this lawyer did to establish influence. First, he began the meeting. Second, he successfully gave instructions, asking people to introduce themselves. Third — and this was the cleverest move — he ended up being the last person to introduce himself, allowing him to make a topic change and then again orient the discussion. Whoever makes topic changes and orienting statements is in control of the meeting.

Follow-Up

The meeting ends. What can advocates do afterward to enhance the chances that their ideas will be adopted? They can follow through in various useful ways.

Write up the minutes. Derk-Jan Eppink worked as a top-level bureaucrat for the European Union for many years. In discussing how power operates, he suggested that the preparation of minutes was the "ideal opportunity to 'adjust' the facts to the wishes of the mandarins [the bureaucrats with influence]. If something is not included in the minutes, it hasn't happened. It no longer exists! Long and difficult discussions can be summarized in a few bland sentences, as though all was sweetness and light. Minutes are the means by which the surreal is allowed to triumph in the [European] Commission. You might think you said one thing but the minutes will prove that you said something else!"[52]

Admittedly, some meeting mavens do adjust minutes to match their goals. But doing so is unethical, and it can backfire. In terms of effective influence, the important reason for preparing the minutes is the opportunity it gives advocates to be in a position of authority. One goal of networking is to make sure that people know and remember you. If you are distributing minutes, everyone hears from you again. If an agenda item needs to be adjusted, you are the person they deal with. The senior boss who receives a copy of the minutes sees your name in the e-mail that includes the minutes.

Follow up on action items. Too often people make commitments in meetings that they forget about as soon as the session ends. At the conclusion of a meeting you might ask, "Who's going to do what?" Then you might volunteer to coordinate the follow-through. That way not only do things get done, but you become the central contact. Everyone now regards you as the go-to person on the issue.

Be sure to follow up immediately on your own commitments. Napoleon once said that the most dangerous moment comes with victory. After you win the battle, you get lax — and that is when your enemy counterattacks. The same can be true in advocacy. When given the green light in a meeting, advocates should act quickly. Not only do decision makers want something done right away, but if advocates wait too long, people might get cold feet, or other issues might be reprioritized. So wise proponents send confirming e-mails immediately, get signatures on agreements swiftly, and make purchases right away.

Publicize results. The meeting is done. The minutes have been written, agreed upon, and distributed. Are you done? No. Now you need to publicize the results of the session. Without being boastful, let people know that your idea was discussed and approved. Put it in writing so others can read about it. The more public the approval, the more difficult it is for people to later oppose your plan.

Lobby. Having an idea adopted at a meeting is only one step in your advocacy campaign. After meetings, successful proponents continue to promote their ideas through one-on-one conversations with other meeting attendees. In these follow-up sessions, they address issues that were raised in sessions, salve wounds, deal with doubts, and respond to further questions. Just because everyone agreed with a proposal in a meeting doesn't mean that it will be executed. After a successful meeting, the work continues. That is when you make the idea a reality.

Meetings are today's coliseum for the gladiators of corporate politics. Adroit advocates have an amazing capacity to get meetings to go their way without irritating others. They dominate without being domineering. Most of us have spent most of our careers developing technical competencies — we are inventive engineers, expert accountants, skilled physicians, proficient managers. But we have spent little time focusing on how to promote our ideas, how to campaign for them, how to manage meetings in their favor, so we are often taken advantage of. By learning the tactics and strategies of advocacy, both in and out of meetings, anyone can advocate for ideas successfully.

Notes

Chapter 1. The Politics of Ideas

1. Hiawatha Bray, "Creation of the World Wide Web: World-Changing Web Was Born 20 Years Ago," *Austin American Statesman*, March 23, 2009.
2. Katie Thomas, "Left Behind: A City Team's Struggle Shows Disparity in Girls' Sports," *New York Times*, June 13, 2009.
3. William S. Hammack, "Black Box," *The Science Show with Robyn Williams*, Radio National, March 27, 2004.
4. Joan Ganz Cooney, interview by Shirley Wershba, April 27, 1998, part 3 of 9, *Archive of American Television*, http://www.emmytvlegends.org/interviews/people/joan-ganz-cooney (accessed November 7, 2009).
5. Michael Davis, *Street Gang: The Complete History of Sesame Street* (New York: Viking, 2008), 63.
6. Harold Evans, "Joan Ganz Cooney: Sesame Street," in *They Made America: From the Steam Engine to the Search Engine: Two Centuries of Innovators* (New York: Little, Brown, 2004), 441.
7. John Love, *McDonald's: Behind the Arches* (New York: Bantam, 1995), 294.
8. David Bornstein, *How to Change the World: Social Entrepreneurs and the Power of New Ideas* (New York: Oxford University Press, 2007), 91.
9. Ashley Halsey, "He's in Deeper Waters Now: New EPA Adviser on Bay's Health Skilled in the Art of Politics," *Washington Post*, March 31, 2009.
10. Peter Whoriskey, "Bright Idea of Tire Reef Now Simply a Blight: Officials Plan Recovery off Florida Coast," *Washington Post*, October 2, 2006.

11. Elisabeth Rosenthal, "Once a Dream Fuel, Palm Oil May Be an Eco-Nightmare," *New York Times*, January 31, 2007.

12. Jena McGregor et al., "How Failure Breeds Success," *Business Week*, July 10, 2006, http://www.businessweek.com/magazine/content/06_28/b3992001.htm (accessed April 14, 2010).

13. Douglas Brinkley, *Wheels of the World: Henry Ford, His Company, and a Century of Progress* (New York: Viking, 2003), 669.

14. Steven Levy, *The Perfect Thing* (New York: Simon and Schuster, 2006), 44.

15. Gary Hamel, "Innovation Now!" *Fast Company*, December 2002, 120.

16. Alan Cane, "Vision Thing: How Foresight Led to a Fortune," *Financial Times* (London), September 23, 2005.

17. Gordon Moore, "An Interview with Gordon Moore," interview by Jill Wolfson and Teo Cervantes, The Tech, http://www.thetech.org/exhibits/online/revolution/moore/ (accessed April 14, 2010).

18. John Boudreau, "Q&A with Apple Co-founder Steve Wozniak," *Seattle Times*, April 10, 2006.

19. John Warnock, "An Interview with John Warnock," interview by Jill Wolfson and Denise Cobb, The Tech, http://www.thetech.org/exhibits/online/revolution/warnock/ (accessed April 14, 2010).

20. Meredith Wadman, "Biology's Bad Boy Is Back," *Fortune*, March 8, 2004, 172.

21. "Koshiba, Tanaka Give Nobel Lectures," *Asahi Shimbun*, December 12, 2002.

22. Stephen Miller, "Former Xerox CEO Funded Fabled PARC but Failed to Harvest Innovations," *Wall Street Journal*, December 23-24, 2006.

23. Douglas Smith and Robert Alexander, *Fumbling the Future: How Xerox Invented, Then Ignored, the First Personal Computer* (New York: Morrow, 1988), 147.

24. Ibid., 150.

25. Michael Hiltzik, *Dealers of Lightning: Xerox PARC and the Dawn of the Computer Age* (New York: HarperBusiness, 1999), 381.

26. Steven Strauss, *The Big Idea* (Chicago: Dearborn, 2002), 158.

27. Everett Rogers, *Diffusion of Innovation* (New York: Free Press, 1993), 161.

28. John K. Borchardt, "Selling Your Ideas," *Rotarian* 168, no. 4 (April 1996): 7.

29. David Strick, "Shuji Nakamura," *Time*, April 9, 2007, 67.

30. Rogers, *Diffusion of Innovation*, 144.

31. Smith and Alexander, *Fumbling the Future*, 196.

32. Michael Useem, *Leading Up: How to Lead Your Boss So You Both Win* (New York: Crown, 2002), 58-63.

33. Amy Joyce, "A Better Way — but You Have to Say It; Keeping Your Good Ideas to Yourself Costs You and the Company," *Washington Post*, May 30, 2004.

34. Seth Godin, *Free Prize Inside: The Next Big Marketing Idea* (New York: Portfolio, 2004), 113.

35. Scott Kirsner, "The Legend of Bob Metcalfe," *Wired*, November 1998.

36. Kortney Stringer and Ann Zimmerman, "Polishing Penny's Image," *Wall Street Journal*, May 7, 2004.

37. Alan Murray, "After the Revolt, Creating a New CEO," *Wall Street Journal*, May 5, 2007.

38. Brian Dumaine, "How Managers Can Succeed through Speed," *Fortune*, February 13, 1989, 54–59.

39. Robert Rubin and Jacob Weisburg, *In an Uncertain World: Tough Choices from Wall Street to Washington* (New York: Random House, 2004), 362.

40. Peter Maas, *The Terrible Hours: The Man behind the Greatest Submarine Rescue in History* (New York: HarperCollins, 1999).

41. Amol Sharma and Stephen J. Norton, "Funding for Basic Science Has Little Traction in Congress," *CQ Weekly*, July 3, 2004, 1612.

42. Gina O'Connor and Mark Rice, "Opportunity Recognition and Breakthrough Innovation in Large Established Firms," *California Management Review* 43, no. 2 (2001): 95–116.

43. Fredric Jablin, "Superior's Upward Influence, Satisfaction, and Openness in Superior-Subordinate Communication: A Reexamination of the 'Pelz Effect,'" *Human Communication Research* 6 (1980): 210–220.

44. Sandra Vandermerwe, "Diffusing New Ideas In-House," *Journal of Product Innovation Management* 4 (1987): 256–264.

45. *Economist Technology Quarterly*, September 6, 2003, 29.

46. Stephen Green, Ann Welsh, and Gordon Dehler, "Advocacy, Performance, and Threshold Influences in Decisions to Terminate New Product Development," *Academy of Management Journal* 46 (2003): 419–434.

47. David Bornstein, *How to Change the World: Social Entrepreneurs and the Power of New Ideas* (New York: Oxford University Press, 2004), 119.

48. Rubin and Weisburg, *In an Uncertain World*, 149.

49. Duksup Shim and Mushin Lee, "Upward Influence Styles of R&D Project Leaders," *IEEE Transactions on Engineering Management* 48 (2001): 394–413.

50. Jane Howell, Christine Shea, and Christopher Higgins, "Champions of Product Innovations: Defining, Developing, and Validating a Measure of Champion Strength," *Journal of Business Venturing* 20 (2005): 641–661.

51. Ibid., 317–341; Shim and Lee, "Upward Influence Styles," 394–413; Filiz Tabak and Steve Barr, "Propensity to Adopt Technological Innovations: The Impact of Personal Characteristics and Organizational Context," *Journal of Engineering and Technology Management* 16 (1999): 247–270.

52. Roderick Magee II, ed., *Strategic Leadership Primer* (Carlisle, PA: United States War College, 1998).

53. Charles Crawford, "Marketing Research and the New Product Failure Rate," *Journal of Marketing* 41 (1977): 51–61.

54. Mark Simon and Susan Houghton, "The Relationship between Overconfidence

and the Introduction of Risky Products: Evidence from a Field Study," *Academy of Management Journal* 46 (2003): 139–149.

55. Jerry Wind and Vijay Mahajan, "Issues and Opportunities in New Product Development," *Journal of Marketing Research* 34 (1997): 9.

56. Isabelle Royer, "Why Bad Projects Are So Hard to Kill," *Harvard Business Review*, February 2003, 48–56.

Chapter 2. Communicate Your Idea with Impact

1. Art Fry, "Art Fry's Invention Has a Way of Sticking Around," interview by Paul Rosenthal, May 20, 2008 (podcast), Lemelson Center, Smithsonian Institution, http://invention.smithsonian.org/video/vid-popup.aspx?clip=1&id=518 (accessed April 23, 2010).

2. Jennifer Samp and Laura Humphreys, " 'I Said What?' Partner Familiarity, Resistance, and the Accuracy of Conversational Recall," *Communication Monographs* 74 (2007): 561–581.

3. Erik Busy and Maria Grabe, "Taking Television Seriously: A Sound Bite and Image Bite Analysis of Presidential Campaign Coverage, 1992–2004," *Journal of Communication* 57 (2007): 652–675.

4. David Stires, "Interview: Fidelity's Harry Lange," *Fortune*, November 14, 2005, http://money.cnn.com/2005/11/14/funds/lange_fortune/index.htm (accessed November 7, 2010).

5. Linda Kaplan, Robin Koval, and Delia Marshall, *Bang: Getting Your Message Heard in a Noisy World* (New York: Currency, 2003), 123.

6. Susan Saegert, Walter Swap, and R. B. Zajonc, "Exposure, Context, and Interpersonal Attraction," *Journal of Personality and Social Psychology* 25 (1973): 234–242.

7. Christian Unkelbach, Klaus Fiedler, and Peter Freytag, "Information Repetition in Evaluative Judgments," *Organizational Behavior and Human Decision Processes* 103 (2007): 37–52.

8. "Less Insult from Injury," *Business Week*, August 14, 2006, 63.

9. Del Jones, "Corning Chief Says Keep Open Mind, Challenge Strategy in Down Times, Concentrate on Keeping Earnings Growth Steady," *USA Today*, June 1, 2001.

10. Charles Berger and Patrick DiBattista, "Communication Failure and Plan Adaptation: If at First You Don't Succeed, Say It Louder and Slower," *Communication Monographs* 60 (1993): 220–238.

11. Erasmus used the word *copia* (abundant) to describe this kind of redundancy. There is no modern word with precisely the same meaning.

12. Joseph O'Connor and John Seymour, *Introducing NLP Neuro-Linguistic Programming* (London: Thorsons, 2003).

13. Joann Peck and Jennifer Wiggins, "It Just Feels Good: Customers' Affective

Response to Touch and Its Influence on Persuasion," *Journal of Marketing* 70 (2006): 56–69.

14. Peter Bloch, Frederic Brunel, and Todd Arnold, "Individual Differences in the Centrality of Visual Product Aesthetics: Concept and Measurement," *Journal of Consumer Research* 29 (2003): 551–565.

15. Donald Phillips, *Lincoln on Leadership: Executive Strategies for Tough Times* (New York: Warner, 1993), 152.

16. Emily Stark, Anita Kim, Chris Miller, and Eugene Borgida, "Effects of Including a Graphic Warning Label in Advertisements for Reduced-Exposure Products: Implications for Persuasion and Policy," *Journal of Applied Social Psychology* 38 (2008): 281–293.

17. Stephen Dubner, "Selling Soap," *New York Times Magazine*, September 24, 2006, 23.

18. Remo Job, Rino Rumiati, and Lorella Lotto, "The Picture Superiority Effect in Categorization: Visual or Semantic," *Journal of Experimental Psychology: Learning, Memory, and Cognition* 18 (1992): 1019–1028.

19. Karine Gallopel-Morvan, Patrick Gabriel, Marine Le Gall-Ely, Sophie Rieunier, and Bertrand Urien, "The Use of Visual Warnings in Social Marketing: The Case of Tobacco," *Journal of Business Research* 64 (2011): 7–11.

20. "Doing eBay's Bidding," *Economist*, November 10, 2001, 75.

21. Renzo Baldasso, "The Role of Visual Representation in the Scientific Revolution: A Historiographic Inquiry," *Centaurus* 48 (2006): 69–88.

22. Sharon McGrayne, *Prometheans in the Lab: Chemistry and the Making of the Modern World* (New York: McGraw-Hill, 2001), 195.

23. David Myers, *Intuition: Its Powers and Perils* (New Haven: Yale University Press, 2002), 124.

24. David Stockman, *The Triumph of Politics* (New York: Harper and Row, 1986), 291.

25. Hannah Chua, J. Frank Yates, and Priti Shah, "Risk Avoidance: Graphs Versus Numbers," *Memory and Cognition* 34 (2006): 399–410.

26. Presentation by L. Stahl at Morgan Stanley, October 19, 2005.

27. Howard Gardner, *Changing Minds: The Art and Science of Changing Our Own and Other People's Minds* (Boston: Harvard Business School Press, 2004), 76.

28. William Immen, "The Energizer Bunny: Edison, Meet Urry," *Toronto Globe and Mail*, October 4, 1999, available at the Kitsap Sun Mobile Web site, http://m.kitsapsun.com/news/1999/oct/04/the-energizer-bunny-edison-meet-urry/ (accessed April 16, 2010).

29. William S. Hammack, "Black Box," *The Science Show with Robyn Williams*, Radio National, March 27, 2004.

30. Andrew Hargadon and Yellowlees Douglas, "When Innovations Meet Institutions: Edison and the Design of the Electric Light," *Administrative Science Quarterly* 46 (2001): 476–501.

31. "Edison's Electric Light: 'The Times' Building Illuminated by Electricity," *New York Times*, September 5, 1882.

32. Warren Hodge, "A Swede Who Filters Diplomacy in a Glass of Water," *New York Times*, August 6, 2005.

33. David Bornstein, *How to Change the World: Social Entrepreneurs and the Power of New Ideas* (New York: Oxford University Press, 2004), 248.

34. John Lyons, "Expensive Energy? Burn Other Stuff, One Firm Decides," *Wall Street Journal*, September 1, 2004.

35. Steven Strauss, *The Big Idea* (Chicago: Dearborn, 2002), 154.

36. Tom Farley, "The Cell-Phone Revolution," *Invention and Technology*, Winter 2007, 31.

37. Harold Evans, *They Made America: From the Steam Engine to the Search Engine: Two Centuries of Innovators* (New York: Little, Brown, 2004), 387.

38. Burkhard Bilger, "Annals of Invention: Hearth Surgery," *New Yorker*, December 21, 2008, 90.

39. John Heritage and David Greatbatch, "Generating Applause: A Study of Rhetoric and Response at Party Political Conferences," *American Journal of Sociology* 92 (1986): 110–157.

40. Frank Luntz, *Words That Work* (New York: Hyperion, 2007), 156.

41. Eric Igou and Herbert Bless, "Inferring the Importance of Arguments: Order Effects and Conversational Rules," *Journal of Experimental Social Psychology* 39 (2003): 91–99.

42. Curtis Haugtvedt and Duane Wegener, "Message Order Effects in Persuasion: An Attitude Strength Perspective," *Journal of Consumer Research* 21 (1994): 205–218.

43. Arlee Johnson, "A Preliminary Investigation of the Relationship between Message Organization and Listener Comprehension," *Central States Speech Journal* 21 (1970): 104–107; James McCroskey and R. Samuel Mehrley, "The Effects of Disorganization and Nonfluency on Attitude Change and Source Credibility," *Speech Monographs* 36 (1969): 13–21.

44. Walter Issacson, *Einstein: His Life and Universe* (New York: Simon and Schuster, 2007), 476.

45. Jane Howell and Christine Shea, "Individual Differences, Environmental Scanning, Innovation Framing, and Champion Behavior: Key Predictors of Project Performance," *Journal of Product Innovation Management* 18 (2001): 15–27.

46. Joel Brinkley, "Diplomatic Memo: A Diplomatic Lone Ranger with 3 × 5 Cards," *New York Times*, April 17, 2005, 10.

47. Sara Kiesler and Jonathon Cummings, "What Do We Know about Proximity and Distance in Work Groups? A Legacy of Research," in *Distributed Work*, ed. Pamela Hinds and Sara Kiesler (Cambridge, MA: MIT Press, 2002), 57–80.

48. Jim Rohwer and Laurie Windham, "GE Digs into Asia," *Fortune*, October 2, 2000, 170.

49. Carol Hymowitz, "American Chiefs Are Taking Top Posts Overseas," *Wall Street Journal*, October 17, 2005.

50. Simon Avery, "Lenovo Spreads Its Multinational Wings, *Globe and Mail*, May 7, 2007.

51. NASA, "Mars Climate Orbiter Failure Board Releases Report, Numerous NASA Actions Underway in Response," November 10, 1999, http://www.spaceref.com/news/viewpr.html?pid=43 (accessed November 7, 2010).

52. Craig Smith, "Beware of Green Hats in China and Other Cross-Cultural Faux-Pas," *New York Times*, April 30, 2002.

53. Laurence Meyer, *A Term at the Fed* (New York: Harper, 2004), 89.

Chapter 3. Frame Your Message

1. A. A. Milne, *Winnie-the-Pooh* (New York: American Book-Stratford Press, 1961), 28.

2. The linguist Jens Allwood reports that English used to have both "thou" and "you." Interestingly, "you" was the more formal of the two.

3. Lara Boroditsky, Lauren Schmidt, and Webb Phillips, "Sex, Syntax, and Semantics," in *Language in Mind: Advances in the Study of Language and Thought*, ed. Dedre Gentner and Susan Goldin-Meadow (Cambridge: MIT Press, 2003), 70.

4. Christopher Federico, "Predicting Attitude Extremity: The Interactive Effects of Schema Development and the Need to Evaluate and Their Mediation by Evaluative Integration," *Personality and Social Psychology Bulletin* 30 (2004): 1281–1294.

5. Michael Marks, Mark Sabella, C. Shawn Burke, and Stephen Zaccaro, "The Impact of Cross-Training on Team Effectiveness," *Journal of Applied Psychology* 87 (2002): 3–13.

6. Philip Bayster and Cameron Ford, "The Impact of Functional Issue Classification on Managerial Decision Processes: A Study in the Telecommunications Industry," *Journal of Managerial Issues* 12, no. 4 (Winter 2000): 468–484.

7. I am grateful to Randall Stutman for his permission to use this exercise.

8. Thomas Lawrence, "Institutional Strategy," *Journal of Management* 25 (1999): 161–188.

9. Janet Guyon, "The Coming Storm over a Cancer Vaccine," *Fortune*, October 31, 2005, 123.

10. Philip Vergragt, "The Social Shaping of Industrial Innovations," *Social Studies of Science* 18 (1988): 500–501.

11. Bernard Barber, "Resistance by Scientists to Scientific Discovery," *Science* 135 (1961): 596–602; Thomas Kuhn, *The Structure of Scientific Revolutions* (Chicago: University of Chicago Press, 1996).

12. Adrienne Carter, "Slimmer Kids, Fatter Profits?" *Business Week*, September 5, 2005, 73.

13. Lorrie Grant, "Container Store's Workers Huddle Up to Help You Out," *USA Today*, April 29, 2002.

14. Ting-I Tsai and Ian Johnson, "As Giants Step In, Asustek Defends a Tiny PC," *Wall Street Journal*, May, 1, 2009.

15. Henry Petroski, *Invention by Design* (Cambridge, MA: Harvard University Press, 1996), 155.

16. For critiques of the broken-window approach, see Ralph Taylor, *Breaking Away from Broken Windows: Baltimore Neighborhoods and the Nationwide Fight against Crime, Grime, Fear, and Decline* (Boulder: Westview, 2001); Bernard Harcourt, *Illusions of Order: The False Promise of Broken Windows Policing* (Cambridge, MA: Harvard University Press, 2001).

17. Peter Chiarelli and Patrick Michaelis, "Winning the Peace," *Military Review*, July–August 1995, 4–17.

18. David Bornstein, *How to Change the World: Social Entrepreneurs and the Power of New Ideas* (New York: Oxford University Press, 2004), 54.

19. Kathleen Jamieson and Paul Waldman, *The Press Effect: Politicians, Journalists, and the Stories That Shape the Political World* (New York: Oxford University Press, 2003).

20. Ann Davis and Randall Smith, "Delayed Reaction: At Morgan Stanley, Board Slowly Faced Its Purcell Problem," *Wall Street Journal*, August 5, 2005.

21. This notion of reframing into realignment and revitalization was taken from a study of how Italian political parties frame issues. See Mario Diani, "Linking Mobilization Frames and Political Opportunities in Italy," *American Sociological Review* 61 (1996): 1053–1069.

22. Jane Dutton and Susan Jackson, "Categorizing Strategic Issues: Links to Organizational Action," *Academy of Management Review* 12 (1987): 76–90.

23. Jane Dutton, "The Making of Organizational Opportunities: An Interpretative Pathway to Organizational Change," *Research in Organizational Behavior* 15 (1993): 195–226.

24. Russell Fazio, J. Richard Eiser, and Natalie Shook, "Attitude Formation through Exploration: Valence Asymmetries," *Journal of Personality and Social Psychology* 87 (2004): 293–311.

25. Amos Tversky and Daniel Kahneman, "The Framing of Decisions and the Psychology of Choice," *Science* 211 (1981): 453–458.

26. George Stephanopoulos, *All Too Human* (New York: Little, Brown, 1999), 350.

27. Beth Meyerowitz and Shelly Chaiken, "The Effect of Message Framing on Breast Self-Examination Attitudes, Intentions, and Behavior," *Journal of Personality and Social Psychology* 52 (1987): 500–510.

28. Larry Tye, *The Father of Spin: Edward L. Bernays and the Birth of Public Relations* (New York: Crown, 1998), 52.

29. Ray Moynihan, Iona Heath, and David Henry, "Selling Sickness: The Pharmaceutical Industry and Disease Mongering," *BMJ USA* 2 (2002): 341.

30. John Trebbel, *A History of Book Publishing in the United States* (New York: Bowker, 1975), 2:286–289.

31. H. Petroski, *The Toothpick: Technology and Culture.* New York: Knopf, 2007), 97, 101.

32. Barton Weitz, "Relationship between Salesperson Performance and Understanding of Customer Decision Making," *Journal of Marketing Research* 15 (1978): 501–516.

Chapter 4. Build Your Reputation, Create a Brand

1. Thomas Robinson, Dina Borzekowski, Donna Matheson, and Helena Kraemer, "Effects of Fast Food Branding on Young Children's Taste Preferences," *Archives of Pediatric and Adolescent Medicine* 8 (2007): 792–797.

2. Cameron Anderson and Aiwa Shirako, "Are Individuals' Reputations Related to Their History of Behavior?" *Journal of Personality and Social Psychology* 94 (2008): 320–333.

3. "Less Insult from Injury," *Bloomberg Businessweek*, August 14, 2006, http://www.businessweek.com/magazine/content/06_33/b3997087.htm (accessed November 25, 2010).

4. Norman Polmar and Thomas Allen, *Rickover* (New York: Simon and Schuster, 1982), 138.

5. "Prince Sadruddin Aga Khan, Refugee Chief, Died on May 12th, Aged 70," *Economist*, May 24, 2003, 86.

6. Tracy Kidder, *The Soul of a New Machine* (New York: Little, Brown, 1981), 141.

7. Martin Kilduff and David Krackhardt, "Bringing the Individual Back In: A Structural Analysis of the Internal Market for Reputation in Organizations," *Academy of Management Journal* 37 (1994): 87–108.

8. Robert Caro, *Master of the Senate* (New York: Vintage, 2002), 389.

9. Stephen Brown, "Tease Your Customers," *Harvard Business School Weekly Knowledge*, October 29, 2001.

10. Anthony Pratkanis and Elliot Aronson, *Age of Propaganda* (New York: Freeman, 2001), 250.

11. Nicholas Lemann, "Kids in the Conference Room," *New Yorker*, October 18 and 25, 1999, 209.

12. Andreas Buchholz and Wolfram Wordemann, *What Makes Winning Brands Different?* (New York: Wiley, 2002), 96.

13. Xin Gea, P. Messinger, and Jin Li, "Influence of Sold-Out Products on Consumer Choice," *Journal of Retailing* 85 (2009): 274–287.

14. "Overcast in Pennsylvania," *New York Times*, June 4, 2005.

15. Jan Englemann, Monica Capra, Charles Noussair, and Gregory Berns, "Expert Financial Advice Neurologically 'Offloads' Financial Decision-Making under Risk," *Public Library of Science One* 4 (2009): e4957.

16. Roderick Kramer, "The Great Intimidators," *Harvard Business Review* 84 (2006): 94.

17. Robert Caro, *The Power Broker* (New York: Vintage, 1975), 92.

18. Linda Kaplan, Robin Koval, and Delia Marshall, *Bang* (New York: Currency, 2003), 176.

19. Robert Coram, *Boyd* (Boston: Little, Brown, 2004), 403.

20. Joan Ganz Cooney, interview by Shirley Wershba, April 27, 1998, part 3 of 9, *Archive of American Television.*

21. Welch Suggs, *A Place on the Team* (Princeton, NJ: Princeton University Press, 2005), 66.

22. Edith Green, interview by Janet Kerr-Tener, Lyndon Baines Johnson Library, August 23, 1985, http://web1.millercenter.org/poh/transcripts/green_edith_1985_0823.pdf (accessed April 17, 2010).

23. Mark Gimein, "Smart Is Not Enough," *Fortune*, January 8, 2001, 130.

24. Clay Chandler, "Full Speed Ahead," *Fortune*, February 7, 2005, 84.

25. Janet Flammang, *Women's Political Voice* (Philadelphia: Temple University Press, 1997), 221.

26. Ann Dowd, "Top of His Game," *Washingtonian*, August 2001, 29.

27. Justin Kruger, Derrick Wirtz, Leaf Van Boven, and William Altermatt, "The Effort Heuristic," *Journal of Experimental Social Psychology* 40 (2004): 91–98.

28. Peter Reingen and Jerome Kernan, "Social Perception and Interpersonal Influence: Some Consequences of the Physical Attractiveness Stereotype in a Personal Selling Setting," *Journal of Consumer Psychology* 2 (1993): 25–38.

29. Gabriel Szulanski, "The Process of Knowledge Transfer: A Diachronic Analysis of Stickiness, Organizational Behavior and Human Decision Processes," *Organizational Behavior and Human Decision Processes* 82 (2000): 9–27.

30. Megan Tschannen-Moran and Wayne Hoy, "A Multidisciplinary Analysis of the Nature, Meaning, and Measurement of Trust," *Review of Educational Research* 70 (2000): 547–593.

31. Joann Lubin, "Managers and Managing — Boss Talk: Mr. Fix-It Shares Secrets about Big Turnarounds; Robert Miller Cleans Up Mess at Federal-Mogul," *Wall Street Journal*, December 27, 2000.

32. David Lidsky, "Transparency: It's Not Just for Shrink Wrap Anymore," *Fast Company*, January 2005, 87.

33. Harry Mills, *Artful Persuasion* (New York: AMACOM, 2000), 22.

34. William Benoit and Kimberly Kennedy, "On Reluctant Testimony," *Communication Quarterly* 47 (1999): 376–387.

35. Elaine Walster, Elliot Aronson, and Darcy Abrahams, "On Increasing the Persuasiveness of a Low Prestige Communicator," *Journal of Experimental Social Psychology* 2 (1966): 325–342.

36. François Duchene, "Jean Monnet's Methods," in *Jean Monnet: The Path to Euro-*

pean Unity, ed. Douglas Brinkley and Clifford Hackett (London: MacMillan, 1991), 197.

37. Walter Friedman, *The Birth of the Salesman* (Cambridge, MA: Harvard University Press, 2004), 24.

38. Chris Matthews, *Hardball* (New York: Touchstone, 1999).

39. John White, *Rejection* (Reading, MA: Addison-Wesley, 1982).

40. Douglas Martin, "Robert Moon, an Inventor of the ZIP Code, Dies at 83," *New York Times*, April 14, 2001, http://www.nytimes.com/2001/04/14/obituaries/14 MOON.html?ex=988734302&ei=1&en=4be29808738ecb46 (accessed April 17, 2010).

41. "Dr. John Eng's Research Found That the Saliva of the Gila Monster Contains a Hormone That Treats Diabetes Better Than Any Other Medicine," *Diabetes in Control*, September 18, 2007, http://www.diabetesincontrol.com/results.php ?storyarticle=5139 (accessed April 17, 2010).

42. Bernie Meyerson, lecture at the University of California, San Diego, December 3, 2003.

43. "Reinventing the Intrapreneur," *Red Herring*, August 31, 2000.

44. Teresa Amabile and Mukti Khaire, "Creativity and the Role of the Leader," *Harvard Business Review*, October 2008, 102.

45. Rajiv Chandrasekaran, "Richard Holbrooke Dies: Veteran U.S. diplomat Brokered Dayton Peace Accords," *Washington Post*, December 14, 2010.

46. Ken Adelman, "Act Cool," *Washingtonian*, March 2001, 29.

Chapter 5. Form Alliances

1. Tracy Kidder, *The Soul of a New Machine* (New York: Little, Brown, 1981), 112.

2. Robert Cialdini, "Indirect Tactics of Image Management: Beyond Basking," in *Impression Management in the Organization*, ed. R. Giacalone and P. Rosenfeld (Hillsdale, NJ: Erlbaum, 1989): 45–56.

3. "Hot Button," *PM Network* 17 (May 2003): 15.

4. Scott Shane, "Are Champions Different from Non-Champions?" *Journal of Business Venturing* 9 (1994): 397–421.

5. Michael Hiltzik, *Dealers of Lightning: Xerox PARC and the Dawn of the Computer Age* (New York: Harper Paperbacks, 2000), 57.

6. Norihiko Shirouzu, "Mr. Fujino's Bumpy Flight Lands Honda in the Jet Age," *Wall Street Journal*, June 18, 2007.

7. Peter Boyer, "Downfall: The Political Scene," *New Yorker*, November 20, 2006, 61.

8. Spencer E. Ante, "The New Blue," *Business Week*, March 17, 2003, 86.

9. Eugene Lewis, *Public Entrepreneurship* (Bloomington: Indiana University Press, 1980), 45.

10. Laura Holson, "Putting a Bolder Face on Google," *New York Times*, March 1, 2009, 8.

11. Everett Rogers, *Diffusion of Innovation* (New York: Free Press, 1993), 145.

12. Bradford Parkinson, "I Had to Sell This to the Air Force, Because the Air Force Didn't Want It," interview by Jim Quinn, *Invention and Technology*, Fall 2004, 60.

13. Elting Morison, *Men, Machines, and Modern Times* (Cambridge, MA: MIT Press, 1966).

14. Brent Schlender and Christopher Tkaczyk, "The Future of Hollywood," *Fortune*, May 29, 2006, 145.

15. James Coleman, Elihu Katz, and Herbert Menzel, *Medical Innovations: A Diffusion Study* (New York: Bobbs-Merrill, 1966).

16. Norman Polmar and Thomas Allen, *Rickover* (New York: Simon and Schuster, 1982), 191.

17. James Carville and Paul Begala, *Buck Up, Suck Up . . . and Come Back When You Foul Up* (New York: Simon and Schuster, 2001), 202.

18. Helen Pauly, "Koss: Riches, Rags, Stability, *Milwaukee Journal*, August 22, 1980.

19. Ian King, "Innovator Gary Martz," *Bloomberg Businessweek*, June 21, 2010, 29.

20. Peter Maas, *The Terrible Hours: The Man behind the Greatest Submarine Rescue in History* (New York: HarperCollins, 1995).

21. Karenna Schiff, *Lighting the Way: Nine Women Who Changed Modern America* (New York: Hyperion, 2006), 110.

22. Reiji Asakura, *Revolutionaries at Sony: The Making of the Sony PlayStation and the Visionaries Who Conquered the World of Video Games* (New York: McGraw-Hill, 2000).

23. Richard Polsky, *Getting to Sesame Street* (New York: Praeger, 1974), 97.

24. Roy Baumeister and Mark Leary, "The Need to Belong: Desire for Interpersonal Attachments as a Fundamental Human Motivation," *Psychological Bulletin* 117 (1995): 497–529.

25. Walter S. Mossberg, "Boss Talk: Shaking Up Sony," *Wall Street Journal*, June 6, 2006.

26. "Out of the Dusty Labs: The Rise and Fall of Corporate R&D," *Economist*, March 3, 2007, 76.

27. S. Markman, "Corporate Championing and Antagonism as Forms of Political Behavior: An R&D Perspective," *Organization Science* 11 (2000): 429–447.

28. Keith Hammonds, "Fast Talk: The Connector," *Fast Company*, March 2007, 46.

29. Jeffery Thieme, Michael Song, and Geon-Cheol Shin, "Project Management Characteristics and New Product Survival," *Journal of Product Innovation Management* 20 (2003): 104–119.

30. Kimberly Collins, "Profitable Gifts," *Perspectives in Biology and Medicine* 47 (2004): 100–109.

31. Steve Vogel, "How the Pentagon Got Its Shape," *Washington Post*, May 27, 2007.

32. Craig Venter, *A Life Decoded* (New York: Viking, 2007), 106.

33. Shona Brown and Kathleen Eisenhardt, "Product Development: Past Research, Present Findings, and Future Directions," *Academy of Management Review* 20 (1995): 343–378.

34. Nanette Byrnes, "Xerox' New Design Team: Customers," *Business Week*, May 7, 2007, 72.

35. Roger Leenders, Jo van Engelen, and Jan Kratzer, "Systematic Design Methods and the Creative Performance of New Product Teams: Do They Contradict or Compliment Each Other?" *Journal of Product Innovation Management* 24 (2007): 166–179.

36. Joseph Bonner and Orville Walker, "Selecting Influential Business-to-Business Customers in New Product Development," *Journal of Product Innovation and Development* 21 (2004): 155–169; Rajesh Sethi, "New Product Quality and Product Development Teams," *Journal of Marketing* 64 (2000): 1–14.

37. Robert Metcalfe, "Invention Is a Flower, Innovation Is a Weed," *MIT Technology Review*, November–December 1999, 54–57.

38. Joseph Weber, Stanley Holmes, and Christopher Palmeri, "'Mosh Pits' of Creativity," *Business Week*, November 7, 2005, 98.

39. Adam Lashinsky, "Razr's Edge," *Fortune*, June 12, 2006, 129.

40. Kipling Williams and Kristin Sommer, "Social Ostracism by Co-workers: Does Rejection Lead to Loafing or Compensation?" *Personality and Social Psychology Bulletin* 23 (1997): 693–706.

41. Ed Sleebos, Naomi Ellemers, and Dick de Gilder, "The Paradox of the Disrespected," *Journal of Experimental Social Psychology* 42 (2006): 413–427.

42. Jean Smith, *FDR* (New York: Random House, 2007), 351.

43. Joe Klein, "Eight Years," *New Yorker*, October 16 and 23, 2000, 192.

44. Fiona Harvey, "The Lessons of St. Patrick, St. Augustine and St. Paul's," *Financial Times*, June 18, 2003.

45. Jeffrey Rosen, "The Dissenter," *New York Times Magazine*, September 23, 2007, 53.

46. Richard Reeves, "President Reagan: The Triumph of Imagination," *Economist*, February 4, 2006, http://www.economist.com/node/5466837 (accessed November 26, 2010).

47. Steven Levy, "The Perfect Thing," *Wired*, www.wired.com/wired/archive/14.11/ipod_pr.html (accessed April 20, 2010).

48. Jonathan Younger, Lucy Walker, and John Arrowood, "Postdecision Dissonance at the Fair," *Personality and Social Psychology Bulletin* 3 (1977): 284–287.

49. Anthony Everitt, *Augustus* (New York: Random House, 2006), 311.

50. Christine Lagarde, "Anne Lauvergeon: A Real Power Player," *Time*, April 18, 2005, 81.

51. Ellen Langer, "The Illusion of Control," *Journal of Personality and Social Psychology* 32 (1975): 311–328.

52. Sheena Iyengar and Mark Lepper, "When Choice Is Demotivating: Can One Desire Too Much of a Good Thing?" *Journal of Personality and Social Psychology* 79 (2000): 995–1006; Erica Goode, "In Weird Math of Choices, 6 Choices Can Beat 600," *New York Times*, January 9, 2001.

53. Sheena Iyengar, Wei Jiang, and Gur Huberman, "How Much Control Is Too Much? Determinants of Individual Contributions in 401(k) Retirement Plans," Pension Research Council Working Paper 2003-10, Pension Research Council, Wharton School, University of Pennsylvania, 2003, http://www.archetype-advi sors.com/Images/Archetype/Participation/how%20much%20is%20too%20m uch.pdf (accessed April 20, 2010).

54. Jane Dutton and Michael Pratt, "Merck & Company, Inc.: From Core Competence to Global Community Involvement," in *Corporate Global Citizenship*, ed. Noel Tichy, Andrew McGill, and Lynda St. Clair (San Francisco: New Lexington Press, 1997), 154.

55. Susan Baer, "U2's Bono in Washington," *Washingtonian*, March 2006, 195.

56. Ibid., 195.

57. Arun Sharma, "Does the Salesperson Like Customers? A Conceptual and Empirical Examination of the Persuasive Effects of Perceptions of the Salesperson's Affect toward Customers," *Psychology and Marketing* 16 (1999): 141–162.

58. Ethan Burris, Matthew Rodgers, Elizabeth Mannix, Michael Hendon, and Jacob Oldroyd, "Playing Favorites: The Influence of Leaders' Inner Circle on Group Processes and Performance," *Personality and Social Psychology Bulletin* 35 (2009): 1244–1257.

59. Richard Johnson, *The Six Men Who Built the Modern Auto Industry* (St. Paul: Motorbooks, 2005), 161.

60. Rick Van Baaren, Rob Holland, Bregje Steenaert, and Ad van Knippenberg, "Mimicry for Money: Behavioral Consequences of Imitation," *Journal of Experimental Social Psychology* 39 (2003): 393–398.

61. Steven Ballmer, "Meetings, Version 2.0, at Microsoft," interview by Adam Bryant, *New York Times*, May 17, 2008.

62. David Drachman, Andre deCarufel, and Chester Insko, "The Extra Credit Effect in Interpersonal Attraction," *Journal of Experimental Social Psychology* 14 (1978): 458–465.

63. John Carlin, *Playing the Enemy* (New York: Penguin, 2008), 34.

64. Daniel Howard, Charles Gengler, and Ambuj Jain, "What's in a Name? A Complimentary Means of Persuasion," *Journal of Consumer Research* 22 (1995): 200–211.

65. Elizabeth Kensinger and Suzanne Corkin, "Effect of Negative Emotional Content on Working Memory and Long-Term Memory," *Emotion* 3 (2003): 378–393.

66. Virginia Cowles, *Winston Churchill* (New York: Gosset, 1953), 237.

67. Kelly Aune and Michael Basil, "A Relational Obligations Explanation for the Foot-in-the-Mouth Effect," *Journal of Applied Social Psychology* 24 (1994): 546–556.

68. Jerry Burger, Nicole Messian, Shebani Patel, Alicia del Prado, and Carmen Anderson, "What a Coincidence! The Effects of Incidental Similarity on Compliance," *Personality and Social Psychology Bulletin* 30 (2004): 35–43.

69. Minda Orina, Wendy Wood, and Jeffry Simpson, "Strategies of Influence in Close Relationships," *Journal of Experimental Social Psychology* 38 (2002): 459–472.

70. Judith White, Renee Tynan, Adam Galinsky, and Leigh Thompson, "Face Threat Sensitivity in Negotiation: Roadblock to Agreement and Joint Gain," *Organizational Behavior and Human Decision Processes* 94 (2004): 102–124.

71. Robert Caro, *The Power Broker* (New York: Vintage, 1975), 187–188.

72. Ted van Dyk, *Heroes, Hacks, and Fools* (Seattle: University of Washington Press, 2007), 30.

73. Ming-Jer Chen, *Inside Chinese Business* (Cambridge, MA: Harvard Business School Press, 2001).

74. Franklin Lavin, "More Than a 'Great Communicator,' " *Wall Street Journal*, June 8, 2004.

75. John Waller, *The Discovery of the Germ* (Cambridge, UK: Icon, 2002), 64.

76. Deborah Ball, "Boss Talk: Stocking a Global Pantry," *Wall Street Journal*, May 24, 2004.

77. Isabel Hilton, "The General in His Labyrinth," *New Yorker*, August 12, 2002, 45.

78. Jon Meacham, *Franklin and Winston: An Intimate Portrait* (New York: Random House, 2004), 85.

Chapter 6. Your Idea Is Only as Good as Its Story

1. Akio Morita, Edwin M. Reingold, and Mitsuko Shimomura, *Made in Japan* (New York: Dutton, 1986), 79.

2. David Rubin, *Memory in Oral Traditions: The Cognitive Psychology of Epics, Ballads, and Counting-Out Rhymes* (New York: Oxford University Press, 1995).

3. Michael Lounsbury and Mary Ann Glynn, "Cultural Entrepreneurship: Stories, Legitimacy, and the Acquisition of Resources," *Strategic Management Journal* 22 (2001): 545–564.

4. Phred Dvorak, "Facing a Slump, Sony to Revamp Its Product Lines," *Wall Street Journal*, September 12, 2003.

5. M. Green and T. Brock, "In the Mind's Eye: Transportation-Imagery Model of Narrative Persuasion," in *Narrative Impact: Social and Cognitive Foundations*, ed. Melanie Green, Jeffery Strange, and Timothy Brock (Mahwah, NJ: Erlbaum, 2002), 315–342.

6. Donald Phillips, *Lincoln on Leadership: Executive Strategies for Tough Times* (New York: Warner, 1993), 155.

7. Dean Simonton, "Group Artistic Creativity: Creative Clusters and Cinematic Success in Feature Films," *Journal of Applied Social Psychology* 34 (2004): 1494–1520.

8. Elizabeth Kensinger and Suzanne Corkin, "Effect of Negative Emotional Content on Working Memory and Long-Term Memory," *Emotion* 3 (2003): 378–393.

9. Robert Caro, *Master of the Senate: The Years of Lyndon Johnson* (New York: Vintage, 2002), 888.

10. Phillips, *Lincoln on Leadership*, 89.

11. Jonathan Karp, "At the Pentagon, an 'Encyclopedia of Ethical Failure,'" *Wall Street Journal*, May 14, 2007.

12. Nancy Pennington and Reid Hastie, "Explaining the Evidence: Tests of the Story Model for Juror Decision-Making," *Journal of Personality and Social Psychology* 62 (1992): 189–206.

13. Cheryl Jorgensen-Earp and Darwin Jorgensen, "Miracle from Mouldy Cheese: Chronological versus Thematic Self-Narratives in the Discovery of Penicillin," *Quarterly Journal of Speech* 88 (2002): 69–90; Eric Lax, *The Mold in Dr. Florey's Coat* (New York: Henry Holt), 2004.

14. Michael Slater and Donna Rouner, "Entertainment-Education and Elaboration Likelihood: Understanding the Processing of Narrative Persuasion," *Communication Theory* 12 (2002): 173–191.

15. Melanie Green and Timothy Brock, "The Role of Transportation in the Persuasiveness of Public Narratives," *Journal of Personality and Social Psychology* 79 (2000): 701–721.

16. Melanie Green and Timothy Brock, "In the Mind's Eye: Transportation-Imagery Model of Narrative Persuasion," in *Narrative Impact: Social and Cognitive Foundations*, ed. Melanie Green, Jeffery Strange, and Timothy Brock (Mahwah, NJ: Erlbaum, 2002), 315–342.

17. M. Sean Limon and Dean Kazoleas, "A Comparison of Exemplar and Statistical Evidence in Reducing Counter-Arguments and Responses to a Message," *Communication Research Reports* 21 (2004): 291–298.

18. Paul Ingrassia and Joseph White, *Comeback: The Fall and Rise of the American Automobile Industry* (New York: Simon and Schuster, 1994), 435. My thanks to Rob Smithson for pointing out this example.

19. Office of the Press Secretary, The White House, "Remarks by the President and the Vice President at Signing of the Don't Ask, Don't Tell Repeal Act of 2010," Department of the Interior, Washington, DC, December 22, 2010, http://www.whitehouse.gov/the-press-office/2010/12/22/remarks-president-and-vice-president-signing-dont-ask-dont-tell-repeal-a (accessed January 16, 2011). Points of applause are omitted.

20. While the core of the story is correct—access to the monasteries at Meteora in Greece was limited to a rope and pulley system up to the 1920s—there are now stairs. Guides often tell visitors the story of fixing the rope only when it is broken.

21. Stanley Meisler, "Man in the Middle: Travels with Kofi Annan," *Smithsonian*, January 2003, 37.

22. Howard Gardner, *Changing Minds: The Art and Science of Changing Our Own and Other People's Mind* (Boston: Harvard Business School Press, 2004), 74.

23. Many Web sites include this story. Here is one: http://www.cojoweb.com/friend ship-week.html (accessed November 25, 2010).

24. Ray Ozzie and Glenn Rifkin, "Speaking Mind to Mind," *New York Times*, December 1, 2002, 14.

25. Henry Cole, "Stories to Live By: A Narrative Approach to Health Behavior Research and Injury Prevention," in *Handbook of Health Behavior Research Methods*, ed. David Gochman (New York: Plenum, 1997): 325–348.

26. Silvia Knobloch, Grit Patzig, Anna-Maria Mende, and Matthias Hastall, "Affective News: Effects of Discourse Structure in Narratives on Suspense, Curiosity, and Enjoyment while Reading News and Novels," *Communication Research* 31 (2004): 259–287.

27. Jeffrey Seglin, "Storytelling Only Works if Tales Are True," *New York Times*, November 19, 2000.

28. Richard Rhodes, *The Making of the Atomic Bomb* (New York: Simon and Schuster, 1985), 313.

29. Carol Hymowitz, "Some Tips from CEOs to Help You to Make a Fresh Start in 2005," *Wall Street Journal*, December 28, 2004.

30. Katrina Brooker, "The UnCEO," *Fortune*, September 16, 2002, 96.

31. A collection is at http://cliffordclavin.com.

Chapter 7. Who's Making the Decision?

1. David Rynecki, "Morgan Stanley's Man on the Spot," *Fortune*, November 15, 2004, 122, 124.

2. Jena McGregor, William Symonds, Dean Foust, Diane Brady, and Moira Herbst, "How Failure Breeds Success," *Business Week*, July 10, 2006, 5.

3. Norihiko Shirouzu, "Mr. Fujino's Bumpy Flight Lands Honda in the Jet Age," *Wall Street Journal*, June 18, 2007.

4. Brent Schlender, "Inside Andy Grove's Latest Crusade," *Fortune*, August 23, 2004, 74.

5. Leonard Susskind, *The Black Hole War* (New York: Little, Brown, 2008), 444.

6. Blair Johnson and Alice Eagly, "Effects of Involvement on Persuasion: A Meta-Analysis," *Psychological Bulletin* 106 (1989): 290–314.

7. Mark Stefik and Barbara Stefik, *Breakthrough: Stories and Strategies of Radical Innovation* (Cambridge, MA: MIT Press, 2004), 78.

8. Alan Deutschman, "The Fabric of Creativity," *Fast Company*, December 2001, 128. In 2003, Gore-Tex sold Glide to Crest.

9. Alice Eagly and Shelly Chaiken, *The Psychology of Attitudes* (New York: Harcourt Brace Jovanovich, 1993).

10. Richard Petty, John Cacioppo, and Martin Heesacker, "Effects of Rhetorical Questions on Persuasion: A Cognitive Response Analysis," *Journal of Personality and Social Psychology* 40 (1981): 432–440.

11. Jerold Hale, Robert Lemieux, and Paul Mongeau, "Cognitive Processing of Fear-Arousing Message Content," *Communication Research* 22 (1995): 459–474.

12. Wesley Moons and Diane Mackie, "Thinking Straight while Seeing Red: The Influence of Anger on Information Processing," *Personality and Social Psychology Bulletin* 33 (2007): 706–720.

13. Joseph Forgas and Rebekah East, "On Being Happy and Gullible: Mood Effects on Skepticism and the Detection of Deception," *Journal of Experimental Social Psychology* 44 (2008): 1362–1367.

14. Stefik and Stefik, *Breakthrough*, 184.

15. Dan Hurley, "Robotic Pancreas: One Man's Quest to Put Millions of Diabetics on Autopilot," *Wired*, April 19, 2010, http://www.wired.com/magazine/2010/04/ff_pancreas/ (accessed June 27, 2010).

16. David Buller, Krystyna Stryzewski, and Jamie Comstock, "Interpersonal Deception I: Deceiver's Reactions to Receivers' Suspicions and Probing," *Communication Monographs* 58 (1991): 1–24.

17. Steven Ballmer, "Meetings, Version 2.0, at Microsoft," interview by Adam Bryant, *New York Times*, May 17, 2008.

18. David Von Drehle, "Roberts Is Defined by His Calm," *Washington Post*, August 28, 2005.

19. Jan Greenberg, *Supreme Conflict* (New York: Penguin, 2007), 189.

20. Robert Coram, *Boyd: The Fighter Pilot Who Changed the Art of War* (Boston: Back Bay Books, 2004), 174.

21. Larry Tracy, *The Shortcut to Persuasive Presentations* (Alexandria, VA: Tracy Presentation Skills, 2003).

22. Walter Friedman, *The Birth of the Salesman* (Cambridge, MA: Harvard University Press, 2004), 217.

23. Sheelah Kolhatkar, "Is California Sold on Governor Meg Whitman?" *Time*, December 14, 2009, 46.

24. Janet Bavelas, Alex Black, Nicole Chovil, and Jennifer Mullett, *Equivocal Communication* (Beverly Hills, CA: Sage, 1990).

25. Robert Woodward, *Maestro* (New York: Touchstone, 2001), 228.

26. Dale Hampel and Judith Dallinger, "On the Etiology of the Rebuff Phenomenon:

Why Are Persuasive Messages Less Polite after Rebuffs?" *Communication Studies* 49 (1998): 305–321.

27. Greg Behrman, *The Most Noble Adventure* (New York: Free Press, 2007), 234.

28. Peggy Noonan, *What I Saw at the Revolution* (New York: Random House, 1990), 56.

29. Jack Valenti, "Vietnam and the Presidency," speech at the John F. Kennedy Presidential Library and Museum, Boston, March 11, 2006, Presidential Libraries and the National Archives.

30. Behrman, *Most Noble Adventure*, 187.

31. John Markoff, "He Helped Build the iPod; Now He Has Built a Rival," *New York Times*, February 27, 2006.

32. Michael Hiltzik, *Dealers of Lightning: Xerox PARC and the Dawn of the Computer Age* (New York: HarperBusiness, 1999), 265.

33. Lena Sun, "Political Realities Stalled Fare Hike," *Washington Post*, September 23, 2007.

34. Justin Kruger and Matt Evans, "If You Don't Want to Be Late, Enumerate: Unpacking Reduces the Planning Fallacy," *Journal of Experimental Social Psychology* 40 (2004): 586–598.

35. Paul Herr, Frank Kardes, and John Kim, "Effects of Word-of-Mouth and Product-Attribute Information on Persuasion: An Accessibility-Diagnosticity Perspective," *Journal of Consumer Research* 17 (1991): 454–462.

36. Elizabeth Kensinger and Suzanne Corkin, "Effect of Negative Emotional Content on Working Memory and Long-Term Memory," *Emotion* 3 (2003): 378–393.

37. Hiltzik, *Dealers of Lightning*, 366.

38. Alexander Rothman and Peter Salovey, "Shaping Perceptions to Motivate Healthy Behavior: The Role of Message Framing," *Psychological Bulletin* 121 (1997): 3–19.

39. Itamar Simonson, "The Influence of Anticipating Regret and Responsibility on Purchase Decisions," *Journal of Consumer Research* 19 (1992): 105–118.

40. Terry Connolly, Lisa Ordonez, and Richard Coughlan, "Regret and Responsibility in the Evaluation of Decision Outcomes," *Organizational Behavior and Human Decision Processes* 70 (1997): 73–85.

41. Daniel Kahneman and Dale Miller, "Norm Theory: Comparing Reality to Its Alternatives," *Psychological Review* 93 (1986): 136–153.

42. Bernard Condon, "The Craftiest Buyer in Banking," *Forbes*, December 25, 2000, 69.

43. Raymond Miles and Charles Snow, *Organizational Strategy, Structure, and Process* (New York: McGraw-Hill, 1978).

44. Bruce Einhorn and Tim Culpan, "Acer: Past Dell, and Chasing HP," *Business Week*, March 8, 2010, 58.

45. Donald Hambreck, "Some Tests of the Effectiveness and Functional Attributes of Miles and Snow's Strategic Types," *Academy of Management Journal* 26 (1983): 5–

25; Alka Citrin, Ruby Lee, and Jim McCullough, "Information Use and New Product Outcomes," *Journal of Product Innovation Management* 24 (2007): 259–273.

46. Abbie Griffin and Albert Page, "PDMA Success Measurement Project: Recommended Measures for Product Development Success and Failure," *Journal of Product Innovation Management* 13 (1996): 478–496; Stanley Slater and John Narver, "Product-Market Strategy and Performance: An Analysis of the Miles and Snow Strategy Types," *European Journal of Marketing* 27 (1993): 33–51.

47. Tim Berners-Lee, *Weaving the Web* (New York: Harper, 1999), 19.

48. Ibid., 32.

49. Thomas Astebro, "Key Success Factors for Technological Entrepreneurs' R&D Projects," *IEEE Transactions on Engineering Management* 51 (2004): 314–321.

50. Rachel Silverman, "GE Goes Back to Future," *Wall Street Journal*, May 7, 2002.

51. Ann Harrington, "Who's Afraid of a New Product?" *Fortune*, November 10, 2003, 190.

Chapter 8. Network!

1. Donald Schon, "Champions for Radical New Inventions," *Harvard Business Review*, March–April 1983, 77–86.

2. Connie Duckworth and Bethany McLean, "Networking Lessons," *Fortune*, November 10, 2003, 192.

3. Ronald Burt, "The Network Structure of Social Capital," in *Research in Organizational Behavior*, ed. Robert Sutton and Barry Staw (Greenwich, CT: JAI Press, 2000) 22; Martin Kilduff and Daniel Brass, "The Social Networks of High and Low Self-Monitors: Implications for Workplace Performance," *Administrative Sciences Quarterly* 46 (2001): 121–146.

4. Fred Luthans, Richard Hodgetts, and Stuart Rosenkrantz, *Real Managers* (Cambridge, MA: Ballinger, 1988).

5. Henk Flap and Beate Volker, "Goal Specific Social Capital and Job Satisfaction: Effects of Different Types of Networks on Instrumental and Social Aspects of Work," *Social Networks* 23 (2001): 297–320.

6. Ronald Burt, "Structural Holes and Good Ideas," *American Journal of Sociology* 110 (2004): 349–399.

7. Dean Simonton, "The Social Context of Career Success and Course for 2026 Scientists and Inventors," *Personality and Social Psychology Bulletin* 18 (1992): 452–463.

8. Isabeli Bouty, "Interpersonal and Interaction Influences on Informal Resource Exchanges between R&D Researchers across Organizational Boundaries," *Academy of Management Journal* 43 (2000): 50–66.

9. Kah-Hin Chai, Mike Gregory, and Yongjiang Shi, "An Exploratory Study of

IntraFirm Process Innovations Transfer in Asia," *IEEE Transactions on Engineering Management* 51 (2004): 364–374; Ken Smith, Chistorpher Collins, and Kevin Clark, "Existing Knowledge, Knowledge Creation Capability, and the Rate of New Product Introduction in High-Technology Firms," *Academy of Management Journal* 48 (2005): 346–357.

10. Jane Howell and Christine Shea, "Individual Differences, Environmental Scanning, Innovation Framing, and Champion Behavior: Key Predictors of Project Performance," *Journal of Product Innovation Management* 18 (2001): 15–27.

11. Gina O'Connor and Mark Rice, "Opportunity Recognition and Breakthrough Innovation in Large Established Firms," *California Management Review* 43 (2001): 108.

12. Jeffrey Travers and Stanley Milgram, "An Experimental Study of the Small World Phenomenon," *Sociometry* 32 (1969): 425–443. For a critique of this study, see Duncan Watts, *Six Degrees: The Science of a Connected Age* (New York: Norton, 2003), 132–135.

13. Randall Stross, *The Wizard of Menlo Park* (New York: Crown, 2007), 47.

14. Thomas Allen, *Managing the Flow of Technology: Technology Transfer and the Dissemination of Technological Information within the R&D Organization* (Cambridge, MA: MIT Press, 1984).

15. Michael Schrage, "I'll Have the Pasta Primavera, with a Side of Strategy," *Fortune*, January 8, 2001, 194.

16. David Rothkopf, *Running the World* (New York: Public Affairs, 2005), 118.

17. Saul Hansell, "Strategy of New Chief at Motorola Appears Poised to Pay Off," *New York Times*, October 29, 2009.

18. Chris Matthews, *Hardball* (New York: Touchstone, 1999), 25.

19. Robert Caro, *Master of the Senate* (New York: Vintage, 2002), 210.

20. William Stevenson and Danna Greenberg, "Agency and Social Network: Strategies of Action in a Social Structure of Position, Opposition, and Opportunity," *Administrative Science Quarterly* 45 (2000): 651–678.

21. Ryan Lizza, "Making It," *New Yorker*, July 21, 2008, 52.

22. David Obstfeld, "Social Networks, the *Tertius Lungens* Orientation, and Involvement in Innovation," *Administrative Sciences Quarterly* 50 (2005): 100–130.

23. Daniel Brass, "Being in the Right Place: A Structural Analysis of Individual Influence in an Organization," *Administrative Sciences Quarterly* 29 (1984): 518–539.

24. Martin Gargiulo, "Two-Step Leverage: Managing Constraints in Organizational Politics," *Administrative Sciences Quarterly* 38 (1993): 1–19.

25. François Duchene, *Jean Monnet* (New York: Norton, 1994), 356.

26. "Israel's Debt to Andrew Jackson," *American Heritage*, April 1977, http://www.americanheritage.com/articles/magazine/ah/1977/5/1977_5_110_print.shtml (accessed April 23, 2010).

27. Robert Lenzner, "Creative Giving," *Forbes*, January 10, 2000, 70.

28. Elsa Walsh, "Kennedy's Hidden Campaign," *New Yorker*, March 31, 1997, 68.

29. Ken Hechler, "Ken Hechler on JFK," interview by John Lilly, West Virginia Division of Culture and History, http://www.wvculture.org/goldenseal/Fall00/hechler.html (accessed April 23, 2010).

30. Mark Granovetter, "The Strength of Weak Ties," *American Journal of Sociology* 78 (1973): 1360-1380.

31. Joel Podolny and James Baron, "Resources and Relationships: Social Networks and Mobility in the Workplace," *American Sociological Review* 62 (1997): 673-693.

32. Ronald Burt, "Structural Holes and Good Ideas," *American Journal of Sociology* 110 (2004): 349-399.

33. Lisa Troy, David Szymanski, and Rajan Varadarajan, "Generating New Product Ideas: An Initial Investigation of the Role of Market Information and Organizational Characteristics," *Journal of the Academy of Marketing Science* 29 (2001): 89-101.

34. Ray Reagan and Ezra Zuckerman, "Network Diversity and Performance: The Social Capital of R&D Units," *Organization Science* 12 (2001): 502-517.

35. John Kimberly and Michael Evanisko, "Organizational Innovation: The Influence of Individual, Organizational, and Contextual Factors on Hospital Adoption of Technological and Administrative Innovations," *Academy of Management Journal* 24 (1981): 689-713.

36. Joseph Bonner and Orville Walker, "Selecting Influential Business-to-Business Customers in New Product Development," *Journal of Product Innovation and Development* 21 (2004): 155-169.

37. Ronald Burt, *Brokerage and Closure: An Introduction to Social Capital* (New York: Oxford University Press, 2005), 90; Michael Erard, "Think Tank," *New York Times*, May 22, 2004.

38. Sharon McGrayne, *Prometheans in the Lab: Chemistry and the Making of the Modern World* (New York: McGraw-Hill, 2001), 186.

39. Ray Reagan and Bill McEvily, "Network Structure and Knowledge Transfer: The Effects of Cohesion and Range," *Administrative Science Quarterly* 48 (2003): 240-267.

40. Ruth Marshall, "Executive Life," *New York Times*, March 23, 2003.

41. Art Fry, "Art Fry's Invention Has a Way of Sticking Around," interview by Paul Rosenthal, May 20, 2008 (podcast), Lemelson Center, Smithsonian Institution, http://invention.smithsonian.org/video/vid-popup.aspx?clip=1&id=518 (accessed April 23, 2010).

42. Ming-Jer Chen, *Inside Chinese Business* (Cambridge, MA: Harvard Business School Press, 2001), 45-65.

43. Sarah Hemming, "A Crowd-Pleaser Who Plays to Her Investors," *Financial Times* (London), May 3, 2005, 14.

44. James Hamilton, *A Life of Discovery* (New York: Random House, 2004), 37.

45. *The Autobiography of Benjamin Franklin*, Archiving Early America, http://early america.com/lives/franklin/chapt9/.

46. Walter Isaacson, "Poor Richard's Flattery," *New York Times*, July 14, 2003.

47. Caro, *Master of the Senate*, 160.

48. George Stephanopoulos, *All Too Human: A Political Education* (Boston: Little, Brown, 1999).

49. Connie Bruck, "The Personal Touch," *New Yorker*, August 13, 2001, 51.

50. Jack Valenti, *This Time, This Place* (New York: Harmony, 2007), 45.

Chapter 9. Timing Is Everything

1. Fiona Harvey, "The Lessons of St. Patrick, St. Augustine and St. Paul's," *Financial Times* (London), June 18, 2003, 5.

2. John Tierney, "Business Sees Its Chance to Be Heard," *New York Times*, January 6, 2003.

3. Ira Breskin, "Responsible Party / Kirk K. Huang; Wiggle Room at Highway Bridges," *New York Times*, May 25, 2003.

4. Udo Zander, and Bruce Kogut, "Knowledge and the Speed of Transfer and Imitation of Organizational Capabilities: An Empirical Test," *Organization Science* 6 (1995): 76–92.

5. Marlene Fiol and Edward O'Connor, "Waking Up! Mindfulness in the Face of Bandwagons," *Academy of Management Review* 28 (2003): 54–70.

6. Eugene Lewis, *Public Entrepreneurship: Toward a Theory of Bureaucratic Political Power* (Bloomington: Indiana University Press, 1980), 180.

7. Diarmuid Jeffreys, *Aspirin* (London: Bloomsbury, 2004), 69–74.

8. Darryl Rehr, "Remington and the Electromatic," http://www.etypewriters.com/ remingtom.htm (accessed November 28, 2010).

9. Erik Hoelzl and George Loewenstein, "Wearing Out Your Shoes to Prevent Someone Else from Stepping into Them: Anticipated Regret and Social Takeover in Sequential Decisions," *Organizational Behavior and Human Decision Processes* 98 (2005): 15–27.

10. Kirk Victor, "Still an Old Boys' Club," *National Journal*, March 12, 2005, 754.

11. Jeff Rhodes, "Willis Hawkins and the Genesis of the Hercules," *Code One* (Third quarter, 2004).

12. Everett Rogers, *Diffusion of Innovations* (New York: Free Press, 1995), 422.

13. Jack Welch, "What I've Learned," interview by Cal Fussman, *Esquire*, January 2004, 95.

14. Katrina Brooker, "The Un-CEO," *Fortune*, September 16, 2002, 92.

15. Robert Harris, "Pirates of the Mediterranean," *New York Times*, September 30, 2006, 23.

16. Ronald Burt, "Social Contagion and Innovation: Cohesion versus Structural Equivalence," *American Journal of Sociology* 92 (1987): 1287–1335.

17. Hubert Gatignon and Thomas Robertson, "Technology Diffusion: An Empirical Test of Competitive Effects," *Journal of Marketing* 53 (1989): 35–49.

18. Tad Friend, "Plugged In," *New Yorker*, August 24, 2009, 52.

19. Davis Dyer, Frederick Dalzell, and Rowena Olegario, *Rising Tide* (Cambridge, MA: Harvard Business School Press, 2004), 74.

20. Hoon-Seok Choi and John Levine, "Minority Influence in Work Teams: The Impact of Newcomers," *Journal of Experimental Social Psychology* 40 (2004): 273–280.

21. Philip Dray, *Stealing God's Thunder* (New York: Random House, 2005), 126.

22. Don Bedwell, "Where Am I?" *Innovation and Technology* (Spring 2007): 29.

23. Matthew Brzezinski, *Red Moon Rising* (New York: Times Books, 2007), 241.

24. Tracy Kidder, *The Soul of a New Machine* (New York: Little, Brown, 1981), 112.

25. Hayagreeva Rao, "Caveat Emptor: The Construction of Nonprofit Consumer Watchdog Organizations," *American Journal of Sociology* 103 (1998): 912–961.

26. Wolfgang Saxon, "Jasper Kane, 101, Biochemist Who Helped Make Antibiotics," *New York Times*, November 20, 2004.

27. "Game On," *Economist*, March 7, 2009, 73.

28. Robert Coram, *Boyd: The Fighter Pilot Who Changed the Art of War* (Boston: Back Bay Books, 2004), 404.

29. Michael Waldman, *POTUS Speaks* (New York: Simon and Schuster, 2000), 122.

30. Jane Dutton, Stephen Stumpf, and David Wagner, "Diagnosing Strategic Issues and Managerial Investment of Resources," in *Advances in Strategic Management*, ed. Paul Shrivastava and Robert Lamb (Greenwich, CT: JAI Press, 1990), 6:143–167.

31. Jane Dutton and Robert Duncan, "The Creation of Momentum for Change through the Process of Strategic Issue Diagnosis," *Strategic Management Journal* 8 (1987): 279–295.

32. Seth Godin, "The Best Things in Life Are Free," *Fast Company*, June 2004, 90.

33. Douglas Smith and Robert Alexander, *Fumbling the Future: How Xerox Invented, Then Ignored, the First Personal Computer* (New York: Morrow, 1988), 242.

34. Darren Rovell, *First in Thirst: How Gatorade Turned the Science of Sweat into a Cultural Phenomenon* (New York: AMACOM, 2006), 14.

35. Ibid., 22.

36. Jane Dutton, Susan Ashford, Regina O'Neill, and Katherine Lawrence, "Moves That Matter: Issue Selling and Organizational Change," *Academy of Management Journal* 44 (2001): 716–736.

37. Henrich Greve, "Performance, Aspirations, and Risky Organizational Change," *Administrative Science Quarterly* 43 (1998): 58–86.

38. Andrew Hargadon and Yellowlees Douglas, "When Innovations Meet Institutions: Edison and the Design of the Electric Light," *Administrative Science Quarterly* 46 (2001): 476–501.

39. Mária Telkes, "Future Uses of Solar Energy," *Bulletin of the Atomic Scientists*, August 1951, 217–219.

40. Stephen Green, Ann Welsh, and Gordon Dehler, "Advocacy, Performance, and Threshold Influences in Decisions to Terminate New Product Development," *Academy of Management Journal* 46 (2003): 419–434.

41. James Thong, "An Integrated Model of Information Systems Adoption in Small Businesses," *Journal of Management Information Systems* 15, no. 4 (March 1999): 187–214.

42. John Kotter, *The General Manager* (New York: Free Press, 1982).

43. Detmar Straub, "The Effects of Culture on IT Diffusion: E-mail and FAX in Japan and the U.S.," *Information Systems Research* 5 (1994): 23–47.

44. Henry Chesbrough, "Graceful Exits and Missed Opportunities: Xerox's Management of Its Technology Spin-Off Organizations," *Business History Review* 76 (Winter 2002): 803–837.

45. Karen Blumenthal, *Let Me Play: The Story of Title IX* (New York: Atheneum, 2005).

46. Steven Levy, "Inside Chrome: The Secret Project to Crush IE and Remake the Web," *Wired*, September 2, 2008, http://www.wired.com/techbiz/it/magazine/16-10/mf_chrome (accessed June 25, 2010).

47. T. Y. Lin, " 'The Father of Prestressed Concrete': Teaching Engineers, Bridging Rivers and Borders, 1931 to 1999," interview by Eleanor Swent, 1999, Regional Oral History Office, University of California, Berkeley, available at Calisphere, a service of the University of California Libraries, http://content.cdlib.org/ark:/13030/kt4w100389/.

48. Chesbrough, "Graceful Exits and Missed Opportunities," 818.

49. Janet Guyo, "The Coming Storm over a Cancer Vaccine," *Fortune*, October 31, 2005, 126.

50. Robert Burgelman and Leonard Sayles, *Inside Corporate Innovation* (New York: Free Press, 1986), 56.

51. Jia Lynn Yang, "The Bottom Line," *Fortune*, September 1, 2008, 112.

52. Nelson Repenning, Paulo Goncalves, and Laura Black, "Past the Tipping Point: The Persistence of Firefighting in Product Development," *California Management Review* 43 (2001): 49.

53. Peter Lewis, "Texas Instruments' Lunatic Fringe," *Fortune*, September 4, 2006, 126.

54. Stephen Humphreys, Henry Moon, Donald Conlon, and David Hofman, "Decision-Making and Behavior Fluidity: How Focus on Completion and

Emphasis on Safety Changes over the Course of Projects," *Organizational Behavior and Human Decision Processes* 93 (2004): 14–27.

55. Om Prakash Kharbanda and Jeffrey Pinto, *What Made Gertie Gallop? Learning from Project Failures* (New York: Van Nostrand, 1996), 138.

56. Reiji Asakura, *Revolutionaries at Sony: The Making of the Sony PlayStation and the Visionaries Who Conquered the World of Video Games* (New York: McGraw-Hill, 2000), 224.

57. Gerardo Okhuysen, Adam Galinsky, and Tamara Uptigrove, "Saving the Worst for Last: The Effect of Time Horizon on the Efficacy of Negotiating Benefit and Burden," *Organizational Behavior and Human Performance* 91 (2003): 269–279.

58. Theodore Rockwell, *The Rickover Effect* (Annapolis, MD: Naval Institute Press, 1992), 209.

59. Art Fry, "Art Fry's Invention Has a Way of Sticking Around," interview by Paul Rosenthal, May 20, 2008 (podcast), Lemelson Center, Smithsonian Institution, http://invention.smithsonian.org/video/vid-popup.aspx?clip=1&id=518 (accessed April 23, 2010).

60. L. Frost, M. Reich, and T. Fujisaki, "A Partnership for Ivermectin: Social Worlds and Boundary Objects," in *Public-Private Partnerships for Public Health*, ed. Michael Reich (Cambridge, MA: Harvard University Press, 2002).

61. Jane Dutton, Susan Ashford, Regina O'Neill, Erika Hayes, and Elizabeth Wierba, "Reading the World: How Middle Managers Assess the Context for Selling Issues to Top Managers," *Strategic Management Journal* 18 (1997): 407–425.

62. Kharbanda and Pinto, *What Made Gertie Gallop?* 290–292.

63. Warren St. John, "Mr. Not-So-Nice Guy in D.C.," *New York Times*, September 15, 2002.

64. Gal Zauberman and John Lynch, "Resource Slack and Propensity to Discount Delayed Investments of Time and Money," *Journal of Experimental Psychology: General* 134 (2005): 23–37.

65. Selin Malkoc, Gal Zauberman, and Canan Ulu, "Consuming Now or Later?" *Psychological Science* 16 (2005): 411–417.

66. Stefan Herzog, Jochim Hansen, and Michaela Wänke, "Temporal Distance and Ease of Recall," *Journal of Experimental Social Psychology* 27 (2007): 433–483.

67. Nicholas Bakalar, "Future Shock Concept Gets a Personal Twist," *New York Times*, February 22, 2004.

68. Drazen Prelec and Duncan Simester, "Always Leave Home Without It," *Marketing Letter* 12 (2001): 5–12; Dilip Soman, "The Effect of Payment Transparency on Consumption: Quasi-Experiments from the Field," *Marketing Letters* 14 (2003): 173–183.

69. Daniel Lyons, "The Stubborn Scientist," *Forbes*, October 4, 1999, 94–95.

70. Tim Palucka, "The Wizard of Octane: Eugène Houdry," *Invention and Technology*, Winter 2005, 39.

Chapter 10. Create Persuasive Messages

1. Davis Dyer, Frederick Dalzell, and Rowena Olegario, *Rising Tide* (Cambridge, MA: Harvard Business School Press, 2004), 151.

2. Steven Johnson, *The Ghost Map* (New York: Riverhead, 2006).

3. Alice Eagly, "Comprehensibility of Persuasive Arguments as a Determinant of Opinion Change," *Journal of Personality and Social Psychology* 29 (1974): 758–773.

4. Scott Hensley, "Side Effects," *Wall Street Journal*, June 13, 2003.

5. Frances Perkins, *The Roosevelt I Knew* (New York: Viking, 1946), 22.

6. Lisa Lindsey and Kimo Ah Yun, "Examining the Persuasive Effects of Statistical Messages: A Test of Mediating Relationships," *Communication Studies* 54 (2003): 306–321.

7. Katie Hafner, "Donald Wilson, 82, Pioneer of a Database, Dies," *New York Times*, November 25, 2006.

8. Mike Allen and Associates, "Effect of Timing of Communicator Identification and Level of Source Credibility on Attitude," *Communication Research Reports* 19 (2002): 46–55.

9. Elizabeth Kolbert, "XXXL," *New Yorker*, July 20, 2009, 75.

10. John Love, *McDonald's* (New York: Bantam, 1995), 296.

11. Norman Polmar and Thomas Allen, *Rickover* (New York: Simon and Schuster, 1982), 103.

12. David Greenberg, *Calvin Coolidge* (New York: Times Books, 2006), 84.

13. Andy Pasztor, "How China Turned Around a Dismal Air-Safety Record," *Wall Street Journal*, October 10, 2007.

14. Jean Smith, *FDR* (New York: Random House, 2007), 169.

15. James Rubin, Richard Amlôt, Lisa Page, and Simon Wessely, "Public Perceptions, Anxiety, and Behaviour Change in Relation to the Swine Flu Outbreak: Cross Sectional Telephone Survey," *BMJ*, July 2, 2009, http://www.bmj.com/cgi/content/abstract/339/jul02_3/b2651 (accessed April 25, 2010).

16. Walter Friedman, *The Birth of the Salesman* (Cambridge, MA: Harvard University Press, 2004), 50.

17. Theodore Rockwell, *The Rickover Effect* (Annapolis: Naval Institute Press, 1992), 93.

18. Louis V. Gerstner Jr., *Who Says Elephants Can't Dance? Inside IBM's Historic Turnaround* (New York: Collins, 2002), 204.

19. "Dihydrogen Monoxide," *Urban Legends Reference Pages*, September 16, 2007, http://www.snopes.com/science/dhmo.asp (accessed December 9, 2010).

20. Sara Silver, "With Uncertain Future, Bell Labs Turns to Commerce," *Wall Street Journal*, August 21, 2006.

21. "Roads to Somewhere," *Economist*, February 16, 2008, 32.

22. David Hardisty and Elke Weber, "Discounting Future Green: Money versus the Environment," *Journal of Experimental Psychology* 138 (2009): 329–340.

23. "Time to Money," *Forbes*, March 22, 1999, 136.

24. Jack Valenti, *This Time, This Place* (New York: Harmony, 2007), 305.

25. Jonathan Freedman and Scott Fraser, "Compliance without Pressure: The Foot-in-the-Door Technique," *Journal of Personality and Social Psychology* 4 (1966): 195–202.

26. Robert Zimmerman, *The Universe in a Mirror* (Princeton, NJ: Princeton University Press, 2008), 53.

27. Robert Cialdini, Joyce Vincent, Stephen Lewis, José Catalan, Diane Wheeler, and Betty Darby, "Reciprocal Concessions Procedure for Inducing Compliance: The Door-in-the-Face Technique," *Journal of Personality and Social Psychology* 34 (1975): 206–215.

28. Irwin Levin, Judy Schreiber, Marco Lauriola, and Gary Gaeth, "A Tale of Two Pizzas: Building Up from a Basic Product versus Scaling Down from a Fully-Loaded Product," *Marketing Letters* 13 (2002): 335–345.

29. Joe Klein, *The Natural* (New York: Doubleday, 2002), 40.

30. Wendy Wood and Jeffrey Quinn, "Forewarned and Forearmed? Two Meta-Analytic Syntheses of Forewarnings of Influence Appeals," *Psychological Bulletin* 129 (2003): 119–138.

31. M. Cruz, "Explicit and Implicit Conclusions in Persuasive Messages," in *Persuasion: Advances through Meta-Analysis*, ed. Mike Allen and Raymond Preiss (Cresskill, NJ: Hampton Press, 1998), 217–230.

32. Michael Santos, Craig Lvee, and Anthony Pratkanis, "Hey, Buddy, Can You Spare Seventeen Cents? Mindful Persuasion and the Pique Technique," *Journal of Applied Social Psychology* 24 (1994): 755–764.

33. Dhruv Grewal, Sukumar Kavanoor, Edward Fern, Carolyn Costley, and James Barnes, "Comparative versus Non-comparative Advertising: A Meta-Analysis," *Journal of Marketing* 61 (1997): 1–15.

34. Mike Allen, "Comparing the Persuasive Effectiveness of One- and Two-Sided Messages," in *Persuasion: Advances through Meta-Analysis*, ed. Mike Allen and Raymond Preiss (Cresskill, NJ: Hampton Press, 1998), 87–98.

35. Ley Killeya and Blair Johnson, "Experimental Induction of Biased Systematic Processing: The Directed-Thought Technique," *Personality and Social Psychological Bulletin* 24 (1998): 17–33.

36. Lara Dolnik, Trevor Case, and Kipling Williams, "Stealing Thunder as a Courtroom Tactic Revisited: Processes and Boundaries," *Law and Human Behavior* 27 (2003): 267–287.

Chapter 11. Make the Idea Matter

1. John Waller, *The Discovery of the Germ* (Cambridge, UK: Icon), 28.

2. Robert Caro, "The Orator of the Dawn," *New Yorker*, March 4, 2002, 55.

3. Jane Dutton, Susan Ashford, Katherine Lawrence, and Kathi Miner-Rubino,

"Red Light, Green Light: Making Sense of the Organizational Context for Issue Selling," *Organizational Science* 13 (2002): 355–369.

4. Jerry Useem, "20 That Made History," *Fortune*, June 27, 2005, 82.

5. Tom Lewis, *Divided Highways* (New York: Viking, 1997), 121.

6. Evan Schwartz, *Juice: The Creative Fuel That Drives World-Class Inventors* (Cambridge, MA: Harvard Business School Press, 2004), 35.

7. Mark Stefik and Barbara Stefik, *Breakthrough: Stories and Strategies of Radical Innovation* (Cambridge, MA: MIT Press, 2004), 185.

8. Michael Beer, Russell Eisenstat, and Derek Schrader, "Why Innovations Sit on the Shelf," Working Knowledge, Harvard Business School, July 19, 2004, http://hbswk.hbs.edu/item/4268.html (accessed December 9, 2010).

9. Susan Hart, Erik Hultink, Nikolaos Tzokas, and Harry Commandeur, "Industrial Companies' Evaluation Criteria in New Product Development Gates," *Journal of Product Innovation Management* 20 (2003): 22–36.

10. Patricia Sellers, "The Trials of John Mack," *Fortune*, September 1, 2003, 106.

11. Leila Abboud, "Economist Strikes Gold in Climate-Change Fight," *Wall Street Journal*, March 13, 2008.

12. James Boswell, *The Life of Samuel Johnson* (New York, Everyman's Library, 1993).

13. Robert Allen, Robert Spohn, and Herbert Wilson, *Selling Dynamics* (New York: McGraw-Hill, 1984).

14. Tim Berners-Lee, *Weaving the Web* (New York: HarperCollins, 1999), 19.

15. Ibid., 42–43.

16. Everett Rogers, *Diffusion of Innovations* (New York: Free Press, 1995).

17. Viswanath Venkatesh, Michael Morris, Gordon Davis, and Fred Davis, "User Acceptance of Information Technology: Toward a Unified View," *MIS Quarterly* 27 (2003): 425–478.

18. Barbara Wejnert, "Integrating Models of Diffusion of Innovations," *Annual Review of Sociology* 28 (2002): 297–326.

19. Choon-Ling Sia, Hock-Hai Teo, Bernard Tan, and Kwok-Kee Wei, "Effects of Environmental Uncertainty on Organizational Intention to Adopt Distributed Work Arrangements," *IEEE Transactions on Engineering Management* 51 (2004): 253–267.

20. William Samuelson and Richard Zeckhauser, "Status Quo Bias in Decision Making," *Journal of Risk and Uncertainty* 1 (1988): 7–59.

21. Rob Walker, "Let There Be Lite," *New York Times Magazine*, December 29, 2002, 39.

22. Therese Louie, Robert Kulik, and Robert Jacobson, "When Bad Things Happen to the Endorsers of Good Products," *Marketing Letters* 12 (2001): 13–23.

23. Bill Pennington, "Golfers Have Their Clothes Laid Out for Them," *New York Times*, July 13, 2009.

24. Andreas Buchholz and Wolfram Wordemann, *What Makes Winning Brands Different* (New York: Wiley, 2002), 25–26.

25. David Rothkopf, *Running the World* (New York: Public Affairs, 2005), 367.

26. Daniel Okrent, *Last Call* (New York: Scribner, 2010).

27. Eric Abrahamson and Charles Fombrun, "Macroculture: Determinants and Consequences," *Academy of Management Review* 19 (1994): 728–755.

28. Richard Weaver, *The Ethics of Rhetoric* (Chicago: H. Regnery, 1953).

29. "The Party's Over," *Economist*, February 1, 2003, 66.

30. Evan Osnos, "The Daley Show," *New Yorker*, March 8, 2010, 40.

31. Samuel Freedman, "How They Overcame," *New York Times*, February 6, 2005.

32. Douglas Smith and Robert Alexander, *Fumbling the Future: How Xerox Invented, Then Ignored, the First Personal Computer* (Lincoln, NE: I-Universe, 1999), 146.

33. Kimberly Collins, "Profitable Gifts," *Perspectives in Biology and Medicine* 47 (2004): 105.

34. George Anders, *Perfect Enough* (New York: Portfolio, 2003), 2.

35. James Twitchell, "Higher Ed, Inc.," *Wilson Quarterly*, Summer, 2004, 57.

36. Michael Barone, "The Loyal Opposition," *Wall Street Journal*, July 6, 2005.

37. John Hocking, Duane Margreiter, and Cal Hylton, "Intra-audience Effects: A Field Test," *Human Communication Research* 3 (1977): 243–249.

38. Robert Cialdini, "Don't Throw in the Towel: Use Social Influence Research," *APS Observer* 18 (2005): 33.

39. Shailagh Murray and Bryan Gruley, "Uneasy Alliance: On Many Campuses Big Brewers Play a Role in New Alcohol Policies," *Wall Street Journal*, November 2, 2000.

40. Wesley Schultz, Jessica Nolan, Robert Cialdini, Noah Goldstein, and Vladas Griskevicius, "The Constructive, Destructive, and Reconstructive Power of Social Norms," *Psychological Science* 18 (2007): 429–434.

41. "Case Studies," National Social Norms Institute, University of Virginia, http://www.socialnorms.org/CaseStudies/casestudies.php (accessed April 28, 2010).

42. Daniel Campbell-Meiklejohn, Dominik Bach, Andreas Roepstorff, Raymond Dolan, and Chris Frith, "How the Opinion of Others Affects Our Valuation of Objects," *Current Biology* 20 (2010): 1–6.

43. Robert Caro, *Master of the Senate* (New York: Vintage, 2002), 340.

44. Jamie Dean, "Bruised Reed," *World Magazine*, November 19, 2005, http://www.worldmag.com/articles/11278 (accessed April 28, 2010).

45. Claire Miller, "eBay Highlights Conservation as a Benefit of Buying Used," *New York Times*, March 8, 2010, B8.

46. Paul Krugman, "For Richer," *New York Times Magazine*, October 20, 2002, 77.

Chapter 12. Make a Memorable Case

1. Paul Herr, Frank Kardes, and John Kim, "Effects of Word-of-Mouth and Product-Attribute Information on Persuasion: An Accessibility-Diagnosticity Perspective," *Journal of Consumer Research* 17 (1991): 454–462.

2. Mark Landler, "A German Banker on Welfare among Miami's Palms," *New York Times*, October 17, 2003.

3. Christian Warren, *Brush with Death* (Baltimore, MD: Johns Hopkins University Press, 2000), 218.

4. "Those Costly Weapons against Dust Mites May Not Be Worth It," *Wall Street Journal*, February 18, 2000.

5. Ronald Reagan, Address Before a Joint Session of the Congress on the Program for Economic Recovery, February 18, 1981, The American Presidency Project, http://www.presidency.ucsb.edu/ws/index.php?pid=43425 (accessed January 16, 2011). Points of audience reaction are omitted.

6. Corey Kilgannon, "Get That Oak an Accountant," *New York Times*, May 12, 2003.

7. David A. Fahrenthold, "U.S. Suggests White Roofs to Curtail Climate Change," *Washington Post*, June 14, 2008.

8. David Williams, "Is Your Desk Making You Sick?" *CNN*, November 13, 2006, http://www.cnn.com/2004/HEALTH/12/13/cold.flu.desk/index.html (accessed April 28, 2010).

9. Nutrition Action Health Letter, Center for Science in the Public Interest, Washington, DC, June 1996.

10. "Chewing the Fat," *Time*, August 1, 1994, 12.

11. Francine Russo, "The Clinical Trials Bottleneck," *Atlantic Monthly*, May 1999, 36.

12. Itamar Simonson and Amos Tversky, "Choice in Context: Tradeoff Contrast and Extremeness Aversion," *Journal of Marketing Research* 29 (1992): 281–295.

13. Gregory Northcraft and Margaret Neale, "Experts, Amateurs, and Real Estate: An Anchoring-and-Adjustment Perspective on Property Pricing Decisions," *Organizational Behavior and Human Decision Processes* 39 (1987): 84–97.

14. Cari Tuna, "Picking Big 'Peers' to Set Pay," *Wall Street Journal*, August 17, 2009.

15. Art Fry, "Art Fry's Invention Has a Way of Sticking Around," interview by Paul Rosenthal, May 20, 2008 (podcast), Lemelson Center, Smithsonian Institution, http://invention.smithsonian.org/video/vid-popup.aspx?clip=1&id=518 (accessed April 28, 2010).

16. Claudia Deutsch, "A Spotlight on the Green Side of Bottled Water," *New York Times*, November 3, 2007.

17. Adam Galinsky and Thomas Mussweiler, "First Offers as Anchors: The Role of Perspective-Taking and Negotiator Focus," *Journal of Personality and Social Psychology* 81 (2001): 657–669.

18. Ian Parker, "The Bright Side," *New Yorker*, November 10, 2008, 56.

19. Marwan Sinaceur, Chip Heath, and Steve Cole, "Emotional and Deliberative Reactions to a Public Crisis," *Psychological Science* 16 (2005): 247–254.

20. Frank Luntz, *Words That Work: It's Not What You Say, It's What People Hear* (New York: Hyperion, 2007), 46.

21. G. Bruce Knecht, *Hooked* (Emmaus, PA: Rodale, 2007).

22. William D. Cohan, "Paradise Lost," *Fortune*, February 6, 2008, http://money.cnn .com/2008/02/04/lifestyle/paradise_lost.fortune/index.htm (accessed April 28, 2010).

23. Brian Wansink, *Mindless Eating* (New York: Bantam, 2006), 19.

24. Eric Anderson and Duncan Simester, "Mind Your Pricing Cues," *Harvard Business Review*, September 2003, 98.

25. Steve Vogel, "Naval Surface Warfare Center at Indian Head Mourns Loss of Its Energetic Champion," *Washington Post*, February 18, 1999.

26. Michael Korda, *Ulysses S. Grant: The Unlikely Hero* (New York: Harper Perennial, 2004), 69.

27. Jill Jonnes, "New York Unplugged," *New York Times*, August 13, 2004.

28. Jill Jonnes, *Empires of Light: Edison, Tesla, Westinghouse, and the Race to Electrify the World* (New York: Random House, 2004), 207.

29. Tom McNichol, *AC/DC: The Savage Tale of the First Standards War* (San Francisco: Jossey-Bass, 2006), 56.

30. Steven Ginsberg, "New Tactics for Dealing with Traffic," *Washington Post*, December 29, 2003.

31. Steve Sasson, "We Had No Idea," *Plugged In*, October 16, 2007, http://steve sasson.pluggedin.kodak.com/ (accessed April 28, 2010).

32. Jared Sandberg, "Slogans Don't Always Make It So," *Wall Street Journal*, October 18, 2005.

33. Hyunjin Song and Norbert Schwartz, "If It's Difficult to Pronounce, It Must Be Risky: Fluency, Familiarity, and Risk Perception," *Psychological Science* 20 (2009): 135–138.

34. Ibid., 135–138.

35. Adam Alter and Daniel Oppenheimer, "Predicting Short-Term Stock Fluctuations by Using Processing Fluency," *Proceedings of the National Academy of Sciences* 103 (2006): 9369–9372.

36. Peggy Lee, "What's in a Name.com? The Effects of '.com' Name Changes on Stock Prices and Trading Activity," *Strategic Management Journal* 22 (2001): 793–804.

37. Theo Frances, "Mutual Funds Change Monikers, but Not Holdings, to Woo Money," *Wall Street Journal*, March 14, 2003.

38. Ken Adelman, "Sage of Pennsylvania Avenue," *Washingtonian*, March 2003, 30.

39. Louis V. Gerstner Jr., *Who Says Elephants Can't Dance? Inside IBM's Historic Turnaround* (New York: Collins, 2002), 173.

40. Kery Murakami, "SLUT — Streetcar's Unfortunate Acronym Seems Here to Stay," *Seattle PI*, http://seattlepi.nwsource.com/local/332081_slut18.html (accessed April 28, 2010).

41. Jim Yardley, "First Comes the Car, Then the $10,000 License Plate," *New York*

Times, July 5, 2006, http://www.nytimes.com/2006/07/05/world/asia/05china.html (accessed April 28, 2010).

42. Douglas Burgess, *Seize the Trident: The Race for Super-Liner Supremacy and How It Altered the Great War* (New York: McGraw-Hill, 2005), 36.

43. Thomas Hine, *The Total Package* (Boston: Little, Brown, 1995), 85.

44. McNichol, *AC/DC*, 57.

45. "A Trolley Too Far," *Economist*, February 10, 2007, 58.

46. Anne Kornblut, "Bush Ad Plays on Kerry Windsurfing," *Boston Globe*, September 23, 2004.

47. Michael Waldman, *POTUS Speaks: Finding the Words That Defined the Clinton Presidency* (New York: Simon and Schuster, 2000), 126.

48. Pradeep Sopory and James Dillard, "The Persuasive Effects of Metaphor: A Meta-Analysis," *Human Communication Research* 28 (2002): 382–419.

49. D. Gentner and D. Gentner, "Flowing Water and Teeming Crowds: Mental Models of Electricity," in *Mental Models*, ed. Dedre Gentner and Albert Stevens (Hillsdale, NJ: Erlbaum, 1983), 99–129.

50. James Aley, "Heads We Win, Tails We Win," *Fortune*, March 3, 2003, 146.

51. Donald Phillips, *Lincoln on Leadership: Executive Strategies for Tough Times* (New York: Warner, 1993), 91.

52. Karenna Gore Schiff, *Lighting the Way: Nine Women Who Changed Modern America* (New York: Hyperion, 2006), 114.

53. Janice L. Krieger, Roxanne L. Parrott, and Jon F. Nussbaum, "Metaphor Use and Health Literacy: A Pilot Study of Strategies to Explain Randomization in Cancer Clinical Trials," *Journal of Health Communication*, January 2011, available at http://www.informaworld.com/smpp/content~db=all~content=a930475136~frm=titlelink (accessed December 20, 2010).

54. Steven Clayman, "Defining Moments, Presidential Debates, and Dynamics of Quotability," *Journal of Communication* 45 (Summer 1995): 118–146.

55. Lisa Endlich, *Goldman Sachs: The Culture of Success* (New York: Touchstone, 2000), 128.

56. My thanks to Angus Warren, Hui Lu, Ritu Pahwa, and Dana Rosenfeld for the figure of speech.

57. Victor Ottati, Susan Rhoads, and Arthur Graesser, "The Effects of Metaphor on Processing Style in a Persuasion Task: A Motivational Resonance Model," *Journal of Personality and Social Psychology* 77 (1999): 688–697.

58. P. Sopory and J. Dillard, "Figurative Language," in *The Persuasion Handbook: Developments in Theory and Practice*, ed. James Dillard and Michael Pfau (Thousand Oaks, CA: Sage, 2002), 407–426.

59. Ted van Dyk, *Heroes, Hacks, and Fools* (Seattle: University of Washington Press, 2007), 23.

60. Office of the Press Secretary, The White House, "Remarks by the President at a

DNC Finance Event in Atlanta Georgia," Hyatt Regency Hotel, Atlanta, Georgia, August 2, 2010, http://www.whitehouse.gov/the-press-office/remarks-president-a-dnc-finance-event-atlanta-georgia (accessed January 16, 2011). Points of audience reaction are omitted.

Chapter 13. Demonstrate Confidence

1. Ellen Langer, "The Illusion of Control," *Journal of Personality and Social Psychology* 32 (1975): 311–328.
2. Elizabeth Tenney, Barbara Spellman, and Robert MacCoun, "The Benefits of Knowing What You Know (and What You Don't): How Calibration Affects Credibility," *Journal of Experimental Social Psychology* 44 (2008): 1368–1375.
3. Bonnie Erickson, Allan Lind, Bruce Johnson, and William O'Barr, "Speech Style and Impression Formation in a Court Setting: The Effects of 'Powerful' and 'Powerless' Speech," *Journal of Experimental Social Psychology* 14 (1978): 266–279.
4. Linda Carli, "Gender, Language, and Influence," *Journal of Personality and Social Psychology* 59 (1990): 941–951.
5. Brian Cutler, Steven Penrod, and Thomas Stuve, "Juror Decision Making in Eyewitness Identification Cases," *Law and Human Behavior* 12 (1988): 41–55.
6. George Anders, *Perfect Enough* (New York: Portfolio, 2003), 73.
7. Reiji Asakura, *Revolutionaries at Sony* (New York: McGraw-Hill, 2000), 182.
8. Daniel Ames and Francis Flynn, "What Breaks a Leader: The Curvilinear Relation between Assertiveness and Leadership," *Journal of Personality and Social Psychology* 92 (2007): 307–324.
9. Tenney, Spellman, and MacCoun, "Benefits of Knowing."
10. Claudia Dreifus, "Here's the Nobel: Now Explain It to Your Grandmother," *New York Times*, December 7, 2004.
11. Margaret Thatcher, *The Downing Street Years* (New York: HarperCollins, 1993), 4–5; emphasis added.
12. Lawrence Hosman, "Language and Persuasion," in *Handbook of Persuasion*, ed. James Dillard and Michael Pfau (Thousand Oaks, CA: Sage, 2002), 371–444.
13. William O'Barr, *Linguistic Evidence: Language, Power, and Strategy in the Courtroom* (New York: Academic Press, 1982); Daniel Oppenheimer, "Consequences of Erudite Vernacular Utilized Irrespective of Necessity: Problems with Using Long Words Needlessly," *Applied Cognitive Psychology* 20 (2006): 139–156.
14. Rachel Simmons, Peter Gordon, and Dianne Chambless, "Pronouns in Marital Interaction," *Psychological Science* 16 (2005): 932–936.
15. Minda Orina, Wendy Woods, and Jeffry Simpson, "Strategies of Influence in Close Relationships," *Journal of Experimental Social Psychology* 38 (2002): 459–472.
16. Carl M. Cannon, "Soul of a Conservative," *National Journal*, June 14, 2005, 1453.

17. Peter Andersen and Tammy Blackburn, "An Experimental Study of Language Intensity and Response Rate in E-mail Surveys," *Communication Reports* 17 (2004): 73–82.

18. Ashlee Vance and Brad Stone, "A Little Chip Designed by Apple Itself," February 1, 2010, *New York Times*, http://www.nytimes.com/2010/02/02/technology/business-computing/02chip.html (accessed December 10, 2010). I added the emphasis after viewing the speech on YouTube.

19. Elizabeth Loftus and John Palmer, "Reconstruction of Automobile Destruction: An Example of the Interaction between Language and Memory," *Journal of Verbal Learning and Verbal Behavior* 13 (1974): 585–589.

20. Hosman, "Language and Persuasion."

21. Michael Burgoon, Stephen Jones, and Diane Stewart, "Toward a Message Centered Theory of Persuasion: Three Empirical Investigations of Language Intensity," *Human Communication Research* 1 (1975): 240–256.

22. John Wright and Lawrence Hosman, "Language Style and Sex Bias in the Courtroom: The Effects of Male and Female Use of Hedges and Intensifiers in Impression Formation," *Southern Speech Communication Journal* 48 (1983): 137–152.

23. Jakob Jensen, "Scientific Uncertainty in News Coverage of Cancer Research," *Human Communication Research* 34 (2008): 347–369; Amanda Durik, Anne Britt, Rebecca Reynolds, and Jennifer Storey, "The Effects of Hedges in Persuasive Arguments: A Nuanced Analysis of Language," *Journal of Language and Social Psychology* 27 (2008): 217–234.

24. "Transcript: Bush News Conference Q & A" (provided by Federal Document Clearing House), ABC News, April 13, 2004, http://abcnews.go.com/WNT/story?id=131608&page=4 (accessed December 10, 2010).

25. Norman Mendoza, Harmon Hasch, Bruce Ponder, and Victor Carrillo, "Well . . . Ah . . . : Hesitations and Hedges as an Influence on Jurors' Decisions," *Journal of Applied Social Psychology* 30 (2000): 2610–2621.

26. Herbert Clark and Fox Tree, "Using *Uh* and *Um* in Spontaneous Speech," *Cognition* 84 (2002): 73–111.

27. Peter Kollock, Philip Blumstein, and Pepper Schwartz, "Sex and Power in Interaction," *American Sociological Review* 50 (1985): 34–46.

28. Philip Collard, Martin Corley, Lucy MacGregor, and David Donaldson, "Attention Orienting Effects of Hesitations in Speech: Evidence from ERPs," *Journal of Experimental Psychology: Learning, Memory, and Cognition* 34 (2008): 696–702.

29. Elizabeth Tenney, Robert MacCoun, Barbara Spellman, and Reid Hastie, "Calibration Trumps Confidence as a Basis for Witness Credibility," *Psychological Science* 18 (2007): 46–50.

30. Kevin Blankenship and Thomas Holtgraves "The Role of Different Markers of Linguistic Powerlessness in Persuasion," *Journal of Language and Social Psychology* 24 (2005): 3–24.

31. Jeremy Rosenberg and Richard Tunney, "Human Vocabulary Use as Display," *Evolutionary Psychology* 6 (2008): 538–549.

32. John A. Bargh, Mark Chen, and Lara Burrows "Automaticity of Social Behavior: Direct Effects of Trait Construct and Stereotype Activation on Action," *Journal of Personality and Social Psychology* 71 (1996): 230–244.

33. John Bargh, Peter Gollwitzer, Annette Lee-Chai, Kimberly Barndollar, and Roman Trotschel, "The Automated Will: Nonconscious Activation and the Pursuit of Behavioral Goals," *Journal of Personality and Social Psychology* 81 (2001): 1014–1027.

34. Keith D. Ciani and Kennon M. Sheldon, "A versus F: The Effects of Implicit Letter Priming on Cognitive Performance," *British Journal of Educational Psychology* 80 (March 2010): 99–119.

35. Nicholas Epley and Thomas Gilovich, "Just Going Along: Nonconscious Priming and Conformity to Social Pressure," *Journal of Experimental Social Psychology* 35 (1999): 578–589.

36. Jacob Jacoby, Maragert Nelson, and Wayne Hoyer, "Corrective Advertising and Affirmative Disclosure Statements: Their Potential for Confusing and Misleading the Consumer," *Journal of Marketing* 46 (1982): 61–72.

37. Joe Magee, "Seeing Power in Action: The Roles of Deliberation, Implementation, and Action in Inferences of Power," *Journal of Experimental Social Psychology* 45 (2009): 1–14.

38. Brad Bell and Elizabeth Loftus, "Trivial Persuasion in the Courtroom: The Power of (a Few) Minor Details," *Journal of Personality and Social Psychology* 56 (1999): 669–679.

39. Judith Hall, Erik Coats, and Lavonia Smith, "Nonverbal Behavior and the Vertical Dimension of Social Relations: A Meta-Analysis," *Psychological Bulletin* 131 (2005): 898–924.

40. Kyle Tusing and James Dillard, "The Sounds of Dominance: Vocal Precursors of Perceived Dominance during Interpersonal Influence," *Human Communication Research* 26 (2000): 148–171.

41. John Vann, Robert Rogers, and John Penrod, "The Cognitive Effects of Time-Compressed Advertising," *Journal of Advertising* 16 (1987): 10–19.

42. Stephen Smith and David Shaffer, "Speed of Speech and Persuasion: Evidence for Multiple Effects," *Personality and Social Psychology Bulletin* 21 (1995): 1051–1060.

43. David Buller and Kelly Aune, "The Effects of Vocalics and Nonverbal Sensitivity on Compliance: A Speech Accommodation Perspective," *Human Communication Research* 14 (1988): 301–332.

44. Lynn Neary, "The Man Who Signed His Name 'A. Lincoln,'" *Book Tour*, NPR, February 24, 2009, http://www.npr.org/templates/story/story.php?storyId=100899483 (accessed April 30, 2010).

45. Smith and Shaffer, "Speed of Speech and Persuasion."

46. Michael Pratt, Ann Krane, and Janet Kendall, "Triggering a Schema: The Role of Italics and Intonation in the Interpretation of Ambiguous Discourse," *American Educational Research Journal* 18 (1981): 303–315.

47. Matthew McGlone and Jessica Tofighbakhsh, "Birds of a Feather Flock Together Conjointly," *Psychological Science* 11 (2000): 424–428.

48. Miron Zuckerman and Kunitate Miyake, "The Attractive Voice: What Makes It So?" *Journal of Nonverbal Behavior* 17 (1993): 119–135.

49. Daphne Bugental, David Beaulieu, Alex Schwartz, and Rebecca Dragosits, "Domain-Specific Responses to Power-Based Interaction," *Journal of Experimental Social Psychology* 45 (2009): 386–391.

50. Hall, Coats, and Smith, "Nonverbal Behavior."

51. Robert Caro, *Master of the Senate* (New York: Vintage, 2002), 419.

52. Dana Carney, Amy Cuddy, and Andy Yap, "Power Posing: Brief Nonverbal Displays Affect Neuroendocrine Levels and Risk Tolerance," *Psychological Science* 21 (2010): 1363–1369.

53. John Hall Gladstone, *Michael Faraday* (London: MacMillan, 1874), 104.

Chapter 14. Steer Meetings Your Way

1. Elizabeth Drew, *On the Edge: The Clinton Presidency* (New York: Touchstone, 1995), 65.

2. Robert Woodward, *Maestro* (New York: Touchstone, 2000), 67.

3. Laurence Meyer, *A Term at the Fed* (New York: HarperCollins, 2004), 50.

4. Carl von Clausewitz, *On War* (Princeton, NJ: Princeton University Press, 1989), 573.

5. Theodore Rockwell, *The Rickover Effect* (Annapolis: Naval Institute Press, 1992), 233.

6. Chen-Bo Zhong, Vanessa Bohns, and Francesca Gino, "Good Lamps Are the Best Police: Darkness Increases Dishonesty and Self-Interested Behavior," *Psychological Science* 21 (2010): 311–314.

7. Rockwell, *Rickover Effect*, 168.

8. Miles Unger, *Magnifico* (New York: Simon and Schuster, 2008), 189.

9. Wilbert van Vree, *Meetings, Manners, and Civilization* (London: Leicester University Press, 1999).

10. Christian Warren, *Brush with Death* (Baltimore, MD: Johns Hopkins University Press, 2000), 217.

11. François Duchene, *Jean Monnet* (New York: Norton, 1994), 155.

12. Michael Davis, *Street Gang* (New York: Viking, 2009), 115.

13. Ann Schlosser and Sharon Shavitt, "Anticipating Discussion about a Product: Rehearsing What to Say Can Affect Your Judgments," *Journal of Consumer Research* 29 (2002): 101–115.

14. Neil Irwin and David Cho, "Paulson's Change in Rescue Tactics," *Washington Post*, October 15, 2008, A25.

15. Peggy Noonan, *What I Saw at the Revolution* (New York: Random House, 1990), 241.

16. François Duchene, "Jean Monnet's Methods," in *Jean Monnet: The Path to European Unity*, ed. Douglas Brinkley and Clifford Hackett (London: MacMillan, 1991), 197.

17. David Hirshleifer and Tyler Shumway, "Good Day Sunshine: Stock Returns and the Weather," *Journal of Finance* 58 (2003): 1009–1032.

18. Marieke De Vries, Rob Holland, Troy Chenier, Mark Starr, and Piotr Winkielman, "Happiness Cools the Warm Glow of Familiarity: Psychophysiological Evidence That Mood Modulates the Familiarity-Affect Link," *Psychological Science* 21, no. 3 (2010): 321–328.

19. Linda Isbell, "Not All Happy People Are Lazy or Stupid: Evidence of Systematic Processing in Happy Moods," *Journal of Experimental Social Psychology* 40 (2004): 341–349.

20. Joseph Forgas, "Feeling and Speaking: Mood Effects on Verbal Communication Strategies," *Personality and Social Psychology Bulletin* 25 (1999): 850–863.

21. Camiel Beukeboom and Gün Semin, "How Mood Turns on Language," *Journal of Experimental Social Psychology* 42 (2006): 553–566.

22. G. Razran, "Conditioned Response Changes in Rating and Appraising Sociopolitical Slogans," *Psychological Bulletin* 37 (1940): 481.

23. Nora Volkow, Gene-Jack Wang, Joanna Fowler, Jean Logan, Millard Jayne, Dinko Franceschi, Cristopher Wong, Samuel Gatley, Andrew Gifford, Yu-Shin Ding, and Naomi Pappas, " 'Nonhedonic' Food Motivation in Humans Involves Dopamine in the Dorsal Striatum and Methylphenidate Amplifies This Effect," *Synapse* 44 (2002): 175–180.

24. Lawrence Williams and John Bargh, "Experiencing Physical Warmth Promotes Interpersonal Warmth," *Science* 322 (2008): 606–607.

25. Pearl Martin, Victoria Hamilton, Blake McKimmie, Deborah Terry, and Robin Martin, "Effects of Caffeine on Persuasion and Attitude Change: The Role of Secondary Tasks in Manipulating Systematic Message Processing," *European Journal of Social Psychology* 37 (2006): 320–338.

26. Joshua Ackerman, Christopher Nocera, and John Bargh, "Incidental Haptic Sensations Influence Social Judgments and Decisions," *Science* 328 (2010): 1712–1715.

27. Fred Moody, *I Sing the Body Electric* (New York: Viking, 1995), 78.

28. Ryan Lizza, "Money Talks," *New Yorker*, May 4, 2009, 53.

29. Priya Raghubir and Ana Valenzuela, "Center-of-Attention: Position Biases in Decision-Making," *Organizational Behavior and Human Decision Processes* 99 (2006):

66–80; Shelley Taylor and Susan Fiske, "Point of View and Perceptions of Causality," *Journal of Personality and Social Psychology* 32 (1975): 439–445.

30. Ted van Dyk, *Heroes, Hacks, and Fools* (Seattle: University of Washington Press, 2007), 23.

31. Daniele Marzoli and Luca Tommasi, "Side Biases in Humans (*Homo sapiens*): Three Ecological Studies on Hemispheric Asymmetries," *Naturwissenschaften*, 96 (2009): 1099–1106.

32. Raghubir and Valenzuela, "Center-of-Attention."

33. "A New Seating Chart," *Wall Street Journal*, March 9, 2007, http://blogs.wsj .com/washwire/2007/03/09/a-new-seating-chart/ (accessed April 30, 2009).

34. Charles Handy, *Myself and Other More Important Matters* (New York: Amacon, 2008), 95.

35. "The Fascination of the Abomination," *New York Times*, February 1, 1989.

36. Jerry Burger, Shelley Soroka, Katrina Gonzago, Emily Murphy, and Emily Somervell, "The Effect of Fleeting Attraction on Compliance to Requests," *Personality and Social Psychology Bulletin* 27 (2001): 1578–1586; Dariusz Dolinski, Magdalena Nawrat, and Izabela Rudak, "Dialogue Involvement as a Social Influence Technique," *Personality and Social Psychology Bulletin* 27 (2001): 1395–1406.

37. Janet Holmes and Maria Stubbe, *Power and Politeness in the Workplace* (London: Pearson, 2003).

38. Arie Kruglanski and Donna Webster, "Motivated Closing of the Mind: Seizing and Freezing," *Psychological Review* 103 (1996): 263–283.

39. Bridget Murray, "A Ticking Clock Means a Creativity Drop," *Monitor on Psychology* 33 (2002): 24.

40. Robert Caro, *Master of the Senate* (New York: Vintage, 2002), 136.

41. Eli Saslow, "A Rising Political Star Adopts a Low-Key Strategy," *Washington Post*, October 17, 2008.

42. Carmine Gallo, *Ten Simple Secrets of the World's Greatest Business Communicators* (Naperville, IL: Sourcebook, 2005), 13.

43. Chris Hughes, "Boy Wonder," *Fast Company*, April 2009, 65.

44. Neil Rackham, *SPIN Selling* (New York: McGraw-Hill, 1998).

45. Ayumi Yamada, "Appreciating Art Verbally: Verbalization Can Make a Work of Art Be Both Undeservedly Loved and Unjustly Maligned," *Journal of Experimental Social Psychology* 45 (2009): 1140–1143.

46. Antonio Pierro, Lucia Mannetti, Eraldo De Grade, Stefano Livi, and Arie Kruglanski, "Autocracy Bias in Informal Groups under Need for Closure," *Personality and Social Psychology Bulletin* 29 (2003): 405–417; Don Willard and Fred Strodtbeck, "Latency of Verbal Response and Participation in Small Groups," *Sociometry* 35 (1972): 161–175.

47. Judith Hall, Erik Coats, and Lavonia Smith, "Nonverbal Behavior and the

Vertical Dimension of Social Relations: A Meta-Analysis," *Psychological Bulletin* 131 (2005): 898–924.

48. Pablo Briñol and Richard Petty, "Overt Head Movement and Persuasion: A Self-Validation Analysis," *Journal of Personality and Social Psychology* 84 (2003): 1123–1139.

49. Nicholas Gueguen, "Mimicry and Seduction: An Evaluation in a Courtship Setting," *Social Influence* 4 (2009): 249–255.

50. Derek Rucker and Richard Petty, "When Resistance Is Futile: Consequences of Failed Counterarguing for Attitude Certainty," *Journal of Personality and Social Psychology* 86 (2004): 219–235.

51. David Greenberg, *Calvin Coolidge* (New York: Times Books, 2006), 9.

52. Derk-Jan Eppink, *Life of a European Mandarin* (Tielt, Belgiun: Lannoo, 2007), 218.

Index

Page numbers for illustrations are in **boldface.**